## The Allocation of Regulatory Competence in the EU Emissions Trading Scheme

The European Union's Emissions Trading Scheme (EU ETS) is the world's largest carbon market. This book offers a new perspective on the EU ETS as a multi-level governance regime, in which the regulatory process is comprised of three distinct 'competences' – norm setting, implementation and enforcement. Are these competences best combined in a single regulator at one level of government or would they be better allocated among a variety of regulators at different levels of government? The combined legal, economic, and political analysis in this book reveals that the actual allocation of competences within the EU ETS diverges from a hypothetical ideal allocation in important ways, and provides a political economy explanation for the existing allocation of norm setting, implementation and enforcement competences among various levels of European government.

**Josephine van Zeben** is a visiting postdoctoral researcher at The Vincent and Elinor Ostrom Workshop in Political Theory and Policy Analysis, Indiana University at Bloomington. Since 2012, she has been teaching environmental regulation at ETH Zurich as a guest lecturer.

Cambridge Studies in European Law and Policy

This series aims to produce original works which contain
a critical analysis of the state of the law in particular areas
of European Law and set out different perspectives and
suggestions for its future development. It also aims to encourage
a range of work on law, legal institutions and legal phenomena in
Europe, including 'law in context' approaches. The titles in the series
will be of interest to academics; policymakers; policy formers who are
interested in European legal, commercial, and political affairs;
practising lawyers including the judiciary; and advanced law students
and researchers.

*Joint Editors*

Professor Dr Laurence Gormley, *University of Groningen*
Professor Jo Shaw, *University of Edinburgh*

*Editorial advisory board*

Professor Richard Bellamy, *University College London*
Professor Catherine Barnard, *University of Cambridge*
Professor Marise Cremona, *European University Institute, Florence*
Professor Alan Dashwood, *University of Cambridge*
Professor Dr Jacqueline Dutheil de la Rochère, *Université de Paris II,*
*Director of the Centre de Droit Européen, Paris*
Dr Andrew Drzemczewski, *Council of Europe, Strasbourg*
Sir David Edward, *KCMG, QC, former Judge, Court of Justice of the*
*European Communities, Luxembourg*
Professor Dr Walter Baron van Gerven, *Emeritus Professor, Leuven*
*and Maastricht, and former Advocate General, Court of Justice of the European*
*Communities*
Professor Daniel Halberstam, *University of Michigan*
Professor Dr Ingolf Pernice, *Director of the Walter Hallstein Institut,*
*Humboldt University*
Michel Petite, *Former Director-General of the Legal Service, Commission of the*
*European Communities, Brussels*
Professor Dr Sinisa Rodin, *University of Zagreb*
Professor Neil Walker, *University of Edinburgh*

Books in the series

*EU Enlargement and the Constitutions of Central and Eastern Europe*
Anneli Albi

*Social Rights and Market Freedom in the European Constitution: A Labour Law Perspective*
Stefano Giubboni

*The Constitution for Europe: A Legal Analysis*
Jean-Claude Piris

*The European Convention on Human Rights: Achievements, Problems and Prospects*
Steven Greer

*European Broadcasting Law and Policy*
Jackie Harrison and Lorna Woods

*The Transformation of Citizenship in the European Union: Electoral Rights and the Restructuring of Political Space*
Jo Shaw

*Implementing EU Pollution Control: Law and Integration*
Bettina Lange

*The Evolving European Union: Migration Law and Policy*
Dora Kostakopoulou

*Ethical Dimensions of the Foreign Policy of the European Union: A Legal Appraisal*
Urfan Khaliq

*The European Civil Code: The Way Forward*
Hugh Collins

*State and Market in European Union Law*
Wolf Sauter and Harm Schepel

*The Ethos of Europe: Values, Law and Justice in the EU*
Andrew Williams

*The European Union's Fight Against Corruption: The Evolving Policy Towards Member States and Candidate Countries*
Patrycja Szarek-Mason

*The Lisbon Treaty: A Legal and Political Analysis*
Jean-Claude Piris

*New Governance and the Transformation of European Law: Coordinating EU Social Law and Policy*
Mark Dawson

*The Limits of Legal Reasoning and the European Court of Justice*
Gerard Conway

*International Trade Disputes and EU Liability*
Anne Thies

*The Allocation of Regulatory Competence in the EU Emissions Trading Scheme*
Josephine van Zeben

# The Allocation of Regulatory Competence in the EU Emissions Trading Scheme

Josephine van Zeben

**CAMBRIDGE**
UNIVERSITY PRESS

University Printing House, Cambridge CB2 8BS, United Kingdom

One Liberty Plaza, 20th Floor, New York, NY 10006, USA

477 Williamstown Road, Port Melbourne, VIC 3207, Australia

314-321, 3rd Floor, Plot 3, Splendor Forum, Jasola District Centre, New Delhi - 110025, India

79 Anson Road, #06-04/06, Singapore 079906

Cambridge University Press is part of the University of Cambridge.

It furthers the University's mission by disseminating knowledge in the pursuit of education, learning and research at the highest international levels of excellence.

www.cambridge.org
Information on this title: www.cambridge.org/9781107042261

© Josephine van Zeben 2014

This publication is in copyright. Subject to statutory exception and to the provisions of relevant collective licensing agreements, no reproduction of any part may take place without the written permission of Cambridge University Press.

First published 2014

*A catalogue record for this publication is available from the British Library*

*Library of Congress Cataloging in Publication data*
Zeben, Josephine A.W. van, 1984– author.
The allocation of regulatory competence in the EU emissions trading scheme / Josephine van Zeben.
    pages   cm. – (Cambridge studies in European law and policy)
Includes bibliographical references and index.
ISBN 978-1-107-04226-1 (hardback)
1.  Emissions trading–Law and legislation–European Union countries.
2.  Climatic changes–Government policy–European Union countries.
3.  Jurisdiction–European Union countries.   I.  Title.
KJE6249.Z43 2014
363.738'747094–dc23
2013041795

ISBN  978-1-107-04226-1  Hardback

Cambridge University Press has no responsibility for the persistence or accuracy of URLs for external or third-party internet websites referred to in this publication, and does not guarantee that any content on such websites is, or will remain, accurate or appropriate.

# Contents

| | |
|---|---|
| *Series editors' preface* | *page* ix |
| *Acknowledgements* | xi |
| *Table of cases* | xiv |
| *Table of legislation* | xvi |
| *List of abbreviations* | xxii |
| *List of figures* | xxiv |
| *List of tables* | xxv |

| | | |
|---|---|---|
| **Introduction: A changing (regulatory) climate** | | 1 |
| | 1 Competence allocation | 6 |
| | 2 Regulatory functioning | 11 |
| | 3 Structural overview | 13 |
| **1** | **From competing jurisdictions to competing competences: The allocation of regulatory competences** | 18 |
| | 1 Competing jurisdictions | 19 |
| | 2 Competing competences: A competence allocation approach | 44 |
| | 3 Interacting competences | 65 |
| | 4 Conclusions | 73 |
| **2** | **Optimal competence allocation for the EU ETS** | 75 |
| | 1 Regulatory dimensions of climate change | 76 |
| | 2 Competence allocation scenarios for the EU ETS | 89 |
| | 3 Conclusions | 105 |

vii

## 3 Regulatory competence allocation in the EU ETS (2005–2012)    108
1 Regulatory competence allocation in the EU ETS    109
2 Regulatory functioning    126
3 Conclusions    141

## 4 Regulatory competence allocation in the EU ETS (2013 onwards)    144
1 Regulatory competence allocation in the EU ETS    145
2 Regulatory functioning    163
3 Conclusions    174

## 5 A political economy explanation for competence allocation in the EU ETS    176
1 A political economy perspective of environmental policy    177
2 A political economy perspective of the EU ETS    190
3 Conclusions    210

## Epilogue: Climate realities and regulatory theories    213
1 The EU ETS: Taking the long way home?    215
2 Regulatory theories: Extensions    219

*Bibliography*    224
*Index*    249

# Series editors' preface

Given that climate change is probably the most important challenge facing mankind, the mechanisms that are developed to respond to that challenge need to be appropriate, effective, and implemented correctly. In this light, the EU Emissions Trading Scheme is of enormous practical importance, and its functioning is rightly the focus of legal, economic, environmental and policy analysis. In this context the allocation of competence across various levels of governance plays a vital role in contributing to the effectiveness of the regime.

Josephine van Zeben examines the economic and legal scholarship on competence allocation, before turning to examine climate change as a regulatory problem, and the substantive elements of regulatory competences as they relate to the EU Emissions Trading Scheme, looking at the role of public actors in the regulatory process. She then turns to benchmarking in order to assess the functioning of that scheme. She looks at the chronological development of the phases of the scheme, analysing the pitfalls and under-performance experienced in the first trading period. She notes that in the second trading period clashes between allocation preferences at European and national level became more apparent, while in both periods the allocation of enforcement competences at national level also gave rise to problems. She also discusses the new approaches which entered into force in 2013. The focus then changes to look at the problems she has identified through a political economy lens, which brings into sharp relief the differences between the optimal competence allocation model and the real-life experiences with the EU Emissions Trading Scheme. The competence allocation perspective enables van Zeben to proffer various suggestions for institutional improvements in this new third trading phase.

Van Zeben's work is an important interdisciplinary contribution to European law and policy, promoting the dialogue between lawyers and political economists. Her discussion is refreshing, stimulating, and grounded in meticulous research; it offers solutions, not merely an analysis of problems; it should be of interest to all those involved in Emissions Trading, as well as to lawmakers, policymakers, and economists concerned to know about the effectiveness or otherwise of the EU Emissions Trading Scheme and its institutional and governance arrangements. Accordingly, it gives us great pleasure to welcome the publication of this book in the *Cambridge Studies in European Law and Policy* series.

Laurence Gormley
Jo Shaw

# Acknowledgements

The success of this book should be measured by the quality of its ideas and the extent to which they speak for themselves. These acknowledgements will therefore not include a list of disclaimers – anyone who has ever attempted to complete a manuscript is aware of the inherent incompleteness of the final result and the continuous desire to build on, and improve, one's work. Rather, these acknowledgements, themselves hopelessly incompletely, mean to highlight some of the people and institutions that have enabled me to join the world of ideas that is academia and put some of my ideas on paper.

The book was initially written as a Ph.D. thesis at the Amsterdam Center for Law and Economics (ACLE) and the Amsterdam Center for Environmental Law and Sustainability (ACELS) at the University of Amsterdam, which I defended in May 2012. The members of my reading committee – Daniel Cole, Deirdre Curtin, Jan Jans, Ans Kolk, Sandrine Maljean-Dubois, Benjamin van Rooij and Rosa Uylenburg – generously took the time to read and assess my work. Their comments have greatly improved the quality of my work and are reflected in the revisions that turned the manuscript into a book. The encyclopedic knowledge of all things European and environmental of my co-supervisor Marc Pallemaerts (ACELS) has provided crucial guidance through the jungle of climate change regulation. My colleagues at the ACLE and ACELS, and the University of Amsterdam more generally, have been a source of inspiration and support for which I am deeply grateful.

I had the privilege of spending the academic year 2010–11 at New York University School of Law as a Hauser Global Research Scholar. My time there has helped shape the ideas in my dissertation in important ways, not least due to the supervision and advice of Richard Stewart. The collegiality of the other Hauser fellows made this one of the

xii ACKNOWLEDGEMENTS

most stimulating years of my (academic) life. The advice of Jennifer Arlen, before, during and after my visit at NYU has armed me with an understanding of American academia that has proven invaluable. The colleagues and friends whom I have met through the Society for Environmental Law and Economics (SELE) and the Ius Commune Research School make academia a great place. After completing my Ph.D., I joined the Amsterdam Center for European Law and Governance (ACELG), first as a lecturer in European Union law and later as a postdoctoral researcher and assistant research director. Under Deirdre Curtin's leadership, the ACELG is one of the most exciting places for European Union research in Europe.

Although this book closely reflects the ideas of the original doctoral dissertation, some revisions have been included, reflecting valuable comments from my reading committee and anonymous reviewers at Cambridge University Press, and incorporating legal developments that have taken place between May 2012 and July 2013. These revisions were mostly made during my visiting postdoctoral research position at the Vincent and Elinor Ostrom Workshop in Political Theory and Policy Analysis at Indiana University, Bloomington, which has been generously supported by the Niels Stensen Fellowship. The Ostrom Workshop has been a unique place to pursue my postdoctoral research: aside from the warm atmosphere created by the vibrant and welcoming Workshop community, Vincent and Elinor Ostrom's intellectual heritage provides an incredibly rich basis for my ongoing interdisciplinary work. Dan Cole's mentorship has been a continuing source of support and inspiration throughout my Ph.D. and my postdoctoral work, and I will sorely miss our daily conversations as I prepare to move to Harvard Law School in September 2013. My American adventures would not have been possible, nor quite as exciting, without the advice and friendship of Burney Fischer, Shi-Ling Hsu, Mike McGinnis, Jonathan Nash, Arden Rowell, Keith Taylor, Tom Ulen and the Law and Economics lunch group at IU.

Being able to develop my doctoral dissertation into a book under the guidance of Cambridge University Press has been a privilege, and I am very grateful for the efforts of the entire editorial team. A special debt is owed to the editors of the Cambridge Studies in European Law and Policy, Laurence Gormley and Jo Shaw, for their faith in the original manuscript and their decision to add it to this great Cambridge series.

Most importantly, I want to thank my 'promotor', my supervisor, Giuseppe Dari-Mattiacci of the ACLE. Giuseppe, thank you for pushing me out of my comfort zone, for raising the bar, and for helping me exceed my own expectations. The lessons you taught me about research, and myself, are invaluable and have shaped my understanding of what it means to be an academic. You never imposed your ideas on me but rather challenged me to think deeper, further and better. The intellectual standards that you set for yourself continue to form the 'moral fibre' of my work and aspirations as an academic. I hope this book does justice to your teachings. The only disclaimer in these acknowledgements should be that any remaining errors are my own.

A special word of gratitude to my friends and family for their patience and their support for my ambitions, even when pursuing these ambitions has meant long periods away from the people closest to me. You are all vital parts of my life and happiness, and your continued presence, often from afar, enables me to fulfil whatever potential I have been given. The loving and unfaltering support from my parents, Thea and Gert Jan, has provided me with the confidence to pursue numerous ideas, including my dissertation, and I hope this book makes them proud. I am extremely grateful for my two brothers: for Joris, in ways that I cannot even start to describe, and for Pieter, whose completely different perspective on life challenges and educates me on a daily basis. Last but not least, my life, and in many ways this book, is better because of Christopher.

# Table of cases

## European Union

Case C-72/95, *Aannemersbedrijf P. K. Kraaijeveld BV e.a.* v. *Gedeputeerde Staten van Zuid-Holland* [1996] ECR I-05403 219

Case C-366/10, *Air Transport Association of America and others* v. *The Secretary of State for Energy and Climate Change* [2010] OJ C 260/12 91, 210, 217

Case C-127/07, *Arcelor Atlantique and Lorraine and others* [2008] OJ C44/8 117

Case C-73/08, *Bressol and Others and Céline Chaverot and Others* v. *Gouvernement de la Communauté française* [2010] ECR I-2735 5

Case T-499/07, *Bulgaria* v. *Commission* [2008] OJ C64/50 136

Case T-500/07, *Bulgaria* v. *Commission* [2008] OJ C64/51 136

Case 9/74, *Casagrande* v. *Landeshaupttstadt München* [1974] ECR 773 42

Case C-236/92, *Comitato di Coordinamento per la Difesa della Cava and others* v. *Regione Lombardia and others* [1994] ECR I-03463 219

Case C-431/92, *Commission* v. *Germany* [1995] ECR I-2189 219

Case T-387/04, *EnBW Energie Baden-Württemberg* v. *Commission* [2007] ECR II-1195 138

Case T-263/07, *Estonia* v. *European Commission* [2009] ECR II-03463 15, 136, 137, 166

Case C-505/09P, *European Commission* v. *Estonia* [2009] not yet reported, 137

Case C-504/09P, *European Commission* v. *Poland* [2011] OJ C370, 137

Case C-279/93, *Finanzamt Köln-Altstadt* v. *Roland Schumacker* [1995] ECR I-225 5

Case T-374/04, *Germany* v. *European Commission* [2007] ECR II-4431 115, 118, 136

Cases 3/76, 4/76 and 6/76 (joined), *Kramer* [1976] ECR 1279 83

Case T-251/00, *Lagardere and Canal \+* v. *European Commission* [2002] ECR II-4825 136

Case T-369/07, *Latvia* v. *European Commission* [2011] ECR II-01039 136

xiv

Case T-183/07, *Poland* v. *European Commission* [2009] ECR II-03395 15, 136, 137, 166

Case 65/81, *Reina* v. *Landeskredit Bank Baden-Württemberg* [1982] ECR 336 42

Case T-483/07, *Romania* v. *Commission* [2008] OJ C51/56 136

Case T-484/07, *Romania* v. *Commission* [2008] OJ C51/57 136

Case C-415/93, *Royal Club Liegois SA* v. *Jean-Marc Bosman* [1995] ECR I-04921 42

Case T-178/05, *United Kingdom* v. *European Commission* [2005] ECR II-4807 135, 136

Case T-27/07, *U.S. Steel Kosice* v. *European Commission* [2007] ECR II-128 138

## International Court of Justice

*Reparation for Injuries Suffered in the Service of the United Nations*, Advisory Opinion of 11 April 1949, ICJ Reports 1949, 174 80

# Table of legislation

## European Union documents

Protocol No. 1 on the role of national parliaments in the European Union OJ 2008 No. C155 41

Protocol No. 2 on the application of the principles of subsidiarity and proportionality OJ 2008 No. C155 41, 42

Protocol No. 25 on the exercise of shared competences, OJ 2008 No. C155 41

Declaration No. 18 in relation to the delimitation of competences, OJ 2010 No. C83 41

Treaty on European Union (consolidated version), OJ 2012 C 326 6, 9, 11, 20, 41, 82, 113

Treaty on the Functioning of the European Union (consolidated version, 2012), OJ 2012 C 326 6, 41, 43, 82, 83, 84, 113, 118, 167, 168, 220

## Regulations

Commission Regulation No. 2216/2004 of 21 December 2004 for a standardized and secured system of registries pursuant to Directive 2003/87/EC of the European Parliament and of the Council and Decision No. 280/2004/EC of the European Parliament and of the Council, OJ 2004 No. L386 124

Council Regulation 401/2009 of 23 April 2009 on the European Environment Agency and the European Environment Information and Observation Network, OJ 2009 No. L126 141

Commission Regulation No. 920/2010 of 7 October 2010 for a standardized and secured system of registries pursuant to Directive 2003/87/EC of the European Parliament and of the Council and Decision No.

280/2004/EC of the European Parliament and of the Council, OJ 2010 No. L270 157

Commission Regulation 1031/2010 of 12 November 2010 on the timing, administration and other aspects of auctioning of greenhouse gas emission allowances pursuant to Directive 2003/87/EC of the European Parliament and of the Council establishing a scheme for greenhouse gas emission allowances trading within the Community, OJ 2010 No. L302, 155, 156, 157, 158, 168, 170

Commission Regulation No. 600/2012 of 21 June 2012 on the verification of greenhouse gas emission reports and tonne-kilometre reports and the accreditation of verifiers pursuant to Directive 2003/87/EC of the European Parliament and of the Council, SEC/2012/0176 final 133

Commission Regulation No. 601/2012 of 21 June 2012 on the monitoring and reporting of greenhouse gas emissions pursuant to Directive 2003/87/EC of the European Parliament and of the Council OJ 2012 No. L181 162, 171

## Directives

Council Directive 2001/77/EC of 27 September 2001 on promotion of electricity produced from renewable energy sources in internal electricity market, OJ 2001 No. L283 115, 149

Council Directive 2002/91/EC of 16 December 2002 on energy performance of buildings, OJ 2003 No. L1 115

Council Directive 2003/6/EC of 28 January 2003 on insider dealing and market manipulation (market abuse), OJ 2003 No. L96 161, 170

Council Directive 2003/87/EC of 13 October 2003 establishing a scheme for greenhouse gas emission allowance trading within the Community and amending Council Directive 96/61/EC, OJ 2003 No. L275 86, 152, 169

Council Directive 2004/39/EC of 21 April 2004 on financial instruments amending Council Directives 85/611/EEC and 93/6/EEC and Directive 2000/12/EC of the European Parliament and of the Council and repealing Council Directive 93/22/EEC, OJ 2004 No. L145 119, 161, 170

Council Directive 2004/101/EC of 27 October 2004 amending Directive 2003/87/EC in respect of the Kyoto Protocol's project mechanisms, OJ 2004 No. L338 (Linking Directive) 86, 117

Council Directive 2005/60/EC of 26 October 2005 on the prevention of the use of the financial system for the purpose of money laundering and terrorist financing, OJ 2005 No. L309 170

xviii    TABLE OF LEGISLATION

Council Directive 2008/101/EC of 19 November 2008 amending Directive 2003/87/EC so as to include aviation activities in the scheme for greenhouse gas emission allowance trading within the Community, OJ 2009 No. L83 90, 151, 157, 159

Council Directive 2009/28/EC of 23 April 2009 on the promotion of the use of energy from renewable sources and amending and subsequently repealing Directives 2001/77/EC and 2003/30/EC, OJ 2009 L140 16, 149, 204

Council Directive 2009/31/EC of 23 April 2009 on the geological storage of carbon dioxide and amending Council Directive 85/337/EEC, European Parliament and Council Directives 2000/60/EC, 2001/80/EC, 2004/35/EC, 2006/12/EC, 2008/1/EC and Regulation (EC) No. 1013/2006, OJ 2009 No. L140 149, 165, 204, 205

## Decisions

Commission Decision 2000/479/EC of 17 July 2000 on the implementation of a European pollutant emission register (EPER) according to Article 15 of Council Directive 96/61/EC concerning integrated pollution prevention and control (IPCC) (notified under document number C(2000) 2004 OJ 2000 No. L192 36, 218

Council Decision 2002/358/CE of 25 April 2002 concerning the approval, on behalf of the European Community, of the Kyoto Protocol to the United Nations Framework Convention on Climate Change and the joint fulfilment of commitments thereunder [Burden Sharing Agreement], OJ 2002 No. L130 86, 111

Commission Decision 2004/156/EC of 29 January 2004 establishing guidelines for the monitoring and reporting of greenhouse gas emissions pursuant to Directive 2003/87/EC of the European Parliament and of the Council, OJ 2004 No. L59 120, 121, 123, 141, 199, 206

Decision 208/2004/EC of the European Parliament and of the Council of 11 February 2004 concerning a mechanism for monitoring Community greenhouse gas emissions and for implementing the Kyoto Protocol, OJ 2004 No. L49 142

European Commission Decision 2005/166/EC of 10 February 2005 laying down rules implementing Decision No. 280/2004/EC of the European Parliament and of the Council concerning a mechanism for monitoring Community greenhouse gas emissions and for implementing the Kyoto Protocol, OJ 2005 No. L55 113

Commission Decision 2006/944/EC of 14 December 2006 determining the respective emission levels allocated to the Community and each of its Member States under the Kyoto Protocol pursuant to Council Decision 2002/358/EC, OJ 2006 L358 112

Commission Decision 2007/589/EC of 18 July 2007 establishing guidelines for the monitoring and reporting of greenhouse gas emissions pursuant to Directive 2003/87/EC of the European Parliament and the Council, OJ 2007 No. L229 120, 121, 122, 141, 160

Commission Decision 2009/73/EC of 17 December 2008 amending Decision 2007/589/EC as regards the inclusion of monitoring and reporting guidelines for emissions of nitrous oxide, OJ 2009 No. L24 120, 122

Commission Decision 2009/339/EC of 16 April 2009 amending Decision 2007/589/EC as regards the inclusion of monitoring and reporting guidelines for emissions and tonne-kilometre data from aviation activities, OJ 2009 No. L103 120, 159, 160

Commission Decision 406/2009/EC of 23 April 2009 on the effort of Member States to reduce their greenhouse gas emissions to meet the Community's greenhouse gas emission reduction commitments up to 2020, OJ 2009 No. L140 149–151, 166, 167, 204

Commission Decision 2010/2/EC of 24 December 2009 determining, pursuant to Directive 2003/87/EC of the European Parliament and of the Council, a list of sectors and subsectors which are deemed to be exposed to a significant risk of carbon leakage, OJ 2010 No. L1 208

Commission Decision 2010/345/EU of 8 June 2010 amending Decision 2007/589/EC as regards the inclusion of monitoring and reporting guidelines for greenhouse gas emissions from the capture, transport and geological storage of carbon dioxide, OJ 2010 No. L229 120, 122

Commission Decision of 17 August 2012 amending Decisions 2010/2/EU and 2011/278/EU as regards the sectors and subsectors which are deemed to be exposed to a significant risk of carbon leakage, OJ 2012 No. L241 165

## Communications

Commission Communication, 'Environmental Taxes and Charges in the Single Market', COM(1987) 9 final 114

Commission Communication, 'Preparing for Implementation of the Kyoto Protocol', COM(1999) 230 final 114

Commission Communication, 'Greenhouse gas emissions trading within the European Union (Green Paper)', COM(2000) 87 final 114, 193

Commission Communication, European Governance (White Paper), COM(2001) 428 final 41

Commission Communication, Proposal of 23 October 2001 for a Directive of the European Parliament and of the Council establishing a scheme for greenhouse gas emission allowance trading within the Community and amending Council Directive 96/61/EC, COM(2001) 581 final 132

Commission Communication on guidance to assist Member States in the implementation for the criteria listed in Annex III to Directive 2003/87/EC and on the circumstances under which force major is demonstrated, COM(2003) 830 final 118

Commission Communication on Building a Global Carbon Market – Report pursuant to Article 30 of Directive 2003/87/EC, COM(2006) 676 final 139, 202

Commission Communication on the assessment of national allocation plans for the allocation of greenhouse gas emission allowances in the second period of the EU Emissions Trading Scheme, COM(2006) 725 final 207

Commission Communication on rights-based management tools in fisheries, COM(2007) 73 final 87

Commission Communication, '20 20 by 2020 – Europe's climate change opportunity', COM (2008) 13 final 87, 111

Commission Communication, Proposal of 23 January 2008 for a Directive amending Directive 2003/87/EC so as to improve and extend the greenhouse gas emission allowance trading system of the Community, COM(2008) 30 final 130, 154, 165, 172, 204

Commission Communication, Impact Assessment of 23 January 2008 accompanying the Proposal for a Directive of the European Parliament and of the Council amending Directive 2003/87/EC so as to improve and extend the EU greenhouse gas emission allowance trading system, COM(2008) 16 final 130, 138, 168, 169, 172, 207

Commission Communication, 'Analysis of options to move beyond 20% greenhouse gas emission reductions and assessing the risk of carbon leakage', COM(2010) 265 final 151

Commission Communication, 'Towards an enhanced market oversight framework for the EU Emissions Trading Scheme', COM(2010) 796 final 124, 133, 160, 161, 206

Commission Communication, 'A Roadmap for moving to a competitive low carbon economy in 2050', COM(2011) 112 final 164, 165

Commission Communication, Proposal of 20 October 2011 for a Regulation of the European Parliament and of the Council on insider dealing and market manipulation (market abuse), COM(2011) 651 final 206

Commission Communication, Proposal of 20 October 2011 for a Regulation of the European Parliament and of the Council on markets in financial instruments and amending Regulation [EMIR] on OTC derivatives, central counterparties and trade repositories, COM(2011) 652 final 206

Commission Communication, Proposal of 20 October 2011 for a Directive of the European Parliament and of the Council on criminal sanctions for insider dealing and market manipulation, COM(2011) 654 final 206

Commission Communication, Proposal of 20 October 2011 for a Directive of the European Parliament and of the Council on markets in financial instruments repealing Directive 2004/39/EC of the European Parliament and of the Council (Recast), COM(2011) 656 final 162, 170, 171, 206

Commission Communication, 'The State of the European carbon market in 2012', COM(2012) 652 final 216

## National legislation

United States Constitution, adopted 17 September 1787, ratified 28 September 1787 9

Scotland Act (1998, c.46) 53

California Global Warming Solutions Act of 2006 35

Greenhouse gas emissions reductions, in California Health and Safety Code, Division 25.5 Part 4, Section 38562(d)(1)) 35

Act 695 on the greenhouse gas emissions trading scheme, Journal of Law (Poland) 122, 28 April 2011 134

## International documents

United Nations Framework Convention on Climate Change, conclusion 5 May 1992, entry into force 21 March 1994, United Nations Treaty Series I-30822 4, 58, 80, 84, 110, 111, 127, 140

Kyoto Protocol to the United Nations Framework Convention on Climate Change, conclusion 11 December 1997, entry into force 16 February 2005, United Nations Treaties A-30822 4, 80, 84, 85, 86, 111, 112, 113, 127, 146

# Abbreviations

| | |
|---|---|
| AAU | Assigned Amount Unit |
| CDM | Clean Development Mechanism |
| CJEU | Court of Justice of the European Union |
| CMP | COP serving as the Meeting of the Parties to the Kyoto Protocol |
| COP | Conference of the Parties |
| DG | Directorate General |
| ECCP | European Climate Change Programme |
| EEA | European Economic Area |
| EPA | Environmental Protection Agency (United States) |
| ESA | Effort Sharing Agreement |
| EU | European Union |
| EU12 | EU candidate countries before the enlargement on 1 January 1995 |
| EU15 | EU Member States before the enlargement on 1 May 2004 |
| EU27 | EU Member States after the enlargement on 1 January 2007 |
| EU28 | EU Member States after the enlargement on 1 July 2013 |
| EUA | EU Emission Allowance |
| EUAA | EU Aviation Emission Allowance |
| EU ETS | European Union Emissions Trading Scheme |
| IPCC | Intergovernmental Panel on Climate Change |
| JI | Joint Implementation |
| MiFID | Markets in Financial Instruments Directive |
| MS | Member State |
| NAP | National Allocation Plan |
| OECD | Organization for Economic Co-operation and Development |
| QELRO | Quantified Emission Limitation or Reduction Objective |

| | |
|---|---|
| RGGI | Regional Greenhouse Gas Initiative |
| SBI | Subsidiary Body for Implementation |
| SBSTA | Subsidiary Body for Scientific and Technological Advice |
| TEC | Treaty establishing the European Community |
| TEU | Treaty on European Union |
| TFEU | Treaty on the Functioning of the European Union |
| UN | United Nations |
| UNDP | United Nations Development Programme |
| UNEP | United Nations Environment Programme |
| UNFCCC | United Nations Framework Convention on Climate Change |

# Figures

| | | |
|---|---|---|
| I.1 | Optimal pollution norm | *page* 8 |
| 1.1 | Competence allocation choices | 53 |
| 2.1 | Scenario 1 (global norm setting) | 89 |
| 2.2 | Scenario 2 (regional norm setting) | 89 |
| 2.3 | Independent optimal allocation under global or regional norm setting | 98 |
| 2.4 | Divergence between regional and global norms | 101 |
| 2.5 | Interactions between implementation (I) and enforcement (E) | 102 |
| 2.6 | Optimal allocation under global or regional norm setting | 106 |
| 3.1 | Competence allocation in Phases I and II of the EU ETS | 126 |
| 4.1 | The revised EU ETS Directive and the Effort Sharing Agreement | 152 |
| 4.2 | Competence allocation in Phase III of the EU ETS | 163 |

# Tables

| | | |
|---|---|---:|
| 1.1 | Working definitions of regulatory competences | *page* 48 |
| 1.2 | Relevant regulated activity characteristics | 56 |
| 1.3 | Welfare implications | 71 |
| 2.1 | Regulatory competences for climate change mitigation | 88 |

# Introduction
## A changing (regulatory) climate

Climate change has become the greatest regulatory challenge of our time. The inevitability of climate change is now universally accepted by governmental leaders, but their responses to the accompanying economic and societal changes differ widely. In 2003, Vladimir Putin remarked that a temperature rise of one or two degrees would not be so bad for a country like Russia: less money could be spent on fur coats, and the grain harvest would go up.[1] In stark contrast with this devil-may-care attitude is the reality of a country such as the Maldives, which will vanish due to a rise in sea level if temperatures increase by more than 1.5 degrees Celsius. Whereas small temperature rises may indeed result in more arable land, lower electricity bills or profitable new trade routes, such as the Northwest Passage over the Arctic,[2] the likelihood of relatively large temperature rises (above two degrees Celsius) is increasing and their effects are much less benevolent. Recent studies have shown that an average temperature increase of 1.8 to 4.0 degrees Celsius, compared to 1980s levels, may be expected by the end of the century.[3]

---

[1] Russian President, World Climate Change Conference, Moscow, 29 September–3 October 2003.

[2] The Northwest Passage is a sea route through the Arctic Ocean, connecting the Atlantic and Pacific Oceans. Until 2009, the Arctic pack ice prevented regular marine shipping throughout most of the year, but climate change has reduced the pack ice, and this Arctic shrinkage has made the waterways more navigable. See generally S. G. Borgerson, 'Artic Meltdown: The Economic and Security Implications of Global Warming' 87 (2008) *Foreign Affairs* 63–77.

[3] R. K. Pachauri and A. Reisinger (eds.), *Climate Change 2007: Synthesis Report. Contribution of Working Groups I, II and III to the Fourth Assessment Report of the Intergovernmental Panel on Climate Change* (Geneva: Intergovernmental Panel on Climate Change, 2008).

This 'global warming' is only a small part of the climate change dynamic, and in many ways a misnomer: the average mean temperature increases that are quoted by media and politicians will not be dispersed evenly. Rather, we will see more extreme weather patterns due to ecosystems' inability to absorb the rapid changes in temperature that we are set to experience. As a consequence, climates and ecosystems are changed suddenly and irreparably. Agricultural conditions in Russia may improve in terms of temperature, but may also suffer from excessive, or insufficient, rainfall. Significant climate change will give rise to food, water and clean air scarcity and is likely to lead to the destruction of people's livelihoods or homes due to phenomena such as rising sea levels or desertification.[4] Even if the consequences and their distribution cannot be entirely predicted, it has become clear that everyone, regardless of geographic location or socio-economic status, will be affected by climate change.

The mitigation and adaptation of climate change has become a focal point for scientists, politicians, entrepreneurs, environmental interest groups and many others. Meaningful mitigation of climate change would necessitate significant changes in our energy consumption patterns, which are difficult to achieve in light of the economic and geo-political interests at play and the relatively low (direct) costs of energy use. As a consequence, attention is shifting to our ability to adapt to climate change, for instance through political cooperation or technological innovation. In comparison to the futuristic scientific advances that are being made,[5] the contributions of social scientists to the mitigation of, and adaptation to, climate change may appear rather academic and abstract. Yet, the vast amount of law, economics and political science scholarship in this area focuses on an equally powerful tool for climate change mitigation and adaptation: regulation.

---

[4] The South Pacific nation of Tuvalu is expected to disappear due to rising sea levels within the next century. See http://media.adelaidenow.com.au/multimedia/2008/10/tuvalu/tuvalu-perthnow.html.

[5] A recent example is Stratospheric Shield proposed by Intellectual Ventures, also known as the 'garden hose to the sky' project. By injecting large amounts of sulphur dioxide aerosols into the stratosphere, less sunlight would reach Earth, which would provide a temporary cooling effect (sulphur dioxide remains in the stratosphere for two years). See Intellectual Ventures Report, *The Stratospheric Shield: A practical, low-cost way to reverse catastrophic warming of the Arctic – or the entire planet* (2009), http://intellectualventureslab.com/wp-content/uploads/2009/10/Stratoshield-white-paper-300dpi.pdf.

The regulatory complexity of climate change mirrors its scientific complexity, involving numerous institutions, at multiple levels of governance.[6] The aim of this regulation is to incentivize parties, private and public, to change their climate change-related behaviour in significant ways. Regulation can help us adapt to the effects of climate change by stimulating investments in new technologies, or clarifying the legal status of people who have become displaced due to the effects of climate change (so-called climate refugees).[7] Regulation can also help mitigate the causes of climate change by putting in place liability rules for climate change,[8] or incentivizing the reduction of greenhouse gas emissions. These emission reductions may be achieved by raising the cost of emitting greenhouse gases, and/or spurring on technological innovations, such as low-carbon fuels, that may replace existing high-carbon fuel sources.

The global nature of climate change requires us to reassess the roles of regulators at various levels of governance. Although climate change is considered a 'global' problem, the costs and benefits of climate change are distributed unequally across the globe. This inequality is complicated further by the fact that those who historically contributed most to climate change through greenhouse gas emitting activities, such as (western) Europe and the United States, are not necessarily faced with the most extreme consequences of climate change. Since it is not in one's self-interest to stop engaging in an activity that results in a net benefit, the ability to 'externalize' the costs of greenhouse gas emitting activities necessitates regulatory intervention. Even if we were able to overcome the collective action problem of climate change – no single

---

[6] These developments run parallel to the more general trend of the emergence of so-called 'post-national' rulemaking, which questions the traditionally central role of the state in regulation. See e.g. B. Kingsbury, N. Krisch, and R. B. Stewart, 'The Emergence of Global Administrative Law' (2005) 68 *Law and Contemporary Problems* 15–61; A. Slaughter, *A New World Order* (Princeton University Press, 2004); J. Scott, 'The Multi-Level Governance of Climate Change', in P. Craig and G. de Búrca (eds.), *The Evolution of EU Law* (Oxford University Press, 2011) 805–835.

[7] See F. Biermann and I. Boas, 'Preparing for a Warmer World: Towards a Global Governance System to Protect Climate Refugees' (2010) 10 *Global Environmental Politics* 60–88.

[8] See R. Lefeber, *An Inconvenient Responsibility* (Amsterdam: Eleven International Publishing, 2009); M. Faure and A. Nollkaemper, 'International Liability as an Instrument to Prevent and Compensate for Climate Change' (2007) 26 *Stanford Environmental Law Journal* 123–179; E. Kosolapova, 'Liability for Climate Change-Related Damage in Domestic Courts: Claims for Compensation in the USA', in Michael Faure and Marjan Peeters (eds.) *Climate Change Liability* (Cheltenham: Edward Elgar, 2011), 189–205.

4    A CHANGING (REGULATORY) CLIMATE

country is willing (or able) to address climate change alone – we would still have to address the related problem of 'free riding', where countries will attempt to benefit from the actions of others without contributing to the solution themselves.

Notwithstanding the politics, the unprecedented scale and complexity of climate change as a regulatory problem challenges established approaches to regulation and governance. The diversity, complexity and uncertainty associated with climate change make the design of effective climate change regulation a daunting task, but also provide opportunities for experimentation. The increased application of so-called market-based instruments has been spurred on by the need for 'new' regulatory tools.[9] Emission trading schemes, a type of market-based instrument also known as tradable permit schemes, have been considered particularly promising in the cost-effective mitigation of greenhouse gas emissions – the main cause of anthropogenic climate change.[10] However, our limited practical experience with emissions trading has rendered mixed results.[11]

At the time of writing, the United Nations Framework Convention on Climate Change (UNFCCC) and its Kyoto Protocol remain the most important international treaties for the mitigation and adaptation of climate change.[12] The European Union and its Member States are parties to both, and developed the European Union Emissions Trading Scheme (EU ETS), in part, as a method to meet their reduction targets under the Kyoto Protocol in a cost-effective manner.[13] The EU ETS is a traditional cap-and-trade scheme that caps the amount of $CO_2$ that may be emitted by a specified group of actors. In turn, these actors may decide to buy additional permits from other actors, or abate their emissions in order to fulfil their reduction requirements. The EU ETS is the largest

---

[9] As discussed further in Chapter 1, emission trading schemes are in fact not 'new' regulatory instruments, but their scope and application have expanded significantly within the environmental sphere.

[10] For a critique of the somewhat romanticized view on emission trading schemes and their potential for climate change mitigation, see S. Bogojević, *Emissions Trading Schemes: Markets, States and Law* (Oxford: Hart Publishing, 2013).

[11] The US Acid Rain Program has been considered particularly successful, see A. D. Ellerman *et al.*, *Markets for Clean Air: The U.S. Acid Rain Program* (Cambridge University Press, 2000).

[12] United Nations Framework Convention on Climate Change (1994) and Kyoto Protocol to the United Nations Framework Convention on Climate Change, conclusion 11 December 1997, entry into force 16 February 2005, United Nations Treaties A-30822.

[13] See Chapter 3.

cap-and-trade system currently in operation: in 2010, the EU ETS market volume amounted to 5.5 billion tonnes of $CO_2$ with a weighted average price of €14.5/tonne, accounting for 80 per cent of global transacted volume.[14] The EU ETS can moreover be conceptualized as a multi-level regulatory tool: its functioning depends on the actions and cooperation of regulators at several different levels of governance.

This book takes a closer look at the practice of competence allocation in the EU ETS, and shows that its functioning can be improved, or undermined, by the way in which competences – i.e. norm setting, implementation and enforcement – are allocated across governance levels.[15] Since its inception in 2005, the EU ETS has gone through three trading phases: the 'learning by doing' phase from 2005 to 2007; the 'Kyoto commitment' phase between 2008 and 2012; and the 'post-Kyoto' phase, which started in 2013. In each trading phase, the EU ETS underwent significant institutional changes, making it a particularly rich case study with respect to competence allocation. We will see that the de facto competence allocation in the EU ETS tends to diverge from the theoretically optimal, as well as the *de jure*, allocation.[16] In order to explain this divergence and the resulting problems, the discussion on competence allocation is supplemented by a political economy analysis of the EU ETS. This political economy view of the EU ETS shows how the relative strength and position of certain interest groups within the

---

[14] The volume of carbon rights traded throughout the world amounted to €93 billion in 2010, see G. Turner, 'Value of the Global Carbon Market Increases by 5% in 2010 but Volumes Decline', *Bloomberg New Energy Memo* (6 January 2011). By means of comparison, the market share of the Regional Greenhouse Gas Initiative (RGGI) in the United States dropped from 9 per cent to less than 1 per cent in 2010 due to the lack of prospects for a federal cap-and-trade scheme in the United States. The projected value of the world's carbon markets in 2020 is €1.7 trillion, provided that other markets are implemented by e.g. Japan and Australia.

[15] In this book, the term 'competence' is used to refer to the exercise of government authority, primarily by public actors. The usage of this term is based on the working language of the European Court of Justice – *compétence*/competence as opposed to *pouvoirs*/powers – in line with the European context of the EU ETS and as exemplified by the cases C279/93 *Schumacker* [1995]: 'Il convient de constater que si, en l'état actuel du droit communautaire, la matière des impôts directs ne relève pas en tant que telle du domaine de la *compétence* de la Communauté, il n'en reste pas moins que les Etats membres doivent exercer leurs *compétences* retenues dans le respect du droit communautaire' (emphasis added) and C73/08, *Bressol* [2010]: 'il convient de rappeler que si le droit de L'Union ne porte pas atteinte à la *compétence* des Etats membres [...] il demeure toutefois que, dans l'exercice de cette *compétence*, ces Etats doivent respecter le droit de L'Union.' (emphasis added).

[16] See Chapters 3 and 4.

6   A CHANGING (REGULATORY) CLIMATE

regulatory process influenced the design, implementation and enforcement of the trading scheme.

## 1 Competence allocation

Article 1 of the Treaty on European Union (TEU) states that the Member States confer upon the EU 'competences to attain objectives they have in common'.[17] It then goes on to state that the Union 'shall pursue its objectives by appropriate means commensurate with the competences conferred upon it'.[18] In a number of policy areas, the EU's competence is exclusive, and as such takes precedence over the Member States.[19] Similarly, there are shared competence areas where the roles of the EU and the Member States are determined by the principle of subsidiarity.[20] Despite the centrality of 'competence allocation' within the European Union, there is little guidance within the European Treaties as to the 'content' of these competences. While it is clear that either the EU or the Member States are empowered to act within specific policy areas, it is not self-evident what such action entails.

This inflation of competence allocation into the unitary act of assigning policy-making powers to a regulator is mimicked by the two main bodies of economic and legal literature that address this topic: the economic theory of federalism and legal federalism.[21] Both theories (implicitly) adhere to the simplifying assumption that one jurisdiction

---

[17] Article 1 of the Treaty on European Union, OJ C 326, 26.10.2012.

[18] Article 3(6) of the TEU.

[19] Article 3 of the Treaty on the Functioning of the European Union (TFEU), OJ C 326, 26.10.2012. In most other areas, Member States are obliged to exercise their powers in compliance with EU law, see e.g. L. Azoulai, 'The "Retained Powers" Formula in the Case Law of the European Court of Justice: EU Law as Total Law?' (2011) 4(2) *European Journal of Legal Studies* 192–219.

[20] Article 5 of the TEU; Article 4 of the TFEU.

[21] Within European legal literature, these topics are mostly found in the subsidiarity discussions. See generally K. van Kersbergen and B. Verbeek, 'The Politics of Subsidiarity in the European Union' (1994) 32 *Journal of Common Market Studies* 215–236; J. Golub, 'Sovereignty and Subsidiarity in EU Environmental Policy' (1996) 44 *Political Studies* 686–703; D. Benson and A. Jordan, 'Understanding Task Allocation in the European Union: Exploring the Value of Federal Theory' (2008) 15 *Journal of European Public Policy* 78–97. Another important approach within European law and governance is the multi-level governance methodology, as developed by G. Marks, L. Hooghe, and K. Blank, 'European Integration from the 1980s: State-Centric v. Multi-level Governance' (1996) 34 *Journal of Common Market Studies* 341–378; G. Marks, 'An Actor-centred Approach to Multi-level Governance' (1996) 6 *Regional & Federal Studies* 20–38.

controls the entire regulatory process, through 'policy-making'. Thus, questions of competence allocation focus on whether 'policy-making' is centralized or decentralized. There is little differentiation between the processes that constitute policy-making, i.e. norm setting, implementation and enforcement.[22]

Within the economic theory of federalism, there is a rebuttable presumption in favour of decentralization. This presumption is based primarily on the, presumed, heterogeneous preferences of different localities. Since centralized provision of public goods necessarily entails uniformity, the local provision of public goods is preferable, as this will better accommodate these heterogeneous preferences.[23] In addition, the diversity in local goods provision will allow citizens – i.e. 'consumers' of the public goods provided – to move to a different locality that provides a different set of goods.[24] The situation changes, however, when there are spillovers, or externalities, between localities. To illustrate the concept of externalities, which is central to the problem of climate change, let us consider a typical transboundary regulatory problem:

Two jurisdictions (A and B) share a common river. Jurisdiction A engages in an economic activity that provides certain economic and/or social benefits to its own jurisdiction. However, this activity comes with a cost, namely pollution. This pollution is transboundary in the sense that the common river causes (some of) the pollution to move from jurisdiction A to jurisdiction B, which consequently has to bear part of the costs of pollution.

In this classic externalities problem, A will 'produce' too much of the polluting activity since it does not have to bear the full costs of this activity, while receiving the full benefits of the activity.[25] This means that when A decides on the production norm, it would set it at $Q^A$ (see Figure 1). This level of activity ($Q^A$) is higher than the optimum ($Q^*$)

---

[22] There are important exceptions to this generalization, particularly with respect to legal literature on types of federalism and constitutionalism. However, the focus of these writings is on how the competences should be divided, based on the constitutional setting of the legal system at hand. The approach taken in this book is an extra-legal one, based on normative criteria outside the legal framework of the available regulatory system(s).

[23] See e.g. W. E. Oates, 'An Essay on Fiscal Federalism' (1999) 37 *Journal of Economic Literature* 1120–1149. For an in-depth discussion on the literature, see Chapter 1.

[24] See C. Tiebout, 'A Pure Theory of Local Expenditures' (1956) 64 *The Journal of Political Economy* 416–424.

[25] See A. C. Pigou, *The Economics of Welfare*, 4th edn (London: Macmillan, 1932); R. H. Coase, 'The Problem of Social Cost' (1960) 3 *The Journal of Law and Economics* 1–44.

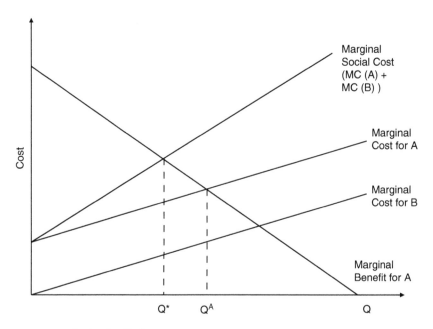

FIGURE I.1 *Optimal pollution norm*

since A does not take account of B's costs. If B were able to set the production norm of A's activity, it would reduce the activity to zero since B only bears the costs from the activity and none of the benefits of the activity.[26] This disregards the benefits that the activity produces in jurisdiction A and as such is also sub-optimal. Thus we can only arrive at the social optimum (Q*) when a regulator, whose jurisdiction spans the geographical area where both the costs and benefits of the activity materialize, sets the standard.

This simplified approach shows the effect of externalities on the determination of objective and subjective optima in the provision and regulation of public goods. If we consider the case of climate change, it is easy to envisage how country A (e.g. the United States of America) would have little interest in limiting its polluting but profitable economic activity when most of the damage is born by country B (e.g. Tuvalu). However, what this example does not show is that in order for the optimal norm to be maintained, its implementation and enforcement

---

[26] In reality, B is likely to enjoy some beneficial side-effects of jurisdiction A's success, for instance in the form of regional stability or touristic spending.

may also have to be 'centralized',[27] so as to prevent a similar externalities problem at a later stage of the regulatory process. Country A does not only lack the incentives to set the socially optimal norm, but also to implement and enforce this norm. The decentralization of policy-making largely ignores the distinction between these different phases and fails to recognize that, for instance, decentralized implementation and enforcement may well undermine centralized enforcement.

The legal approach to competence allocation focuses on the particulars of the legal framework at hand, rather than on abstract jurisdictions. As such, it centres on those constitutional principles that refer to the division of competence between levels of governance. For the European Union, the principle of subsidiarity sets out the division of competence for areas that are not exclusively in the hands of the EU or the Member States.[28] Similarly, the 'doctrine of enumerated powers' is a founding principle in the United States Constitution.[29] Aside from constitutional doctrine, legal scholarship is increasingly influenced by economic theory, as exemplified by the development of the so-called 'race-to-the-bottom' hypothesis.[30] The race-to-the-bottom hypothesis posits that jurisdictions will compete with each other for investments and consumers (citizens/voters). In our example, this could mean that jurisdictions A and B adopt increasingly lenient pollution norms in order to attract industry investment, for example. Alternatively, they could adopt increasingly stringent regulations, attracting a certain group of citizen-voters, which would lead to a 'race-to-the-top' in terms of environmental quality. This type of competition is facilitated by the presence of externalities as jurisdictions are able to externalize

---

[27] The terms 'centralization' and 'decentralization' assume a binary choice between the levels of government. It is easy to imagine a situation where the regulator overseeing jurisdictions A and B still operates at a relatively 'decentralized' level of governance. The oversimplification created by the use of centralization/decentralization terminology will be discussed in more detail in Chapters 1 and 2.

[28] See Article 5 of the TEU (on subsidiarity), as well as Articles 3 and 4 of the TEU (on competence allocation generally).

[29] See Tenth Amendment to the United States Constitution (1787), adopted 17 September 1787, ratified 28 September 1787, ('[t]he powers not delegated to the United States by the Constitution, nor prohibited by it to the States, are reserved to the States respectively, or to the people.')

[30] See R. B. Stewart, 'Environmental Regulation and International Competitiveness' (1993) 102 *The Yale Law Journal* 41–75; D. Esty, 'Revitalizing Environmental Federalism' (1996) 95 *Michigan Law Review* 570–653 as quoted in G. Porter, 'Trade Competition and Pollution Standards: "Race to the Bottom" or "Stuck at the Bottom"' (1998) 8 *Journal of Environment and Development* 133–151.

some of the costs of their under- or over-regulation on neighbouring jurisdictions.[31] Notwithstanding the increased application of economic approaches and criteria, legal theories of federalism continue to focus primarily on legal arguments founded in relevant constitutional provisions. Legal scholarship better captures the rich complexity of regulatory arrangements but its case-specific focus prevents the development of a more general theory.[32]

There are additional differences between economic and legal theories of federalism: firstly, the economic approach labels regulatory systems as 'federal' when, as a matter of fact, competences are divided between two or more regulators in a hierarchical setting. Thus, from an economic perspective certain systems may be considered 'federal', even if the constitution of that system does not provide for an expressly 'federal' relationship between different governance levels. The framework for competence allocation developed in this book similarly does not set out to determine whether the division of competences within a legal system is in line with the underlying constitutional arrangements, i.e. whether it is internally coherent. Rather it applies a de facto approach, which allows us to consider relationships between levels of governance that are part of more than one legal system. For instance, both the international legal regime – in the form of the United Nations – as well as the European legal order will be discussed, since they both form part of the regulatory context of climate change mitigation.

The scenarios of competence allocation developed in this book are more elaborate than models typically applied within economic theory. Rather than having a binary option between centralization and decentralization, additional levels of governance are included in order to more closely reflect regulatory reality. Also, close attention is paid to the legal rules that provide the framework for the EU ETS. Nevertheless, these scenarios inherently simplify the reality of competence allocation and should therefore not be mistaken for 'the total view' of the

---

[31] See R. L. Revesz, 'The Race to the Bottom and Federal Environmental Regulation: A Response to Critics' (1997) 82 *Minnesota Law Review* 535–564; R. Revesz and K. Engel, 'State Environmental Standard-Setting: Is There a "Race" and Is It "To the Bottom"?' (1997) 48 *Hastings Law Journal* 271–398.

[32] K. M. Holland, F. L. Morton, and B. Galligan (eds.), *Federalism and the Environment: Environmental Policymaking in Australia, Canada, and the United States* (Westport, CT: Greenwood, 1996) find that while there is an immense literature on various aspects of federalism, there is little systematic, comparative research assessing the impact of federalism on regulation.

phenomenon.[33] Likewise, the interactions between actors in these models are based on the assumption of rationality – a simplification of human behaviour.[34] The resulting model of interactions can, however, provide useful insights; a city map will help you find your way despite its being a simplification of reality.[35]

## 2 Regulatory functioning

A second normative difference between economic and legal theories of federalism lies in their interpretation and valuation of 'optimality'. Economic theory of federalism focuses on the efficiency of allocation, as is evidenced by the emphasis on accommodating heterogeneous circumstances and economies of scale.[36] Legal theory, on the other hand, focuses on internal consistency, i.e. is the distribution of power in line with relevant principles set out in the system's constitution? For the purposes of the current framework, which is developed in order to assess the performance of the EU ETS, the legal principles of allocation can be found in the European Treaties and the EU ETS Directives.[37]

However, our goal is not to determine the consistency of allocation with these constitutional principles, but rather to explain (sub)optimal performance of the EU ETS as a regulatory tool for cost-effective climate change mitigation. Thus 'optimal' competence allocation is not a goal in itself but a proxy for regulatory functioning. In light of our assumption that the functioning of the EU ETS is affected by its institutional setting, we must specify our criterion of optimality to reflect those regulatory challenges that are particularly relevant for the EU ETS context. Combining the regulatory context of the EU ETS and

---

[33] G. Calabresi and A. D. Melamed, 'Property Rules, Liability Rules and Inalienability: One View of the Cathedral' (1972) 85 *Harvard Law Review* 1089–1128 ('[M]odels can be mistaken for the total view of phenomena, like legal relationships, which are too complex to be painted in any one picture.')

[34] See generally V. L. Smith, *Rationality in Economics: Constructivist and Ecological Forms* (Cambridge University Press, 2008).

[35] However, we must not feel compelled to force situations into a box that does not fit simply because we have created the box. A point also made by Calabresi and Melamed, 'Property Rules, Liability Rules and Inalienability', 1128: '[M]odels generate boxes into which one then feels compelled to force situations which do not truly fit.'

[36] See literature discussed in Chapter 1.

[37] See Article 5(3) TEU and e.g. Article 3d(4) Council Directive 2009/29/EC amending Directive 2003/87/EC so as to improve and extend the greenhouse gas emission allowance trading scheme of the Community, OJ 2009 No. L140, 23 April 2009.

lessons from existing law and economics scholarship, three determinants for optimal regulatory functioning for the EU ETS can be identified:[38]

(i) The system's ability to 'internalize' and capture externalities;
(ii) The system's ability to accommodate heterogeneity of conditions and preferences; and
(iii) The system's ability to maximize economies of scale and/or scope.

A 'first-best' competence allocation scenario would be able to fulfil all three of these conditions at each stage of the regulatory process, i.e. during norm setting, implementation and enforcement. Yet, more often than not, an allocation will only be able to reflect one or two of these goals, not all of them simultaneously. In this case, a decision will have to be made as to which of these three goals is most important considering the nature of the regulatory problem, and the role of the relevant competence in addressing this problem. Ranking these goals as 'first-order' and 'second-order' considerations facilitates this trade-off. For example, for norm setting, the need to capture all externalities of the regulated activity may be considered a first-order consideration in light of the characteristics of climate change. In the context of the EU ETS this would mean setting an emission reduction norm that reflects the global social optimum by incorporating all costs and benefits of greenhouse gas-emitting activities, not just those of one country or region. This aim is most likely to be achieved at the global international level.[39]

Once the allocation of norm-setting competences is in line with this first-order consideration, second-order considerations (the accommodation of heterogeneous conditions and preferences, and the possibility of achieving economies of scale and/or scope) can be incorporated in the competence allocation decision. The labelling of these considerations as first and second order reflects a normative distinction between the necessary and the desirable: the allocation of norm-setting powers must ensure the capture of externalities, and preferably take account of heterogeneous conditions or economies of scale/scope. In those cases where competence allocation cannot optimize considerations across

---

[38] Additional determinants may be envisaged e.g. if one adopts an intra-legal, rather than extra-legal, perspective.

[39] In practice, the allocation of competences at a global level does not guarantee successful norm setting, as discussed in Chapters 2, 3 and 4.

all dimensions, instrument choice can help to accommodate secondary considerations.

The combined first-best allocation for each competence may result in a fragmented system of allocation, where each competence is allocated at a different level of governance. In such a fragmented system, regulators at different governance levels are likely to interact with each other in order to fulfil their respective tasks. Depending on the incentives of the regulator, the amount of discretion, and the methods of oversight at each level, these interactions may lead to a sub-optimal situation, where regulators may enforce too much or too little. Some of these interactions can be regulated through improved oversight rules or providing incentives for the regulators. In some cases, the first-best individual competence allocation may have to be reconsidered. For instance, a unified system of allocation may be preferable, in order to overcome the negative interactions between different governance levels.[40] The proposed model of competence allocation thus considers both the allocation of individual competences as well as their interaction.

## 3 Structural overview

The structure of this book is based on a number of intersecting questions on competence allocation and regulatory functioning in the context of the EU ETS.

Chapter 1 sets out the existing economic and legal scholarship on competence allocation, which frames our debate. It also develops the theoretical framework for competence allocation. From this framework we can distil the first-best allocation of regulatory competences based on the following three conditions: (i) capturing relevant externalities, (ii) accommodating heterogeneity of conditions and preferences and (iii) maximizing potential economies of scale and/or scope. When the resulting allocation is fragmented, the welfare implications of the interactions between regulators are compared with those of a unified system of allocation.

In order for this framework to provide a benchmark for competence allocation in the EU ETS, its parameters have to be tailored more

---

[40] In a unified system, different actors at the same regulatory level may be responsible for the executing of specific competences. We assume that the preferences and goals of regulators at the same level of governance are aligned. This simplifying assumption is discussed in more detail in Chapters 1 and 2.

precisely to the regulatory context of climate change. Chapter 2 therefore considers the defining characteristics of climate change as a regulatory problem, which allows us to determine the trade-offs between regulatory considerations (i.e. the capture of externalities, heterogeneity and economies of scale/scope). In addition, we can specify the substantive elements of the regulatory competences as they relate to the EU ETS: norm setting as the determination of emission reduction norms for a specific region or country; implementation as the distribution of this norm between individual emitters and creating the institutional structure of the emissions trading scheme; and enforcement as those processes that enforce the distribution made under implementation through verification and penalties, and oversight of the market in which emission permits are traded.

From these building blocks we create two benchmark scenarios against which we can assess the functioning of the EU ETS. In the first scenario, we assume that norm setting takes place at the global level (i.e. through the UNFCCC), and that implementation and enforcement are decentralized at the European or national level (i.e. European Member State). This first scenario corresponds with the situation under the first two trading phases of the EU ETS between 2005 and 2012. The second scenario assumes that norm setting takes place at the regional (European) level, combined with implementation and enforcement taking place at the European or national level, which is in line with the EU ETS practice from 2013 onwards.

It is important to stress that the focus of this book is limited to the role of public actors in the regulatory process. As with all forms of regulation, the role of private parties within market-based instruments is of great interest when considering its functioning and should be viewed as distinct from that of public parties. Moreover, private parties participate increasingly within regulatory processes on different levels of governance with varying degrees of success. Their potential with respect to, for instance, enforcement is increasingly recognized and should be more fully exploited in order to improve enforcement practices. However, since the regulatory competences discussed here are traditionally the prerogative of public actors, a framework of regulatory functioning based on competence allocation must start with their respective roles. Furthermore, the incentive structures for these two groups are distinctly different, which makes a combined analysis of these roles undesirable. Therefore the role of private actors will only be included in those circumstances where the analysis of public regulatory action benefits from an explicit mention.

Chapters 3 and 4 follow the chronological development of the EU ETS, distinguishing between periods of global norm setting (Phases I and II) and regional norm setting (Phase III onwards). In both these periods, the allocation of implementation and enforcement competences diverges from our theoretical first-best scenario. The effects of this divergence are particularly clear in Phases I and II, where the implementation of the EU ETS, with respect to the allocation of emission allowances, has proven to be a strategic pitfall within the regulatory process. In the first trading period, the decentralized national implementation of the EU ETS led to a situation of over-allocation. This under-performance can partly be explained by the incentives of the EU Member States to protect their national industries under the EU ETS. In addition, this type of over-allocation requires asymmetric information between the European level and national level regarding the actual emissions of individual actors.[41]

In the second trading period, these information problems had been partly resolved, which led to more explicit clashes between the allocation preferences at the European level and the national level. The European Commission questioned the allocation strategies of individual countries, replacing nationally collected data with data gathered by European institutions. This led to legal action before the European courts regarding the division of implementation competences between the European and national level.[42] The allocation of enforcement competences at the national level has also caused several problems during the first two trading phases. The regulation of a European market in emission allowances by national agencies gives rise to a potential externalities problem: when the activities of a trader on a national segment of the market primarily affect actors in other national segments, the incentives of national enforcers to intervene are lower than when damage manifests in their own jurisdiction. Significant changes have been put in place for the third trading phase of the EU ETS, with important implementation and enforcement competences shifting to the European level. Whether these changes, in force since January 2013, will result in the improved performance of the EU ETS remains to be seen.

---

[41] See Chapter 3.
[42] See inter alia Case T-183/07, *Poland v. European Commission* [2009] ECR II-03395; Case T-263/07, *Estonia v. European Commission* [2009] ECR II-03463. See in detail Chapter 3.

Recent experiences with the EU ETS underline the importance of the instrument choice and design elements of the EU ETS. Whereas initially the shift of implementation competence appeared to be sufficient to overcome over-allocation issues, especially combined with a move away from 'grandfathering'[43] in favour of the auctioning of allowances, the continued economic downturn has aggravated the problem of over-allocation. The European Commission proposed a temporary solution to over-allocation through the 'back loading' of allowances – a process that reduces the number of allowances on the market – but this proposal was met with resistance from the European Parliament.[44] While competence allocation can explain regulatory successes and failures along several dimensions, it does not explain the divergence between our first-best allocation and actual allocation in the EU ETS or the design choices made by the respective regulators.

Chapter 5 turns to answer these questions via a political economy approach, by studying 'the collective or political processes through which public economic decisions are made'.[45] Since the 1970s, political economy has developed as a branch of economics, and social science generally, that examines how political forces, organized in 'interest groups', affect the design and choice of policies, especially insofar as these policies concern the distribution of scarce resources in society. The positive models developed within political economy hold explanatory value for the sharp contrast(s) between the real-life experiences with the EU ETS and the optimal competence allocation model developed in this book. Capture theory and public choice models are particularly adept at shedding light on the developments within the EU ETS.[46] During the first two phases, the design and competence allocation of the EU ETS appeared to favour industrial rather than environmental or consumer interests. This has changed towards the third phase and we

---

[43] Under a grandfathering regime, allowances are given to market incumbents for free.

[44] See e.g. MEMO/13/343, 'Commissioner Hedegaard's Statement on Today's Vote by the European Parliament on the Backloading Proposal', 16 April 2013.

[45] W. E. Oates and P. R. Portney, 'The Political Economy of Environmental Policy', in K.-G. Maler and J. R. Vincent (eds.), *Handbook of Environmental Economics* (Amsterdam: Elsevier Science B.V., 2003), 325–350, 327.

[46] There are three main political economy models that explain the creation of social policy: those of the median-voter, capture theory, and public choice. The median-voter model provides some important insights into the more general questions regarding the adoption of e.g. environmental measures, but once questions of stringency of regulatory norms or instrument choice are raised, the model's predictive value becomes less clear. See generally Oates and Portney, *ibid.*, 329 (on the explanatory value of the median-voter model for environmental programmes

will see that the maturation of the EU ETS market is partly responsible for this change.

The epilogue reflects on the continuing importance of competence allocation for the EU ETS. The changes made at the end of the second trading phase with respect to cap-setting and allowance allocation were meant to remedy the problems of the first phase. Yet, despite the pre-emptive changes in the design of the EU ETS, the first months of the third trading phase have been far from uneventful and have been marked by political debate on further legislative changes to, inter alia, the centralized cap.[47] The future of the EU ETS remains uncertain and the research for this book was concluded at a particularly precarious point in its colourful development.[48] The competence allocation perspective offers several suggestions for institutional improvements as the EU ETS enters its third trading phase.

A final remark is warranted regarding the position of this book within legal, economic, and law and economics scholarship. Any academic that attempts to produce a work that claims to incorporate approaches of two or more disciplines, or uses the methodology of one (economics) to analyse another (law) will inevitably struggle to completely satisfy either audience. In this respect, this book's aspirations are in equal parts modest and ambitious. According to Goethe, 'we see only what we know'. Thus, if a lawyer turns to this book for a detailed overview of the legal particularities of the EU ETS, and finds exactly that, I consider this book a success. However, I believe that interdisciplinary work can expand what we know, and thus what we see. Therefore, I hope that a lawyer's intuitions regarding the political process surrounding the creation of laws may be formalized in our political economy analysis, or find a supplementary normative framework for the allocation of competences within the European Union. Conversely, economists or political scientists may gain additional insights into the legal rules that operationalize the EU ETS. Ultimately, I hope this book contributes to the ever-growing interdisciplinary dialogue between lawyers, economists and political scientists.

in particular). A more detailed discussion of the various contributions of political economy can be found in Chapter 5.

[47] See note 44 and the discussion in the Epilogue, section 1 for more detail.

[48] Research for this book was completed in July 2013.

# 1 From competing jurisdictions to competing competences

## The allocation of regulatory competences

The aim of this chapter is to depict the landscape in which our approach to competence allocation is developed. To that end, it surveys the existing economic and legal scholarship on competence allocation, which frames our debate. The main contribution of this theoretical framework compared to existing theories is the focus on the fragmentation of the regulatory framework into different competences, which can be allocated to different levels of governance. These competences play different roles in the regulatory system, and their optimal allocation level may differ accordingly. This fragmentation is increasingly recognized by other scholars in specific regulatory contexts,[1] but is yet to be incorporated in a general theoretic framework. Aside from providing an overview of the most important contributions from economic and legal theories on federalism, we also consider several streams from political science such as multi-level governance and polycentric theory, insofar as they have influenced legal understanding on competence allocation.

Together with Chapter 2, this chapter forms the theoretical and normative framework against which the European Union Emissions

---

[1] See e.g. Oates and Portney, 'The Political Economy of Environmental Policy', 342–343: 'We can envision a system of environmental policy-making in which the central government sets standards and oversees measures to address explicitly national pollution problems and intervenes in cases where (like acid rain) polluting activities in one jurisdiction impose substantial damages elsewhere. In addition, the central government would provide basic support for research and the dissemination of information on environmental problems, since these are activities that benefit everyone. At the same time, decentralized levels of government would set their own standards and establish their own programs for managing those dimensions of environmental quality that are primarily contained within their own boundaries (for instance, the standards that a local landfill might have to meet).'

Trading Scheme (EU ETS) will be analysed in subsequent chapters. This extended framework of competence allocation allows us to consider, first, the advantages and disadvantages of centralizing or decentralizing ('(de)centralizing') certain competences, and second, possible strategic interactions between regulatory competences, depending on their relative allocation. By including these two dimensions – allocation and interaction – we aim to 'perceive relationships which have been ignored'[2] by existing literature on legal and economic theories of federalism. Finally, the role of instrument choice is made explicit. Regulatory tools affect the regulatory system's ability to accommodate heterogeneity and costs, as well as the ability of implementers or enforcers, for example, to externalize certain costs onto others. As such, instrument choice can be used to nuance our earlier, more general observations regarding the optimal allocation of competences. Specific attention is given to cap-and-trade, a form of market-based regulation, since this is the method of regulation under the EU ETS.

# 1 Competing jurisdictions

From the mid-eighteenth century onwards, the question as to which regulatory body, at which degree of centralization, should carry out certain regulatory functions has become an increasingly important part of the intellectual and political debate. Inspired by Montesquieu's arguments on the virtues of the *separation* and *division* of powers, the American Founding Fathers drew strict dividing lines between the branches of government, as well as between the powers of the United States government and the state governments.[3] The 1787 American Constitution provides that the United States Congress can only exercise those powers specified in the Constitution and that all other powers belong exclusively to the state governments as reserved powers: the so-called doctrine of enumerated powers.[4] Tocqueville also considered

---

[2] Calabresi and Melamed, 'Property Rules, Liability Rules and Inalienability', 1090: 'We then analyse aspects of the pollution problem and of criminal sanctions in order to demonstrate how the model enables us to perceive relationships which have been ignored by writers in those fields.'

[3] See C. de Montesquieu, *The Spirit of the Laws*, T. Nugent (trans.) (New York: MacMillan, 1949) (arguing in 1748 that a separation of powers could function as a guard against tyranny).

[4] See US Constitution (1787), Article I, section 1 ('All legislative Powers herein granted shall be vested in a Congress of the United States.'); Article I, section 8 (detailing seventeen separate legislative powers which are expressly enumerated); the Tenth

the division of powers between the federal and state level one of the key virtues of the American legal and political system,[5] and the United States federal model may be said to have inspired many consequent federalist systems. In the European Union, the principle of subsidiarity strives to maintain a high level of decentralization in ways reminiscent of the doctrine of enumerated powers.[6]

The relative popularity of government through a combination of shared and self-rule has given rise to a rich body of economic, political and legal scholarship, which all claim the term 'federalism' as characteristic for their respective fields of research. Over time, great normative value has become attached to the term. For political and legal scholars, 'federalism' stands for the theory (and/or advocacy) of a political order with principles for dividing final authority between member units and common institutions.[7] Yet within legal scholarship, drawing a comparison between the federal system of the United States and the 'multi-level' system of the European Union is precarious since many European lawyers and politicians continue to reject the characterization of the European Union as a federal system.[8] Looking beyond the

Amendment ('[t]he powers not delegated to the United States by the Constitution, nor prohibited by it to the States, are reserved to the States respectively, or to the people'). Cf. US Constitution (1787), Article I, section 8, clause 18 (stating that Congress has the power '[t]o make all Laws which shall be deemed necessary and proper for carrying into Execution the foregoing Powers, and all other Powers vested by this Constitution in the Government of the United States, or in any Department or Officer thereof.')

[5] A. de Tocqueville, *Democracy in America*, vol. I, J. P. Mayer (ed.) and G. Lawrence (trans.) (London: Fontana Press, 1994).

[6] Within the European Union, the allocation of (legislative) competences in different policy areas is subjected to the 'subsidiarity' test, which dictates that 'in areas which do not fall within its exclusive competence, the Union shall act only if and insofar as the objectives of the proposed action cannot be sufficiently achieved by the Member States, either at the central level or the regional or local level, but rather, by reason of the scale or effects of the proposed action, be better achieved at Union level'. See Article 5(3) of the TEU.

[7] K. Lenaerts, 'Constitutionalism and the Many Faces of Federalism' (1990) 38 *American Journal of Comparative Law* 205–264.

[8] Marks *et al.*, 'European Integration from the 1980s'; B. Kohler-Koch, 'Catching up with Change: The Transformation of Governance in the European Union' (1996) 3 *Journal of European Public Policy* 359–380; E. Grande, 'The State and Interest Groups in a Framework of Multi-Level Decision-Making: The Case of the European Union' (1996) 3 *Journal of European Public Policy* 365–390. See generally D. J. Elazar, *Exploring Federalism* (Tuscaloosa: The University of Alabama Press, 1987) and R. L. Watts, 'The Theoretical and Practical Implications of Asymmetrical Federalism' in R. Agranoff (ed.) *Accommodating Diversity: Asymmetry in Federal States* (Baden-Baden, Germany: Nomos Verlagsgesellschaft, 1999) (discussing the different species of a federal order, such as federations, unions, confederations, leagues and decentralized unions). T. A. Börzel

legal classification of the European governance model,[9] the de facto competence division between different regulatory levels within the European Union is strongly reminiscent of a 'federal' construct.

When viewed from the perspective of the economic theory of federalism, the term becomes less of a political statement and more a question of the factual division of labour between different regulatory levels. The economic theory of federalism presents positive theories for the impact of (de)centralization on regulation focusing on the efficiency of (de)centralized public good provision. Some of the considerations introduced by the economic theory of federalism have now become common parlance in some areas of legal scholarship focused on federalism. European legal scholarship has also been profoundly influenced by so-called 'multi-level governance' scholarship that speaks to the *sui generis* nature of the European Union as a legal and political entity.[10] In multi-level governance theory, there is more prominence for non-state actors and state actors beyond the national level. This section will introduce the main arguments of these theories, which provide the foundation for a theoretical framework of competing *competences*, as opposed to jurisdictions.

## A  Economic theory of federalism

The economic theory of federalism encompasses an incredibly rich body of literature that comprises various fields of economic research, including in particular public economics, fiscal federalism, public finance, and increasingly also the economics of information, organization theory, public choice and principal–agent theory.[11] The main analytical endeavour of this field has been to 'enrich our understanding at a conceptual level of the structure and working of multi-level

---

and T. Risse, 'Who is Afraid of a European Federation? How to Constitutionalise a Multi-Level Governance System' *Harvard Jean Monnet Working Paper* (Symposium), No.7/00 (2000).

[9] See e.g. Marks *et al.*, 'European Integration from the 1980s'; Kohler-Koch, 'Catching up with Change'; Grande, 'The State and Interest Groups in a Framework of Multi-Level Decision-Making'. See *generally* Elazar, 'Exploring Federalism' and Watts, 'Asymmetrical Federalism' (discussing the different species of a federal order, such as federations, unions, confederations, leagues and decentralized unions).

[10] R. Eising and B. Kohler-Koch (eds.), *The Transformation of Governance in the European Union* (London: Routledge, 2004), at xi.

[11] W. E. Oates, 'Toward A Second-Generation Theory of Fiscal Federalism' (2005) 12 *International Tax and Public Finance* 349–373; Y. Qian and B. R. Weinga, 'Federalism as a Commitment to Preserving Market Incentives' (1997) 11 *Journal of Economic Perspectives* 83–92.

government'.[12] I will discuss the main findings and contributions of these works by looking first at the initial studies that form the basis of the economic theory of federalism, the so-called 'fiscal federalism' literature as developed in the 1970s. This discussion is followed by an overview of the more recent additions and developments in the field; the 'second-generation theory of fiscal federalism'.[13]

## 1 First generation: 'Fiscal' federalism

In the 1950s and 1960s, Paul Samuelson, Kenneth Arrow and Richard Musgrave made important contributions to the field of public finance, which would later be the foundation for the normative economic work on (fiscal) federalism. The combination of Samuelson's work on public goods,[14] Arrow's treatise on the conceptualization of the roles of the private and public sector,[15] and Musgrave's on public finance,[16] set out a model of regulation where the public sector should step in, in the event that private provision of public goods had resulted in market failure. Based on the implicit assumption that the relevant level of government would provide such goods while seeking to maximize social welfare, it followed that for public goods whose pattern of consumption is less than national, local (decentralized) provision of these goods could result in improved social welfare, as compared to a national uniform level of public good provision.

In 1972, Wallace Oates formalized this proposition in his 'Decentralization Theorem' (DT).[17] In its most basic form, the DT finds that, in the absence of spillovers or externalities, the local provision of public goods will be Pareto superior to centralized provision of public goods,[18] given that centralized provision is presumed to be synonymous

---

[12] Oates, 'Toward A Second-Generation Theory', 349.

[13] *Ibid.*

[14] P. A. Samuelson, 'The Pure Theory of Public Expenditures' (1954) 4 *Review of Economics and Statistics* 387–389; P. A. Samuelson, 'Diagrammatic Exposition of a Theory of Public Expenditure' (1955) 37 *Review of Economics and Statistics* 350–356.

[15] K. Arrow, 'The Organization of Economic Activity: Issues Pertinent to the Choice of Market Versus Non-Market Allocation', in Joint Economic Committee, *The Analysis and Evaluation of Public Expenditures: The PPB System*, vol. I (Washington, DC: U.S. GPO, 1970).

[16] R. Musgrave, *The Theory of Public Finance* (New York: McGraw Hill, 1959); R. Musgrave, 'The Voluntary Exchange Theory of Public Economy' (1939) 53 *Quarterly Journal of Economics* 213–237.

[17] W. E. Oates, *Fiscal Federalism* (New York: Harcourt Brace Jovanovich, 1972).

[18] 'Pareto optimality or efficiency' refers to a state of the world where no more changes to the allocation of goods among a set of individuals could be made without at least

with a uniform level of output across jurisdictions.[19] The assumption that centralization equates to uniformity is justified by reference to the fact that proximity of local governments to their constituents gives them superior knowledge of their preferences and conditions,[20] and that it might be politically costly to differentiate between jurisdictions at the central level.[21]

Tiebout's well-known 'voting-with-the-feet' model also argues in favour of local provision of public goods.[22] Samuelson's earlier work claims that decentralization would not result in an efficient provision of public goods, due in part to the lack of incentives for parties to make their preferences for goods explicit;[23] in Tiebout's model, the decentralized provision of *local* public goods is Pareto-efficient under certain, rather restrictive, conditions.[24] This efficiency would be achieved through the relocation of citizen-consumers between localities that each offer a different mix of public goods, assuming there are no

one person being better off and no other individual worse off. If a situation is Pareto superior to another, it means that there are still Pareto improvements to be made, i.e. individuals could still be made better off without making another individual worse off. Pareto efficiency does not incorporate a sense of equity, or other socially desirable aspects of distribution.

[19] See also Oates, *Fiscal Federalism*; and Oates, 'Toward a Second-Generation Theory', 352–353 ('[U]nder certain conditions, a varied pattern of local outputs in accordance with local tastes will be Pareto superior to an outcome characterized by a centrally determined, uniform level of output across all jurisdictions.')

[20] See also R. P. Inman and D. L. Rubinfeld, 'Federalism', in B. Bouckaert and G. De Geest (eds.), *Encyclopedia of Law and Economics* (Cheltenham: Edward Elgar Publishing, 2000), 661–691 (who argue that participation of interest groups and individuals may rise with increased decentralization and this increased political participation may place more pressure on the local regulator to conform to local preferences). Conversely, one may also argue that the likelihood of regulatory capture increases when the links between the regulator and regulated are closer. See G. J. Stigler, 'The Theory of Economic Regulation' (1971) 2 *The Bell Journal of Economics and Management Science* 3–21, 3 ('as a rule, regulation is acquired by the industry and is designed and operated primarily for its benefit'); E. Dal Bo, 'Regulatory Capture: A Review' (2006) 22 *Oxford Review of Economic Policy* 203–225 at 203 (regulatory capture broadly refers to 'the process through which special interests affect state intervention in any of its forms'. More narrowly defined, regulatory capture refers to the process 'through which regulated monopolies end up manipulating the state agencies that are supposed to control them').

[21] Oates, 'Toward A Second-Generation Theory', 353.

[22] Tiebout, 'A Pure Theory of Local Expenditures'.

[23] *Ibid.*, 416–424. Compare Samuelson, 'The Pure Theory of Public Expenditures'.

[24] Tiebout, *ibid.*, 419. (The assumptions are that: 1) consumer-voters are fully mobile, 2) consumer-voters have full knowledge of differences between communities, 3) there is a large number of communities to choose from, 4) there are no employment-related restrictions, 5) public services exhibit no external economies or diseconomies between communities, 6) for every preference pattern there is an optimal community

externalities and the number of localities is at least equal to the types of citizen-consumers.[25] An important difference between Tiebout's theory and Oates' DT is that Oates assumes there would exist a 'systematic difference in tastes across jurisdictions',[26] even without mobile individuals, whereas Tiebout partly ascribed differences in local preferences to the local differentiation of public goods supply.[27] Although the latter may appear to be counter-intuitive, following Tiebout's assumption of perfect mobility between jurisdictions, local governments may be considered as firms each offering a different mix of public goods products in order to cater to the entire range of 'consumers' (citizens).

These theories accumulate in an important normative finding of the economic theory of federalism: the geographical area in which the benefits of public good materialize should be matched by the geographical scope of the governmental jurisdiction, which typically results in decentralization.[28] There are, however, cases where the provision of 'local' public goods produces interjurisdictional spillovers: benefits (or costs) that materialize in other jurisdictions.[29] In the presence of such spillovers, Oates' DT considers the decision between centralization and decentralization to be a trade-off, which depends on the extent of heterogeneity of preferences and the degree of spillovers.[30] Still, spillovers do not dictate centralization; introducing subsidies from the central

---

size which is determined by the number of residents for which this bundle of preferences can be produced at the lowest average cost, 7) communities under the optimum size will seek to attract new residents to lower average costs).

[25] See also D. Mueller, *Public Choice III* (Cambridge University Press, 2003), 192 onwards (which discusses the effects of the level of rental income of the individual joining an optimal size community. It is submitted that if an individual has a high enough rental income, the welfare of the existing member will always be increased, even if this individual brings the community over its optimal size. The full effects of rents in relation to voting-with-the-feet are beyond the scope of this book but are well set out in Mueller, above.)

[26] Oates, 'Toward A Second-Generation Theory', 354.

[27] P. Seabright, 'Centralised and Decentralised Regulation in the European Union' in P. Newman (ed.) *The New Palgrave Dictionary of Economics and the Law* (London: Macmillan, 1998), 214.

[28] See also M. Olson, 'The Principle of "Fiscal Equivalence": The Division of Responsibilities among Different Levels of Government' (1969) 59 *American Economic Review, Papers and Proceedings* 479–487 (referring to this phenomenon as 'fiscal equivalence').

[29] Tiebout's model (1956) relies on the explicit assumption that there are no externalities (Tiebout, 'A Pure Theory of Local Expenditures').

[30] See also T. Besley and S. Coate, 'Centralized Versus Decentralized Provision of Local Public Goods: A Political Economy Approach' (2003) 87 *Journal of Public Economics* 2611–2637 at 2612.

government to the decentralized governments could cause them to internalize the benefits without the need for centralization.[31]

In brief, the findings and recommendations of the first generation of fiscal federalism for the assignment of public responsibility to different levels of government can be summarized as follows:

Services should be provided by the smallest jurisdiction that encompasses the geographical expanse of the benefits and costs associated with the service. In this way, all the benefits and costs are internalized, and, at the same time, we can take full advantage of tailoring service levels to the particular tastes and other circumstances that characterize the individual jurisdictions. Rather than providing a uniform level of public outputs over a large area, we can increase social welfare by differentiating these outputs in accord with local preferences and conditions.[32]

## 2 The second-generation theory

From the 1980s onwards, the findings of fiscal federalism have been enriched and challenged by economic scholarship from other related fields, such as political economy.[33] The 'second-generation theory of fiscal federalism' covers many different aspects of fiscal federalism theory, parts of which, such as discussion regarding the structure of fiscal institutions, fall outside the scope of this overview.[34] Of these new perspectives, the public choice and political economy work regarding the objectives of political participants, the application of the principal–agent model, and the role of information are particularly relevant to our framework, since they go to the heart of some of the assumptions underlying the first generation of the economic theory of federalism.

One of the central precepts of the economic theory of federalism, as developed in the 1950s and 1960s, was the assumption that government agencies would seek to maximize social welfare. This assumption

---

[31] A. C. Pigou, 'The Laws of Diminishing and Decreasing Costs' (1927) 37 *The Economic Journal* 188–197; Oates, 'Toward A Second-Generation Theory' (on the Pigouvian theory of subsidies); cf. D. W. Carlton and G. C. Loury, 'The Limitations of Pigouvian Taxes as a Long-Run Remedy for Externalities' (1980) 97 *The Quarterly Journal of Economics* 559–566 (showing that a Pigouvian tax will only provide a socially efficient allocation of resources in the long run if it is supplemented with a lump sum tax-subsidy scheme for participating firms.

[32] W. E. Oates, 'On Environmental Federalism' (1997) 83(7) *Virginia Law Review* 1321–1329 at 1323.

[33] Political economy theories will be discussed in more detail in Chapter 5. The overview in the present chapter focuses on those parts of political economy that have particular implications for the economic theory of federalism.

[34] For an extensive overview see Oates, 'Toward A Second-Generation Theory'.

was challenged with the emergence of public choice, starting with Niskanen in the 1970s. Niskanen formalized the theory of budget maximization, which characterized public agents as seeking to maximize their budgets, rather than social welfare.[35] Budgets are considered a proxy for other objectives that (employees of) governmental agencies may aspire to, such as power and influence, larger salaries and larger staffs. Brennan and Buchanan offered another perspective in the 1980s, describing the public sector as a 'Leviathan' that seeks to better its own position and has characteristics of a monopoly.[36] Moving away from the assumption that governmental agencies seek to maximize social welfare and focusing instead on the individual objectives that participants of the political process may have changed the role of decentralization; for Brennan and Buchanan decentralization becomes a way to limit the monopoly of the government by introducing competition between decentralized governments.[37]

Beyond these public choice insights into the incentives of elected officials and bureaucrats, the political economy approach to fiscal federalism provides additional insights into the behaviour of voters. The first-generation literature provides a normative trade-off between inefficiencies due to lack of preference consideration (centralization), and inefficiencies due to spillovers (decentralization). Political economy suggests a trade-off between local 'accountability' (sensitivity to local preferences) versus 'a coordination of policies under centralization that serves to internalize interjurisdictional interdependencies' (capture of externalities).[38] This approach moves away from the assumption of uniformity as a result of centralization and adds further elements to the trade-off between centralization and decentralization. This does not necessarily change the outcome of the analysis but it does offer some additional and different solutions.[39] One such solution

---

[35] W. A. Niskanen, 'Nonmarket Decision Making: The Peculiar Economics of Bureaucracy' (1968) 58 *The American Economic Review* 293–305; W. A. Niskanen, *Bureaucracy and Representative Government* (Chicago, IL: Aldine Atherton, 1971).

[36] G. Brennan and J. M. Buchanan, *The Power to Tax: Analytical Foundations of a Fiscal Constitution* (Cambridge University Press, 1980).

[37] See also Oates, 'Toward A Second-Generation Theory', 355. The succes of decentralization in constraining the central government has been contested by empirical work on this, see W. E. Oates 'Searching for Leviathan: An Empirical Study' (1985) 75 *The American Economic Review* 748–757.

[38] Oates, 'Toward A Second-Generation Theory', 357.

[39] Besley and Coate, 'Centralized Versus Decentralized Provision of Local Public Goods', 2628 ('[T]he key insight remains that heterogeneity of preferences and spillovers are correctly at the heart of the debate about the gains from centralization.')

comes from the application of the principal–agent model to the public sector.[40]

The principal–agent model can be shaped in two different ways: by considering central government as principal and local government as agent,[41] or by viewing the different levels of government as agents of the electorate.[42] In both cases, questions as to what extent these 'contracts' between the principal (central government or the electorate) and the agent (local or central/local government respectively) are complete and/or enforceable prove problematic. With respect to cooperation between different (sovereign) jurisdictions in order to overcome problems of interjurisdictional spillovers – as opposed to resolving this problem through centralization – political economy scholars identify a set of problems, which complement the efficiency consideration of fiscal federalism. These problems can prevent effective cooperation between different decentralized jurisdictions,[43] leading to a situation of 'forced' centralization. Examples of such situations are those where a coordinated agreement cannot be reached due to a 'tragedy of the commons',[44] collective action

---

[40] S. A. Ross, 'The Economic Theory of Agency: The Principal's Problem' (1973) 63 *American Economic Review*, 134–139.

[41] See also R. Inman, 'Transfers and Bailouts: Enforcing Local Fiscal Discipline with Lessons from U.S. Federalism' in J. Rodden (ed.) *Enforcing the Hard Budget Constraint* (Cambridge, MA: MIT Press, 2003) 35–83, who labels this 'administrative federalism'.

[42] See e.g. M. Tomassi *et al.*, 'Political Institutions, Policymaking Processes, and Policy Outcomes: An Intertemporal Transactions Framework' Leitner Program in International and Comparative Political Economy Working Paper 2003-03, Yale University (2003) (Tomassi uses a common agency model to capture the problem of the control of public officials by citizens through the design of an optimal contract and finds that decentralization may be preferable even in case of perfect homogeniety of preferences across local jurisdictions) and P. Seabright, 'Accountability and Decentralisation in Government: An Incomplete Contracts Model' (1996) 40 *European Economic Review* 61–89 (viewing elections as incomplete contracts, where centralization allows for better capture of externalities and decentralization allows for greater accountability).

[43] Seabright, 'Centralised and Decentralised Regulation', 215.

[44] G. Hardin, 'The Tragedy of the Commons' (1968) 162 *Science* 1243–1248, at 1244 ('Picture a pasture open to all … A rational herdsman concludes that the only sensible course for him to pursue is to add another animal to his herd. And another; and another … Each man is locked into a system that compels him to increase his herd without limit – in a world that is limited. Ruin is the destination toward which all men rush, each pursuing his own best interest in a society that believes in the freedom of the commons. Freedom in the commons brings ruin to all'); cf. P. Dasgupta, *The Control of Resources* (Cambridge, MA: Harvard University Press, 1982) ('It would be difficult to locate another passage of comparable length and fame

28    FROM COMPETING JURISDICTIONS TO COMPETING COMPETENCES

problems,[45] the presence of a prisoner's dilemma,[46] or more general free-rider-type situations.[47]

Another addition to the federalism literature is on the role of information based on microeconomic theory and industrial organization scholarship. There are various ways in which information impacts on (de)centralization choices, going back to the problem of information asymmetries, which formed the basis for the assumption that local governments would be better informed regarding the preferences of their constituents, and the related cost functions, based on their proximity to the issues as compared to central government. The study of the costs of information and regulation more generally forms part of the work by Vincent and Elinor Ostrom, who consider the nature of the public good provided, i.e. the type of services rendered, to change the relative advantages of (de)centralization.[48] Traditionally, the provision of public goods was viewed as organized solely through government institutions, which delivered services through public administration.[49] As early as 1977, the

     containing as many errors as the one above') and R. N. Stavins, 'The Problem of the Commons: Still Unsettled after 100 Years' (2011) 101 *American Economic Review* 81–108 at 88–89 ('Ruin is not the outcome of the commons, but rather excessive employment of capital and labor, small profits for participants, and an excessively depleted resource stock. Those are bad enough'); M. Olson, *The Logic of Collective Action: Public Goods and the Theory of Groups* (Cambridge, MA: Harvard University Press, 1965); E. Ostrom, 'Reflections on "Some Unsettled Problems of Irrigation"' (2011) 101(1) *American Economic Review* 49–63 at 49–50 (providing an excellent literature overview of the commons problem with respect to water scarcity in the United States).

[45] Olson, *The Logic of Collective Action*; A. R. Poteete, M. A. Janssen, and E. Ostrom (eds.), *Working Together: Collective Action, the Commons, and Multiple Methods in Practice* (Princeton University Press, 2010); E. Ostrom, 'Analysing Collective Action' (2010) 41(s1) *Agricultural Economics* 155–166; C. F. Camerer, *Behavioral Game Theory: Experiments in Strategic Interaction* (Princeton, NJ: Cloth, 2003) and C. A. Holt, *Markets, Games, and Strategic Behavior* (Boston, MA: Pearson-Addison Wesley, 2007) (experimental research on collective action problems).

[46] R. M. Dawes, 'The Commons Dilemma Game' 13 *ORI Research Bulletin* (1973) 1–12.

[47] R. F. Homans and J. E. Wilen, 'A Model of Regulated Open Access Resource Use' (1997) 32(1) *Journal of Environmental Economics and Management* 1–21 and D. M. Smith and J. E. Wilen, 'Economic Impacts of Marine Reserves: The Importance of Spatial Behavior' (2003) 46(2) *Journal of Environmental Economics and Management* 183–206 (on the challenges of regulated open-access fishery); E. Ostrom, *Governing the Commons* (Cambridge University Press, 1990), 8 (arguing that for problems which 'cannot be solved by cooperation … the rationale for government with major coercive powers is overwhelming.')

[48] V. Ostrom, *The Intellectual Crisis in American Public Administration* (Tuscaloosa: University of Alabama Press, 1974), 68–69.

[49] V. Ostrom and E. Ostrom, 'Public Good and Public Choices', in M. McGinnis and E. Ostrom (eds.), *Polycentricity and Local Public Economies* (Ann Arbor: University of Michigan Press, 1999) 75–103, at 75.

Ostroms challenged this assumption, pointing out that the public economy need not be an exclusive government monopoly, but can be a mixed economy with substantial private participation in the delivery of public services.[50]

Elinor Ostrom further qualifies this work by stating that it is the regulatory cost involved, such as monitoring and enforcement costs, as well as costs connected with changing existing institutional arrangements, that are important in judging institutional arrangements.[51] Based on these considerations, regional and national governments are considered most useful as facilitators, providing the basic needs and boundary conditions for local governments.[52] A danger of this approach, as recognized by Ostrom, is that when these arrangements become standardized, the effectiveness and fairness as perceived by the local regulators is reduced, which can result in high monitoring and enforcement costs of the said rules.[53] This analysis hints at the fact that the regulatory process should be seen as involving different steps and that the (de)centralization debate should take account of more than the policy-making competences and take account of broader implementation and enforcement competences.

A related issue is the potential for economics of scale and/or scope in centralized decision-making.[54] In situations where the regulation of public good provision requires technologies that involve large-scale investments, or a high level of expertise,[55] the centralization of scientific research, data collection and technical analysis may significantly

---

[50] *Ibid.* The production and provision of public services through many different collective consumption units is a theme that can be found throughout Vincent Ostrom's work on polycentrism, an additional political theory that is discussed together with multi-level governance theory in part 3 of this section.

[51] E. Ostrom, *Governing the Commons.*   [52] *Ibid.*, 214.   [53] *Ibid.*

[54] A. Alesina, I. Angeloni and F. Etro, 'International Unions' (2005) 95(3) *American Economic Review* 602–615. (Their paper characterizes the benefit of centralization as the possibility of exploiting economies of scale in the central allocation of policy responsibilities. It characterizes the costs of harmonization, principally, as those related to dealing with heterogeneity of preferences across the regions); K. Griffin, 'Economic Development in a Changing World' (1981) 9 *World Development* 221–320; Seabright, 'Centralised and Decentralised Regulation'.

[55] R. W. Hahn, 'Economic Prescriptions for Environmental Problems: How the Patient Followed the Doctor's Orders' (1989) 3 *The Journal of Economic Perspectives* 95–114 at 111: 'It might seem, for example, that if the problem is local, then the logical choice for addressing the problem is the local regulatory body. However, this is not always true. Perhaps the problem may require a level of technical expertise that does not reside at the local level, in which case some higher level of government involvement may be required.'

reduce information costs.[56] Moreover, economies of scope may occur when certain policy responsibilities require a fixed resource that can also be used for another policy responsibility at no additional costs.[57] For example, the expertise needed for banking and insurance sector regulation is comparable and may share many common costs.[58] One may also consider 'content-based' economies of scope, which occur when policies are combined to reinforce each other, or less ambitiously, care is taken to prevent policies from cancelling each other out.

A final consideration in the field of economic theories of federalism relates to risk diversification.[59] Arcuri and Dari-Mattiacci, building on the Condorcet Jury Theorem, explicitly applied the issue of risk diversification to the choice between centralization and decentralization.[60] Their model shows that centralization more often succeeds at delivering the 'right' decision in terms of policy as compared to decentralized systems due to the possibility of pooling expertise at the central level, *ceteris paribus*. However, the consequences of an erroneous decision at the centralized level can be global, rather than locally confined. They conclude that in the case of independent risks, the choice between centralization and decentralization depends on the level of scientific expertise available: if advanced expertise is available, centralization guarantees more accurate decisions and less risk. Centralization continues to deliver more accurate results where there is less available expertise, but decentralization lowers the risk that comes with an erroneous decision.[61] Risk diversification is also discussed in the field of organization economics where the possibility to lower risk plays a role

---

[56] J. H. Adler, 'Jurisdictional Mismatch in Environmental Federalism' (2005) 14 *New York University Environmental Law Journal* 131–178 at 145 (referring specifically to environmental regulation). See also Congressional Budget Office, *Federalism and Environmental Protection: Case Studies for Drinking Water and Ground-level Ozone* (Washington, DC: Congress of the United States, 1997).

[57] E. Carbonara, B. Luppi, and F. Parisi, 'Optimal Territorial Scope of Laws' University of Minnesota Law School, Legal Studies Research Paper No. 08–44 (2008), 3 (defining economies of scope as a situation where 'creating and enforcing two or more policies together costs less than doing so separately'.)

[58] *Ibid.*

[59] F. H. Knight, *Risk, Uncertainty, and Profit* (Boston, MA: Hart Schaffner and Marx, 1921).

[60] A. Arcuri and G. Dari-Mattiacci, 'Centralization versus Decentralization as a Risk-Return Trade-off' (2010) 53 *Journal of Law and Economics*, 359–378; J. M. Condorcet, *Essay on the Application of Analysis to the Probability of Majority Decisions* (Paris, 1785).

[61] Arcuri and Dari-Mattiacci, 'Centralization versus Decentralization', 374.

in deciding between coordinated and independent action of division in multidivisional organizations.[62]

## 3 Economic views on competence allocation

The rich economic theory of federalism literature draws from various streams of economic sub-disciplines. The selective summary given here aims to highlight that there are certain shared considerations on which these different approaches base their preference for (de)centralization, even if their application and outcome is different. Essentially, these considerations can be grouped as follows: the accommodation of heterogeneous preferences and conditions of different jurisdictions; the need to capture (possible) externalities; the aim to maximize economies of scale and/or scope; and allowing for risk diversification. The theoretically optimal allocation of powers cannot be given at the hand of these principles without specific regard to the circumstances under which (de)centralization occurs – particularly with respect to the type of regulatory problem at hand.[63] Moreover, little to no distinction continues to be made between regulatory competences; (de)centralization is assumed to take place for the whole of the regulatory process or not at all. Within the second generation literature on the economic theory of federalism, a move towards greater precision of the federalism models has been achieved through the understanding of governmental agencies and voters alike as groups with their own interest and maximization functions, as compared to the earlier assumption of governments as social welfare maximizers.

---

[62] R. Alonso, W. Dessein and N. Matouschek, 'When does Coordination Require Centralization?' (2008) 98 (1) *American Economic Review*, 145–179.

[63] Most empirical studies remain inconclusive as to the effects of (de)centralization. See e.g. K. Strumpf and F. Oberholzer-Gee, 'Endogenous Policy Decentralization: Testing the Central Tenet of Economic Federalism' (2002) 110 *Journal of Political Economy* 1–36 (reviewing the assignment of regulatory responsibility to the various levels of government in the case of liquor control in the United States, finding that there is indeed a tendency for US States with more heterogeneous preferences to decentralize liquor control); A. Estache and S. Sinha, 'Does Decentralization Increase Spending on Public Infrastructure?' World Bank Policy Research Working Paper No. 1457 (1995); E. Fiske, *Decentralization of Education: Politics and Consensus* (Washington, DC: World Bank, 1996); F. Fleurke, 'Effecten van Decentralisatie' (1995) 49(2) *Bestuurswetenschap* 101–137; V. Ostrom and R. Bish, *Comparing Urban Service Delivery Systems: Structure and Performance* (Beverly Hills, CA: Sage, 1977); R. Prud'homme, 'The Dangers of Decentralization' (1995) 10 *The World Bank Research Observer* 201–220; and H. Werlin, 'Linking Decentralization and Centralization: A Critique of the New Development Administration' (1992) 12(3) *Public Administration and Development: An International Journal of Training, Research, and Practice* 223–236.

## B The 'legalization' of federalism

Policymakers and lawyers have been careful to emphasize the restricted relevance of economic considerations for the (de)centralization of legal and/or political decisions. With respect to environmental policy, for example, the United States Congressional Budget Office has stated that '[e]conomic analysis cannot prescribe which level of government should be making the various decisions about environmental protection.'[64] However, the office qualified this statement by acknowledging that '[e]conomics does, however, help to answer the question of which level of government is most likely to make efficient choices about environmental protection – that is, choices that balance all of the relevant benefits and costs.'[65] Despite the general scepticism towards the use of economics in competence allocation decisions, legal scholarship has increasingly found application for some of the lessons of the economic theory of federalism, for instance in the areas of competition, financial and environmental law. Given the application of our theoretical framework to climate change regulation, particular attention is paid to developments in the area of environmental law, where some of the ideas first expressed in economic and fiscal federalism have been applied and developed with great success. Most of this research originates from the United States, whereas the focus of our inquiry is the EU ETS, which is governed primarily by European law. We will therefore also pay close attention to the legal scholarship regarding competence allocation in the European Union, as influenced by multi-level governance theory.

## 1 The 'race-to-the-bottom' hypothesis and regulatory experimentation

The most important link between economic and legal scholarship is the race-to-the-bottom hypothesis as developed in, primarily, American legal literature on the environment.[66] The race-to-the-bottom hypothesis posits that jurisdictions will compete with each other for investments and/or certain groups of voters/consumers by providing a relatively higher or lower level of public good provision than competing or surrounding jurisdictions.[67] Applied to environmental regulation, this hypothesis predicts a downwards spiral in the

---

[64] Congressional Budget Office, *Federalism and Environmental Protection*, at xi.

[65] *Ibid.*, at xi.  [66] Oates, 'Fiscal Decentralization'.

[67] In a globalized economy, there need not be geographical proximity between jurisdictions for there to be competition between them.

provision of environmental protection when environmental policy-making is decentralized since localities will have incentives to lower their standards in order to attract more (industrial) investment, to the detriment of environmental quality.[68] However, empirical evidence shows no conclusive proof that allowing for decentralized environmental policy leads to 'pollution havens',[69] or 'hot spots'.[70] When they are found, they are more likely to be created by low tax rates on capital rather than by pollution control costs, since the latter comprises a relatively small part of the total production costs of manufacturing industries and therefore does not dictate location decisions.[71] Put differently, environmental regulation is only one area of regulation in which jurisdictions can compete with each other; therefore the only

[68] See for instance W. E. Oates and R. M. Schwab, 'Economic Competition Among Jurisdictions: Efficiency Enhancing or Distortion Inducing?' (1988) 35 *Journal of Public Economics* 333–354; W. E. Oates, 'A Reconsideration of Environmental Federalism' in J. List and A. de Zeeuw (eds.), *Recent Advances in Environmental Economics* (Cheltenham: Edward Elgar, 2002), 9 (on race-to-the-bottom), 16–17 (on empirical studies on race-to-the-bottom); see also Stewart, 'Environmental Regulation' and Esty, 'Revitalizing Environmental Federalism', 570.

[69] The location of emissions may still be relevant for other environmental considerations such as the creation of so-called hot spots or smog development. See e.g. R. Revesz, *Environmental Law and Policy* (New York: Foundation Press, 2008), 450 (discussing the possibility of hot spots in the context of interstate air pollution), and N. O. Keohane and S. M. Olmstead, *Markets and the Environment* (Washington, DC: Island Press, 2007) 173–177.

[70] H. Sigman, 'Decentralization and Environmental Quality: An International Analysis of Water Pollution', National Bureau of Economic Research Working Papers 13098 (2007), who finds that states do not use the control of their programmes to undercut federal environmental standards under 'authorization' from the US federal government, at 23: 'The results support the model's prediction that the stronger the environmental preferences are in the state, the sooner the state will authorize. This association arises for authorization under both the CWA and the RCA. Although our main finding contradicts the conventional wisdom that authorization worsens the environment, it is consistent with other empirical literature, which often fails to find evidence that decentralization in the U.S. harms the environment.'

[71] On this topic see D. Esty and D. Geradin (eds.), *Regulatory Competition and Economic Integration, Comparative Perspectives* (Oxford University Press, 2001), 282–294. See also R. Revesz and R. N. Stavins, 'Environmental Law' in A. M. Polinsky and S. Shavell (eds.), *The Handbook of Law and Economics* (Amsterdam: Elsevier Science, 2007), 499–589, at 565, who submit that very low capital tax rates will often be combined with high environmental standards, which are defined by equating the willingness to pay for environmental quality with the corresponding change in wages). The debate concerning the race-to-the-bottom continues but the assumption that it is a prime justification for central regulation has been widely discredited. See e.g. Revesz, 'The Race to the Bottom'; Revesz and Engel, 'State Environmental Standard-Setting'.

complete solution for possible race-to-the-bottom behaviour would be total centralization.[72]

Although it is still often referred to, the race-to-the-bottom phenomenon has been partially discredited. Richard Revesz, one of the main legal contributors to this field, has gone as far as to state that 'there is no compelling race-to-the-bottom justification for across-the-board federal minimum standards, which are the cornerstone of federal environmental law in both the United States and the European Union.'[73] One of the main contributors to the fiscal federalism theory, Wallace Oates, has responded to the legal race-to-the-bottom literature on several occasions, finding that interjurisdictional competition should be considered predominantly positive.[74] He further submits that the failure of states to implement stringent standards in certain areas where there is also federal regulation may be due to the fact that the federal standards are already excessively stringent.[75] This latter perspective also shows that there has been a growing appreciation for the possibility of a fragmented regulatory process where federal norm setting may be complemented by state implementation.[76]

There has also been considerable attention for the potential *benefits* of interjurisdictional competition, such as regulatory experimentation, regulatory competition (race-to-the-top),[77] regulatory

---

[72] Revesz, 'The Race to the Bottom', 1338 ('If environmental regulation is federalized, the competition would shift to another arena and the reduction in social welfare implicit in race-to-the-bottom arguments would not be eliminated. The only solution would be total centralization of regulatory and fiscal functions, a policy that would have little, if any, support.')

[73] Revesz, 'The Race to the Bottom', 1337.

[74] Oates, 'Fiscal Decentralization', 1322 (arguing that interjurisdictional competition is generally efficiency enhancing and that 'the fear of a race to the bottom is, in my view, largely misplaced'). He furthermore argues that any distortions, if they do occur, are likely to result in minor deviations from efficient outcomes, see W. E. Oates, 'A Reconsideration of Environmental Federalism' Resources for the Future, Discussion Paper No. 01–54 (2001), at 8.

[75] Oates, 'Fiscal Decentralization', 1326–1327.

[76] G. J. Stigler, 'The Tenable Range of Functions of Local Government', in Joint Economic Committee, Subcommittee on Fiscal Policy, U.S. Congress (ed.), *Federal Expenditure Policy for Economic Growth and Stability* (Washington, DC: US Government Printing Office, 1957) 213–219, at 216: 'Competition among communities offers not obstacles but opportunities to various communities to choose the type and scale of government functions they wish.'

[77] J. P. Trachtman, 'Regulatory Competition and Regulatory Jurisdiction' (2000) 3(2) *Journal of International Economic Law* 331–348 (arguing that regulatory competition always takes place under second-best parameters and involves interpersonal utility comparisons which call for political deliberation rather than scholarly prescription).

cooperation,[78] and the potential facilitation of the adoption of controversial policies through phased adoption. In the case of regulatory experimentation, jurisdictions may learn from each other's experiences, which may eventually improve the practice of regulation as a whole.[79] For instance, in the context of the United States, the decision of some states to establish emission trading schemes with differing designs allowed for learning between these jurisdictions, which is beneficial both for the states themselves, and for a possible federal system that may be developed as a result.[80] Conversely, regulatory competition may give rise to certain 'information externalities' where experimental policies of one jurisdiction may generate valuable information for others, which may result in free-riding behaviour.[81] Aside

[78] See A. O. Sykes, 'Regulatory Competition or Regulatory Harmonization? A Silly Question?' (2000) 3(2) *Journal of International Economic Law* 257–264 on the importance of cooperation between jurisdictions in the presence of important cross-border effects of regulation.

[79] Oates, 'A Reconsideration of Environmental Federalism' (2001) (argues in favour of 'laboratory federalism'); J. Scott, 'In Legal Limbo: Post-Legislative Guidance as a Challenge for European Administrative Law' (2011) 48 *Common Market Law Review* 329–355 at 33 ('Just as federalism is said to offer some advantages, including the possibility for regulatory experimentation and regulatory learning, so too can the multi-level governance associated with a regime complex create incentives and opportunities for regulatory innovation and regulatory learning across different states.'); Oates, 'An Essay on Fiscal Federalism', at 22 (arguing that decentralization can be important in offering an opportunity for experimentation). See also W. B. Buzbee, 'Climate as an Innovation Imperative: Federalism, Institutional Pluralism and Incentive Effects', Public Law & Legal Theory Research Paper Series, No. 10–125, Emory University School of Law (2010), at 17 (arguing that pre-emption by the federal government in the area of environmental protection and especially climate change would negate the many advantages of state involvement in environmental regulation and may eventually lead to regulatory failure: 'Institutional diversity retaining federal, state and local roles would be more stable and conducive to market and regulatory innovation').

[80] At the time of writing, there appears to be a stalemate in US domestic politics regarding the development of a federal cap-and-trade system (see e.g. Stavins, 'The Problem of the Commons', 101), which means that sub-national policies, such as the Regional Greenhouse Gas Initiative remains most promising (put in place by the California Global Warming Solutions Act of 2006: Greenhouse gas emissions reductions, in California Health and Safety Code, Division 25.5, Part 4, Section 38562(d)(1)).

[81] Oates, 'An Essay on Fiscal Federalism', 1133 ('There exists a basic "information externality" in that states that adopt new and experimental policies generate valuable information for others. And this creates a standard sort of incentive for free-riding. From this perspective, we might expect too little experimentation and policy innovation in a highly decentralized public sector. Indeed, as Strumpet shows, it is unclear whether a centralized or decentralized outcome will result in more policy innovation.')

FROM COMPETING JURISDICTIONS TO COMPETING COMPETENCES

from regulatory learning, decentralized policy-making could even result in federal or central regulation on an issue, which would have previously been considered (too) controversial.[82] There have also been signs of regulatory competition between jurisdictions, resulting in a race-to-the-top rather than bottom. An example of this can be found in foreign investment practices where regulatory regimes with a higher degree of legal certainty and better legal and economic institutions are better able to attract foreign investors.[83]

A final cost-based argument, which has found its way into the legal debate, is the role of heterogeneous conditions and the availability of information regarding these conditions to different regulators. In the United States, the variation in environmental circumstance in the different states is considered one of the main reasons for decentralization,[84] especially due to the informational costs this variation imposes on the central level: expertise regarding local circumstances is arguably more costly to acquire at the central level and this problem is not necessarily overcome through centralization.[85]

[82] K. H. Engel, 'Harnessing the Benefits of Dynamic Federalism in Environmental Law' (2006) 56 *Emory Law Journal* 159–188 ('[R]egulatory activity at one level – state or federal – may be a stepping zone to regulation at the governing level that dual federalism proponents label "optimal". Thus, to achieve regulation at the level of government considered optimal, policymaking may need to begin at a different level of government.')

[83] See OECD (2000 onwards).

[84] See e.g. H. N. Butler and J. R. Macey, 'Externalities and the Matching Principle: The Case for Reallocating Environmental Regulatory Authority' (1996) 14 *Yale Law & Policy Review* 24–66, critiquing the centralization of environmental regulatory authority to the federal level in the United States and arguing for reform through market-based regulation, economic property rights or greater state control: 'We conclude that, in every area of pollution, environmental regulation has been centralized beyond any possible justification, resulting in tremendous costs.'

[85] See e.g. J. H. Adler, 'When Is Two a Crowd? The Impact of Federal Action on State Environmental Regulation' (2007) 31 *Harvard Environmental Law Review* 67–114 at 77 ('Environmental knowledge, like economic knowledge, is highly decentralized. Specific knowledge about local ecological conditions ... is more likely to be found at the local level than in a centralized bureaucracy. Due to the decentralized nature of knowledge, one might expect that environmental protections would be adopted first in those areas where local knowledge about the need for such protection is the greatest.'); and Adler, 'Jurisdictional Mismatch' ('[T]he ecological and economic diversity of the nation requires local knowledge and expertise that is often unavailable at the federal level. A more decentralized system is better able to overcome this "knowledge problem" and ensure that regulatory measures take account of local conditions.'). See also Butler and Macey, 'Externalities and the Matching Principle', 27 ('Federal regulators never have been and never will be able to acquire and assimilate the enormous amount of information necessary

## 2 The European perspective: multi-level governance and subsidiarity

Much of the regulatory backdrop for this book is formed by the European Union's legal order. Since the academic and policy discourses in the United States are not necessarily applicable to, or predictive of, those in the EU, this section will discuss some of the methodologies developed in relation to multi-level governance within the EU, specifically those that deal with the nature of governance within the EU and the constitutional legal principles, such as subsidiarity, that govern competence allocation in the EU.

The complex development of the European Communities into the present-day European Union has defied pre-existing theories of governance, such as federalism, which led to the construction of alternative methodologies, of which multi-level governance has been by far the most influential. A multi-level governance system is one of 'continuous negotiation among nested governments at several territorial tiers – supranational, national, regional, and local – as a result of the broad process of institutional creation and decisional reallocation that has pulled some previously centralized functions of the state up to the supranational level and some down to the local/regional level.'[86] From this broad definition, Liesbeth Hooghe and Gary Marks distil two categories of multi-level governance: Type I and Type II systems.[87]

Type I systems carry a strong resemblance to classic models of federalism, whereas Type II systems are less stable, special-purpose, jurisdictions that are not necessarily restricted by pre-existing geographic jurisdictions such as institutions set up to deal with cross-border resource management. Type II jurisdictions are typically nested within larger, general jurisdiction Type I systems. Within Hooghe and Marks' definition, a key feature of Type II systems is 'conflict avoidance'.[88] Since Type II multi-level governance jurisdictions are issue specific, they assume a

---

to make optimal regulatory judgments that reflect the technical requirements of particular locations and pollution sources.'). See also C. J. M. Kimber, 'A Comparison of Environmental Federalism in the United States and the European Union' (1995) 54 *Maryland Law Review* 1658–1690.

[86] G. Marks, 'Structural Policy and Multilevel Governance in the EC: The State of the European Community' in A. Cafruny and G. Rosenthal (eds.) *The State of the European Community: The Maastricht Debate and Beyond* (Boulder, CO: L. Rienner Publishers, 1993) 391–411 at 392.

[87] L. Hooghe and G. Marks, 'Types of Multi-level Governance', in H. Enderlein, S. Wälti, and M. Zürn, *Handbook on Multi-Level Governance* (Cheltenham: Edward Elgar, 2010) 17–31.

[88] *Ibid.*, at 28.

high level of consensus within the jurisdiction, and have less conflict with other jurisdictions since all effects of the actions taken by the Type II jurisdiction are internalized. There is also an important difference in the normative drivers of Type I and Type II multi-level governance systems as compared to polycentric systems. Hooghe and Marks stress:

> Type I and II governance are not different means to the same end. They embody contrasting visions about collective decision-making. Type I jurisdictions are suited to political deliberation about basic value choices in society: who gets what, when, and how … Type II jurisdictions, in contrast, emphasize problem solving … The assumption underlying Type II jurisdictions is that externalities among jurisdictions are sufficiently limited to sustain compartmentalized decision making.[89]

Recent legal scholarship has repositioned the concept of multi-level *governance* as being theoretically distinct from multi-level *regulation*.[90] Whereas 'governance' refers to the mode of government of the modern nation state, which is in a relationship of negotiation and cooperation with private actors in order to ensure the delivery of public goods and services, 'regulation' refers to the control of private behaviour by public agencies to ensure that public interest is not violated in the delivery of public goods and services.[91] Put differently, regulation covers smaller specific action within the broader field of governance.[92] The concept of multi-level regulation, as developed in more depth in a 2012 article by Chowdhury and Wessel, aligns closely with the competence allocation approach developed here. Specifically, Chowdhury and Wessel state:

> Multilevel regulation is a term used to characterise a regulatory space, in which the process of rule making, rule implementation or rule enforcement is dispersed across more than one administrative or territorial level amongst several different actors, both public and private.[93]

Moreover, the relationship between these actors is non-hierarchical and may be independent as both public and private actors are included.

---

[89] *Ibid.*
[90] N. Chowdhury and R. A. Wessel, 'Conceptualising Multilevel Regulation in the EU: A Legal Translation of Multilevel Governance?' (2012) 18 *European Law Journal* 335–357 at 345.
[91] *Ibid.* For a multi-disciplinary overview of literature on governance, see S. Burris, M. Kempa, and C. Shearing, 'Changes in Governance: A Cross-Disciplinary Review of Current Scholarship' (2008) 41 *Akron Law Review* 1–66.
[92] J. Braithwaite, C. Coglianese, and D. Levi-Faur, 'Can Regulation and Governance Make a Difference?' (2007) 1 *Regulation and Governance* 1–7.
[93] Chowdhury and Wessel, 'Conceptualising Multilevel Regulation in the EU', 346.

This is not the case in our competence allocation discussion given the unique structure of their relative incentives. Nevertheless, the fact that the division of the regulatory process into rule formation/making, rules implementation and rule enforcement is considered a core feature of the concept of multi-level regulation shows the growing recognition of the distinctive roles of these steps within the regulatory process.[94]

A more economic theory of European governance, as developed by Bruno Frey and Reiner Eichenberger, is called *functional overlapping competing jurisdictions* (FOCJ).[95] FOCJ is defined as a form of federal governance that is created as a bottom-up response to citizen preferences and as such comes closest to polycentric theory. FOCJ foresees direct access to federal level courts for all citizens, independence of local communities in order to constitute local governance systems, which would also have the right to levy taxes to finance themselves.[96] Although promising, FOCJ theory remains underdeveloped with respect to more practical concerns regarding exit and voice,[97] the presence or absence of constitutional rule-design, and the interaction between public and private actors.

More recently, polycentric theory, as developed by Vincent and Elinor Ostrom and the Bloomington School of Governance,[98] has been used to explain the ongoing development of European Union governance.[99] As the name suggests, a polycentric system is one that encompasses multiple centres of decision-making. The most important ideological difference between polycentricity and other theories of multi-level governance and federalism is that the relationship between these centres need not be hierarchical. In the words of Elinor Ostrom and Michael McGinnis:

---

[94] *Ibid.*, at 347.

[95] B. Frey and R. Eichenberger, 'FOCJ: Competitive Governments for Europe' (1996) 16 *International Review of Law and Economics* 315–327 at 315.

[96] *Ibid.*

[97] A. Hirschman, *Exit, Voice, and Loyalty: Responses to Decline in Firms, Organizations, and States* (Cambridge, MA: Harvard University Press, 1970).

[98] The concept was first introduced by Vincent Ostrom, Charles Tiebout and Robert Warren in their 1961 article, V. Ostrom, C. Tiebout, and R. Warren, 'The Organization of Government in Metropolitan Areas: A Theoretical Inquiry' (1961) 55 *American Political Science Review* 831–842, and consequently developed at the Ostrom Workshop in Political Theory and Policy Analysis in Bloomington.

[99] J. A. W. van Zeben, 'Research Agenda for a Polycentric European Union', The Vincent and Elinor Ostrom Workshop in Political Theory and Policy Analysis Working Paper Series, W13–13 (2013).

[P]olycentricity conveys more than just federalism as it typically is understood. A federal system may consist only of a sequence of neatly nested jurisdictions at the local, state or provincial, and national levels, but *a polycentric system also includes crosscutting jurisdictions specializing in particular policy matters*, such as an agency managing a river basin that cuts across state lines. *In addition, private corporations, voluntary associations, and community-based organizations play critical supporting roles in a polycentric system of governance, even if they have not been assigned public roles in an official manner*.[100]

As compared with federalism, polycentricity thus allows for an additional dimension of crosscutting 'issue-specific' jurisdictions and envisages an explicit role for non-governmental bodies, such as private and community-based organizations. The complementarity between the units of the primary governance partition and the special-purpose secondary governance units may be considered the essence of polycentric governance.[101] This can be interpreted more broadly to mean that Type I and Type II multi-level governance may be considered parts of a 'fuller' polycentric system – Type II multi-level governance does not (necessarily) constitute such a system independently by virtue of being flexible in design and membership. The *raison d'etre* provided by the collective decision-making rationale may be compared with the economic efficiency argument referred to earlier; although this can be an important reason to choose polycentric governance, it is by no means the only reason. The multi-level governance theory as presented by Hooghe and Marks does not appear to leave the same amount of room for individual or community-based discretion in choosing the regulatory goal of the jurisdiction. This can be explained by the descriptive outlook of multi-level governance as compared to polycentric theory: these features have been observed within a set of Type I and Type II jurisdictions and have thereafter been taken as indicative for their existence. Polycentric theory does not make assumptions about the driving force for the creation of these jurisdictions, rather it focuses on the existence of the prerequisites for self-governance to take place, which in turn will give rise to a polycentric system of governance.[102]

---

[100] M. McGinnis and E. Ostrom, 'Reflections on Vincent Ostrom, Public Administration, and Polycentricity' (2012) 72 *Public Administration Review* 15–25 at 15 (emphasis added).

[101] M. McGinnis and M. Hanisch, 'Analyzing Problems of Polycentric Governance in the Growing EU' (2005) Paper presented at the Transcoop Workshop on Problems of Polycentric Governance in the Growing EU, Humboldt University, Berlin (on file with the author), at 24.

[102] This is also an important contrast with the normative claims of multi-level governance theory, which centre around the concept of 'good governance' – also

Notwithstanding the differences between these methodologies, each of them considers flexibility and fluidity key features of European governance. This fluidity is addressed at a later stage of our theoretical framework as well since the dividing line between, especially, norm setting and implementation is not always easily drawn; both competence allocation and competence definition are challenging in the European context. Whereas both the Treaty on European Union (TEU) and the Treaty on the Functioning of the European Union (TFEU) refer to competences and their allocation, neither is explicit about *which* competences are being allocated. Article 1 of the TEU states that the Member States will confer 'competences' to the Union in order to attain goals that they hold in common.[103] In those policy areas that do not fall under the EU's exclusive competence, the Union 'shall act only and insofar as the objectives of the proposed action cannot be sufficiently achieved by the Member States, either at central level or at regional and local level, but can rather, by reason of the scale or effects of the proposed action, be better achieved at Union level.'[104] Together with the principle of conferral and proportionality,[105] this principle of subsidiarity forms the constitutional foundation for competence allocation in the European Union.[106]

Despite its prima facie legal nature, it may be argued that the application and interpretation of the principle of subsidiarity are partly founded on arguments based in economic theory. Protocol No. 2 to the Lisbon Treaty provides guidance for the interpretation of the subsidiarity principle by the European Union institutions.[107] This guidance is mostly

adopted and recognized by the EU Commission in e.g. Commission Communication, European Governance (White Paper), COM(2001) 428 final. The concept of good governance emphasizes elements such as transparency, accountability and citizens' participation but also has an important efficiency component. See R. Riedel, 'Silesian Representations in Brussels: How the Sub-National Authorities Utilise Opportunity Structures in the Multi-Level Governance of the EU', in R. Grzeszczak and I. Karolewski (eds.) *The Multi-level and Polycentric European Union: Legal and Political Studies* (Zurich: Lit Verlag, 2012) 57–76 at 65.

[103] Article 1 of the TEU, read together with Articles 4(1) and 5(1)(2) of the TEU.
[104] Article 5(3) of the TEU.   [105] Article 5(1) of the TEU.
[106] Protocol No. 25 on the exercise of shared competences (OJ 2008 No. C155, 9 May 2008), Declaration No. 18 in relation to the delimitation of competences (OJ 2010 No. C83, 30 March 2010), combined with Protocol No. 1 on the role of national parliaments in the European Union (OJ 2008 No. C155, 9 May 2008) also help to convey the image of a stronger check on the use of competences by the EU. See also H. Vedder, 'The Treaty of Lisbon and European Environmental Law and Policy' (2010) 22 *Journal of Environmental Law* 285–299 at 292–293.
[107] Protocol No. 2 on the application of the principles of subsidiarity and proportionality, OJ 2008 No. C155, 9 May 2008.

procedural, provided through a set of legislative steps for the European institutions to follow. Reference is made to an assessment of the proposal's 'financial impact' and that account should be taken that 'any burden, whether financially or administrative, falling upon the Union, national governments, regional or local authorities, economic operators and citizens should be minimized'.[108] Legal academia and the European Courts continue to provide little guidance regarding the *content* of the principle of subsidiarity, as opposed to its more general political (and strategic) role in the European debate.[109] It therefore remains unclear what form the qualitative and quantitative indicators should take in order to successfully apply the principle of subsidiarity.[110] Gráinne de Búrca has developed several questions, which arguably cover the most important trade-offs under a possible subsidiarity test. Of these five questions, at least two refer explicitly to economic-based arguments: the presence of interjurisdictional externalities, for instance through negative effects on the internal market,[111] and possible economies of scale.[112]

[108] Article 5 of Protocol No. 2.
[109] See for instance I. Maher, 'Legislative Review by the EC Commission: Revision without Radicalism' in J. Shaw and G. More (eds.) *New Legal Dynamics of European Union* (Oxford: Clarendon Press, 1995) 235–253 (arguing that the subsidiarity principle has mainly symbolic and political significance, moving away from centralizing tendencies); G. Bermann, 'Taking Subsidiarity Seriously: Federalism in the European Community and the United States' (1994) 94 *Columbia Law Review* 331–456 (stressing the importance of the subsidiarity principle as a normative procedural requirement); G. de Búrca, 'Reappraising Subsidiarity's Significance after Amsterdam', Harvard Jean Monnet Working Papers, No. 7/99 (1999) (finding that the limited impact of the principle of subsidiarity is due to the wide margin of discretion enjoyed by the European institutions in their interpretation of the Treaties and that the Protocol adds to the open-endedness and vagueness of the subsidiarity principle). Regarding the European Court of Justice's interpretation of the subsidiarity principle, see for instance Case 9/74, *Casagrande* v. *Landeshauptstadt München* [1974] ECR 773, and Case 65/81, *Reina* v. *Landeskredit Bank Baden Baden-Württemberg* [1982] ECR 336; Case C-415/93, *Royal Club Liegois SA* v. *Jean-Marc Bosman* [1995] ECR I-04921, para 72–78. Arcuri and Dari-Mattiacci, 'Centralization versus Decentralization' find that the ECJ tends to allow more decentralization in the presence of high scientific uncertainty.
[110] E. S. Hendriks, 'Modelling Subsidiarity Applying a Continuous CJT to Determine the Optimal Level of Decision Making for Standard Setting', PhD thesis, University of Amsterdam (2010).
[111] Harmonization of European Union law is often justified with reference to the protection of the internal market. See G. Close, 'Harmonisation of Laws: Use or Abuse of the Powers under the EEC Treaty?' (1978) 3 *European Law Review* 461–481 at 470–472; A. Haagsma, 'The European Community's Environmental Policy: A Case-Study in Federalism' (1989) 12 *Fordham International Law Journal* 311–359 at 355; O. Lomas, 'Environmental Protection, Economic Conflict and the European Community' (1988) 3(3) *McGill Law Journal* 506–539 at 511.
[112] See e.g. G. de Búrca, 'Reappraising Subsidiarity's Significance after Amsterdam', at 32 ('How strong and how compelling are the internal-market requirements/competitive

Competences with respect to environmental policy, under which the EU ETS is adopted,[113] are shared with the Member States under Article 4 of the TFEU.[114] Notwithstanding the presence of the subsidiarity principle and its recent elaboration in Protocol No. 2, EU environmental policy remains very centralized since the relatively low requirements under the subsidiarity 'test' are easily fulfilled, particularly in the presence of externalities.[115] Once European laws on environmental policy are adopted, they may overrule Member States' existing environmental legislation and pre-empt new Member State legislation. That said, European legislation in the area of environmental policy often takes the shape of 'minimum harmonization' legislation,[116] which means that Member States remain free to adopt more stringent environmental regulation in addition to the European laws.[117]

## 3 Legal views on competence allocation

Arguments that were first advanced by the economic theory of federalism have found their way into the legal debate. Issues such as externalities, scale economies and information costs are increasingly recognized by legal scholars as impacting on decisions of (de)centralization of regulatory powers, even when this is considered normatively

distortions/trade restrictions/cross-border effects in question? … What are the countervailing arguments in favour of Member State action, e.g. such as the decision of the states to specify expressly in the Treaty that they retain national competence over a closely related or overlapping policy area?')

[113] See extensively Chapter 3.
[114] See also Articles 191–193 of the TFEU.
[115] See also N. de Sadeleer, 'Principle of Subsidiarity and the EU Environmental Policy' (2012) 9 *Journal for European Environmental & Planning Law* 63–70.
[116] Minimum harmonization has given rise to extensive discussions on potential race-to-the-bottom scenarios in the European context. See e.g., M. T. A. Brus, R. R. Raimond and T. G. Drupsteen, 'Balancing National and European Competence in Environmental Law' (1994) 9 *Connecticut Journal of International Law* 633–674 at 647; K. Lenaerts, 'The Principle of Subsidiarity and the Environment in the European Union: Keeping the Balance of Federalism' (1994) 17 *Fordham International Law Journal* 846–895 at 879–82; M. L. Schemmel and B. de Regt, 'The European Court of Justice and the Environmental Protection Policy of the European Community' (1994) 17 *Boston College International & Comparative Law Review* 53–84 at 80; R. B. Stewart, 'Environmental Law in the United States and the European Community: Spillovers, Cooperation, Rivalry, Institutions' (1992) 39 *University of Chicago Legal Forum* 44–46; R. van den Bergh, M. Faure and J. Lefevere, 'The Subsidiarity Principle in European Environmental Law: An Economic Analysis' in E. Eide and R. van den Bergh (eds.), *Law and Economics of the Environment* (Oslo: Juridisk Forlag, 1996), 121–166.
[117] Article 193 of the TFEU. These national laws may not create obstacles to free trade, but see also Article 114 of the TFEU (stating that the EU has to take account of environmental aspects while regulating the internal market).

undesirable. The interpretation of legal principles that speak to the division of powers within a federal-type system, such as the European principle of subsidiarity, no longer depends solely on legal or political argument.[118] Within European legal scholarship, most attention is paid to the constitutional rules that govern the power balance between the European Union and the Member States, and specific cases of competence allocation.[119] In combination with the fluidity of arrangements in the European Union, it continues to be difficult to achieve a systematic differentiation between competences and criteria for their allocation.

## 2 Competing competences: A competence allocation approach

It is important to emphasize that the issue is not whether environmental policy should be centralized or decentralized ... The issue for environmental federalism is the proper assignation of the various roles to the different levels of government.[120]

The premise of this book is that in order to have a more accurate discussion about the optimal division of powers between the central and decentralized level, more attention needs to be paid to the different competences involved in the regulatory process. Rephrasing the federalism question as one that considers competing *competences*, rather than competing *jurisdictions*, we can more precisely consider the (de)-centralization of specific parts of the regulatory process (regulatory competences). Each of these competences differs in their ability to capture externalities, deal with heterogeneous conditions and preferences and achieve economies of scale. It thus cannot be (implicitly) assumed that the centralization of norm setting is sufficient to overcome, for instance, a collective action problem caused by the presence of externalities. The allocation of

[118] A. Alesina, I. Angeloni, and L. Schuknecht, 'What Does the European Union Do?' (2005) 123 *Public Choice* 275–319 (providing empirical evidence on the expansion of the policy-making role of the European Union in the years between 1971 and 2000. They find that in the European Union something seems to have drawn the process of allocation of policy responsibilities away from the optimal balance of economies of scale and the heterogeneity of preferences. Substantial harmonization and centralization have occurred in areas where heterogeneity of preferences is predominant (like social protection or agricultural policy) whereas other areas characterized by strong economies of scale have remained in the local domain (like defence).)
[119] See e.g. European Commission, 'Impact Assessment Guidelines', SEC(2009) 92.
[120] Oates, 'Fiscal Decentralization', 1329.

implementation and enforcement competences must also be discussed since a failure to implement or enforce may negate the centralized norm-setting effort with respect to the relevant externalities.[121]

## A Descriptive variables

This section starts by defining the variables that underlie the theoretical framework of competence allocation: regulatory competences and regulatory levels. Part B then considers the normative trade-offs involved in deciding the optimal division of competences between different regulatory levels. In deciding this optimal allocation, the nature of the regulatory problem and the instrument choice are of particular importance. According to the normative framework given by the economic theory of federalism, the regulatory system should strive to accommodate (i) the heterogeneity of conditions and preferences in different localities; (ii) the presence of externalities; and (iii) achieve economies of scale and/or scope. Some of these aims will be difficult to reconcile, or may even be mutually exclusive. For example, the capture of externalities through centralization may reduce the ability to accommodate heterogeneous conditions. In our framework, the nature of the regulatory problem determines the prioritization of these different criteria. Instrument choice may then help to optimize the allocative situation by allowing for greater flexibility in goal achievement and implementation, i.e. minimizing regulatory costs through flexibility.

## 1 Regulatory competences

The parameters of our 'regulatory competence' variable are formed by three sets of competences that together make up the regulatory process:[122] norm setting, implementation, and enforcement. In order to move forward, working definitions of what these competences entail are essential.

---

[121] This 'second-level' collective action problem can undermine the effectiveness of transboundary environmental policy and has been acknowledged in the academic debate but arguably insufficiently explored. See e.g. A. van Aaken, 'Effectuating Public International Law Through Market Mechanisms?' (2009) 165 *Journal of Institutional and Theoretical Economics* 33–57 at 33 ('Whereas the two-level game of lawmaking procedures is well acknowledged in the scholarship, the two-level game in the second stage, the compliance decision, has not been extensively analysed.') See also O. Ben-Shahar and A. Bradford, 'The Economics of Climate Enforcement' John M. Olin Law and Economics Working Paper No. 512 (2010). See generally Olson, *The Logic of Collective Action.*

[122] The term 'regulation' has become a term of convenience referring to practically any activity, mostly of public actors but increasingly also private parties, which

46    FROM COMPETING JURISDICTIONS TO COMPETING COMPETENCES

*Norm setting* revolves around the establishment of a *primary* regulatory norm that defines the recommended or prescribed behaviour for the regulated parties.[123] Those responsible for setting these behavioural norms will be referred to as 'norm setters' and/or 'policymakers'. Norm setting forms the foundation of the regulatory process, which defines the policy goal that will be pursued. This stage may also involve the choice of regulatory instrument, and the allocation of implementation and enforcement competences to other regulatory institutions. In practice, the allocation of competences is often pre-determined by the constitutional setting of the regulatory activity, i.e. the European Treaties. Put differently, the norm setter is not always empowered to change the constitutional 'rules of the game' when deciding on the primary norm with respect to one particular policy area, such as EU environmental policy. This does not mean that the same (group of) norm setter(s) is not able to change these rules through a separate process, Treaty revision, for instance. This effectively means that for norm setting, competences that are allocated with reference to the principle of subsidiarity only involve the setting of behavioural standards or policy goals, and do not pertain to the allocation of implementation or enforcement competences, or instrument choice.

*Implementation* puts in place the *secondary* regulatory norms, which set out more precise arrangements for both implementation and enforcement processes.[124] As such, implementation operationalizes the norms defined in the norm setting stage. This typically involves a further specification of rules, i.e. standard setting, through more detailed (secondary) legislation. Depending on the pre-existing institutional setting, this process may also include the creation or earmarking of specific agencies

> aims to influence behaviour in order for it to conform to a given standard. Within legal scholarship, a more precise definition, which is commonly referred to, is limited to the regulatory methods of enforcement of conduct requirements or prohibitions by administrative, criminal or civil actions backed by the coercive power of the state, rather than including also norm-based practices and institutions. See R. B. Stewart, 'Enforcement of Transnational Public Regulation' EUI Working Papers, Robert Schuman Centre for Advanced Studies, Private Regulation Series–06 no. 2011/49 (2011), at 2 ('In defining regulation as involving enforcement of conduct requirements or prohibitions, this essay follows what Neil Walker has identified as the narrow view of regulation – one shared by most lawyers – as distinguished from a broader view of regulation that encompasses other norm-based practices and institutions that shape conduct in regular patterns, including much network regulation and elements of new governance.')
> [123] Stewart, 'Enforcement of Transnational Public Regulation', 3.
> [124] *Ibid.*

that become responsible for the administration of different parts of the regulatory process (administration). The dividing line between norm setting and implementation can become murky depending on the level of specificity of the norm setter. For example, if a policymaker decides that the use of renewable energy by consumers must increase by 30 per cent over the next five years, the implementer must decide how to translate this norm into concrete standards for energy providers in terms of energy mix, or a subsidy scheme for private parties, as well as deciding on potential sanctions. If, however, the norm itself is already more specific, for instance a change in the maximum speed limit from 120 km/h to 110 km/h, implementation may be limited to defining sanctions for non-compliance.

Crucially, the implementation process can have undeclared consequences for the allocation of competences, for instance through the assignation of certain agencies as administrators or enforcers, or the method of implementation when instrument choice is left to the implementer. For example, in the area of EU environmental policy the use of directives leaves a large margin of discretion in the implementation of norms insofar as the method of implementation is concerned – this large amount of discretion may mean that implementation, rather than the formulation of the norms, is critical.[125] When the implementation is left to the Member States, this freedom of method can affect norm achievement. These effects cannot always be remedied by infringement procedures by the European Commission since there may not always be an infringement – there can also be more subtle ways to circumvent the intended allocation of competences.[126]

*Enforcement* refers to actions to monitor behaviour in order to ensure compliance with set standards, and the sanctioning of confirmed violations. Enforcement may take place through both formal and informal methods, the former referring primarily to legal processes involving administrative mechanisms, civil action or criminal persecution, whereas the latter includes 'softer' mechanisms such as

---

[125] I. von Homeyer, 'The Evolution of EU Environmental Governance', in Joanne Scott (ed.) *Environmental Protection: European Law and Governance* (Oxford University Press, 2009), 1–23, at 20 (stating that in environmental policy, there are four main reasons for this large amount of discretion: the formulation of targets is typically left to the implementation stage; full implementation often takes twenty or more years; Member States have leeway in the types of instruments to be used; and legislative measures often do not include legally binding obligations).

[126] See also Section 3 of this chapter.

## 48  FROM COMPETING JURISDICTIONS TO COMPETING COMPETENCES

### Table 1.1 Working definitions of regulatory competences

| Competence | Definition |
| --- | --- |
| Norm setting | *Primary* regulatory norm; defines prescribed and recommended behaviour.<br>Cannot prescribe *instrument choice* or *allocation of implementation or enforcement powers.* |
| Implementation | *Secondary* regulatory norm; standard-setting and creation/ distribution administration.<br>*Discretion* regarding operationalization has implications for *allocation of implementation or enforcement powers.* |
| Enforcement | Monitoring and enforcing of behaviour.<br>No *discretion* over the norm; *discretion* over enforcement. |

advice, negotiation, education and persuasion.[127] Despite the arguably important role played by these informal mechanisms, the focus within this paper will be on the formal methods of enforcement provided by the relevant legal framework within which regulation is developed.[128] Within this book, enforcement will therefore refer to both public and private actions that induce compliance on the basis of a governmental mandate.[129] Enforcers are able to differentiate in their enforcement, i.e. let certain violations go unpunished, but cannot change the norm against which the behaviour is measured or the prescribed penalty. The key features of each regulatory competence are summarized in Table 1.1.

---

[127] See also B. van Rooij, *Regulating Land and Pollution in China: Lawmaking, Compliance, and Enforcement; Theory and Cases* (Leiden University Press, 2006) ('Enforcement is here defined as the state's actions to detect violations to stop them, and to prevent further violation from occurring in the future.')

[128] See C. Abbot, *Enforcing Pollution Control Regulation – Strengthening Sanctions and Improving Deterrence* (Oxford: Hart Publishing, 2009), 8–9. See also B. Hutter, *Compliance: Regulation and Environment* (Oxford: Clarendon Press, 1997), as quoted in Abbot, above, 8–9 ('[T]hese [informal enforcement techniques] were used by all law enforcement officials, but came into particular prominence in the regulatory arena.') Ideally, enforcement serves to sanction both existing behaviour and to deter actors from future violations.

[129] Compliance can also be increased through actions by private actors on their own behalf, for instance through tort proceedings, see e.g. S. Shavell, 'Liability for Harm versus Regulation of Safety' (1984) 13 *Journal of Legal Studies* 357–374. These forms of private enforcement fulfil an important ancillary role to 'public' enforcement, both

## 2 Regulatory levels: (de)centralization

The terms centralization and decentralization are ubiquitous in the existing literature, and have taken on a certain 'you know it, when you see it' quality, requiring little to no formal definition.[130] Definitions of the terms are most commonly provided in cases where one specific element or type of (de)centralization is envisaged.[131] Another common feature of discussions on (de)centralization is that the choice is considered dichotomous. We will also assume that the choice that needs to be made is between centralization *or* decentralization, in order not to excessively complicate the framework. However, it must be stressed that centralization and decentralization are better conceptualized as points on a continuum rather than as a binary choice.[132]

Drawing on public administration literature, we find a more general definition of decentralization, which makes an initial distinction between territorial and functional decentralization.[133] Territorial decentralization concerns the distribution of powers between different tiers of government.[134] Functional decentralization, on the other hand, refers to the dispersal of control over particular activities, and is often 'vertical' rather than 'horizontal'. For example, a shift from public to

---

through public and private institutions, and will be discussed where relevant. See also R. D. Cooter, 'Three Effects of Social Norms on Law: Expression, Deterrence, and Internalization' (2000) 79 *Oregon Law Review* 1–22 (discussing the effects of social norms on law, specifically the fact that norms, rather than written laws, may induce changes in behaviour and similarly that social norms may have several effects on law: expression, internalization, and deterrence), and J. A. W. van Zeben, 'The Untapped Potential of Horizontal Private Enforcement within EC Environmental Law' (2010) 5 *The Georgetown International Environmental Law Review* 241–269 (on the role of 'horizontal' private enforcement in European environmental law).

[130] R. M. Bird, 'Threading the Fiscal Labyrinth: Some Issues in Fiscal Decentralization' (1993) 46 *National Tax Journal* 207–227 at 208 ('Decentralization seems often to mean whatever the person using the term wants it to mean.')

[131] For instance, Arcuri and Dari-Mattiacci take centralization to mean a concentration of experts in one single committee as compared to a distribution of the same number of experts among several jurisdictions in the case of decentralization. Arcuri and Dari-Mattiacci, 'Centralization versus Decentralization', 2.

[132] See also P. D. Hutchcroft, 'Centralization and Decentralization in Administration and Politics: Assessing Territorial Dimensions of Authority and Power' (2001) 14 *Governance* 23–53 at 46.

[133] D. A. Rondinelli, 'Government Decentralization in Comparative Perspective: Theory and Practice in Developing Countries' (1981) 47 *International Review of Administrative Sciences* 133–145; H. Maddick, *Democracy, Decentralisation and Development* (London: Asia Publishing House, 1963).

[134] Rondinelli, 'Government Decentralization in Comparative Perspective'.

private ownership could be a form of functional decentralization but does not necessarily imply anything about tiers of government.[135] Given our focus on competence allocation between different levels of government, our theoretical framework clearly draws on territorial, rather than functional decentralization. There is a rich social science literature that further categorizes types of territorial decentralization in different ways.[136] The most influential has been the typology of Rondinelli,[137]

[135] M. Bray, 'Centralization/Decentralization and Privatization/Publicization: Conceptual Issues and the Need for More Research' (1994) 21 *International Journal of Educational Research* 817–824 at 819.

[136] J. M. Cohen and S. B. Peterson, *Administrative Decentralization: Strategies for Developing Countries* (West Hartford: Kumarian Press, 1999), who identify six major approaches to classify decentralization: the 'Historical' approach (types: French, English, Soviet and traditional decentralization); the 'Hierarchy and Function' approach of the Berkeley Decentralization project (types: territorial and functional decentralization); the 'Problem and Value-centered' approach (types: devolution, functional devolution, interest organization, prefectoral deconcentration, ministerial deconcentration, delegation to autonomous agencies, philanthrophy and marketization); the 'Service delivery' approach presented by the United Nations in 1962 (types: local government systems, partnership systems, dual systems and integrated administrative systems); the 'Objective Based' approach (types: administrative (deconcentration, devolution and delegation), political, spatial, market decentralization); and finally the 'Single country experience' approach; D. Tiersman, 'Decentralization and the Quality of Government', UCLA Political Science Working Paper (2002), who identifies five types of political decentralization (structural, decision, resource, electoral and institutional decentralization) and outlines five arguments on how specific types may affect governance, using collected data from 154 countries.

[137] Rondinelli, 'Government Decentralization in Comparative Perspective'; D. A. Rondinelli and J. R. Nellis, 'Assessing Decentralization Policies in Developing Countries: The Case for Cautious Optimism' (1986) 4 *Development Policy Review* 3–23, who expand the original typology to identify four popular typologies of decentralization: devolution, deconcentration, delegation and divestment (or privatization). Devolution refers to a situation in which central government transfers authority for decision-making, finance and management to quasi-autonomous units of local government. Deconcentration occurs when central government disperses responsibilities for certain services to its regional branch offices. This does not involve any transfer of authority to lower levels of government and is unlikely to lead to the potential benefits or pitfalls of decentralization. Delegation refers to the situation in which central government transfers responsibility for decision-making and the administration of public functions to local governments or semi-autonomous organizations (local governments are not wholly controlled by central governments but are ultimately accountable to it). Finally, divestment is the transfer of public services and institutions to private companies and firms. A simplified version of Rondinelli's typology has been adopted by the World Bank in the context of decentralization in developing countries, one of the main fields where decentralization theories have been developed. See A. Parker, 'Decentralization: The Way Forward for Rural Development?' The World Bank Policy Research Working Paper 1475 (1995).

which distinguishes between deconcentration, fiscal decentralization and devolution.[138] These types of decentralization are not mutually exclusive and may take place at the same time.[139] *Deconcentration*, also referred to as administrative decentralization, occurs when agents in higher levels of government move to lower levels. *Fiscal decentralization* then describes the process when higher levels of government cede influence over budgets and financial decisions to lower levels. *Devolution*, or democratic decentralization, occurs when resources, power, and often tasks are shifted to lower-level authorities who are somewhat independent of higher authorities, and who are at least somewhat democratic. Decentralization is an umbrella term, which may refer to any of these processes.

On the basis of this typology, the centralization or decentralization of competences can best be characterized as a process of devolution: the regulator responsible for the execution of a given competence will be presumed to have complete discretion with respect to these competences.[140] The conceptual difference between harmonization and centralization must also be stressed: in the context of this book, the term 'centralization' is used to describe the conferral of discretionary decision-making powers to the central legislator whereas 'harmonization' refers to the conscious effort of the legislator to bring national (or local) laws in line with one another.

The categorization of a certain regulatory level as 'central' or 'decentralized/local' must thus be seen in light of the fact that discussions of federalist systems typically presume a two-layered system.[141] The framework developed in this chapter will be applied to a multi-level system of governance in which one can distil at least three public levels of governance – international, European and national.[142] The simplifying assumption that there are only two levels of governance – the 'central' and 'local' – must thus be abandoned. Furthermore, 'central'

---

[138] See also R. Crook and J. Manor, 'Democratic Decentralization', OED Working Paper Series (2000).

[139] *Ibid.*

[140] As we shall see with reference to the EU ETS, this is not always the case in the European Union where the European institutions can (try to) influence the exercise of e.g. implementation competences by the Member States under a specific set of circumstances.

[141] See e.g. S. Rose-Ackerman, 'Does Federalism Matter? Political Choice in a Federal Republic' (1981) 89 *Journal of Political Economy* 152–165 at 153.

[142] P. Ylvisaker, 'Some Criteria for a "Proper" Areal Division of Governmental Powers' in A. Maass (ed.), *Area and Power: A Theory of Local Government* (Glencoe, IL: Free Press,

52    FROM COMPETING JURISDICTIONS TO COMPETING COMPETENCES

and 'local' are relative terms that depend on the institutional setting of our regulatory problem. The situation of the European Member States may serve as an illustration: until the 1970s, Member States' national parliaments were the 'central' regulatory level in respect of environmental policy, with municipalities and localities serving as their 'local' or decentralized counterparts. However, as the European institutions increased their environmental policy-making, these national parliaments became decentralized implementers and enforcers to the central European policymaker. Thus the 'central' and 'decentralized' level can be defined only within a given regulatory framework and/or with respect to a certain area of regulation.[143]

With respect to the competences that we have identified – norm setting, implementation and enforcement – the terms 'centralized' and 'decentralized' must then be interpreted as follows:

(i)   for *norm setting*, the 'central' and 'local' level are defined relative to the geographical scope of the regulated activity. Thus, if the regulated activity and its effects are restricted to one municipality, and norm setting takes places at the municipal, provincial, national or international level, norm setting may be considered centralized. If on the other hand, the effects of the regulated activity encompass several localities, but norms are set by individual municipalities, norm setting is decentralized;

(ii)  for implementation and enforcement, the decisive factor is the regulator's relative position to the norm setting or the implementer, respectively. Put differently, if norm setting takes place at the national level, and implementation at the municipal level, implementation will be referred to as decentralized, regardless of whether norm setting itself is centralized or decentralized.

Given that we allow for more than two regulatory levels in our theoretical framework, this can also mean that implementation and enforcement are both decentralized, but at different levels. For instance, in the case of a European policy – depending on the regulatory problem this could be the central level – it may be implemented by the

1959). The amount of layers could be increased to include many other (sub-national) levels of governance in the EU as well.

[143] C. Kumar Sharma, 'Decentralization Dilemma: Measuring the Degree and Evaluating the Outcomes' (2006) 1 *The Indian Journal of Political Science* 49–64 (regarding the

|  | Norm Setting | Implementation | Enforcement |
|---|---|---|---|
| Global | $N_C$ | $I_D$ | $E_C$ |
| Regional | $N_D$ | $I_D$ | $E_D$ |

FIGURE 1.1 *Competence allocation choices*

national regulator (decentralized), and enforced by a municipality (also decentralized).[144]

In the remainder of this framework, the terms decentralized and centralized will only be used in general discussions, as soon as more than two levels of governance are involved, they will be referred to by name, e.g. international, regional, or national.[145] Finally, the choice to (de)centralize is made for each competence individually. This can result in a *unified* model of regulation, where all competences are located at the same regulatory level, or a *fragmented* model where some competences

    undesirability of the development of a more general definition given the importance of mapping institutional specificities when giving policy advice).

[144] In this book we take an issue-specific approach to competence allocation. If one were to consider the division of competence between regulatory levels in a multi-level system in a more general way, considerations of the hierarchy between regulatory levels in terms of the possibility for interaction between levels, i.e. whether the division of functions is fluid or pre-determined, also become relevant. See e.g. Rose-Ackerman, 'Does Federalism Matter?', 153–154 (referring to the possibility of pre-emption in hierarchical federal systems). This model should be contrasted with others, which have strict division of functions between high- and low-level governments. See e.g. K. C. Wheare, *Federal Government* (London: Oxford University Press, 1953), 32–33. Recently, concern for strict division of authority has given way to scholarship that recognizes the importance of communication between levels of government. See e.g. M. Grodzins, 'The Federal System' in *The Goals for Americans: Report of President's Commission on National Goals* (New York: Prentice Hall, 1960), 256–282; M. Grodzins, *The American System: A New View of the Government of the United States* (New York: Rand McNally, 1966) and D. J. Elazar, *The American Partnership: Intergovernmental Co-operation in the Nineteenth-Century United States* (Chicago University Press, 1962).

[145] Pre-existing constitutional arrangements may dictate the allocation of competences at certain levels, such as the principle of subsidiarity in the European Union. Comparable constitutional arrangements exist in most federal systems, for instance in the United Kingdom. See Scotland Act (1998), section 54, section 98 and Schedule

54 FROM COMPETING JURISDICTIONS TO COMPETING COMPETENCES

are centralized and others decentralized.[146] Distinguishing between different competences, we are left with a number of potential (de)centralization choices, which are mapped in Figure 1.1.

## B Normative trade-offs

The selection of allocative criteria is an inherently normative exercise, based in part on the researcher's own preferences and experiences. Another important source for identifying criteria within the context of this book is the economic and legal scholarship on federalism.[147] The identification of these considerations only provides us with a trade-off; the optimal division of competences between different levels of governance depends on how these considerations are weighed against each other. Put differently, we must decide how much weight to give to the competing normative criteria in order to use them as a motivation, and standard, for competence allocation decisions.[148]

## 1 Allocative criteria

The allocation of competences within legal scholarship depends on constitutional principles such as the European principles of

---

5 (Reserved Matters) and Schedule 6 (Devolved Issues) (which set out the legislative issues that are reserved or devolved to the Scottish legislator by the British government. Reserved matters include foreign affairs, defence, and the registration and funding of political parties).

[146] The assignment of all competences to the same level of governance will not preclude a fragmentation of these competences among different actors at that same level. Justification of this practice may be found in the separation of powers doctrine as first developed by Montesquieu. See de Montesquieu, *The Spirit of the Laws*.

[147] Aside from the combination that we propose based on the economic theory of federalism, numerous other trade-offs are possible. See e.g. R. Inman and D. Rubinfeld 'Rethinking Federalism' (1997) 11(4) *The Journal of Economic Perspectives* 43–64 at 44 ('[T]hose who value a federal system typically do so for a mix of three reasons: it encourages an *efficient* allocation of national resources; it fosters *political participation* and a sense of the democratic community; and it helps to protect basic *liberties and freedoms*'). The trade-off between efficiency and equity (distributional or otherwise) will not be part of the analysis of this paper. See e.g. Revesz and Stavins, 'Environmental Law', 499, 507 ('The consensus, at least within the realm of environmental policy, is that efficiency and equity ought to be evaluated separately, but there is no consensus on specific criteria that might be used to rank alternatives from an equity perspective'). See also Revesz and Stavins, *ibid.*, 508 onwards for a detailed discussion of cost-benefit analysis in the context of environmental regulation.

[148] *See* L. H. Goulder and I. W. H. Parry, 'Instrument Choice in Environmental Policy' (2008) 2 *Review of Environmental Economics and Policy* 152–174 at 152: 'Beyond the theoretical and empirical challenges involved, there is a sobering conceptual reality:

subsidiarity.[149] Article 5 of the TEU identifies 'reasons of scale or effect' as the deciding factor in subsidiarity assessments. This has mostly been interpreted as referring to the presence of externalities due to certain actions or activities, a threshold that, especially in the area of environmental policy, is easily overcome.[150] Even when there are no environmental externalities *strictu sensu*, one can point at externalities through the creation of de facto trade barriers caused by divergent environmental protection laws.[151] This focus on externalities needs to be qualified insofar as the phrase 'reasons of scale or effect' can, and should, be interpreted as referring to more than the presence of externalities – i.e. the range of criteria should be expanded. The economic theory of federalism is more explicit and identifies several 'conditions', or circumstances, under which decentralization may be preferred over centralization or vice versa.[152] These conditions are:

(i) The level of *heterogeneity* of the conditions and preferences in different localities;
(ii) The presence of *externalities*, and;
(iii) The potential to achieve *economies* of *scale* and/or *scope*.[153]

the absence of an objective procedure for deciding how much weight to give to the competing normative criteria.'

[149] Within the legal literature we also find important discussions pertaining to the accountability and transparency of the regulatory system. Since these discussions relate primarily to procedural elements of the regulatory process, they will not feature within our allocative criteria. This is not to say that accountability and transparency are not influenced by the allocation of competences at different levels, only that the absence or presence of accountability or transparency is an effect of allocation rather than a reason for allocation. When transparency is negatively impacted by a centralized allocation of e.g. implementation, this could be addressed through e.g. the instrument choice or the adoption of procedural rules at the relevant governance level. Heterogeneity, externalities and scale/scope economies, on the other hand, can directly drive the allocation of competences.

[150] De Sadeleer, 'Principle of Subsidiarity', 64.

[151] See also de Sadeleer, 'Principle of Subsidiarity', 65 (referring to the need to ensure a high level of protection for the environment in all Member States and possible distortive effects on interstate competition).

[152] See e.g. Alesina, Angeloni, and Schuknecht, 'What Does the European Union Do?', 277 ('[T]he EU – like any international union – should focus on policy areas where economies of scale are large, and internalizing externalities is important, and delegate to national or even sub-national levels of government the policy prerogatives where heterogeneity of preferences is predominant relative to the benefit of scale.') See also Alesina, Angeloni and Etro, 'International Unions' and A. Alesina and R. Wacziarg, 'Is Europe Going Too Far?' (1999) 51(1) *Carnegie-Rochester Conference Series on Public Policy* 1–42, who formally model these and related concepts.

[153] See note 147.

56    FROM COMPETING JURISDICTIONS TO COMPETING COMPETENCES

A crucial factor in this balancing act is the nature of the regulated activity, or regulatory problem, since its characteristics will determine the relevance of the considerations and their ranking *inter se*. The most important questions that must be answered in light of the above-mentioned trade-offs are:

(i)   Does the regulated activity give rise to externalities, and if so, what is the geographical scope of the activity's effects?
(ii)  Do the causes and/or effects of the regulatory problem differ across regions?
(iii) Are the (negative) effects of the activity immediate or delayed?
(iv)  What information is needed to regulate this activity?[154] Is the information more costly to gather at the central or local level?[155]

These questions can be matched to the allocative criteria above, as set out in Table 1.2.

Table 1.2 Relevant regulated activity characteristics

| Allocative criterion | Activity characteristics |
| --- | --- |
| *Heterogeneity* | Heterogeneous causes and/or effects? |
| *Externalities* | Geographical and socio-economic manifestation of (positive/ negative) externalities. |
| | Temporal dimension of effects: immediate or delayed? |
| *Economies of scale/scope* | Information needed to regulate activity? |
| | Potential cross-over with other policy areas? |

---

[154] Hahn, 'Economic Prescriptions for Environmental Problems', 111 ('It might seem, for example, that if the problem is local, then the logical choice for addressing the problem is the local regulatory body. However, this is not always true. Perhaps the problem may require a level of technical expertise that does not reside at the local level, in which case some higher level of government involvement may be required.')

[155] See e.g. Adler, 'When Is Two a Crowd?', 77 ('Environmental knowledge, like economic knowledge, is highly decentralized. Specific knowledge about local ecological conditions … is more likely to be found at the local level than in a centralized bureaucracy. Due to the decentralized nature of knowledge, one might expect that environmental protections would be adopted first in those areas where local knowledge about the need for such protection is the greatest.') See also J. L. Huffman, 'Making Environmental Regulation More Adoptive through Decentralization: The Case for Subsidiarity' (2005) 52 *University of Kansas Law Review* 1377–1400 at 1378 (Huffman observes 'enforcement is inherently local'.)

## 2 Instrument choice

Regulatory instruments are commonly divided into two groups:[156] command-and-control regulation (such as technology standards and performance standards) and market-based regulation (such as taxes and tradable permits).[157] Command-and-control regulation is easily the most widespread type of regulation, used in various forms in most areas of regulation.[158] As a group, command-and-control regulation broadly covers all regulation that is founded in the prohibition or prescription of specific behaviour, for instance through permits.[159] Of market-based instruments, taxes and tradable permits are most common.[160] The aim

[156] See e.g. R. N. Stavins, 'Market-Based Environmental Policies' Resources for the Future Discussion Paper 98–26 (1998); D. Driesen, 'Is Emissions Trading an Economic Incentive Program?: Replacing the Command and Control/Economic Incentive Dichotomy' (1998) 55 *Washington and Lee Law Review* 289–350; L. H. Goulder, 'The Cost-Effectiveness of Alternative Instruments for Environmental Protection in a Second-Best Setting' (1999) 72 *Journal of Public Economics* 329–360; K. Conrad and M. Schroder, 'Choosing Environmental Policy Instruments Using General Equilibrium Models' (1993) 15 *Journal of Policy Modeling* 521–544; J. Nicolaisen *et al.*, 'Economics and the Environment: A Survey of Issues and Policy Options' OECD Economics Studies No. 16 (1991); D. E. Spulber, 'Effluent Regulation and Long-Run Optimality' (1985) 12 *Journal of Environmental Economics and Management*, 103–116.

[157] For a discussion of further types of regulation, see R. M. Friedman, D. Downing, and E. M. Gunn, 'Environmental Policy Instrument Choice: The Challenge of Competing Goals' (2000) 10 *Duke Environmental Law & Policy Forum* 327–387 at 333–343.

[158] R. N. Stavins, 'Policy Instruments for Climate Change: How Can National Governments Address a Global Problem?' Resources For the Future Discussion Papers 97–11 (1997), 326 ('[W]e may reflect on the fact that despite thirty years of normative arguments from economists, the U.S. political system has typically taken a command-and-control regulatory approach, rather than an economic incentive-based approach to environmental problems.')

[159] These mandates may take numerous shapes, including for instance: obligations of notification, authorization, prohibition and obligation to act. For a description of these instruments, see L. Krämer, *EC Environmental Law* (London: Sweet & Maxwell, 6th edn, 2007), at 65–69.

[160] See generally T. Tietenberg, 'Tradable Permits in Principle and Practice' (2006) 14 *Penn State Environmental Law Review* 251–281; Stavins, 'Policy Instruments for Climate Change', 302–312 (for an overview of market-based policy instruments). On permit trading, see e.g. B. Van Dyke, 'Emissions Trading to Reduce Acid Deposition' (1991) 100 *Yale Law Journal* 2702–2726; G. E. Marchant, 'Global Warming: Freezing Carbon Dioxide Emissions: An Offset Policy for Slowing Global Warming' (1992) 22 *Environmental Law* 623–684; R. B. Stewart, 'Environmental Quality as a National Good in a Federal State' (1997) *University of Chicago Legal Forum*, 199–230; W. F. Pedersen, 'Using Federal Environmental Regulations To Bargain for Private Land Use Control' (2004) 21 *Yale Journal On Regulation* 1–66; R. R. Nordhaus and K. W. Danish, 'Assessing the Options for Designing a Mandatory U.S. Greenhouse Gas Reduction Program' (2005) 32 *B.C. Environmental Affairs Law Review* 97–164; J. V. Kefer, 'Warming up to an International Greenhouse Gas Market: Lessons from the U.S. Acid Rain Experience'

of market-based instruments is to harness the potential of economic incentives and market dynamics in order to induce the potential violator/polluter to behave in the public interest.[161] Market-based regulation is often also referred to as 'incentive-based' regulation, which is arguably more inclusive (not all market-based regulation makes use of a 'market') but also inaccurate: both command-and-control regulation and market-based regulation use incentives (positive or negative) to change the behaviour of regulated parties.

In our framework, instrument choice is considered part of the implementation process, since it forms part of the secondary norms that are needed to shape the regulatory system.[162] That said, in the norm-setting phase, some parameters may already be set for instrument choice, e.g. a number of different tools is selected from which the implementer may then choose to apply one or several.[163] Another important reservation that must be made is that we assume the use of one method of regulation, rather than a combination of tools. Often several instruments are employed to deal with the same regulatory problem, especially if the regulatory problem is particularly complex and encompasses several market failures.[164] This may result in positive and/or negative

(2001) 20 *Stanford Environmental Law Journal* 221–300. On the use of regulatory taxes, see B. Yandle, 'Creative Destruction and Environmental Law' (2002) 10 *Penn State Environmental Law Review* 155–174; R. R. M. Verchick, 'Feathers or Gold? A Civic Economics for Environmental Law' (2001) 25 *Harvard Environmental Law Review* 95–150; K. M. Swenson, 'A Stitch in Time: The Continental Shelf, Environmental Ethics, and Federalism' (1987) 60 *Southern California Law Review* 851–896; E. D. Elliott, 'Goal Analysis versus Institutional Analysis of Toxic Compensation Systems' (1985) 73 *Georgetown Law Journal* 1357–1376; N. Keohane, R. L. Revesz and R. N. Stavins, 'The Choice of Regulatory Instruments in Environmental Policy' (1998) 22 *Harvard Environmental Law Review* 313–367. See also Krämer, *EC Environmental Law*, 73–74 and 330–334 (for a general discussion on the introduction of tradable permits in European environmental regulation).

[161] Pigou, *The Economics of Welfare* (introducing corrective taxes to discourage activities that generate externalities); J. H. Dales, *Pollution, Property, and Prices* (University of Toronto Press, 1968) (showing that transferable property rights could be used to protect the environment against lower aggregate costs instead of command-and-control regulation); see also R. Hahn and R. N. Stavins 'Economic Incentives for Environmental Protection: Integrating Theory and Practice' (1992) 82(2) *The American Economic Review* 464–468 at 464.

[162] See also S. A. Shapiro and R. L. Glicksman, 'Goals, Instruments, and Environmental Policy Choice' (2000) 10 *Duke Environmental Law and Policy Forum* 297–325 at 325 ('Agencies cannot easily obtain the information necessary to determine which instrument minimizes implementation costs.')

[163] This is for instance the case in the context of the UNFCCC (1994).

[164] See generally Goulder and Parry, 'Instrument Choice in Environmental Policy'.

interactions between the different tools. Although this is an important aspect of instrument choice, it goes beyond our point of the interaction between competence allocation and instrument choice.

Instrument choice is influenced by the nature of the regulated activity (e.g. the type of damage – local or transboundary, dispersed or concentrated, immediate or delayed; the number of regulated parties; heterogeneous or homogeneous compliance costs) and the costs of specific regulatory tools.[165] Few attempts have been made to incorporate instrument choice into discussions on (de)centralization,[166] despite its influence on, inter alia, the ability of the regulatory system to accommodate *heterogeneous conditions and preferences* in terms of the regulated *activity*; and the ability of the regulatory system to accommodate *heterogeneous conditions* with respect to the *regulatory costs*.[167] In the trade-off between allocative criteria, the role of instrument choice can be seen to have two effects:

*Effect (i): ability to accommodate heterogeneous conditions and preferences regarding the regulated activity*

When the decision has been taken to centralize norm setting, for instance due to the presence of externalities, Oates' Decentralization Theorem suggests that this centralization must result in uniformity with respect to the norms for different sub-regions.[168] There are many real-life examples to suggest that this presumption of uniformity does not hold in practice. However, even if we were to assume that centralized norm setting will result in a lessened ability to take account of heterogeneous conditions and preferences of different regions that

---

[165] At this point, we do not consider the motivations of the regulator stemming from capture or voting behaviour. Path dependencies may also dictate instrument choice.

[166] See e.g. Inman and Rubinfeld, 'Federalism' (arguing that decentralization is often the more efficient type of regulation in terms of regulatory costs); Hahn, 'Economic Prescriptions for Environmental Problems', 111 ('In addition to selecting an appropriate mix of instruments, attention needs to be given to the effects of having different levels of government implement selected policies').

[167] See e.g. Friedman, Downing, and Gunn, 'Environmental Policy Instrument Choice', 356 ('Another measure of cost-effectiveness is at the firm level – that is, whether the instrument allows a firm to minimize its costs for compliance').

[168] Oates, *Fiscal Federalism*. See also Buzbee, 'Climate as an Innovation Imperative', 17 (arguing that pre-emption by the federal government in the area of environmental protection and especially climate change would negate the many advantages of state involvement in environmental regulation and may eventually lead to regulatory failure.) ('Institutional diversity retaining federal, state and local roles would be more stable and conducive to market and regulatory innovation').

fall under the central regulator's jurisdiction,[169] this problem can be (at least partly) resolved through instrument choice. Depending on the design of a specific emissions trading scheme, there will be much room to accommodate differences in conditions and preferences in sub-regions. If regions are allowed to decide independently how to distribute the reduction obligations of the central cap among different local industries, heterogeneity between localities can be fully observed. This is different for technological standards since here a given standard will apply to every industry member in the relevant jurisdiction. This may result in competitive advantages or disadvantages between industries, or producers within the same industry. Here the presumption of uniformity is hard to disprove with respect to central norm setting, also since differentiation in technological standards can be costly and thus unlikely.

*Effect (ii): accommodating heterogeneous costs*
Regulatory and compliance costs both need to be considered.

*Regulatory costs*
In order to successfully implement and enforce regulation, information is needed about the nature of the regulatory problem, the regulated parties and their behaviour. The costs of obtaining this information vary depending on, for example, the relative distance between the regulator and the regulated parties and problem, the number of regulated sources, the complexity of the regulated activity and the expertise of the regulator in a given area. Economies of scale and scope may occur through the centralization of scientific research and decision-making. Also, economies of scope occur when policies reinforce each other, provided that the central regulator is aware of the most important environmental policies within the jurisdiction. The information needed to

---

[169] See e.g. Butler and Macey, 'Externalities and the Matching Principle', 27 (critiquing the centralization of environmental regulatory authority to the federal level in the United States and arguing for reform through market-based regulation, economic property rights or greater state control: 'We conclude that, in every area of pollution, environmental regulation has been centralized beyond any possible justification, resulting in tremendous costs.') See Adler, 'Jurisdictional Mismatch'. Some have even argued that this is the case regarding air pollution, which is typically considered a transboundary problem. See J. Dwyer, 'The Practice of Federalism under the Clean Air Act' (1995) 54 *Maryland Law Review* 1183–1225 at 1218 (noting that: '[t]he knowledge necessary to administer any air pollution control program … can be found only at the local level.') See also Kimber, 'A Comparison of Environmental Federalism',1661.

create policy is different in nature from that which is needed to implement or enforce it. It has been argued that the economies of scale that are achieved through centralized policy-making are dwarfed by the diseconomies of scale in centralized administration of these rules.[170] Another issue that is frequently raised with respect to information costs is that the information needed to ascertain compliance is predominantly 'local', making centralized enforcement potentially costly.[171] The extent to which this is true depends on the type of information needed, the method of information collection, and whether economies of scale may be achieved. Increasingly, improved technological methods of data collecting and the harnessing of private parties' knowledge are used to reduce these regulatory costs.

Some forms of command-and-control regulation, such as technological standards, require a relatively high level of expertise on the part of the implementing institution since it needs to set specific standards in terms of technology for individual plants, industries and so on. Information costs involved in setting these standards is typically high, which may increase the risk of regulatory capture since regulators may need to rely on information provided by industries, which will attempt to influence the implementer's standard setting to their benefit.[172] On the other hand, the administrative costs of monitoring technological standards can be lower since there only needs to be a check on whether the prescribed technology is in place, in contrast to other forms of regulation where, for instance, the output of an installation may also need to be monitored.[173]

---

[170] Butler and Macey, 'Externalities and the Matching Principle', 145 ('[W]hatever economies of scale associated with the centralization of environmental policy, they are surely overwhelmed by the diseconomies of scale in centralized administration.').

[171] Adler, 'When Is Two a Crowd?', 77. See also Huffman, 'Making Environmental Regulation More Adoptive', 1378 (Huffman observes that 'enforcement is inherently local'.)

[172] See Chapter 5. See also R. Baldwin and M. Cave, *Understanding Regulation: Theory, Strategy and Practice* (Oxford University Press, 1999), 40 (arguing that due to the high level of expertise needed to set these standards, the system is also sensitive to the problem of regulatory capture, where regulators (and thus regulation) are manipulated – through information dissymmetry – to pursue the regulated enterprises' interests rather than the public interest). For certain environmental problems, self-regulation was initially considered an alternative to command-and-control regulation given the information advantages in the case of particularly complex regulatory problems and the relative flexibility of the rule-making process. The risk of regulatory capture in case of self-regulation is, however, considerable.

[173] See D. H. Cole and P. Z. Grossman, 'Toward a total-cost approach to environmental instrument choice' (2002) 20 *Research in Law and Economics* 223–241 (arguing that

The preference of many economists for these market-based instruments is based on the fact that economic theory suggests a much higher cost-effectiveness of these tools compared to command-and-control regulation.[174] However, the theoretical cost-effectiveness of market-based instruments is often not achieved in practice.[175] The implementation of these mechanisms may prove as equally challenging as that of command-and-control regulation since a market may need to be established,[176] or a tax rate determined. Moreover, especially in the case of market-based instruments, sophisticated monitoring and administration are needed, which are costly.[177] For both types of regulatory tools, the type of information needed for implementation and

where monitoring costs are exorbitant, command-and-control regulations may be more effective and more efficient).

[174] See e.g. J. M. Buchanan and G. Tullock, 'Polluters' Profits and Political Response: Direct Controls Versus Taxes' (1975) 65 *The American Economic Review* 139–147 at 139 ('Economists agree on the superior efficacy of penalty taxes as instruments for controlling significant external diseconomies which involve the interaction of many parties. However, political leaders and bureaucratic administrators, charged with doing something about these problems, appear to favour direct controls'); K. R. Richards, 'Framing Environmental Policy Instrument Choice' (2000) 10 *Duke Environmental Law and Policy Forum* 221–286 at 222 ('One consistent message from the environmental economics literature is that incentive-based instruments are more cost-effective means to achieve environmental goals than alternative policy instruments such as technology-based standards'). See also Stewart, 'Enforcement of Transnational Public Regulation', (2011) 8 ('Because of the dysfunctions encountered by governments in attempting to extend and intensify command and control requirements to meet increasingly ambitious regulatory goals, many developed and some developing countries have adopted market-based and information-based regulatory instruments as a supplement or alternative to traditional approaches').

[175] Hahn, 'Economic Prescriptions for Environmental Problems', 107 stresses that most market-based instruments are implemented based on existing regimes, which explains a lot of the difficulties. It also means that their cost savings are generally a lot lower than their theoretic potential; R. W. Hahn, 'The Political Economy of Environmental Regulation: Towards a Unifying Framework' (1990) 65 *Public Choice* 21–47 at 28 ('As several scholars have noted, emissions fees are rarely implemented in ways even remotely resembling their pure form. Consequently, this instrument choice comparison may not be terribly revealing').

[176] Hahn, 'Economic Prescriptions for Environmental Problems', 96 ('Naturally these results are subject to the usual cautions that a competitive market actually must exist for the results to hold true. Perhaps more importantly, the results assume that it is possible to easily monitor and enforce a system of permits or taxes').

[177] Hahn and Stavins 'Economic Incentives', 467 ('Much of the work on markets and emission taxes assumes that there is a reasonably sophisticated environmental control agency that can administer incentive-based programs'); S. A. Shapiro and T. McGarity, 'Not so Paradoxical: The Rationale for Technology-based Regulation' (1991) 40 *Duke Law Journal* 729–752 at 748–49 ('Emissions trading … require[s] inspectors to monitor constantly the amount of pollution that a plant emits').

enforcement is an important factor in deciding whether centralized or decentralized competence allocation is preferable. Economies of scale may be achieved in standard setting and information gathering, but enforcement may prove most cost-effective at the decentralized level. In the most basic model, emissions trading and taxes are symmetric in terms of their cost-effectiveness but when faced with actual implementation and enforcement, significant differences appear.[178] In short, (de)-centralized norm setting, implementation or enforcement of these different tools will affect the administrative costs involved, and the extent to which this is the case depends on the type and amount of information that is needed.

*Compliance costs*
If one is faced with heterogeneity of regulated sources and corresponding differences in abatement costs (as in the case of climate change), command-and-control regulation in the form of technology standards may be overly rigid and give rise to excessive compliance costs.[179] One of the key theoretical advantages of tradable permits (or 'emissions

---

[178] Seabright, 'Centralised and Decentralised Regulation', 8 ('First, permits fix the level of pollution control while charges fix the costs of pollution control. Second, in the presence of technological change and without additional government intervention, permits freeze the level of pollution control while charges increase it. Third, with permit systems as adopted, resource transfers are private-to-private, while they are private-to-public with ordinary pollution charges ... permit systems may be more susceptible to strategic behaviour, because of the barriers to entry that implemented forms of these systems frequently provide ... finally, in the presence of uncertainty, either permits or charges can be more efficient, depending upon the relative slopes of the marginal benefit and marginal cost functions and any correlation between them.')

[179] See e.g. J. Scott, *EC Environmental Law* (New York: Longman Publishing Group, 1998), 36 (explaining that in the case of extremely detailed and overly prescriptive standards, dynamic efficiency may suffer and may reduce incentives for technical innovation or other cost-effective responses, which can lead regulated parties to comply in the most minimal way with the set standards); M. Lee, 'From Private to Public: The Multiple Roles of Environmental Liability' (2001) 7 *European Public Law* 375–397; J. Holder and M. Lee, *Environmental Protection, Law and Policy: Texts and Materials* (Cambridge University Press, 2007) at 417; C. R. Sunstein, 'Political Equality and Unintended Consequences' (1994) 94 *Columbia Law Review* 1390–1414 (labelling command-and-control regulation as 'futile and self-defeating'). See also Driesen, 'Is Emissions Trading an Economic Incentive Program?', 289–350 (in-depth discussion of critiques of command-and-control). See generally on the inefficiency of command-and-control regulation: T. Tietenberg, *Emissions Trading: An Exercise in Reforming Pollution Policy*', (Resources for the Future, 1985); B. Ackerman and R. Stewart, 'Reforming Environmental Law' (1985) 37 *Stanford Law Review* 1333–1366; A. McGartland and W. E. Oates, 'Marketable Permits for the Prevention

trading') is the fact that a regulated party (a company or installation) has the flexibility to make a situation-specific calculation regarding the marginal abatement cost,[180] and can decide to buy allowances or abate based on this calculation. This flexibility should lead to a lower overall cost of abatement and the correct allocation of abatement costs to the companies or actors who have lowest marginal abatement costs.[181] In theory, either price-based (taxes) or quantity-based instruments (permits) can be used to meet an abatement goal at the same marginal price, provided there is perfect information.[182]

## 3 Overview

The theoretical framework developed in this section questions the existing legal and economic approaches to (de)centralization decisions, as they fail to distinguish between different stages in the regulatory process. By differentiating between norm setting, implementation and enforcement, the distinctive characteristics of these processes are highlighted and a more precise recommendation of (de)centralization per competence can be given. These recommendations are based on the normative trade-off between accommodating heterogeneous conditions and preferences, capturing externalities, and maximizing economies of scale/scope, based on the economic theory of federalism and legal federalism scholarship. The characteristics of the regulated activity should be decisive in determining the ranking of these allocative criteria. For example, if the problem is inherently local, without any externalities, accommodating heterogeneous conditions and preferences will be the

of Environmental Deterioration' (1985) 12 *Journal of Environmental Economics and Management* 207–228; R. B. Stewart, 'Economics, Environment, and the Limits of Legal Control' (1985) 9 *Harvard Environmental Law Review* 1–22. See also C. Hepburn, 'Regulation by Prices, Quantities, or Both: a Review of Instrument Choice' (2006) 22 *Oxford Review of Economic Policy* 226–247.

[180] The reduction in pollution per unit of production.
[181] See e.g. M. L. Weitzman, 'Prices vs. Quantities' (1974) 41 *Review of Economic Studies* 477–491.
[182] See Richards, 'Framing Environmental Policy', 244; Weitzman, 'Prices vs. Quantities', 480 ('In an environment of complete knowledge and perfect certainty there is a formal identity between the use of prices and quantities as planning instruments'). Cf. Hahn, 'Economic Prescriptions for Environmental Problems', 108 ('On the whole, there is more evidence for cost savings with marketable permits than with charges'). Hahn argues that this is due to the different role that taxes and permits play in meeting environmental objectives, since charges are used primarily to improve environmental quality by redistributing revenues, whereas marketable permits are used primarily to promote cost savings.

first-order consideration. Instrument choice can then be used to minimize regulatory costs and achieve economies of scale and/or scope. Conversely, if the problem is a transboundary one, the capture of externalities will be the first-order consideration, and the accommodation of heterogeneity and the realization of economies are second order. Also here, instrument choice may help optimize the regulatory process. The application of this framework ultimately depends on particulars of the regulatory setting, in our case that of the EU ETS, as will be set out in Chapter 2.

## 3 Interacting competences

Applying our criteria for competence allocation can result in a fragmented system within which competences are divided over several governance levels. In such a fragmented system, interactions are set to occur between the agencies that are assigned these regulatory competences. These interactions are highly dependent on the characteristics of the relevant agencies,[183] and the way in which they give shape to their relative competences. The aim of this framework is to make potential interactions explicit and to consider the way in which these interactions can strengthen, or undermine, regulatory functioning within the system. Therefore we adopt several simplifying assumptions regarding the nature of the interactions.

First, we assume there are no strategic interactions in case of a unified system on the *competence dimension*. We define a unified system as one where there is either a single regulator exercising all competences, or a number of different regulators at the same governance level, whose actions and interests are perfectly aligned. For instance, within a nation state, norm setting, implementation and enforcement competences

---

[183] The methodology applied in this section is closely linked to the principal–agent paradigm that is present in much of the economic literature on policy interactions. However, since this framework does not attempt to provide a formal model of the relationship between different agencies, and since we are dealing with a myriad of different relationships, depending on which legal framework we refer to (e.g. European Union and its citizens or Member States, the United Nations and its parties, nation states and their constituents), we use the term 'agencies' rather than agents since our primary interest does not lie with the principal–agent relationship. For an overview on the principal–agent paradigm, see L. Toth, 'Agency Issues within Public Agencies: Performance Effects of External Budget Assignment' University of Amsterdam (2012) (who notes that there is relatively little work on public agencies as multi-level hierarchies).

are typically divided between the executive, legislative and judiciary. The theoretical literature on the incentives of these agencies typically shows that there are large variations in their motivation and incentives, the promotion of their respective mandates or the professional advancement of people working in these bodies, for example.[184] Since our focus is on the interaction between the competences, we side-step this more general discussion of the characteristics and incentives of agencies and instead assume that any negative or positive interaction is dependent only on the type of agency – social welfare maximizing or rent seeking – and the type of competence.

Second, and relatedly, we assume that interactions will take place when the interests of agencies located at different governance levels are not aligned, as can be the case with a fragmented allocation. The resulting interactions may undermine the functioning of the system as a whole, particularly across the dimensions on which the independent competence allocation was based, such as externalities capture. This may necessitate a change in the competence allocation, even when this allocation was considered optimal in light of the relative (dis)advantages of (de)centralization of the individual competences when considered in isolation.

Third, we assume that there is no multi-tasking in the agencies, i.e. they are assigned only one task and do not need to consider whether to prioritize tasks within their relative budget constraints.[185] That said, an agency could be constricted in the performance of its task (i.e. norm setting, implementation or enforcement) due to budget constraints.

## A  Interacting regulators

In the existing legal literature, a competitive or cooperative interaction between regulatory agencies or levels is typically discussed as a manifestation of the constitutional framework underlying a specific federalist system,[186] and/or refers to the competence to regulate a specific

---

[184] See e.g. M. Dewatripont, I. Jewitt and J. Tirole 'The Economics of Career Concerns, Part II: Application to Missions and Accountability of Government Agencies' (1999) 66 *Review of Economic Studies* 199–217 (finding that motivation in public agencies is largely driven by career concerns and mission motivation).

[185] For a more elaborate treatment of this possibility, see Toth, 'Agency Issues within Public Agencies', focusing on the effects of budget assignment on the quantitative range of activities of regulatory agencies and the welfare effects of such budget settings, finding that resource constraints can change both the kind and the level of public good provision.

[186] See e.g. J. Freeman and J. Rossi, 'Agency Coordination in Shared Regulatory Space' (2012) 125 (5) *Harvard Law Review* 1131–1211.

policy area as a whole (with competing jurisdictions), rather than to interactions between specific competences within a policy area.[187] Our focus on individual competences leads to a different perspective. In the context of competence allocation, the question of interactions becomes relevant as soon as the optimal allocation for each individual competence has been determined and either a 'unitary' or 'fragmented' system has emerged. In the former, all competences are assigned to the same governance level, whereas a fragmented system is characterized by an allocation of competences to different regulatory levels.[188] In light of our first assumption that the interests and preferences of different actors functioning at the same regulatory level are perfectly aligned, it follows that all agencies are of the same type, whereas under fragmentation, there can be as many different types as there are regulatory levels. The diversity in type is not a consequence of fragmentation; the type of agency is an exogenous factor, independent of the competence allocation.

The behaviour of agencies is extremely varied and depends largely on their institutional setting (including its social and cultural characteristics). The purpose of our discussion is not to map all the subtleties involved in these human interactions but to draw a blueprint of agency interactions in a situation of fragmented competence allocation. We therefore distinguish between two types of agencies: benevolent and

[187] See generally E. S. Corwin, 'The Passing of Dual Federalism' (1950) 36 *Virginia Law Review* 1–24 at 17 (introducing the term cooperative federalism); Elazar, *The American Partnership* (introducing the idea that dual federalism is no longer applicable to the federal relationships in the United States but rather cooperative federalism); M. Grodzins, *The American System*. More recently, see J. F. Zimmerman, 'Nation-State Relations: Cooperative Federalism in the Twentieth Century' (2001) 31 *Publius* 15–30 at 30 ('[T]he postulates of a more general federalism theory of national-state relations include dual, cooperative, and coercive elements, and emphasize the importance of the national political process to states and their political subdivisions in preventing enactment of or obtaining relief from pre-emption statutes, their implementing rules and regulations, and mandates and restraints, protection against the exercise of coercive powers by Congress, and enactment of statutes desired by states'). For environmentally based empirical work, see H. Sigman, 'Transboundary Spillovers and Decentralization of Environmental Policies' (2005) 50 *Journal of Environmental Economics and Management* 82–101 at 96: '[M]y empirical results suggest ... the optimal response to free riding may not be centralization, but rather decentralization in combination with more targeted responses to spill overs.'
[188] Assuming two levels of governance – centralized (C) and decentralized (D) – six different fragmented scenarios can be constructed as the vectors (C, D, C), (C, C, D), (C, D, D), (D, C, C), (D, D, C) and (D, C, D).

rent-seeking agencies.[189] A benevolent agency is assumed to (try to) act in a social welfare maximizing way.[190] Conversely, a rent-seeking agency sets out to create value for itself, which probably (but not necessarily) leads to socially inefficient outcomes.[191] A first-best scenario would assume a benevolent agency with full information. In this case, the allocation of competences can be based purely on the (dis)advantages of (de)centralization of the individual competences since there will be no distortions by the agencies, their actions being fully informed and welfare maximizing. If, however, we are dealing with a rent-seeking agency, certain (fragmented) allocations may be better than others, depending on the type of regulatory authority exercised by the agency, and the resulting relationship between the competences.[192]

## B Interacting competences

The regulatory agencies referred to above interact with each other on the basis of the regulatory competence(s) that have been assigned to them. Since we distinguish between three different competences, there can be two sets of interactions (under a fully fragmented system): one

---

[189] F. Parisi, N. Schulz, and J. Klick, 'Two Dimensions of Regulatory Competition' (2006) 26 *International Review of Law and Economics* 56–66 at 63–4. (They identify one additional group of agencies, so-called shirking agencies, which lack sufficient incentives to intervene or regulate, which will lead to an inefficient level of regulation. To help reduce the complexity of our analysis we will focus on rent-seeking and benevolent agencies since these two categories cover the vast majority of agencies in our regulatory context of climate change.)

[190] Social welfare refers to the overall welfare of society. See A. K. Sen, 'Distribution, Transitivity and Little's Welfare Criteria' (1963) 73 *Economic Journal* 771–78 at 771–78; A. K. Sen, *Choice, Welfare and Measurement* (Cambridge, MA: MIT Press, 1982); P. A. Samuelson, *Foundations of Economic Analysis* (Cambridge, MA: Harvard University Press, 1947); K. J. Arrow, *Social Choice and Individual Values* (New Haven, CT: Yale University Press, 1951); F. M. Bator, 'The Simple Analytics of Welfare Maximization' (1957) 47(1) *The American Economic Review* 22–59.

[191] See e.g. A. O'M. Bowman, 'Horizontal Federalism: Exploring Interstate Interactions' (2004) 14 *Journal of Public Administration Research and Theory* 535–546 at 544, on horizontal interstate cooperation in the United States, arguing that this cooperation can offer an alternative to federal legislation, finding that the cooperative aspect of horizontal federalism is relatively unstable: 'more capable states cooperate by engaging in multistate legal action, and less capable states cooperate by adopting uniform state laws'. Moreover: 'Because self-interest is the impetus for state action, the likelihood of coordinated, collaborative action across the fifty states is always problematic' (at 545).

[192] Determining an agency's type is an empirical question, which must be answered for each specific regulatory context. See e.g. T. Yang, 'International Treaty Enforcement as a Public Good: Institutional Deterrent Sanctions in International Environmental Agreements' (2006) 27 *Michigan Journal of International Law* 1131–1184 at 1156 ('As

between the norm setter and the implementer, and one between the implementer and the enforcer.[193] These interactions are sequential rather than simultaneous insofar as implementation action can only be taken once norms are set, and enforcement can only take place once the norms are implemented. Having made these preliminary observations, we must identify a driver for interaction between regulatory competences that is founded on the characteristics of the competences, rather than on (only) those of the agencies.

One of the few theoretical contributions on this topic is a 2006 model by Parisi, Schulz and Klick.[194] Their model of regulatory competition distinguishes between positive and negative types of regulatory *authority* (i.e. different effects of regulatory action), and between alternative and concurrent regulatory *competences* (i.e. ways in which different competences relate to each other).[195] Positive *authority* refers to the permitting of a certain activity that would otherwise be restricted, whereas negative *authority* involves the restriction of an otherwise permissible activity.[196] In the case of *alternative competences*, an action of 'one among multiple bodies is sufficient to give effects to a regulatory act':[197] i.e. an 'either/or' situation. In the case of *complementary competences*, all regulatory agents must choose to, for example, permit or restrict an activity in order for the regulatory act to take effect:[198] i.e. an 'and/and' situation. A 'regulatory competence' describes an agency's ability to permit or restrict a certain activity, for instance, rather than a specific step in a larger regulatory chain.

Given these parameters of regulatory authority and competence, regulatory competition between agencies takes place based on the possibility of rent extraction. Rent extraction is a positive externality which one regulatory agent creates for another by taking a certain course of action. For instance, in the case of a positive authority and concurrent

---

    a public good, treaty enforcement must overcome collective action difficulties in getting states to contribute to the cost of enforcement.')

[193] These interactions could be extended to include possible feedback effects between the enforcer and the norm setter.

[194] Parisi, Schulz and Klick, 'Two Dimensions'.

[195] *Ibid.*, 58. See also W. B. Buzbee, 'Recognizing the Regulatory Commons: A Theory of Regulatory Gaps' (2003) 89 *Iowa Law Review* 1–64, arguing that these dynamics may give rise to regulatory gaps rather than over-regulation: 'The regulatory commons dynamic creates analogous disincentives [to the tragedy-of-the-commons] for potential regulators to make such political investments where a regulatory opportunity is shared by many.'

[196] Parisi, Schulz and Klick, 'Two Dimensions', 57.   [197] *Ibid.*, 58.   [198] *Ibid.*, 58.

competences, the approval of a permit by one regulator increases the value of the second approval for the applicant since both approvals are needed to make use of the permit. This in turn increases the exploitable rent for the second regulator.[199] If, however, the first agency would deny the permit, there are no rents left for the second regulator since their approval will not 'activate' the permit. Similarly, in the case of positive authority coupled with alternative competence, the approval by one agent destroys the rents for the other agent since only one approval is needed. In both situations, we are dealing with a negative regulatory externality. Generally speaking, in the case of alternative competences, the decision of one regulator to permit or restrict an activity destroys the exploitable rent of the other competence holder since the activity can only be permitted or restricted once. If, on the other hand, the competences are concurrent, the activity can only be permitted if all regulators agree, which means that the approval of the 'first' competence holder increases the exploitable rent for the second regulator.

It follows from this that regulators will seek to maximize their rents through over- or under-regulation of a certain activity: in situations of alternative competence, agencies will exercise their regulatory power more than optimally from the point of view of the regulators' joint interests, and less than optimally in concurrent competence situations.[200] The answer to the question as to whether this over- or under-regulation is welfare improving or diminishing goes back to the type of agency. The welfare implications of competence allocation to benevolent and rent-seeking agencies under the Parisi *et al.* model are summarized in Table 1.3. The welfare outcomes under different competence allocations are ordered relative to the baseline of unified regulatory competence ($W_0$). The first two rows assume that the allocation of competence (in the sense of the competences being alternative or concurrent) is fixed, and only the type of authority may be chosen. The third and fourth rows assume the opposite. Thus, for rent-seeking agencies holding alternative competences, positive authority ($W_P$) is welfare increasing as compared to a unified ($W_0$) or negative authority ($W_N$), and unified allocation ($W_0$) is preferred to negative authority ($W_N$). In the case of benevolent agencies, we find that unified allocation is always welfare improving over a fragmented system.

In the Parisi *et al.* model either the nature of the regulatory activity or the type of competence can be taken as exogenous.[201] In our framework

---

[199] For other examples see *ibid.*, 59 onwards.   [200] *Ibid.*, 61.   [201] *Ibid.*, 64.

## 3 INTERACTING COMPETENCES 71

Table 1.3 Welfare implications

| | Welfare results | |
| --- | --- | --- |
| | Rent-seeking agencies | Benevolent agencies |
| Alternative authority | $W_P>W_0>W_N$ | $W_0>W_P\ W_0>W_N$ |
| Concurrent authority | $W_N>W_0>W_P$ | $W_0>W_P\ W_0>W_N$ |
| Positive action | $W_A>W_0>W_C$ | $W_0>W_A\ W_0>W_C$ |
| Negative action | $W_C>W_0>W_A$ | $W_0>W_A\ W_0>W_C$ |

Source: Adapted from Parisi, Schultz and Klick, 'Two Dimensions', 64.

of competence allocation, the relationship between the competences is endogenous, depending on the nature of the regulatory competences, i.e. what does each regulatory competence entail in terms of responsibilities? In addition, the relationship between implementation and enforcement will always be imperfectly alternative or concurrent.[202] Implementation and enforcement are not perfectly alternative since the action to permit or prohibit by the implementer does not destroy all exploitable rents for the enforcer: under both positive and negative authority, the enforcer could choose to non-enforce against non-compliant behaviour if provided with side-payments or other types of rents. However, since the enforcer cannot enforce against behaviour that has not already been either permitted or prohibited by the implementer, the competences are also not concurrent.

Despite these differences, we can draw certain conclusions regarding the impact of competence interactions for regulatory functioning: depending on (i) the type of regulatory agency, and (ii) the type of regulatory authority, the fragmentation of competences among different levels of governance can be welfare increasing or decreasing relative to a situation of unified competence allocation (see third and fourth line of Table 1.3). This could mean that even if the fragmentation of competences is preferable based on individual competence allocation

---

[202] For norm setting and implementation the situation is closer to one of perfect complementarity: under negative authority, the competences are imperfectly concurrent since a blanket restriction of behaviour would destroy rents. However, in most cases, norm setting determines to what extent the behaviour must be reduced or which behaviour must be prohibited, and the implementer determines to whom the prohibition applies, or which parties must restrict their behaviour.

considerations, unification may be welfare improving. The actual consequences of these interactions will depend on the specific regulatory context.

## C Instrument choice

The choice of regulatory tool is instrumental in the relationship between the implementer and the enforcer since it is one of the factors that determines to what extent under- or over-permitting or restricting is able to take place.[203] With respect to enforcement, the pay-offs of enforcement agents are influenced by the (perceived) likelihood that implementers will detect or correct their action or inaction.[204] This problem will manifest itself differently depending on the level of governance: sovereign parties to an international agreement may be less responsive to pressure to enforce than states in a federal setting where there may be specific provisions for failure to enforce.[205] Regardless of the governance level, the two main factors that influence the relationship between implementer and enforcer are information and discretion. These two factors are interrelated since tools that allow for a greater amount of discretion or flexibility are typically applied to more complex regulatory situations where the information is relatively asymmetrical.[206] Similarly, it may be argued that the more a regulatory tool allows for discretion on the part of the enforcer or the regulated party, the more likely it is that information asymmetries exist,

---

[203] The relationship between norm setter and implementer is not influenced in the same way by instrument choice since we assume that the implementer, not the norm setter, makes the choice of instrument. The norm setter may give a range of regulatory tools to choose from but this choice will not influence the relationship between the norm setter and the implementer in the way it does the implementer and enforcer relationship. Allowing for multiple interactions between the norm setter and the implementer, the range of regulatory tools allowed for by the norm setter could be influenced by the implementer/enforcer interaction once it becomes clear that certain instruments enhance sub-optimal results.

[204] And more generally whether the implementer has set upper and lower limits for e.g. fines. See also G. Spagnolo, 'Divede et Impera: Optimal Leniency Programmes' CEPR Discussion Papers 4840, C.E.P.R. (2004).

[205] See e.g. C. Lin, 'How Should Standards Be Set and Met?: An Incomplete Contracting Approach to Delegation in Regulation' (2010) 10 *The B.E. Journal of Economic Analysis & Policy* 1–17; J.-M. Burniaux *et al.*, 'The Economics of Climate Change Mitigation: How to Build the Necessary Global Action in a Cost-Effective Manner' Economics Department Working Papers No. 701 (2009) (arguing that the difficulty of enforcing international rules against sovereign states makes international carbon trading dependent on negotiation and consensus building).

[206] See Section 2.B.2 above.

are maintained or created. Flexible instruments are typically applied in situations where there is a high level of technical complexity, and/or heterogeneous circumstances among the regulated parties that make it difficult and costly to determine the right standard or type of activity for each party.[207] Depending on the relative levels of governance on which the implementer and the enforcer are active, the relative distance between the implementer or enforcer to the regulated party in these cases may mean that, for example, the implementer has relatively less insight into the activities of the regulated party, which plays into possible rent-seeking behaviour at the enforcement level.

Another important factor is the possibility to externalize certain regulatory costs onto others. For instance, the likelihood of under-enforcement is increased when the costs of this under-enforcement can be externalized onto other parties. When fines are paid to the enforcer and form part of that enforcer's budget, the pay-offs for non-enforcement in the form of rents have to be higher since the cost of non-enforcing the rents is a decrease in the enforcer's budget. Alternatively, when the enforcement takes the form of market-oversight, as is the case for tradable permits, the non-enforcement of certain types of market abuse will be externalized to other market participants, some of which may even be located outside the jurisdiction of the enforcer in case of an international market with national or regional enforcers. In this case, the pay-offs to the enforcer can be lower than in the case of fines since the cost of non-enforcement is externalized. The safeguards that can be put in place to limit these risks depend on the legal framework in which these competences are exercised, and the way in which competences have been delegated to different actors.[208]

## 4 Conclusions

The theoretical framework developed in this chapter questions the existing approach to (de)centralization decisions, which fails to distinguish between different stages in the regulatory process. By differentiating between norm setting, implementation and enforcement, the distinctive characteristics of these processes are highlighted and a more precise recommendation of (de)centralization per competence can be

---

[207] See Richards, 'Framing Environmental Policy', 237 (on the allocation of regulatory and abatement costs).
[208] See section 3.B.

given. These recommendations are based on the normative trade-off between accommodating heterogeneous conditions and preferences, capturing externalities, and maximizing economies of scale and scope, as developed within the economic theory of federalism and legal federalism scholarship. Whether this optimal allocation takes the shape of a fully (de)centralized allocation or a fragmented allocation among several levels of governance depends on the regulatory problem at hand, and the instrument used for its regulation.

Aside from the advantages and disadvantages of individual competence allocation, we have also considered the interactions between these competences and their potential consequences. By distinguishing between positive and negative authority, and the alternative or concurrent nature of the regulatory competences, and accounting for the benevolent or rent-seeking identity of the regulatory agency, it is shown that in certain cases unified or fragmented allocation have welfare increasing or decreasing effects beyond the considerations that determined the individual allocation.

Instrument choice plays an important role with respect to interactions as well since it may mitigate or aggravate to what extent these interactions can play themselves out. Instruments allowing higher levels of discretion, combined with information asymmetries, make it more likely for interactions between the implementer and the enforcer to occur. The effect of instrument choice on the interaction between the norm setter and implementer is less pronounced since we assume that instrument choice is part of the implementation stage. The optimal allocation of competences across different governance levels will depend on the concrete regulatory context and the nature of the regulatory problem itself. In the next chapter, we apply the theoretical framework to the mitigation of climate change through the EU ETS.

# 2 Optimal competence allocation for the EU ETS

The primary aim of the European Union Emissions Trading Scheme (EU ETS) is to ensure the reduction of greenhouse gas emissions, in an effort to contribute to national, regional and global climate change mitigation efforts. In order to understand the multi-layered regulatory framework that has developed with respect to climate change mitigation and adaptation, we must first take a closer look at the characteristics of climate change as a regulatory problem. This chapter will then set out the regulatory levels, tools and competences involved in climate change mitigation, particularly through the reduction of greenhouse gas emissions. Once the regulatory context of climate change is provided, we can specify the parameters of our competence allocation framework in order to develop two scenarios of competence allocation for the EU ETS. These scenarios reflect the two most prevalent states of the world in terms of competence allocation at the time of writing: global or regional norm setting, combined with regional or national implementation and/or enforcement. In both scenarios, optimal competence allocation is based on the allocation's ability to ensure (i) the capture of externalities, (ii) the accommodation of heterogeneity in conditions and preferences; and (iii) the maximization to economies of scale and/or scope. In addition, potential strategic interactions under fragmented allocation are mapped. The resulting scenarios will later be used as a benchmark against which the functioning of the EU ETS, in different trading phases, can be compared.

# 1 Regulatory dimensions of climate change

[T]here is the clearest possible distinction between the apparent normative simplicity of environmental issues, and the appalling complexity of the law required to realise environmental objectives[1]

At first glance, the science that underlies our present-day understanding of anthropogenic climate change is deceptively straightforward: the emission of so-called 'greenhouse gases' – increasingly caused by human activity – affects the global climate, which results in more extreme weather patterns and an overall rise in global temperatures.[2] Since the effects of these temperature increases are considered disruptive, and potentially threatening, to our way of life, any further rise in temperatures needs to be minimized through the reduction and capture of greenhouse gas emissions. However, as soon as we step away from this technical reading of the causes and effects of, and solution for, climate change, the problem quickly becomes highly complex. There are many scientific uncertainties regarding the long-term effects and costs of climate change and its mitigation; numerous and diverse contributing activities, and potentially regulated parties; and an unequal distribution of mitigation and adaptation costs. These factors make the 'apparent normative simplicity' of climate change into a highly complex regulatory problem. Section A will set out the key characteristics of climate change as a regulatory problem. This will be followed by a discussion of the regulatory levels, tools and competences involved in international climate regulation (in sections B, C and D, respectively).[3]

---

[1] Scott, *EC Environmental Law*, 2.
[2] See Intergovernmental Panel on Climate Change, Assessment Reports (2007) at www. ipcc.ch/publications_and_data/publications_and_data_reports.shtml. Rather than revisit the threshold question as to whether the causal connection between human activity and climate change is accurate or whether climate change is in fact occurring at all, we accept that there is a need for regulation of this problem and focus on how best to mitigate its effect and adapt to it.
[3] Climate change law and policy is an incredibly rich field of study, with important contributions taking place at the regional and sub-national level. These sub-national efforts are largely outside the scope of the current discussion. For further reading, see e.g. H. M. Osofsky, 'Multiscalar Governance and Climate Change: Reflections on the Role of States and Cities at Copenhagen' (2010) 25 *Maryland Journal of International Law* 64–85; H. M. Osofsky, 'Is Climate Change "International"?: Litigation's Diagonal Regulatory Role' (2009) 49 *Virginia Journal of International Law* 585–650; and E. Ostrom, 'A Polycentric Approach for Coping with Climate Change', World Bank Policy Research Working Paper Series, No. 5095 (2008).

## A Climate change as a regulatory problem

Since the explicit acknowledgement of the existence of anthropogenic climate change in the 1970s, the mitigation of and adaptation to climate change have come to dominate the international environmental regulatory agenda.[4] The emission of greenhouse gases is considered the primary cause of climate change, with emissions originating primarily, though not exclusively, from the burning of fossil fuels.[5] Since the Industrial Revolution these emissions have increased exponentially, especially in the United States and western European countries. In the last couple of decades the emissions of 'developing' countries have come close to taking over this position due to their economic growth and their corresponding increase in energy consumption.[6] Notwithstanding this recent increase in energy consumption in some developing countries, the contribution of countries to the problem of climate change varies hugely. If we consider the emission of $CO_2$, one of the most important greenhouse gases, we find that the entire African continent is responsible for only 3.6 per cent of total $CO_2$ emissions, while it represents 14 per cent of the world's population.[7] By comparison, in 2010, China was responsible for 26.2 per cent of emissions, the United States for 17.6 per cent and the European Union for 13.8 per cent, while constituting roughly 20 per cent, 5 per cent and 11 per cent, respectively, of the world's population.[8]

The costs and benefits of climate change inducing activities are divided in a similarly uneven fashion: some countries benefit from the activities causing climate change and/or the changes in climate

---

[4] In 1979, the first World Climate Conference took place in Geneva and led to the establishment of the World Climate Programme and the World Climate Research Programme as well as to the creation of the Intergovernmental Panel on Climate Change (IPCC) and the United Nations Environmental Programme (UNEP) in 1988.

[5] Climate change was referred to in early scientific work such as that of J. Fourier, 'Mémoire sur les Températures du Globe Terrestre et des Espaces Planétaires' (1827) 7 *Mémoires de l'Académie Royale des Sciences* 569–604 (the first mention of a 'greenhouse' gas effect); S. Arrhenius, 'On the Influence of Carbonic Acid in the Air upon the Temperature of the Ground' (1896) 41(5) *Philosophical Magazine and Journal of Science* 237–276 at 270 (linking the greenhouse gas effect to the emission of 'carbon acid' (now known as $CO_2$) released by the burning of fossil fuels such as coal); and more recently the IPCC (2007).

[6] China has already overtaken the United States as the largest greenhouse gas emitter. Some report that this happened as early as 2006, others quote 2011.

[7] http://maps.grida.no/go/graphic/ emissions_of_carbon_dioxide_in_africa_and_selected_oecd_countries

[8] See http://mdgs.un.org/unsd/mdg/SeriesDetail.aspx?srid=749.

themselves, whereas others suffer.[9] Due to the transboundary nature of climate change and the uneven spread of its effects, states fail to independently capture the full effects of a greenhouse gas emitting (or reducing) activity. The transboundary externalities involved in climate change mean that some countries have an incentive to undersupply the public good of regulation, whereas others (although admittedly very few) may oversupply it – a market failure in terms of the provision of regulation.[10] This problem of externalities is augmented by the fact that action on climate change is considered to be ineffective without the participation of the largest greenhouse gas emitters.[11] Yet, the countries that emit most greenhouse gases have limited incentives to participate in regulation since their relative economic prosperity means that they will be able to adapt to most of the climate change effects that may take place in their jurisdiction. Conversely, those countries most affected by climate change, such as small island states, contribute relatively little to the problem and are unable to unilaterally reverse these trends. Furthermore, these nations often lack the capacity to adapt to climate change. This leads to a complex collective action problem where the incentives to free ride on other parties' actions are significant.

Moreover, many of the activities that have led to the current situation have taken place in the past.[12] This has led developing countries to argue that they have an 'equitable entitlement' to emit an amount of greenhouse gases comparable to those emitted by developed countries in order to reach a similar level of economic development. However, climate change is a so-called 'stock problem', rather than a 'flow problem', which means that greenhouse gases remain in the atmosphere

---

[9] See e.g. R. S. J. Tol, 'The Economic Effects of Climate Change' (2009) 23 *Journal of Economic Perspectives* 29–51; R. S. J. Tol, *et al.*, 'Distributional Aspects of Climate Change Impacts' (2004) 14 *Global Environmental Change* 259–272.

[10] See also R. B. Stewart, 'Enforcement of Transnational Public Regulation', in F. Cafaggi (ed.), *Enforcement of Transnational Regulation: Ensuring Compliance in a Global World* (Cheltenham: Edward Elgar Publishing, 2012), 41–74 ('Transnational regulatory regimes are (in ideal theory) established to address twin institutional failures: (1) market failures; and (2) decentralization failures resulting from the inability of states acting independently though purely domestic measures to adequately or properly regulate market actors in circumstances of global economic regulation and transnational externalities.')

[11] These importantly include the 'developing' countries such as China, India and Brazil. See also D. H. Cole, 'Climate Change and Collective Action' (2008) 61(1) *Current Legal Problems* 229–264.

[12] The main increase came with the Industrial Revolution, see R. J. Andres *et al.*, 'Carbon Dioxide Emissions from Fossil-fuel Use, 1751–1950' (1999) 51B *Tellus* 759–765.

for decades and their accumulation, as well as their emission, causes climate change.[13] Further complicating factors are the uncertainty and heterogeneity of the causes and effects of climate change.[14] It is unclear where and when most of the effects of climate change will occur and how extreme the consequences of our inaction or actions will be. The price of present-day mitigating action may appear exceedingly high as compared to future adaptation, depending on what discount rates one applies to the expected future harm.[15] Finally, the large number of heterogeneous public and private activities that contribute to the causes in varying degrees requires regulation through many different tools, which may interfere with each other – a single 'magic bullet' solution is unlikely.[16]

In brief, 'perfect' climate change policy would have to overcome the collective action problem; take account of diverging mitigation and adaptation costs of different actors; balance the current and future costs of action and inaction; and arguably take account of certain equity issues, such as democratic accountability, social (or distributional) justice, and intergenerational justice.[17] Due to the collective action and free-riding elements of this solution, international agreement on climate change policy is particularly important, and difficult to achieve.

## B Regulatory levels

Mitigation and adaptation strategies for climate change encompass many regulatory levels, from the international to the local, supplemented by numerous private initiatives.[18] The scenarios we develop in

[13] Stavins, 'The Problem of the Commons', 98.
[14] See e.g. Tol, 'Economic Effects of Climate Change'; Tol *et al.*, 'Distributional Aspects of Climate Change Impacts'.
[15] See R. G. Newell and W. A. Pizer, 'Uncertain Discount Rates in Climate Policy Analysis' (2004) 32(4) *Energy Policy* 519–529 (giving a good overview of the challenges in this area).
[16] See J. E. Vinuales, 'Legal Techniques for Dealing with Scientific Uncertainty in Environmental Law' (2010) 43 *Vanderbilt Journal of Transnational Law* 437–503 (describing the different ways in which scientific uncertainty is dealt with in environmental law with specific reference to ten legal techniques, including: precautionary reasoning; framework-protocol approach; advisory scientific bodies; law-making by treaty bodies; managerial approaches to compliance; prior informed consent; environmental impact assessment and monitoring; provisional measures; evidence; and facilitated liability).
[17] See e.g. W. N. Adger, *et al.* (eds.), *Fairness in Adaptation to Climate Change* (Cambridge, MA: MIT Press, 2006).
[18] R. B. Stewart, M. Oppenheimer, and B. Rudyk, 'Building Blocks for Global Climate Protection' NYU Law and Economics Research Paper No. 12–43 (2012).

section 2.2 are limited in scope insofar as they consider only public regulation taking place at the global level (i.e. United Nations), regional level (i.e. European) and national level (i.e. European Member State). In this sub-section, we will briefly discuss the most important actors responsible for norm setting, implementation and enforcement at these levels.

## 1 The UN framework convention on climate change

Since climate change is a global problem, the United Nations is arguably the only existing framework within which 'central' regulation on climate change can take place, as it is the only organization of which virtually all recognized sovereign nations are a member.[19] Within the UN framework, international norm setting and policy-making regarding climate change mitigation and adaptation have taken place primarily under the auspices of the United Nations Framework Convention on Climate Change (UNFCCC), signed at the Earth Summit in Rio de Janeiro in 1992. With 194 parties, the UNFCCC enjoys near-universal membership, as does the Kyoto Protocol with 192 parties. In 1997, the Kyoto Protocol made the broad commitment to the stabilization of greenhouse gases under the UNFCCC more concrete by setting legally binding emission reduction targets for the so-called Annex I countries (including mostly the 1992 OECD members and some 'economies in transition', such as the Russian Federation).[20]

In both the UNFCCC and the Kyoto Protocol framework, the key policy-making decisions are taken through a so-called Conference of the Parties (COP). For the UNFCCC, this body consists of all countries that are party to the convention. In annual meetings, the COP reviews the national implementation of the UNFCCC commitments and decides on possible additional measures needed to assure the achievement of the ultimate objective of the convention. The COP of the Kyoto Protocol is referred to as the 'COP serving as the meeting of the Parties to the Kyoto Protocol' (CMP). The CMP also meets annually, in the same period

---

[19] The exception is the Vatican City. Several other states do not enjoy internationally recognized sovereignty, notably Palestine. See *Reparation for Injuries Suffered in the Service of the United Nations*, Advisory Opinion of 11 April 1949, ICJ Reports 1949, 174 (about the UN being an international organization).

[20] Article 17 and Annex I of the Kyoto Protocol. The OECD members are furthermore listed in Annex II of the UNFCCC, requiring them to assist in the mitigation and adaptation of developing countries to climate change and to promote and develop environmentally friendly technologies in developing countries and economies in transition.

# 1 REGULATORY DIMENSIONS OF CLIMATE CHANGE 81

as the COP, and any countries that are not party to the Kyoto Protocol, but are party to the UNFCCC, may request observer status to the CMP.[21] The principal task of the CMP has been the renegotiation of country-specific emission reduction targets for specific commitment periods under the Kyoto Protocol.

In addition, there are two permanent subsidiary bodies under the convention: the Subsidiary Body for Scientific and Technological Advice (SBSTA), and the Subsidiary Body for Implementation (SBI). These bodies, composed of national experts in the respective fields, are responsible for advising the COP in accordance with their mandate. The SBSTA deals with scientific, technological and methodological matters, importantly including the development and transfer of technologies, and works on guidelines for preparing national communications and emission inventories. It moreover translates the technical advice of the IPCC into concrete policy advice.[22] The SBI, on the other hand, advises on all matters related to the implementation of the convention. One of the key parts of this task is the review of national emission reports in order to assess the convention's effectiveness. The SBSTA and the SBI also serve the CMP of the Kyoto Protocol.

## 2 The European Union and its Member States

The UN can only act as the implementer and enforcer of its norms in a limited set of circumstances, which means that regulation under its auspices is typically restricted to norm setting.[23] This has also been the case within the context of the UNFCCC, where the UNFCCC COP, Kyoto Protocol CMP and related UN bodies play a limited role in the

---

[21] The CMP has taken important steps towards the implementation of the Protocol through the adoption of, for instance, the so-called 'Marrakesh accords' on land use. See Marrakesh accords on land-use (2001), available at http://unfccc.int/cop7/documents/accords_draft.pdf.

[22] See IPCC Assessment reports, available at www.ipcc.ch/publications_and_data/publications_and_data.shtml#.UoP_R5TXS5I.

[23] Since the United Nations' police force is dependent on the political mandate and practical support of the UN Members, the political agreements made in the General Assembly and the Security Council (and at times through the Secretary General) are very difficult to enforce by the United Nations. Even for those Security Council resolutions that are 'self-executing' or otherwise considered a rule of international law, the enforcement is dependent on the actions of the Members, e.g. peace-keeping missions are formed by national forces. Arguably, the UN tribunals form an exception to this situation since they in fact enforce international law against parties. However, even in this case, the execution of judgments is often dependent on the cooperation of national governments.

implementation and enforcement of the UNFCCC and Kyoto Protocol commitments.[24] Especially with respect to the mitigation of greenhouse gas emissions, implementation and enforcement is seen to take place at the hands of the parties. Our discussion of the decentralized implementation and enforcement of emission reduction norms as set under the UNFCCC/Kyoto Protocol therefore focuses on the efforts undertaken by the European Union (EU) and its Member States.

The EU and its Member States function within a unique institutional structure that cannot be categorized as a federation, or a classic international organization, such as the United Nations. The countries that make up the European Union, the Member States, remain sovereign nation states that have delegated regulatory competences in certain areas to the European institutions.[25] In some areas this means that the European policymaker has the exclusive competence to regulate that policy area,[26] in others the competences are shared between the European level and the Member States.[27] There are four principal institutions at the European level: the European Council, the European Parliament, the Council of the European Union and the European Commission. These four institutions are responsible for creating policies and laws for the whole of the EU. Other important institutions are the Court of Justice of the EU (CJEU) and the General Court.[28] The Court of Justice is the final arbiter of European law and, with respect to implementation practices, has exclusive jurisdiction with respect to actions for failure to fulfil an obligation, i.e. failure of an EU Member State to apply EU law.[29] Aside from these 'core' institutions, there are numerous other bodies that play specialized roles within the European governmental system, such as the European Economic and Social Committee and the Committee of the Regions, which have an advisory capacity to the Parliament, Council and Commission; the European Central Bank,

---

[24] For the work of the UNFCCC Compliance Committee, see decisions listed under http://unfccc.int/kyoto_protocol/compliance/items/2875.php.

[25] Article 1 of the TEU.

[26] See Articles 2(1) and 3(1) of the TFEU.

[27] See Articles 2(2) and 4 of the TFEU.

[28] The General Court has been given a mandate to deal with cases that are brought by private parties, companies and certain organizations, as well as cases related to competition law in order to alleviate the pressure on the Court of Justice, see Protocol No. 3 (1998), Article 54.

[29] Articles 263 and 258–260 of the TFEU. The Court of Justice also rules on requests for preliminary rulings, actions for annulment, actions for failure to act and direct actions brought by individuals, companies or organizations against EU decisions or actions. Articles 267–269 of the TFEU.

which is responsible for European monetary policy; the European Ombudsman; and the European External Action Service, which assists the High Representative of the Union for Foreign Affairs and Security Policy, who in turn conducts the common foreign and security policy, ensuring the consistency of EU external action.

The entry into force of the Treaty of Lisbon in 2009 has had several consequences for environmental and energy policy, shaping the relevant policy areas for climate change commitments. In terms of the division and sharing of competences, the status of environmental policy as a shared competence remains unaltered. Energy policy, however, is explicitly referred to as a shared competence for the first time.[30] In terms of norm-setting procedures, there are several changes in the Treaty of Lisbon but none of these appear to impact significantly on environmental legislation.[31] The co-decision procedure (now 'the ordinary legislative procedure')[32] remains the primary method of environmental legislation. Under this procedure, the European Commission proposes new laws, which are then adopted by the European Parliament and the Council of the European Union, with the latter acting by qualified majority.[33] The Commission and Member States are responsible for the implementation of European laws, and the Commission is empowered to oversee the implementation efforts of the Member States.

A final element to consider in the relationship between the European institutions and the Member States is the role of the Court of Justice in the enforcement of Member State implementation responsibilities. Under Article 258 of the TFEU (ex. Article 226 of the Treaty establishing the European Community (TEC)), the Commission can bring an infringement procedure against a Member State that fails to apply European (environmental) law. This procedure has been shortened in the Treaty of Lisbon, which means that the Commission is able to bring a case before the Court of Justice sooner than was possible under Article 228 of the TEC.[34] In addition, Article 260(3) of the TFEU allows the Commission to

---

[30] Article 4(2)(e) and (i) of the TFEU, (environment and energy respectively). The EU has exclusive competence with respect to the conservation of marine biological resources under the common fisheries policy (Article 3(1)(d) of the TFEU, cf. Cases 3/76, 4/76 and 6/76 (joined), *Kramer* [1976] ECR 1279.

[31] Vedder, 'The Treaty of Lisbon', 293.

[32] Article 289 of the TFEU in connection with Article 294.

[33] Article 284 of the TFEU. The European Council cannot pass any laws, as opposed to the Council of the EU, and rather is responsible more generally for political agenda setting.

[34] Article 260, second paragraph, of the TFEU. A specialized procedure has also been introduced for the non-communication of implementation measures for directives.

apply directly for the imposition of a lump sum or penalty payment in case of infringement. Traditionally, the Commission has been the main party to confront the Member States over the lack of, or faulty, implementation of EU environmental law.[35]

## C Regulatory tools

The overarching policy objective put in place by the UNFCCC is the 'stabilization of greenhouse gas concentrations in the atmosphere at a level that would prevent dangerous anthropogenic interference with the climate system'.[36] The Kyoto Protocol attached concrete reduction norms to this objective by committing the Annex I parties to the convention to reduce their 'aggregate anthropogenic carbon dioxide equivalent emissions of the greenhouse gases listed in Annex A' to the assigned amounts.[37] These reductions were calculated pursuant to the quantified emission limitation and reduction commitments contained in Annex B and were aimed at reducing the overall emissions of greenhouse gases by at least 5 per cent below 1990 levels in the commitment period 2008 to 2012. The implementation of the country-specific goals set by the Kyoto Protocol was left to the individual parties, or groups of parties.[38] Since these goals are to be met primarily through domestic implementation measures, the Protocol does not prescribe the use of any specific instruments. It does, however, provide for several 'new' market-based mechanisms to be developed, which are meant to stimulate green investments abroad and enhance cost-effectiveness: Emissions Trading,[39] the Clean Development Mechanism (CDM),[40] and Joint Implementation (JI).[41]

---

[35] This may change slightly with the revised text of Article 263 of the TFEU. See extensively van Zeben, 'Untapped Potential of Horizontal Private Enforcement'.

[36] Article 2 of the UNFCCC.

[37] Article 3(1) of the Kyoto Protocol.

[38] *Ibid.* ('The Parties included in Annex I shall, individually or jointly, ensure that their aggregate anthropogenic carbon dioxide equivalent emissions of the greenhouse gases listed in Annex A do not exceed their assigned amounts'). Article 4(1) of the Kyoto Protocol states: 'Any Parties included in Annex I that have reached an agreement to fulfil their commitments under Article 3 jointly, shall be deemed to have met those commitments provided that their total combined aggregate anthropogenic carbon dioxide equivalent emissions of the greenhouse gases listed in Annex A do not exceed their assigned amounts'.

[39] Article 17 of the Kyoto Protocol; Conference of the Parties serving as the meeting of the Parties to the Kyoto Protocol (CMP) (30 November 2005); Conference of the Parties serving as the meeting of the Parties to the Kyoto Protocol (CMP) (17–18 December 2004).

[40] Article 12 of the Kyoto Protocol.   [41] Article 6 of the Kyoto Protocol.

# 1 REGULATORY DIMENSIONS OF CLIMATE CHANGE 85

The CDM is aimed at assisting non-Annex I parties in achieving sustainable development and contributing to the prevention of dangerous climate change. It also allows Annex I parties to comply with their emission reduction targets in a cost-effective way; through investing in CDM projects, these countries obtain 'certified emission reductions', which, subject to certain conditions, go towards their emission reduction targets.[42] Joint Implementation is similarly directed at facilitating the reduction commitments of the Annex I parties. Under JI, the parties may invest in other Annex I parties as an alternative to domestic emission reduction, which may lower the cost of complying with their reduction commitments. Joint Implementation projects are primarily aimed at promoting projects in the so-called 'economies in transition' listed in Annex B of the Kyoto Protocol.[43] Since the JI-investment country also has its own reduction targets, the process of receiving credits for JI projects has to ensure that the total amount of emission credits among the Annex I parties does not change. This is achieved by assigning host countries a number of 'Assigned Amount Units' (AAUs), determined on the basis of its 1990 greenhouse gas emission levels.[44] The 'Emission Reduction Units' that are awarded to

---

[42] See C. Streck, 'The Governance of the Clean Development Mechanism: The Case for Strength And Stability' (2007) 2 *Environmental Liability* 91–100; M. Netto, and K. U. B. Schmidt, 'The CDM Project Cycle and the Role of the UNFCCC Secretariat' in D. Freestone and C. Streck (eds.), *Legal Aspects of Carbon Trading: Kyoto, Copenhagen, and Beyond* (Oxford University Press, 2009) 213–230; M. Krey and H. Santen, 'Trying to Catch up with the Executive Board: Regulatory Decision-making and its Impact on CDM Performance' in D. Freestone and C. Streck (eds.), *Legal Aspects of Carbon Trading: Kyoto, Copenhagen, and Beyond* (Oxford University Press, 2009) 231–247; E. Paulsson, 'A Review of the CDM Literature: from Fine-tuning to Critical Scrutiny?' (2009) 9(1) *International Environmental Agreements: Politics, Law and Economics* 63–80; A. Vasa and A. Michaelowa, 'Uncertainty in Climate Policy – Impacts on Market Mechanisms', in G. Gramelsberger and J. Feichter (eds.), *Climate Change and Policy* (Heidelberg: Springer, 2011), 127–144; M. von Unger and C. Streck, 'An Appellate Body for the Clean Development Mechanism: A Due Process Requirement' (2009) 1 *Carbon and Climate Law Review* 31–44.

[43] See S. Simonetti, 'Access to Justice for the Private Sector in Joint Implementation Projects under the Kyoto Protocol: A Brief Study of Possible Disputes and Remedies Available to Private Participants in International Carbon Emission Reduction Projects' Robert Schuman Center for Advanced Studies, Florence School of Regulation 2010/08, EUI (2010); J. Hoogzaad and C. Streck, 'A Mechanism with a Bright Future: Joint Implementation', in D. Freestone and C. Streck (eds.), *Legal Aspects of Carbon Trading: Kyoto, Copenhagen, and Beyond* (Oxford University Press, 2009) 176–194.

[44] The initial assigned amount of AAUs is equal to a country's 1990 level of greenhouse gas emissions, less 5 per cent, multiplied over five years. This formula is set out in Article 3(1) of the Kyoto Protocol. Each AAU is worth 1 tonne of $CO_2$ equivalent.

the JI-investment country as the result of a successful project come from this pool of AAUs; since both units represent one tonne of $CO_2$ equivalent, the total amount of emission credits among the parties remains the same.

The implementation of the parties' commitments through these mechanisms, and any additional national measures, is subject to mandatory reporting,[45] review,[46] and enforcement by the bodies of the Protocol.[47] Articles 3(1) and 4(1) of the Protocol provide that parties may choose to achieve their emission reduction goals both individually and jointly.[48] These provisions are the basis for the European action through the EU ETS, the targets of which are directly linked to the Kyoto Protocol commitments. Many of the EU Member States were included in Annex I of the Kyoto Protocol, which led to an agreement to combine efforts at the European level.[49] The EU has implemented, and is making use of, all three of the market-based instruments mentioned in the Kyoto Protocol;[50] we will focus on implementation through emissions trading. Under emissions trading, regulators set a *cap* that places an absolute limit on aggregate emissions for certain sectors.[51] This cap is subdivided into a number of tradable permits that entitle the holder to engage in the regulated activity. In the context of the EU ETS, these permits convey the right to emit a certain amount of $CO_2$; other tradable permit schemes, for instance in fishery, allow the permit holder

---

[45] Articles 5, 7 and 13–17 of the Kyoto Protocol.

[46] Articles 8 and 22 of the Kyoto Protocol.

[47] Articles 18 and 27 of the Kyoto Protocol.

[48] See Article 3(1) of the Kyoto Protocol.

[49] Council Decision 2002/358/CE of 25 April 2002 concerning the approval, on behalf of the European Community, of the Kyoto Protocol to the United Nations Framework Convention on Climate Change and the joint fulfilment of commitments thereunder [Burden Sharing Agreement], OJ 2002 No. L130.

[50] Council Directive 2003/87/EC of 13 October 2003 establishing a scheme for greenhouse gas emission allowance trading within the Community and amending Council Directive 96/61/EC, OJ 2003 No. L275; and Council Directive 2004/101/EC of 27 October 2004 amending Directive 2003/87/EC in respect of the Kyoto Protocol's project mechanisms, OJ 2004 No. L338, 13 November 2004 [Linking Directive].

[51] See e.g. Coase, 'The Problem of Social Cost'; Dales, *Pollution, Property, and Prices*; J. H. Dales, 'Land, Water and Ownership' (1968) 1 *Canadian Journal of Economics* 791–804; W. J. Baumol and W. E. Oates, 'The Use of Standards and Prices for Protection of the Environment' (1971) 73(1) *The Swedish Journal of Economics* 42–45; W. D. Montgomery, 'Markets in Licenses and Efficient Pollution Control Programs' (1972) 5(3) *Journal of Economic Theory* 395–418; R. Hahn, and R. Noll, 'Designing a Market for Tradable Emissions Permits' in W. Maget (ed.), *Reform of Environmental Regulation* (Cambridge: Ballinger, 1982) 119–146.

## 1 REGULATORY DIMENSIONS OF CLIMATE CHANGE

to fish a certain amount of a certain species.[52] All actors included in the system are assigned a number of permits, either through grand-fathering (which means that the permits are given away for free),[53] or through auctioning. Once the initial allocation has taken place, the parties can *trade* the permits on the relevant market if they wish to emit more or less than permitted through their initial allocation.[54] The theory behind economic instruments such as emissions trading sug-gests that the economy-wide pricing of carbon is the most cost-effective method to secure meaningful $CO_2$ reductions, especially in industrial-ized countries.[55]

---

[52] Fishing quotas are exceedingly common. Under these schemes, a maximum quota is imposed which is then divided between the different fishermen in a certain region or fleet. See E. S. Amundsen, T. Bjorndal and J. M. Conrad, 'Open Access Harvesting of the Northeast Atlantic Minke Whale' (1995) 6(2) *Environmental and Resource Economics* 167–185; C. Costello, S. D. Gaines and J. Lynham, 'Can Catch Shares Prevent Fisheries Collapse?' (2008) 321 *Science* 1678–1681; Commission Communication of 26 February 2007 on rights-based management tools in fisheries, COM(2007) 73 final.

[53] E. Woerdman, A. Arcuri and S. Clò, 'Emissions Trading and the Polluter-Pays Principle: Do Polluters Pay under Grandfathering?' (2008) 4(2) *Review of Law and Economics* 565–590.

[54] J. Jaffe, M. Ranson and R. N. Stavins 'Linking Tradable Permit Systems: A Key Element of Emerging International Climate Policy Architecture' (2009) 36 *Ecology Law Quarterly* 789–808 at 789 ('A cap-and-trade system constrains the aggregate emissions of regulated sources by creating a limited number of tradable emission allowances, which emission sources must secure and surrender in number equal to their emissions.'); T. Tietenberg, 'The Tradable-Permits Approach to Protecting the Commons: Lessons for Climate Change' (2003) 19(3) *Oxford Review of Economic Policy* 400–419 ('In an emissions trading or cap-and-trade scheme, a limit on access to a resource (the cap) is defined and then allocated among users in the form of permits. Compliance is established by comparing actual emissions with permits surrendered including any permits traded within the cap'); R. N. Stavins, 'Experience with Market-Based Environmental Policy Instruments', Resources for the Future Discussion Paper 01-58 (2001) ('A. Under a tradable permit system, an allowable overall level of pollution is established and allocated among firms in the form of permits. Firms that keep their emission levels below their allotted level may sell their surplus permits to other firms or use them to offset excess emissions in other parts of their facilities.')

[55] G. Metcalf, 'Reacting to Greenhouse Gas Emissions: A Carbon Tax to Meet Emission Targets' Discussion Paper Series, Department of Economics 0731, Tufts University (2009); L. Kaplow, 'Taxes, Permits, and Climate Change' NBER Working Papers 16268, National Bureau of Economic Research (2010); see also R. G. Newell and R. N. Stavins, 'Cost Heterogeneity and the Potential Savings from Market-Based Policies' (2003) 23(1) *Journal of Regulatory Economics* 43–59 (arguing that the ubiquitous nature of energy generation and use and the diversity of $CO_2$ sources in a modern economy mean that conventional technology and performance standards would be infeasible and – in any event – excessively costly). For an

## 88    OPTIMAL COMPETENCE ALLOCATION FOR THE EU ETS

Table 2.1 Regulatory competences for climate change mitigation

| Competence | Definition |
| --- | --- |
| Norm setting | Determining of emission reduction norms for specific countries and/or regions. |
| | Set of suggested instruments (emissions trading, CDM and JI) that can form the basis for further implementation rules. |
| Implementation | Norm distribution: translation of country or regional norms to specific reduction norms for certain industries/sectors of the economy. |
| | Allowance allocation through free allocation or auctioning. |
| | Creation of institutional and administrative structure for regulatory instrument, including market creation. |
| Enforcement | Verification of behaviour and penalizing non-compliance with respect to the distribution made as part of the implementation process. |
| | Market oversight. |

## D Regulatory competences

As set out in Chapter 1, in the abstract, norm setting refers to the primary regulatory norm that defines prescribed and recommended behaviour, but does not necessarily prescribe instrument choice or the allocation of implementation or enforcement powers. Implementation refers to the secondary regulatory norm whereby standard-setting and administration of the system are put in place. The implementer has discretion regarding operationalization, which has implications for the allocation of implementation or enforcement powers. Enforcement covers the monitoring and enforcement of behaviour, with the enforcer having no discretion over the norm, only over the level of enforcement. In Table 2.1, these abstract definitions of regulatory competences are tailored to the context of climate change mitigation through the reduction of greenhouse gases by means of emissions trading.

---

insightful discussion of the similarities and differences between emissions trading and the imposition of (environmental) taxes, see Stavins, 'The Problem of the Commons', 100–101.

## 2 Competence allocation scenarios for the EU ETS

From these building blocks – regulatory competences, levels and tools – two scenarios of competence allocation can be constructed. The key difference between these two scenarios is the locus of norm-setting powers. Scenario 1 places the norm-setting competence at the global (i.e. UN) level, whereas Scenario 2 places it at the regional (i.e. EU) level. In both scenarios, implementation and enforcement are assumed to be located at either the regional or national level (the EU or Member State respectively). Figures 2.1 and 2.2 are a schematic representation of these two scenarios.

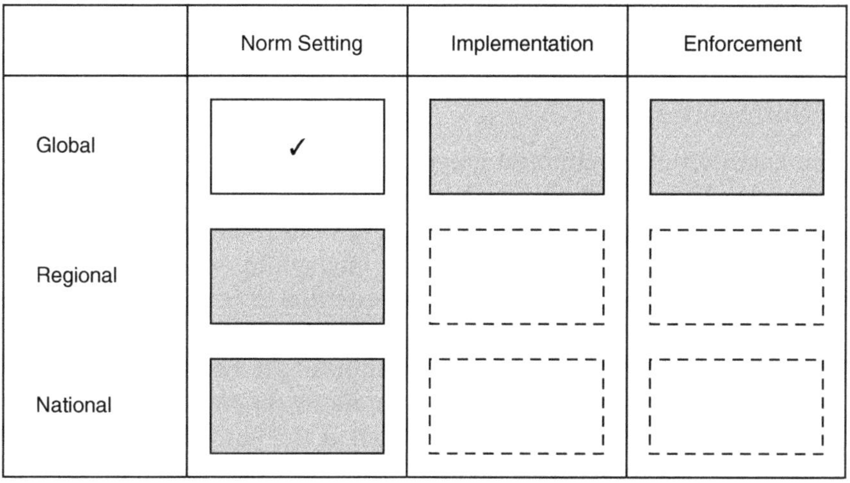

| | Norm Setting | Implementation | Enforcement |
|---|---|---|---|
| Global | ✓ | | |
| Regional | | | |
| National | | | |

FIGURE 2.1 *Scenario 1 (global norm setting)*

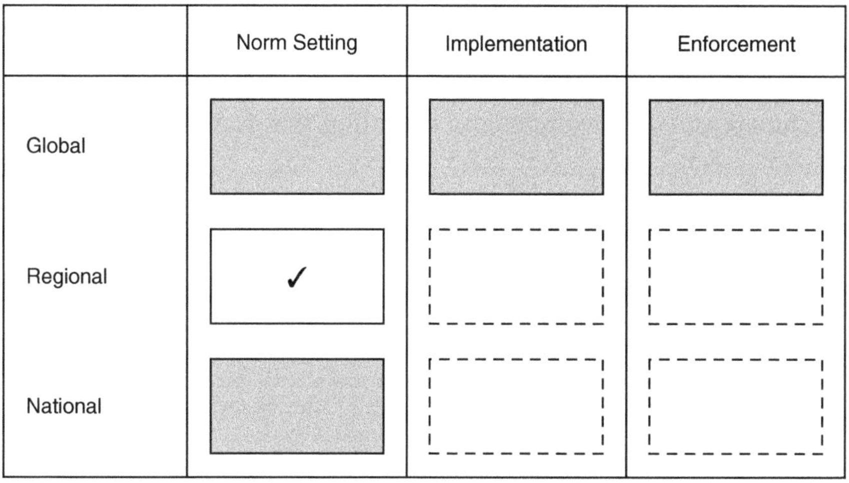

| | Norm Setting | Implementation | Enforcement |
|---|---|---|---|
| Global | | | |
| Regional | ✓ | | |
| National | | | |

FIGURE 2.2 *Scenario 2 (regional norm setting)*

These scenarios correspond to regulatory practice in the EU ETS during the different trading phases between 2005 and 2020, and form the basis for our discussion on optimal competence allocation. Optimality is determined here by the allocation's ability to capture externalities, accommodate heterogeneous conditions and preferences and maximize economies of scale and/or scope. Now that the regulatory characteristics of climate change mitigation, and the regulatory competences involved, have been provided, we can apply each consideration to the different stages of the regulatory process. In doing so, the respective roles of these competences within the regulatory process determine the relative weight of these criteria.

## A Competence-specific allocation

## 1 Norm setting

The emission of greenhouse gases gives rise to externalities at a global scale. The extent to which countries engage in greenhouse gas emitting activities varies substantially, as does their experience of the consequences of emission, i.e. climate change. In order to capture all externalities and overcome the consequential collective action problem, norms should be set by a regulator that incorporates all costs and benefits of climate change and greenhouse gas emitting activities.[56] Moreover, as a practical matter, the regulator should have jurisdiction to set such norms – a regional body such as the European Union could not have the authority to set emission reduction norms for countries outside the EU.[57] These preconditions necessitate norm setting at the *global* level. Only at the global level will norm setting be able to secure the internalization of environmental and economic externalities caused by greenhouse gas emission and overcome the collective action problem. Since the presence of externalities is central to the regulatory problem of climate change, a competence allocation that facilitates the capture

---

[56] It must be noted that we assume that Coasian bargaining between individual nations would be unsuccessful, see Inman and Rubinfeld, 'Rethinking Federalism', 49.

[57] Nevertheless, the EU's decision to include aviation emissions into the ambit of the EU ETS extends to non-EU carriers who land or depart from a European airport. The ETS sectors now also include the aviation sector from 2012 onwards. See Council Directive 2008/101/EC of 19 November 2008 amending Directive 2003/87/EC so as to include aviation activities in the scheme for greenhouse gas emission allowance trading within the Community, OJ 2009 No. L8, 13 January 2009 and the consequent case C-366/10 *Air Transport Association of America and Others* v. *The Secretary of State for Energy and Climate Change*, OJ 2010 C 260/12, of 21 December 2011.

of externalities takes precedence over, for example, an allocation that accommodates heterogeneity. Accommodating heterogeneous circumstances and preferences, and economies of scale and scope are thus 'second-order' considerations, which may act as additional considerations once the capture of externalities is secured.

The heterogeneous causes and effects of climate change and greenhouse gas emitting activities make a uniform approach to greenhouse gas emission reductions undesirable. However, global norm setting need not be synonymous with uniform norm setting: there can be differentiation in norms for different regions or countries. Ecologically, the location of greenhouse gas emission and reduction is immaterial; the location of emission matters in terms of other pollution effects, but not in terms of mitigating climate change. Therefore, any absolute reduction in greenhouse gases will have a positive effect on climate change. Moreover, economies of scope are possible through the combination of greenhouse gas mitigation policies and other, more general, air pollution policies. The environmental and scientific information and research needed to set these norms are subject to potentially large economies of scale, compared to the national collection of similar information.[58] In addition, these economies at the global level could overcome capacity problems at the national or regional level (e.g. in the least developed countries).

The optimality of *global* norm setting is based on its ability to internalize the global externalities of the greenhouse gas emitting activities that lead to climate change. This allocation is confirmed across all second-order considerations. With respect to accommodating heterogeneous preferences/conditions, regional norm setting could be equivalent to global norm setting, but not on the externalities dimension. National norm setting would also accommodate heterogeneity but fail to fulfil the externalities consideration, and would undermine

---

[58] A related consideration is the element of 'risk'. Following Arcuri and Dari-Mattiacci's ('Centralization versus Decentralization') categorization, climate change is partly a weakest link risk – if one country or region gets it wrong, provided it is of significant size, the error causes a global failure – and partly a majority risk – if more countries get it wrong than get it right, there is also global failure. Since it may be assumed that the world is risk averse towards getting the solutions for climate change 'wrong', global norm setting is preferable since it provides the highest likelihood of the 'right' regulatory norm as the global level represents the largest pool of experts. See also G. Dari-Mattiacci, E. S. Hendriks and M. Havinga, 'A Generalized Jury Theorem' Amsterdam Law School Research Paper No. 2011–39, University of Amsterdam (2011).

economies of scale and scope. On the norm-setting dimension, our second scenario of regional norm setting must therefore be considered second best.

## 2 Implementation

The collective action problem with respect to setting correct emissions reduction norms is overcome through global (or imperfectly through regional) norm setting. However, the implementation of these norms through their distribution among sectors of the economy, or specific installations, can also give rise to externalities. In this case, the externalities are caused by the costs of regulation as borne by different sectors of a global, regional or national economy. If the distribution of emission rights takes place at the national level, the implementer may have reasons to distribute them in a way that protects certain national industries. This could be sub-optimal with respect to the cost-effectiveness of emission reduction, i.e. shifting emission obligations from energy plants to the housing sector increases costs, both in terms of monitoring (regulatory costs) and in terms of compliance (the marginal abatement costs for the energy sector are often lower than that of the housing sector, for example). If the distribution takes place at the regional or global level, the protection of national interests becomes more difficult. Few parties in the global or regional process will have sufficient bargaining power to manipulate the process to their advantage. This increases the likelihood of cost-effectiveness distribution among sectors and/or installations (i.e. stricter distribution for sectors with lower marginal abatement costs). Emissions trading allows parties to choose the most cost-effective mitigation strategy for their respective situation (in contrast to more prescriptive methods of regulation such as technology standards). As a consequence, the presence of heterogeneous conditions does not necessitate the allocation of implementation competences at the national level: the regional and global level can distribute the norm after which local preferences can manifest themselves in the market.

In order to effectively distribute the global or regional norms, the implementer needs access to the marginal abatement costs of different industries. Aside from distribution, additional information is required for the allocation on allowances, which varies depending on how the individual permits are assigned. Most tradable permits schemes make use of a benchmark, which means that the implementer bases his plant specific allocation decision on average technology and abatement costs.[59] Depending on what type of benchmark is used, e.g. a Best Available Technology (BAT), historical or technology benchmark, different information is needed, some of which may also be obtained from the regulated parties themselves. The collection of such data is likely to be least costly at the national level due to the relative proximity to the sources, and potential pre-existing data collection obligations and efforts under comparable environmental or economic policies. Naturally, national circumstances may vary in this respect; depending on the number of sources, the size of the country and the administrative capacity, an even more localized approach may be preferable.[60] Any advantage of the national level over the regional, or global, level is reduced further after the initial distribution. Once the emissions trading scheme has been put in place, the information needed for the continuation of the scheme, for the renewal of individual permits, for instance, can also be collected at the regional or global level with potential scale advantages.

The externalities that may arise in the implementation stage lead to higher costs for norm achievement, which makes regional or global norm distribution more appealing. With respect to the second-order considerations, only economies of scale in terms of information gathering give a strong indication for national implementation since the information needed (especially in the putting in place of the emissions trading regime) is most easily gathered at the national level, and there are no apparent scale economies at the regional or global level during that initial phase. Heterogeneous preferences and conditions can be accommodated through instrument choice for emissions trading, which means that there is no strong indication for competence allocation at any level with respect to this dimension. On balance, these considerations speak in favour of a *regional* or *global* implementation, as the informational cost savings will likely be outweighed by the

---

[59] D. N. Dewees, 'Tradable Pollution Permits', in P. Newman (ed.) *The New Palgrave Dictionary of Economics and the Law* (London: MacMillan, 1998), vol. III, 596–601 at 598 ('If Tradable Pollution Permits are to be used, less information is required. The agency needs only to know the technology and cost of abatement for the average plant, and the range of variation among plants. It does not need to know these data for any specific plant, since a plant that cannot abate in the short run or that experiences high costs can simply buy more permits. The reduced information requirements for TPPs should reduce the time required to set emission limits and reduce the costs of that process both for the agency and for the affected sources.')

[60] See Dwyer, 'The Practice of Federalism', 1218.

94    OPTIMAL COMPETENCE ALLOCATION FOR THE EU ETS

cost-effectiveness of regional/global norm distribution as compared to national distribution.[61]

## 3 Enforcement

The possibility of externalizing costs continues to be a concern at the enforcement stage. With respect to emissions trading, there are two types of behaviour that enforcement is set to regulate: (i) emissions that exceed the amount available to the installation on the basis of the permits that it holds, and (ii) activities that constitute market abuse within the ETS market. The effects of the non- or under-enforcement against these two types of behaviour differ in terms of who is affected by the result, both positively and negatively, which in turn affects their preferred allocation.

The enforcement of a tradable permits scheme, like more traditional forms of regulation, involves the monitoring of parties' behaviour and the imposition of penalties in case of non-compliance. The incentives created by tradable permits greatly depend on the market price of emission permits – a higher permit price raises the marginal price of emission, which affects parties' abatement choices. In order for the market to convey a strong price signal, parties need to be sure that there is effective monitoring and enforcement of emissions. Failure to maintain strong enforcement methods may lead to a drop in market prices since parties may be tempted to falsify their emission reports, which leads to artificial drops in demand and a lack of real reductions.[62]

Assuming that excessive emissions (i.e. emitting without surrendering enough permits) are penalized by the imposition of fines,[63] the sub-optimal enforcement of excessive emissions can be reflected in the budget of the enforcer. Fines typically do not go directly into the budget of the enforcer. However, the enforcer may be expected to maintain a certain level of compliance or receive other benefits from a strong

---

[61] This conclusion is based on a characterization of the national agency as optimizing the social welfare within its own territory, which rationally leads to a maximization of the benefits of greenhouse gas emitting activities and a discounting of its costs.

[62] J. K. Stranlund, C. A. Chavez and B. Field, 'Enforcing Emissions Trading Programs: Theory, Practice and Performance' (2002) 30(3) *Policy Studies Journal* 343–361 (empirical review of the Sulfur Dioxide Allowance Program and the Regional Clean Air Incentives Market Program in the United States, which shows the importance of prevailing market prices, accurately measuring firms' emissions and the importance of implementing enforcement strategies that remove the incentives firms may have to falsify emissions reports).

[63] See e.g. Article 16 of Council Directive 2003/87/EC (for penalties within the EU ETS).

enforcement record through reputation or personal advancement in the regulatory system.[64] The costs of sub-optimal enforcement incurred by the enforcer may be compensated by bribes or votes, assuming that these regulators are elected to office (if not, there is no value in terms of votes, only bribes or other side payments).

The sub-optimal enforcement of activities that constitute market abuse, such as the sale of permits that had already been surrendered,[65] creates even larger potential externalities since the effects can be externalized on other jurisdictions in the case of a regional or global market with national enforcers. This is partly an interaction issue:[66] if the enforcement takes place at the same level as the implementation and norm setting and there is only trading on that level, global, regional, or national respectively, this problem does not materialize. This is one of the dimensions in which market-based instruments differ from command-and-control regulation since the latter only involves the monitoring of installation-specific behaviour, not behaviour that may affect a secondary market created by the regulation.

The monitoring and enforcement abilities of global regulatory agencies are typically under-developed as compared to those of national actors. It has been argued that market-based instruments require relatively less monitoring and enforcement capabilities and that fewer opportunities for corruption arise, making market-based instruments a more feasible option for global regulators.[67] Closer examination shows that credible enforcement threats and expert oversight remain crucial to ensure the proper functioning of these mechanisms and as

---

[64] G. S. Becker and G. J. Stigler, 'Law Enforcement, Malfeasance, and Compensation of Enforcers' (1974) 3 *Journal of Legal Studies* 1–18 at 3–4 ('There is, second, the structure of incentives to honesty embedded in the remuneration of enforcers. The correlation between the gain to enforcers from enforcing laws and the gain to violators from successful violation is almost certainly positive. But the variation in the gain to violators is often much greater than that to enforcers from preventing or punishing violations, so that the quality of enforcement would tend to decline as the gain to violators increased.')

[65] The Hungarian government engaged in this 'recycling of certified emissions reductions' under the EU ETS in 2010. See Euractiv, 'Hungary's sale of "used" $CO_2$ credits worries carbon traders' (22 March 2010), www.euractiv.com/climate-environment/hungarys-sale-used-co2-credits-worries-carbon-traders-news-368250.

[66] See Chapter 4, section 2.B.

[67] Stewart, 'Enforcement of Transnational Public Regulation' (2012), at 51 ('In the global setting, on the other hand, the problem is the relative weakness of institutions. Market-based and information-based programs can potentially address both types of problems.')

such pose different but similar challenges to the regulatory agents;[68] effective enforcement for tradable permit schemes requires significant expenditure.[69] The monitoring and verification of allowances in the enforcement phase require installation-specific information. Whether it will be more cost-effective to obtain this information locally or at a more central level will depend partly on the pre-existing expertise and administrative capacity at these levels and in part on the available technology for monitoring and verification. Technological equipment can supply information to enforcers at different locations or levels of governance, which means that there is no necessary bias in favour of centralization or decentralization. Scale economies may apply to monitoring and verification at the central level, especially with respect to the monitoring of transactions that cross jurisdictional lines. A global or regional approach may bring down costs significantly due to scale economies and possible pre-existing expertise in terms of interjurisdictional market administration at the central level, especially in terms

---

[68] See also Stewart, 'Enforcement of Transnational Public Regulation' (2012), at 51 ('A significant feature of these instruments is that the regulatory markets operate transnationally, with purchases and sales occurring across jurisdictions as well as within participating jurisdictions. This necessitates effective transnational administrative authorities to ensure the uniform and proper functioning of transnational markets and, with them, of the component domestic markets.') See conversely, van Aaken, 'Effectuating Public International Law' (on the use of *existing* markets in the enforcement of public international law as opposed to the creation of regulatory markets such as those related to emissions trading).

[69] There is a big disparity between the theory and the practice of market-based regulation, which reduces the schemes' cost-effectiveness. See Hahn, 'Economic Prescriptions for Environmental Problems', 107, who stresses that most market-based instruments are implemented based on existing regimes, which explains a lot of the difficulties. It also means that their cost savings are generally a lot lower than their theoretic potential; Hahn, above, at 28 ('As several scholars have noted, emissions fees are rarely implemented in ways even remotely resembling their pure form. Consequently, this instrument choice comparison may not be terribly revealing.') This gap can be explained in part through the need for sophisticated monitoring and administration under these programmes, which are not always available or are simply costly. Hahn and Stavins 'Economic Incentives', 467 ('Much of the work on markets and emission taxes assumes that there is a reasonably sophisticated environmental control agency that can administer incentive-based programs'); Shapiro and McGarity, 'Not so Paradoxical', 748–749 ('Emissions trading … require[s] inspectors to monitor constantly the amount of pollution that a plant emits.'); Hahn, 'Economic Prescriptions for Environmental Problems', 96 ('Naturally these results are subject to the usual cautions that a competitive market actually must exist for the results to hold true. Perhaps more importantly, the results assume that it is possible to easily monitor and enforce a system of permits or taxes.')

of developing markets, trade rules, regulatory oversight rules and auctions.[70]

Considering these criteria, the optimal level of enforcement is rather indeterminate. The optimal level depends on additional information regarding level-specific administrative capacities, the build-up of the market and information flows. The most significant indicator based on the need to capture externalities is that enforcement powers should be allocated at *a regulatory level equivalent to the geographical scope of the market.*

## 4 Independently optimal allocation

In conceptualizing our discussion on optimal competence allocation with respect to the EU ETS, two scenarios were put forward: one taking global norm setting combined with regional and/or national implementation and/or enforcement as a starting point, another combining regional norm setting with regional and/or national implementation and/or enforcement. We have considered the relative strengths and weaknesses of these respective allocations along three dimensions: externalities capture, accommodation of heterogeneity, and maximization of economies of scale/scope. Figure 2.3 summarizes the optimal allocation for the EU ETS under these two scenarios.

Under the global scenario, there is some fragmentation resulting from our assumption that there cannot be global implementation or enforcement. In the case of a global market, global enforcement would have been preferable. In the regional (EU) scenario, the regional norm setting at the European level is a second-best scenario compared to global norm setting. Because implementation and enforcement are not possible at the global level, regional implementation is preferable under both scenarios. Enforcement, on the other hand, can take place both at the regional or national level, dependent on the size of the market. If we take the EU ETS market as the relevant market, the optimal allocation for the market oversight aspects of enforcement is at the European level. The enforcement of individual installations' compliance can take place at the national level, particularly in the early stages of the market's development where more local information may be needed.

---

[70] Cf. Oates, 'A Reconsideration of Environmental Federalism' (2002), at 24 ('As an aside, the expertise argument surely carries little weight in the case for harmonization in the European context, where member states have plenty of experts.')

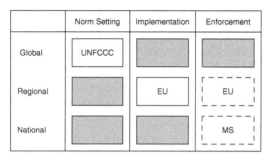

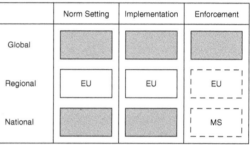

FIGURE 2.3 *Independent optimal allocation under global or regional norm setting*

## B Interactions

In this section, we consider the welfare implications of the interactions resulting from the independent competence allocation under the global and regional norm-setting scenarios. The interactions in our stylized scenarios of competence allocation are based on the following assumptions.

First, we assume that when norm setting takes place at the global level it reflects the global social optimum since the global norm setter is a benevolent actor with full information. Relatedly, we assume that the optimal norm for individual countries or regions diverts from the global social optimum (individually optimal norms may be higher or lower, depending on relevant costs and benefits).

Second, we assume that agencies at the regional and national level are rent-seekers. As a result, agencies will pursue the course of action that provides them with the highest rents. This may result in these agencies actively engaging with a course of action that ensures that the national, regional or global social optimum will be attained, or they may display 'shirking' behaviour, where they under-achieve relative to the social optimum.

## 2 COMPETENCE ALLOCATION SCENARIOS FOR THE EU ETS     99

Finally, over-achieving – setting a standard above the social optimum for a specific country or region – is only possible for regional norm setting. In order for a region to over-achieve, the regional norm would have to be more stringent than the social optimum for that region, i.e. the norm that would have been set for the region by the global norm setter.[71] Moreover, it is not possible to over-achieve in the implementation or enforcement stage – any over-achieving in the implementation stage, through a stricter than optimal distribution to a certain sector, for example, would only result in a non-cost-efficient distribution of reduction burdens. Implementation can thus only be a distribution of the norm, not a further raising of the norm, and enforcement only concerns the enforcement of the distribution of the norm, not the norm itself.

In the context of emissions trading, the authority installed in the regulatory actors is a positive one: a certain level of greenhouse gas emitting activity is permitted and the permits are paid for on the market or in auctions. This positive authority is divided among the norm setter, implementer and enforcer. The interactions between the norm setter and the implementer, and the implementer and the enforcer, respectively, can be conceptualized as follows:[72]

(i)   *Concurrent competence* between norm setter and implementer: Both norm setting and norm distribution are necessary to give effect to the positive regulatory authority of permitting certain greenhouse gas emitting activities, and action by the norm setter creates exploitable rents for the implementer;

(ii)  *Imperfectly alternative competence* between the implementer and enforcer: Both actions are necessary to give effect to the regulatory authority since a permit without enforcement loses its coercive nature. However, once the implementer assigns a permit, the rents for the enforcer are destroyed unless the regulated party's individually optimal distribution of permits differs, and is higher than, the (potentially socially optimal) distribution of the implementer. In this case, the regulated party will attempt to convince the enforcer to under-enforce, which creates a rent for the enforcer.

---

[71] The purpose of such over-achieving could be to counter-balance under-achieving in other regions and is thus unlikely since it would allow free riding by others.

[72] This scenario does not incorporate the possibility of a feedback effect from the enforcement or implementation phase to the norm-setting phase.

Sub-sections 1 and 2 will elaborate on these interactions under our two scenarios of global and regional norm setting.

## 1 Norm setting and implementation

The main difference between the global and regional norm-setting scenarios lies in the interactions between the norm setter and the implementer:[73] in the case of global norm setting, i.e. by the UNFCCC and Kyoto Protocol, there can never be coordination with the implementer since implementation is presumed to take place at the regional (EU) level, or national (MS) level.[74] In the regional norm-setting scenario, there can be a unified model of competence allocation when implementation also takes place at the regional level. Since norm setting and implementation are concurrent competences, both agencies have to take action in order to give effect to their positive regulatory authority. Consequently, the norm setter's actions create exploitable rents for the implementer. These rents will be relatively larger for implementers at the national level since the externalities dimension of the climate change problem is such that the socially optimal norm (sought by the global norm setter) and individually optimal norms for nations (used by the national implementers) tend to diverge.

These interactions would result in under-permitting when there is a fragmented allocation of global norm setting coupled with either regional or national implementation, or regional norm setting combined with national implementation. 'Under-permitting' refers to a situation in which too few emission allowances are assigned in light of the norm. Put differently, based on a balancing of costs and benefits of the polluting activity, more pollution could still be permitted before equilibrium between the marginal costs and benefits of the activity is achieved. The welfare implications of this under-permitting depend on the type of regulatory agent we are dealing with at the norm setting and implementation stage. If we consider the agents as rent-seeking, under-permitting lowers the total surplus and has negative welfare implications.[75] In the case of climate change, the presence of externalities

---

[73] Since we assume no direct link between the norm setter and the enforcer, the question as to whether there is coordination (through unified allocation) between these two parties falls outside the scope of the current discussion.

[74] On coordination and fragmentation, see section 3.

[75] Parisi, Schulz, and Klick, 'Two Dimensions', 64. In the case of these 'shirking agencies', under-permitting due to the combination of positive authority and concurrent authority can be considered welfare improving, since it counterbalances

## 2 COMPETENCE ALLOCATION SCENARIOS FOR THE EU ETS

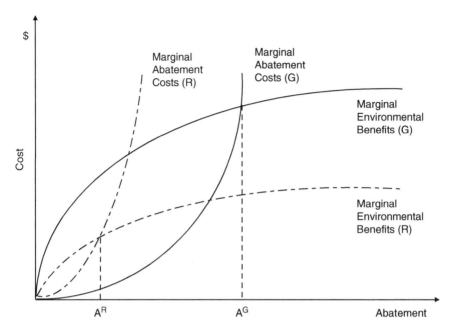

FIGURE 2.4 *Divergence between regional and global norms*

makes it more likely that agencies fail to intervene effectively with respect to the regulated activity (i.e. activities that emit greenhouse gases and require a permit), which would result in over-permitting. Both a unified method of competence allocation, as well as alternative competence, would be welfare improving compared to fragmented concurrent allocation.

There is an assumption that the norm reflecting the (global) social optimum does not hold for regional norm setting, since the regional norm setter will not take account of the externalities caused by its (lack of) abatement. Thus in this case, under-permitting at the implementation stage (i.e. a more restrictive abatement) would result in welfare improvements in some cases or for some regions. As the marginal abatement costs (MAC) curves in Figure 2.4 show, the regional optimum ($A^R$) can lie below the global social optimum ($A^G$), in which case the abatement level under regional norm setting will be lower than the social optimum. In this situation under-permitting, resulting in more

the initial lack of incentives of the shirking agencies not to intervene effectively. However, since we assume that the global norm reflects the social optimum, 'under-permitting' always refers to a move away from the social optimum and this will always be welfare decreasing.

abatement, will bring $A^R$ closer to $A^G$.[76] For this under-permitting to be welfare improving, enforcement would have to be in line with implementation decisions, which depends on the interaction between implementer and enforcer.

## 2 Implementation and enforcement

The dynamics between implementation and enforcement competences are imperfectly alternative rather than concurrent: the positive regulatory authority of the implementer and enforcer is alternative insofar as the allocation of a permit to a party by the implementer destroys exploitable rents for the enforcer. The alternative nature of the competences is imperfect, however, since (i) both competences are needed to give effect to the positive authority – without enforcement, the coercive nature of the permit becomes moot – and (ii) in the case of under-permitting, which is expected through the concurrent nature of norm setting and implementation, rents remain for the enforcer since under-enforcement would allow parties to engage in the activity despite their lack of permit (creating a concurrent rather than alternative situation).

| E \ I | Centralized (EU) | Decentralized (MS) |
|---|---|---|
| Centralized (EU) | 1 | 3 |
| Decentralized (MS) | 2 | 1 |

FIGURE 2.5 *Interactions between implementation (I) and enforcement (E)*

Under both scenarios (global or regional norm setting), the interaction between implementation and enforcement plays out between the regional and national level. Figure 2.5 thus captures the three

---

[76] There are also regions for which one may expect the abatement optimum to lie above the global social optimum since the marginal environmental benefits of abatement for that region are larger than for other regions.

different combinations of interaction that are possible under the two scenarios.

### 1: Unified competence allocation: decentralized or centralized implementation and enforcement

In situations of centralized (regional) or decentralized (national) implementation *and* enforcement, the interests of the implementer and the enforcer are coordinated, i.e. perfectly aligned. In the case of *regionalized* (EU) implementation and enforcement combined with global norm setting, the under-permitting that took place through the norm setting/implementation interaction may be expected to continue in enforcement. Under regional norm setting, this allocation means complete coordination between norm setter, implementer and enforcer.

When implementation and enforcement are *decentralized* at the national level, norm setting and implementation will also result in under-permitting, which will be more severe under the global norm-setting scenario than under the regional norm-setting scenario since the divergence between the optimal permitting amount is wider. The aligned interest of the implementer and the enforcer will result in the enforcement of the sub-optimal distribution under both scenarios, which is welfare diminishing.

### 2 and 3: Fragmented competence allocation

Under alternative positive authority, permission is given by the implementer and cannot be taken away by the enforcer (i.e. alternative competences). However, if the implementer distributes the permits in a manner that is sub-optimal for a specific party, rents may remain available for the enforcer when non-compliant behaviour (behaviour that exceeds the permits given) is sub-optimally enforced (i.e. over-permitted).[77]

---

[77] See also H. Chang, H. Sigman and L. Traub, 'Endogenous Decentralization in Federal Environmental Policies' U. of Penn, Inst. For Law and Econ. Research Paper No. 12–25 (2012), which provides further insights regarding the interactions of competences at different levels with reference to particular regulatory situations. Specifically, it discusses the practice of authorization in the United States, where states are given authority to implement and enforce federal law (i.e. norms), at 1 ('In addition to exploring the role of environmental preferences, we test a few other hypotheses about the determinants of authorization. We find that states with greater potential to generate interstate externalities may authorize somewhat later, suggesting federal efforts to limit negative externalities among the states. We also find that the size and tax or legislative capacity of state governments, however, do not have a statistically significant effect on the speed of authorization.')

*2: Centralized implementation, decentralized enforcement*
Under global norm setting, regional implementation entails some degree of under-permitting, whereas under regional norm setting there will be no under-permitting due to coordination between the norm setter and the implementer. The under-permitting under the global scenario results in exploitable rents at the enforcement stage for parties who deviate from the norm. This means there are incentives for sub-optimal enforcement. This is in line with the predicted outcome of the interactions in the Parisi *et al.* model: the combination of positive authority and alternative competence results in over-permitting. The extent to which it is possible for these dynamics to balance each other out depends on the exact content of the enforcement competence(s). Also, the presence of information asymmetries between the norm setter and the implementer and oversight measures of the implementer over the enforcer is relevant.

*3: Decentralized implementation, centralized enforcement*
Decentralized (national) implementation suggests a sub-optimal distribution, i.e. under-permitting. Regional enforcement cannot counterbalance under-permitting in the same manner as under the centralized implementation/decentralized enforcement model since we assume that the enforcer can only (under-)enforce the distribution set by the implementer, not over-enforce this distribution in favour of the norm set by the norm setter.

## 3 Interactive optimal allocation

In our discussion of interactions, we have taken into account the nature of the competences and to what extent under- and over-permitting might be considered welfare improving. Prima facie, alternative competences should render superior results over unified and concurrent competence for rent-seeking agencies from a welfare perspective, which means there is no interaction-based reason why national enforcement coupled with regional implementation needs to be replaced with unified allocation at the regional level.[78] However, given the fact that we are dealing with *imperfectly* alternative competences, and the fact that under-permitting may have taken place in the implementation stage, the remaining exploitable rents suggest that unified allocation at the regional level is welfare enhancing.

---

[78] See section 2.B, and generally Parisi, Schulz, and Klick, 'Two Dimensions', 64.

Moreover, our interaction framework considers only the most rudimentary tasks of the norm setter, implementer and enforcer. This is especially relevant for the implementation stage since the effective implementation of a cap-and-trade system requires more than norm distribution; for instance, a benchmark must be set in order to ascertain the number of permits that are to be allocated to each emitter included in the system. Also, the method of allocation must be decided upon. Depending on the chosen method, provisions for grandfathering and/or auctioning must be made. Moreover, the regulatory framework for a secondary market on which the permits can be traded must be created, which involves the adoption of legal rules as well as the creation of institutions for market oversight or the alteration of existing institutions' mandates. With respect to enforcement, the fact that costs of over-permitting can be externalized to other market participants when the enforcer's jurisdiction is smaller than that of the market (e.g. in the case of national enforcement combined with a European or global market) strengthens the case in favour of matching jurisdictions for the enforcer and the market. The latter interaction is unique to market-based instruments such as emissions trading.

## 3 Conclusions

The increasing fragmentation of regulatory power between different levels of governance reflects the growing complexity of regulatory arrangements at the national and international level.[79] As a consequence, legislative competences are seldom located at one single level of governance. Increasingly, certain competences are centralized (e.g. placed in the hands of a regional or global institution) while others are decentralized (e.g. at the national or local level). This means that some of our assumptions regarding regulatory functioning must be updated accordingly by recognizing the relative costs and benefits of (de)centralization of norm setting, implementation and enforcement competences. In many policy areas, a fragmentation of regulatory competences between different levels can be beneficial since it may bring down regulatory costs, while externalities of the regulated activity are captured due to centralized policy-making. In this chapter, the general framework for competence allocation, as set out in Chapter 1, has been

[79] See e.g. A. Nollkaemper, and D. Jacobs, 'Shared Responsibility in International Law: A Concept Paper', ACIL Research Paper No 2011–07 (SHARES Series) (2011).

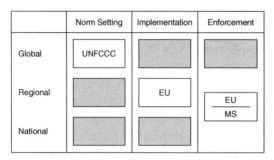

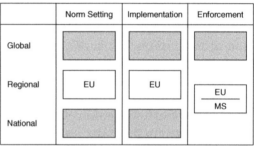

FIGURE 2.6 *Optimal allocation under global or regional norm setting*

tailored to the particularities of greenhouse gases mitigation through emissions trading. The resulting scenarios of optimal allocation will serve as benchmarks for our discussion of the competence allocation practice in the EU ETS (Chapters 3 and 4).

Given the regulatory characteristics of climate change, and specifically the mitigation of greenhouse gases emissions, the prima facie optimal allocation is a combination of global norm setting with regional implementation and enforcement, provided that tradable permits is the method of regulation and the emissions market is regional (Figure 2.6 – top). This allocation is supported by the welfare implications of interactions between the competences. Figure 2.6 (top) shows a role for both the European and the Member State level with respect to enforcement. We have distinguished between two enforcement activities under emissions trading: those that pertain to market oversight and those related to the compliance behaviour of individual installations. The shared allocation of enforcement competences reflects the differing possibilities of externalizing the costs of sub-optimal enforcement with respect to these activities. Market oversight activities are best regionalized (assuming a regional market), which is supported by second-order considerations of economies of scale and scope, whereas installation-specific oversight is best kept at the Member State level.

Due to the challenges of achieving global consensus, particularly with respect to binding emission reductions, we have also considered a second-best scenario with regional norm setting (Figure 2.6 – bottom). The optimal implementation and enforcement allocations under this scenario remain the same as under the global norm-setting scenario. The following chapters will show whether these theoretical optima are adhered to in practice with respect to the EU ETS and with what result.

# 3 Regulatory competence allocation in the EU ETS (2005–2012)

The framework developed in the previous two chapters sets out relevant variables for deciding on regulatory competence allocation. In determining and weighing these variables, we defined the regulatory context as the mitigation of climate change through the reduction of greenhouse gas emissions. In addition, we focused on emissions trading as the regulatory method to achieve this aim. In the coming two chapters, we compare our regulatory scenarios to the practice of regulatory competence allocation in relation to the European Union Emissions Trading Scheme (EU ETS). The application of our theoretical framework to the EU ETS reflects its centrality in regional (and indirectly global) efforts to mitigate greenhouse gas emissions – especially $CO_2$ – as one of the main causes of climate change.

The EU ETS is the largest cap-and-trade system currently in operation: in 2010, the EU ETS market volume amounted to 5.5 billion tonnes of $CO_2$ with a weighted average price of €14.5/tonne, accounting for 80 per cent of global transacted volume.[1] Despite this prima facie success in terms of market creation, the environmental and economic benefits of the EU ETS have been called into question. Criticisms concerning the EU ETS predominantly focus on the stringency of the EU ETS cap and/or the pricing of the emission allowances,[2] or more generally the

---

[1] Turner, 'Value of the Global Carbon Market'. By means of comparison, the market share of the Regional Greenhouse Gas Initiative (RGGI) in the United States dropped from 9 per cent to less than 1 per cent in 2010 due to the lack of prospects for a federal cap-and-trade scheme in the United States. The projected value of the world's carbon markets in 2020 is €1.7 trillion, provided that other markets are implemented by e.g. Japan and Australia.

[2] See e.g. S. Clò, 'Assessing the European Emissions Trading Scheme Effectiveness in Reaching the Kyoto Target: An Analysis of the Cap Stringency', Rotterdam Institute of Law and Economics Working Paper Series, No.14 (2008).

appropriateness of a tradable permits system for addressing the problem of greenhouse gas emissions.[3] Rather than addressing these criticisms by providing an additional analysis of the substantive laws underlying the EU ETS, this book focuses on the division of competences among levels of governance, and considers how possible deviations from the optimum appear to influence its functioning.

Thus far, the EU ETS has gone through three trading phases: the 'learning by doing' phase from 2005 to 2007; the 'Kyoto commitment' phase between 2008 and 2012; and the 'post-Kyoto' phase, which started in 2013. These trading phases differ significantly with respect to regulatory competence allocation; for instance, in the first two phases there is global norm setting by the United Nations Framework Convention on Climate Change (UNFCCC) and the Kyoto Protocol, whereas there is regional norm setting by the European Union in the third trading phase. This difference provides an invaluable comparison in regulatory functioning linked with competence allocation within one regulatory instrument. In this chapter, the regulatory framework of the first two trading phases is set out (2005–2012). A discussion of the design of the third trading phase (2013 onwards) follows in Chapter 4. Both chapters start by setting out the allocation of norm setting, implementation and enforcement competences with respect to the EU ETS, followed by an assessment of this allocation as compared with the optimal allocation in our global and regional norm-setting scenarios, both with respect to independent allocation considerations and interactions. Insofar as the actual and first-best allocations differ, possible positive or negative effects of this divergence are also discussed.

## 1 Regulatory competence allocation in the EU ETS

In order to determine an optimal allocation in the setting of our theoretical framework, we defined norm setting as the determination of an emissions reduction norm, implementation as the distribution of the norm, and enforcement as activities that penalize non-compliance with the norm distribution. The regulatory reality of greenhouse gas

---

[3] See e.g. B. D. Solomon and R. Lee, 'Emissions Trading Systems and Environmental Justice' (2000) 42(8) *Environmental Justice* 32–45; L. N. Chinn, 'Can the Market be Fair and Efficient? An Environmental Justice Critique of Emissions Trading' (1999) 26(1) *Ecology Law Quarterly* 80–125.

reduction through emissions trading does not always adhere to these strict divisions between the different competences. This is particularly true when implementation and/or enforcement involve the translation of international or European commitments into European or national law. Our discussion regarding the EU ETS will focus on the 'core' competences as described in our theoretical framework. However, where relevant, other aspects of the regulatory process will also be discussed in order to reflect the division of competences as realistically as possible. This both enriches and complicates our later comparison with the theoretical optimum, which is based on a simplified competence model. In this section, we set out the allocation of competences with respect to the EU ETS; specifically, we describe the emission reduction norms determined under the norm-setting process (section 1.A), their implementation through distribution and other operationalizing processes (section 1.B), and their enforcement through monitoring, verification and penalties (section 1.C).

## A Norm setting

The Conference of the Parties under the UNFCCC has been the international norm setting and policy-making body on the mitigation of, and adaption to, climate change.[4] The overarching policy objective put in place by the UNFCCC is the 'stabilization of greenhouse gas concentrations in the atmosphere at a level that would prevent dangerous anthropogenic interference with the climate system'.[5] Several additional commitments are listed under Article 4 of the UNFCCC, which are to be fulfilled by all parties 'on the basis of equity and in accordance with their common but differentiated responsibilities, and respective capabilities'.[6] These commitments include the development and publication of national inventories of anthropogenic emissions, the formulation and implementation of programmes to mitigate climate change through anthropogenic emissions and cooperate in the transfer of technologies and practices to control or reduce anthropogenic emissions, with additional reduction commitments for the developed country parties.[7] Aside from the general obligations contained in the UNFCCC, the

---

[4] For a detailed discussion of the institutions of the UNFCCC and the Kyoto Protocol, see Chapter 2, section 1.B.
[5] Article 2 of the UNFCCC.   [6] See Article 3(1) of the UNFCCC.
[7] Article 4(1) and (2)(a) of the UNFCCC.

# 1 REGULATORY COMPETENCE ALLOCATION IN THE EU ETS

1997 Kyoto Protocol sets legally binding emission reduction targets for the so-called Annex I countries.[8]

The implementation process of the goals set by the UNFCCC, and specifically the emission reduction goals under the Kyoto Protocol, were part of the reason for the development of the EU ETS. The UNFCCC commits both the EU and its Member States to develop national inventories on greenhouse gas emissions, and to develop national, and/or regional, programmes for the mitigation of climate change through the reduction of greenhouse gas emissions.[9] The Kyoto Protocol imposes additional responsibilities on the EU and its Member States in terms of specific emission reduction goals.[10] Both the monitoring and reporting commitments and the reduction commitments are reflected in the climate change agenda of the EU generally, and the EU ETS specifically.[11]

At the time of signing the Kyoto Protocol, the EU consisted of 15 Member States ('the EU15').[12] When the EU and the EU15 ratified the Protocol, they notified the Secretariat that their obligations would be fulfilled jointly under Article 3(1) of the Kyoto Protocol.[13] The consequently adopted Burden Sharing Agreement, or the EU Bubble, can be considered a first step towards implementation.[14] The main consequence of the Burden Sharing Agreement with respect to the fulfilment of commitments under the Kyoto Protocol is that the EU and the Member States are jointly liable for the achievement of an 8 per cent reduction as compared to 1990 levels. Possible non-compliance of individual targets is immaterial; as long as this collective goal is reached, the EU and the EU15 will be considered in compliance with

---

[8] Article 17 and Annex I of the Kyoto Protocol. The OECD members are furthermore listed in Annex II of the UNFCCC, requiring them to assist in the mitigation of and adaptation of developing countries to climate change and to promote and develop environmentally friendly technologies in developing countries and economies in transition.

[9] Article 4(1) of the UNFCCC.

[10] Annex I of the Kyoto Protocol.

[11] See e.g. Commission Communication, '20 20 by 2020 – Europe's climate change opportunity' COM 30 (2008) 13 final.

[12] The Member States in question are: Austria, Belgium, Denmark, Finland, France, Germany, Greece, Ireland, Italy, Luxembourg, the Netherlands, Portugal, Spain, Sweden and the United Kingdom of Great Britain and Northern Ireland.

[13] Conference of the Parties (12 June 2002).

[14] Council Decision 2002/358/CE of 25 April 2002 concerning the approval, on behalf of the European Community, of the Kyoto Protocol to the United Nations Framework Convention on Climate Change and the joint fulfilment of commitments thereunder [Burden Sharing Agreement], OJ 2002 No. L130.

international law as contained in the Kyoto Protocol.[15] The Burden Sharing Agreement assigns quantified emission limitation or reduction objectives (QELROs) to each Member State based on considerations of equity and efficiency,[16] which combined will lead to the 8 per cent reduction obligation under the Kyoto Protocol.[17]

Through enlargements in 2004 and 2007, a total of 12 new Member States joined the EU. Ten of these Member States have individual reduction targets ranging between 6 and 8 per cent; Malta and Cyprus have no reduction targets since they were not Annex I parties.[18] Despite the changed composition of the EU, the enlargements did not result in an alteration of the Burden Sharing Agreement. The 'blocking clause' in Article 4(4) of the Kyoto Protocol prevents any changes to the EU Burden Sharing Agreement, either temporal or geographical.[19] Significantly, Commission Decision 2006/944/EC, which sets out the emission levels 'allocated to the European Community and Member States in terms of tonnes of $CO_2$ equivalent for the first QELR commitment period' under the Kyoto Protocol, assigned emission levels to both the EU12 and the EU15.[20] There has been much debate regarding the extent to which the EU12 can be held responsible for the EU and EU15's commitments

[15] Article 4(5) and (6) of the Kyoto Protocol. Importantly, this does not exclude the Member States' responsibility to fulfil their emission reductions under the EU Burden Sharing Agreement under European law. See L. Massai, *The Kyoto Protocol in the EU: European Community and Member States under International and European Law* (The Hague: T.M.C. Asser Press, 2011), 220.

[16] Officially these commitments are referred to as 'quantified emission limitation or reduction commitments (QELRs), however the term QELROs has been adopted for ease of use.

[17] See Annex II of the Burden Sharing Agreement. These QELROs vary from an increase of 25 per cent relative to 1990 levels to a reduction of 28 per cent. Much has been written about the role of the 'equity' and 'efficiency' considerations leading up to the Burden Sharing Agreement. For more detail, see P. Marklund and E. Samakovlis, 'What is Driving the EU Burden-Sharing Agreement: Efficiency or Equity?' (2007) 85 *Journal of Environmental Management* 317–329.

[18] Malta became an Annex I party in 2010, and Cyprus was added in Durban.

[19] Article 4(4) of the Kyoto Protocol reads as follows: 'If Parties acting jointly do so in the framework of, and together with, a regional economic integration organization, any alteration in the composition of the organization after adoption of this Protocol shall not affect existing commitments under this Protocol. Any alteration in the composition of the organization shall only apply for the purposes of those commitments under Article 3 that are adopted subsequent to that alteration.'

[20] Commission Decision 2006/944/EC of 14 December 2006 determining the respective emission levels allocated to the Community and each of its Member States under the Kyoto Protocol pursuant to Council Decision 2002/358/EC, OJ 2006 L358, 16 December 2006.

to the Kyoto reduction goals.[21] References made to the principle of loyal cooperation in Article 10 of the Treaty establishing the European Community (TEC),[22] which is explicitly referred to in Preamble 10 to the Burden Sharing Agreement,[23] and reference to 'all' Member States in Article 21 of Decision 2005/166/EC, for example, suggest that the EC12 are also expected to contribute to the achievement of the Kyoto commitments, or at the very least, to not jeopardize it.[24] Put differently, under EU law, the EU12 could be considered co-responsible in the event of failure by the Union and the EU15 to meet their joint reduction commitments under the Kyoto Protocol.[25] However, reference to, and/or reliance on, Article 10 TEC leaves the situation under international law unaltered; the latter remains decided by the provisions in Article 4 of the Kyoto Protocol.[26] Neither situation applies to the non-Annex I Member States, which are exempt from these responsibilities under international and EU law. As for the responsibilities beyond the emission reduction targets, such as those concerning reporting, the EU and the Member States can be held accountable both jointly or individually at the international level.[27]

---

[21] Massai, *The Kyoto Protocol in the EU*; A-S. Tabau, *La mise en œuvre du Protocole de Kyoto en Europe* (Paris: Bruylant, 2011).

[22] Now repealed in substance by Article 4(3) of the TEU, ('Pursuant to the principle of *sincere* cooperation, the Union and the Member States shall, in full mutual respect, assist each other in carrying out tasks which flow from the Treaties. The Member States shall take any appropriate measure, general or particular, to ensure fulfilment of the obligations arising out of the Treaties or resulting from the acts of the institutions of the Union. The Member States shall facilitate the achievement of the Union's tasks and refrain from any measure which could jeopardise the attainment of the Union's objectives.')

[23] The preamble of the Burden Sharing Agreement refers to the 'Member States individually and collectively', without distinguishing between the EU15 and the EU12. Article 10 of the TEC, OJ 2006 No. C321, 29 December 2006, reads 'Member States shall take all appropriate measures, whether general or particular, to ensure fulfilment of the obligations arising out of this Treaty or resulting from action taken by the institutions of the Community. They shall facilitate the achievement of the Community's tasks. They shall abstain from any measure which could jeopardise the attainment of the objectives of this Treaty.'

[24] European Commission Decision 2005/166/EC of 10 February 2005 laying down rules implementing Decision No. 280/2004/EC of the European Parliament and of the Council concerning a mechanism for monitoring Community greenhouse gas emissions and for implementing the Kyoto Protocol, OJ 2005 No. L.55, 1 March 2005.

[25] Massai, *The Kyoto Protocol in the EU*, 225.

[26] Especially Article 4(6) of the Kyoto Protocol.

[27] Article 24(3) of the Kyoto Protocol, combined with Article 4(2)(e) of the TFEU.

## B Implementation

In order to fully understand the implementation process of the EU ETS, we need to nuance our portrayal of the creation of the EU ETS as a direct result of the policy-making and goal setting that took place during the UNFCCC and Kyoto Protocol processes. Aside from being legally bound to the reduction goals adopted in the Kyoto Protocol and its emphasis on flexible (market-based) mechanisms, there were several other factors that contributed to the adoption of the EU ETS. In the preparation of the ratification of the Kyoto Protocol, the European Commission released several communications and green papers regarding the future implementation of the Protocol and the role of emissions trading in this process.[28] First of all, to the frustration of the European Commission, all attempts to institute a European-wide environmental tax had thus far failed.[29] Although reluctant, the Member States did not have the same level of hostility towards a tradable permits scheme.[30] The Commission successfully used this fact, combined with arguments regarding the certain environmental benefits and cost-effectiveness of the scheme,[31] and the international opportunities provided by the leadership role left vacant by the United States in lieu of their ratification

[28] Commission Communication, 'Preparing for Implementation of the Kyoto Protocol' COM (1999) 230; Commission Communication, 'Greenhouse gas emissions trading within the European Union (Green Paper)' COM (2000) 87 final; European Commission, Proposal for a Directive of the European Parliament and of the Council establishing a scheme for greenhouse gas emission allowance trading within the Community and amending Council Directive 96/61/EC, COM (2001) 581 final, 2001/0245 (COD).

[29] See e.g. Commission Communication, 'Environmental Taxes and Charges in the Single Market', COM (97) 9 final (1997).

[30] During this process, the European Commission played an active role in mobilizing the, initially reluctant, Member States behind the emissions trading scheme. See Environmental Commissioner Ritt Bjerregaard, as quoted in J. B. Skjærseth and J. Wettestad, *EU Emissions Trading: Initiation, Decision-Making and Implementation*, (Aldershot: Ashgate Publishing Limited, 2008). The Commission emphasized the certainty regarding the environmental benefits, which would result from the scheme and opportunities for cost-effective implementation, *ibid.*, at 39. See also U. Collier, 'The European Union's Climate Change Policy: Limiting Emissions or Limiting Powers?' (1996) 3 *Journal of European Public Policy* 122–138; J. B. Skjærseth, 'The Climate Policy of the EC: Too Hot to Handle?' (1994) 32 *Journal of Common Market Studies* 25–45.

[31] European Commission, COM (2000) 87 final, at 4 ('it enables cost-effective implementation of the overall target'). The goal of cost-effectiveness is now also included in Article 1 of Council Directive 2003/87/EC.

of the Kyoto Protocol, to push for the adoption of an emissions trading scheme.[32]

The European commitments under the UNFCCC and Kyoto Protocol go beyond greenhouse mitigation and are captured by several European-level environmental and energy related policies.[33] Within this broader climate change programme, we focus on the implementation of the Kyoto Protocol's emission reduction goals by means of emissions trading under the EU ETS. In discussing these secondary norms,[34] it is important to separate cap distribution (implementation) from cap setting (norm setting). It may furthermore be helpful to distinguish substantive from procedural implementation rules. All rules, standards and provisions created to operationalize the distribution of the norm (in this case the 'cap', or the achievement of the QERLOs) are part of the implementation process. Within this body of rules, substantive rules are those decisions that relate to the division of the cap between the different countries, industries and individual actors; the allocation of the corresponding permits; and consequent provisions regarding grandfathering benchmarks and assignation of carbon leakage sensitive sectors. Procedural rules are those provisions that speak to the process through which the substantive rules are achieved. The most important example of these are the rules concerning grandfathering and auctioning of allowances ('allowance allocation'), something which is especially important with respect to the changes in the third trading phase. Finally, those who create these rules may not be responsible for their execution or application, so this aspect of implementation will also be discussed separately.

---

[32] Case T-374/04, *Germany* v. *European Commission* [2007] ECR II-4431, at para. 124 (The EU ETS has been, and continues to be, the key instrument in 'reduc[ing] greenhouse gas emissions substantially in order to fulfil the commitments of the Community and its Member States under the Kyoto Protocol').

[33] The extensive package of measures adopted after the adoption of the Kyoto Protocol by the EU went beyond the EU ETS and also consolidated many other environmental and energy related policies that had been part of policy debate before and notwithstanding the international UNFCCC-based policy-making. See e.g. European Council Directive 2001/77/EC of 27 September 2001 on promotion of electricity produced from renewable energy sources in internal electricity market, OJ 2001 No. L283, 27 October 2001 *and* Council Directive 2002/91/EC of 16 December 2002 on energy performance of buildings, OJ 2003 No. L1, 4 January 2003.

[34] Stewart, 'Enforcement of Transnational Public Regulation' (2012), 6 ('[M]ore specific regulatory norms in the form of regulations, standards and guidelines and periodically revise them in light of evolving conditions and accumulating experience.')

## 1 Substantive rules: cap-division

The EU ETS is modelled on a traditional cap-and-trade system, where a *cap* is set for a certain type of emission – in this case, the emission of $CO_2$. This cap is subdivided into single units (emission allowances, e.g. for one tonne of $CO_2$ equivalent) that are allocated, for free or through auction, to parties covered by the system. The parties may decide to use the permits to cover their own emissions or to sell them to others (*trade*) while reducing their own emissions. The key substantive rules contained in Directive 2003/87/EC, which puts in place the EU ETS, relate to (i) the earmarking of so-called 'ETS sectors' and (ii) the subdivision of the national caps between specific actors within these ETS industries and so-called 'non-ETS sectors'.[35] This subdivision of the cap is the equivalent to our theoretical distribution of the norm and forms the most important substantive implementation competence. Although the directive that creates the EU ETS was proposed, drafted and adopted at the European level, cap-division was placed in the hands of the Member States through their control over the National Allocation Plans (NAPs).[36]

National Allocation Plans were the core feature of the EU ETS during the first and second trading phase. In these plans, each Member State set out the total quantity of allowances that it intended to allocate for the relevant trading period and how it would allocate them. The number of allowances available for allocation in each NAP depended on the respective Member States' obligations as set out in the Burden Sharing Agreement. NAPs cover only $CO_2$ emissions from installations in the ETS sectors,[37] in line with the chosen 'step-by-step' approach where select greenhouse gases in select sectors were regulated and

---

[35] The ETS sectors are those listed in Annex I of Council Directive 2003/87/EC. See S. Clò, 'The Effectiveness of the EU Emissions Trading Scheme' (2009) 9 *Climate Policy* 227–241 at 227 ('According to the cost-effectiveness approach, the ETS sectors should bear a higher emissions reduction burden than non-ETS sectors, rather than vice versa.')

[36] Article 9 (1) of Council Directive 2003/87/EC.

[37] The greenhouse gases covered by the Kyoto Protocol are carbon dioxide, methane, nitrous oxide, hydrofluorocarbons, perfluorocarbons, and sulphur hexafluoride. The aggregate target is based on the carbon dioxide equivalent of each of the greenhouse gases. These gases are supposed to be monitored throughout the trading phases. The greenhouse gases covered by the EU ETS, however, are those set out in Annex I of Council Directive 2003/87/EC. For the first two phases, the EU ETS primarily covers $CO_2$; in Council Directive 2009/29/EC nitrous oxide and perfluorocarbons were added to Annex I.

this list was then gradually expanded.[38] Initially, the only greenhouse gas included was $CO_2$, produced by energy activities, the production and processing of ferrous metals, the cement industry, the glass and ceramic industry, and pulp and paper production, based on the relatively low marginal abatement costs of these industries.[39] By the end of the second trading phase, the EU ETS had become operational in thirty countries: the EU27 and the European Economic Area (EEA) countries Iceland, Liechtenstein and Norway.[40]

The step-by-step approach makes it difficult to assess the likelihood of a Member State achieving its Kyoto objectives based on its NAP; Member States also have to adopt measures for non-ETS sectors and other greenhouse gases but these national strategies are included in the NAPs.[41] The amount of allowances allocated through NAPs therefore has direct relevance for all other sectors of a Member State's economy since any emission reduction not required from the ETS sectors needs to take place in non-ETS sectors, which means that the reduction burden shifts to non-ETS sectors which have higher marginal abatement costs. The linkage of the EU ETS with the Kyoto Protocol's flexible instruments, Joint Implementation and Clean Development Mechanisms, provides additional opportunities for sectors and Member States to fulfil their obligations through reductions outside of the EU.[42]

---

[38] This differential treatment was challenged by one of the companies covered by the system through a preliminary ruling procedure before the European Court of Justice. See Case C-127/07, *Arcelor Atlantique and Lorraine and others* [2008] OJ C44 8, at para. 47, 64–65 (the Court held that the difference in direct emissions between the steel sector and the non-ferrous metal sector, the treatment of which was at issue in this case, was so substantial that different treatment was justified, especially in light of the 'step-by-step approach'. In respect of the chemical sector, the main consideration was the sheer size of the industry, which would have made the initial administrative burden of the EU ETS politically unacceptable and the fact that the advantages of excluding it at the start of the implementation of the scheme thus outweighed the advantages of inclusion.)

[39] Annex I of Council Directive 2003/87/EC.

[40] Due to their status as members of the EEA, Iceland, Liechtenstein and Norway are subject to a number of European environmental directives, the scope of which can be extended by a decision by the EEA Joint Committee. See EEA Joint Committee (2007) (extending the scope of the EU ETS).

[41] For a full analysis of the relative role of the EU ETS in Member States' programmes to achieve their Kyoto objectives see A. Gilbert, J. W. Bode and D. Phylipsen, *Analysis of the National Allocation Plans for the EU Emissions Trading Scheme* (London: Ecofys, 2004).

[42] Council Directive 2004/101/EC. See generally J. B. Skjærseth and J. Wettestad, 'The EU Emissions Trading System Revised (Directive 2009/29/EC)', in M. Pallemaerts and S. Oberthür (eds.), *The New Climate Policies of the European Union: Internal Legislation and Climate Diplomacy* (Brussels: VUB Press, 2010) 65–93, at 69 onwards.

# REGULATORY COMPETENCE ALLOCATION IN THE EU ETS (2005–2012)

The European Commission was able to exercise some powers of review over the NAPs through the twelve criteria set out in Annex II of Directive 2003/87/EC, including: consistency with the proportional share that the allowances represent in comparison to sources not covered by the directive; consistency with actual and projected progress towards fulfilling the commitments of the Member State; consistency of NAPs with other Community instruments; and non-discrimination between companies and sectors.[43] On the basis of these criteria, the Commission may review the NAPs and reject them when considered incompatible with one or more of the criteria.[44] Only once the Commission has approved the NAP can the Member State issue the allowances to the installations through an Article 11 allocation decision.[45] Overall, the substantive cap-division competences during the first and second phases may be considered to have been placed in the hands of the Member States, i.e. at the national level.

## 2 Procedural rules: allowance allocation

Only those installations that have received a greenhouse gas emissions permit will be assigned allowances by the Member States. The greenhouse gas permit is not a tradable right, but rather a prerequisite to hold tradable greenhouse gas allowances. The application and assignment of permits takes place under Articles 4 and 5 of Directive 2003/87/EC and is left to the discretion of the Member States in line with the conditions of Article 6 of the directive.[46] In accordance with Articles 10 and 11 of Directive 2003/87/EC, the Member States were to allocate at least 95 per cent (Phase I) or 90 per cent (Phase II) of the tradable allowances free of

---

[43] For a full overview of the criteria see Annex II of Council Directive 2003/87/EC.

[44] Article 9(3) of Council Directive 2003/87/EC.

[45] Article 11 of Council Directive 2003/87/EC. In order to provide guidance for the Member States as to the relative importance of the Annex III criteria and their interpretation, the Commission published a Communication (Commission Communication on guidance to assist Member States in the implementation for the criteria listed in Annex III to Directive 2003/87/EC and on the circumstances under which force major is demonstrated, Brussels, 7 January 2004, COM (2003) 830 final). Despite the fact that these Guidelines do not constitute a measure of secondary legislation as provided for in Article 288 of the TFEU, and thus have no 'general' legal effect, they do bind the Commission in terms of their review discretion. See Case T-374/04, *Germany v. European Commission* [2007] ECR II-4431, at para. 110.

[46] One of the conditions of Article 6 is that the permitting authority must be satisfied that the operator is capable of fulfilling its monitoring and reporting obligations (Article 6(1) of Council Directive 2003/87/EC). See also Article 8 of Council Directive 2003/87/EC.

charge. Allocation criteria commonly used by Member States included the 'Business as Usual' criterion, historic emissions, projected sector growth or a combination of these. The Commission could see whether the allocation criteria applied by Member States were in line with the Annex III criteria but could only reject the NAP as a whole. These procedural rules were thus created primarily at the national Member State level.

## 3 Execution: institutions

During the first two trading phases, the Council Directive placed responsibility for the execution of the implementation of the EU ETS with the Member States. Article 18 of Directive 2003/87/EC explicitly provides that Member States shall make the 'appropriate administrative arrangements, including the designation of the appropriate competent authority or authorities, for the implementation of the rules of this Directive.'[47] Member States are also required to put in place registries that oversee the accounting of allowance trades.[48] In respect to the latter, there has been some centralization through the adoption of standardized electronic databases provided by the Commission.[49] Also, Member States are allowed to maintain their registries together with one or more other Member States.[50] Apart from the decentralized registries and authorities put in place by the Member States, the Commission has been made responsible for designating a Central Administrator 'to maintain an independent transaction log recording the issue, transfer and cancellation of allowances.'[51] This Central Administrator conducts automated checks on transactions and reports irregularities to the

[47] Article 18 of Council Directive 2003/87/EC. European Commission, COM (2001) 581 final, at 10 (suggesting that Member States could choose to use those authorities responsible for the allocation of IPCC permits to give out EU ETS permits as well).

[48] Article 19(1) of Common position adopted by the Council on 18 March 2003 with a view to the adoption of Directive of the European Parliament and of the Council establishing a scheme for greenhouse gas emission allowance trading within the Community and amending Council Directive 96/61/EC, 15792/1/02/REV1.

[49] Article 19(1) of Common position, 15792/1/02/REV1; see Council Directive 2004/39/ EC of 21 April 2004 on markets in financial instruments amending Council Directives 85/611/EEC and 93/6EEC and Directive 2000/12/EC of the European Parliament and of the Council and repealing Council Directive 93/22/EEC, OJ 2004 No. L145, 30 April 2004.

[50] Article 19(1) of Common position adopted by the Council on 18 March 2003.

[51] Article 20 (1) of Common position. See also European Commission, COM (2001) 581 final, Part 6, page 42 onwards (on the financial burden of the European-level administration of the EU ETS).

relevant Member State, which is then responsible for following up on the matter.[52]

## C Enforcement

The enforcement processes within the EU ETS introduce an additional level of governance – the private party level – through its reliance on operators for monitoring and verification. Specifically, operators of installations covered by the EU ETS are obliged to monitor and report emissions in line with set requirements.[53] Third parties, typically private firms, then verify the resulting reports. This may lead to the imposition of penalties in those cases where the allowances surrendered by the installation are not in line with its obligations.[54] We will discuss these verification and sanctioning competences, as well as the private party monitoring and reporting obligations by referring to the primary rules set out by the directive and the extensive guidance provided through several Commission Decisions.[55]

## 1 Monitoring and reporting

Article 14 of Directive 2003/87/EC imposes a two-sided responsibility in respect of monitoring and reporting: the installations must gather and provide the information as set out in Annex IV to the directive and further clarified in Commission guidelines,[56] and the Member States must ensure that these monitoring and reporting duties are complied

---

[52] Article 20(2) of Common position adopted by the Council on 18 March 2003.
[53] Article 14 of Council Directive 2003/87/EC.
[54] Articles 15 and 16 of Council Directive 2003/87/EC.
[55] All are legally binding. Commission Decision 2004/156/EC of 29 January 2004 establishing guidelines for the monitoring and reporting of greenhouse gas emissions pursuant to Directive 2003/87/EC of the European Parliament and of the Council, OJ 2004 No. L59, 26 February 2004; Commission Decision 2007/589/EC of 18 July 2007 establishing guidelines for the monitoring and reporting of greenhouse gas emissions pursuant to Directive 2003/87/EC of the European Parliament and the Council, OJ 2007 No. L229, 31 August 2007; Commission Decision 2009/73/EC of 17 December 2008 amending Decision 2007/589/EC as regards the inclusion of monitoring and reporting guidelines for emissions of nitrous oxide, OJ 2009 No. L24, 28 January 2009; Commission Decision 2009/339/EC of 16 April 2009 amending Decision 2007/589/EC as regards the inclusion of monitoring and reporting guidelines for emissions and tonne-kilometre data from aviation activities, OJ 2009 No. L103, 23 April 2009; Commission Decision 2010/345/EU of 8 June 2010 amending Decision 2007/589/EC as regards the inclusion of monitoring and reporting guidelines for greenhouse gas emissions from the capture, transport and geological storage of carbon dioxide, OJ 2010 No. L229, 22 June 2010.
[56] Article 14(1) of Council Directive 2003/87/EC.

with, in accordance with the said guidelines.[57] Many of these elements are standardized in order to reduce monitoring costs, but some non-common fuels cannot be measured through these default factors.[58]

Large-scale changes were adopted in respect of the monitoring and verification procedures when the Commission guidelines in Decision 2004/156/EC were replaced by Decision 2007/589/EC of 18 July 2007.[59] These changes came into effect between Phases I and II in order to reduce the burden on installations and to provide greater clarity and cost-effectiveness.[60] The key changes in the revised guidelines aimed to: bring the guidelines closer to common industrial practices regarding monitoring and reporting; make the guidelines more cost effective, especially for small emitters and installations using biomass fuels; better align the guidelines with reporting made by Member States under national greenhouse gas inventory requirements; increase the accuracy, credibility and integrity of the system; and strengthen the verification procedures.[61]

Those guidelines contained in Annex I to the Decision are generally applicable, but the majority of the guidelines – Annexes II to XI – are activity-specific. The reason for this activity-specific approach can be found in the methodologies employed for measuring emissions, which are composed of the following variables: activity data, emission factors, composition data, oxidation and conversion factors.[62] Each monitoring approach is referred to as a different 'tier', which in turn reflects a certain level of accuracy.[63] The appropriate tier depends on the type of activity

---

[57] Article 14(2) and (3) of Council Directive 2003/87/EC.
[58] One of the building blocks of the monitoring process is the calculation of emissions, which is based on the formula: activity data x emission factor x oxidation factor. See Annex IV of Council Directive 2003/87/EC. Default factors are acceptable for all fuels except non-commercial ones (waste fuels such as tyres and industrial process gases). Seam-specific defaults for coal, and EU-specific or producer country-specific defaults for natural gas is further elaborated. IPCC default values are acceptable for refinery products. The emission factor for biomass is zero.
[59] Commission Decision 2004/156/EC and Commission Decision 2007/589/EC of 18 July 2007 establishing guidelines for the monitoring and reporting of greenhouse gas emissions pursuant to Directive 2003/87/EC of the European Parliament and the Council, OJ 2007 No. L229, 31 August 2007, respectively.
[60] Preamble 3 of Commission Decision 2007/589/EC.
[61] Commission reporting on the revised Guidelines as made public on http://ec.europa.eu/clima/policies/ets/monitoring/documentation_En.htm.
[62] For descriptions of these variables, see Annex I, para. 5 of Commission Decision 2007/589/EC, 13–14.
[63] See in detail Commission Decision 2007/589/EC, 14.

engaged in by the monitored facility,[64] and each emissions permit must contain monitoring requirements, specifying the monitoring methodology and frequency as set out in Article 6(2)(c) of Directive 2003/87/EC.[65] The tier approach is based on the IPCC Inventory Guidelines,[66] and aims for installations to be placed in the highest tiers, if technically feasible at reasonable cost.[67]

The monitoring plans must be approved by the competent authority of the relevant Member State based on the criteria contained in Annex I.[68] The monitoring activities provide the basis for the emission report which must be compiled every year covering the emissions of a calendar year in a reporting year – i.e. trading phase.[69] The reporting requirements for installations are furthermore supplemented by the reporting format as set out in Section 14 of the Decision. During 2008 and 2009, the scope of the Decision was extended to include the monitoring and reporting on activities emitting nitrous oxide ($N_2O$),[70] emissions and tonne-kilometre data from aviation activities,[71] and emissions from capturing, transporting and the geological storage of $CO_2$.[72] In order to lessen the administrative burden placed on installations and to harmonize approaches in the Member States, the Commission has published electronic templates for monitoring plans, but only for those emissions coming from aviation activities.[73]

## 2 Verification and penalties

Member States must ensure that the reports submitted by the operators are verified so as to guarantee that emissions have been monitored in accordance with the guidelines and that reliable and correct

---

[64] Minimum requirements can be found in Commission Decision 2007/589/EC of 18 July 2007, Table 1, Annex I, at 16–18.

[65] Article 6(2)(c) of Council Directive 2003/87/EC ('Greenhouse gas emissions permits shall contain the following … (c) monitoring requirements, specifying monitoring methodology and frequency'). Article 6(2)(d) also refers to reporting requirements.

[66] S. Eggleston *et al.* (eds.), '2006 IPCC Guidelines for National Greenhouse Gas Inventories', Intergovernmental Panel on Climate Change (2006).

[67] M. Loprieno, 'Data Consistency between National GHG Inventories and Reporting under the EU ETS: Differences and Similarities, Outlook to Changes', Second Workshop, Copenhagen (13 September 2007).

[68] See specifically, Annex I, para. 4.3 of Commission Decision 2007/589/EC, 3.

[69] Annex I, section 8 of Commission Decision 2007/589/EC.

[70] Commission Decision 2009/73/EC.   [71] *Ibid.*

[72] Commission Decision 2010/345/EU.

[73] This technology was also used in the US sulphur allowances programme. See Tietenberg, 'Tradable Permits', 257 ('According to Kruget *et al.* (1999), the

## 1 REGULATORY COMPETENCE ALLOCATION IN THE EU ETS    123

emission data will be reported.[74] Verification is a multi-segmented process, which includes strategic analysis, risk analysis, verification, internal verification and a verification report.[75] This process may moreover include on-site visits in order to inspect the operation of meters and monitoring systems.[76] Verification cannot be carried out by the national authorities involved in the issuing of allowances; Article 15 stipulates that 'Member States shall ensure that the reports submitted by operators ... are verified in accordance with the criteria set out in Annex V, *and that the competent authority is informed thereof.*'[77] The directive does not set any specific standards as to the nature or person of the verifier, meaning that the verifier may be either a private or public body, provided that it is independent from the operator.[78] If the verifier finds that the reported facts do not contain any 'material misstatements', i.e. any misstatements that lead to an aggregate error or omission in the total emissions figure greater than 5 per cent, the report can be validated as reliable.[79] In the case of non-satisfactory verification, the Member States can bar the operator from making further transfers of allowances until a report has been verified as satisfactory.[80]

In terms of penalties, significant discretion has been placed in the hands of the Member States. In the case of a failure to surrender sufficient allowances, Member States must publish the names of operators in breach,[81] and hold operators liable for the payment of an excess emissions penalty.[82] The latter penalty does not release the operator

---

development of this technology has increased administrative efficiency, lowered transaction costs and provided greater environmental accountability.')

[74] Annex I, Section 10.4.1 of Council Directive 2003/87/EC.

[75] Annex I, Section 10.4.2 of Commission Decision 2004/156/EC.

[76] Annex I, Section 10.4.2(c) of Council Directive 2003/87/EC.

[77] Article 15 of Council Directive 2003/87/EC (emphasis added).

[78] Annex V of Council Directive 2003/87/EC.

[79] Annex V, sub. 3 of Council Directive 2003/87/EC; Commission Decision 2004/156/EC, at 19.

[80] Article 15(2) of Council Directive 2003/87/EC.

[81] Article 16(2) of Council Directive 2003/87/EC. See also S. G. Badrinath and P. J. Bolster, 'The Role of Market Forces in EPA Enforcement Activity' (1996) 10 *Journal of Regulatory Economics* 165–181 (empirical study showing that stock market reactions to Environmental Protection Agency (EPA) judicial actions on publicly traded firms appear to reinforce the intent of EPA enforcement efforts through a significant decline of 0.43 per cent in firm value and are more pronounced for citations under the Clean Air Act, as well as repeat violators and more recent EPA actions).

[82] Article 16(3) of Council Directive 2003/87/EC.

from the obligation to surrender the excess allowances the next calendar year.[83] The penalty for failure to surrender sufficient allowances was harmonized in both trading phases, and the penalty increased from €40 per tonne/$CO_2$ equivalent in the first trading phase to €100 in the second trading phase.[84] The Member States furthermore retain full discretion regarding penalties applicable to infringements of national provisions adopted pursuant to Revised Directive 2003/87, but the penalties must be notified to the Commission.[85]

Due to the focus on the verification and enforcement of the installations and their respective emissions, the supervision of the EU ETS market itself – the integrity of the market in terms of the quality and nature of the allowances traded – has arguably been considered secondary to the checking of the installations since initially no specific provisions regarding fraud, insider trading and manipulation were adopted.[86] This apparent regulatory gap in terms of oversight and enforcement has led to a number of high profile cases involving VAT fraud[87] and allowances theft.[88] The latter case resulted in the temporary closure of several of

---

[83] Article 16(3) of Council Directive 2003/87/EC. See Tietenberg, 'Tradable Permits'. (Tietenberg argues that penalties should be commensurate with the danger posed by non-compliance. This does not imply that penalties have to be unrealistically high but rather that efficient penalties incorporate a financial penalty for non-compliance as well as the forfeiture of a number of future allowances to compensate.)

[84] Article 16(3) and (4) of Council Directive 2003/87/EC.

[85] Article 16(1) of Council Directive 2003/87/EC.

[86] The Community Independent Transaction Log (CITL) does provide annual data on the independently verified emissions of all installations covered by the EU ETS, see Annex XVI point 4(a) of Commission Regulation No. 2216/2004 of 21 December 2004 for a standardized and secure system of registries pursuant to Directive 2003/87/ EC of the European Parliament and of the Council and Decision No 280/2004/EC of the European Parliament and of the Council, OJ 2004 No. L386 1. Article 12(1)(a) of Council Directive 2003/87/EC provides that the Commission shall examine whether the market for emission allowances is sufficiently protected from insider dealing and market manipulation and, if appropriate, shall bring forward proposals to ensure such protection. Commission Communication of 21 December 2010, 'Towards an enhanced market oversight framework for the EU Emissions Trading Scheme', COM(2010) 796 final, represents the first effort in this examination.

[87] See Commission Communication of 21 December 2010, at 6. See also EurActiv, 'EU moves to tackle carbon trading fraud' (1 October 2009), www.euractiv.com/en/climate-change/eu-moves-tackle-carbon-trading-fraud/article-185933; EurActiv, 'EU approves revised ETS rules to combat cyber crime' (18 February 2010), www.euractiv.com/en/climate-environment/eu-approves-revised-ets-rules-combat-cyber-crime-news-260461.

[88] This 'theft' occurred through so-called 'phishing attacks', see Commission Communication of 21 December 2010. See also EurActiv, 'Great carbon theft may have netted €28m of permits' (21 January 2011), www.euractiv.com/climate-environment/great-carbon-theft-may-netted-28-news-501455. Another problem has been the 'recycling' of certified emission reductions.

the European registries, which meant a complete stop in trading for several days.[89] In December 2010, the Commission released a statement, together with a Communication,[90] in which it was acknowledged that the EU ETS market had become 'a potential target of fraudulent practices' and that as such 'it is critical that it continues to be subject to appropriate and effective regulatory oversight'.[91] The accompanying Communication started work on a legislative proposal, which was proposed in 2011 and takes effect for the third trading phase.[92]

## D EU ETS competence allocation – Phases I and II

Within the reality of the EU ETS, the dividing lines between norm setting, implementation and enforcement are less easily drawn. At times, the distinction between norm setting and implementation seems rather pedantic, and the de facto division of powers with respect to certain competences appears to differ from the *de jure* situation. The latter is particularly true for the implementation and enforcement competences allocated between the European institutions and the Member States. Through the Burden Sharing Agreement, the Member States placed some of the cap-division competences in the hands of the European regulator, rather than fulfilling their national targets individually. Also, the fact that the founding legislation for the EU ETS – Directive 2003/87/EC – is a European instrument, created and adopted by European institutions, points towards a European-based implementation. However, despite the fact that the European Member States have agreed to combine their reduction targets and other commitments under the Kyoto Protocol and UNFCCC respectively, the most important implementation and enforcement competences remain in the hands of the individual Member States. The European institutions play a coordinating and facilitating role at best, without substantial means for correction of national implementation and enforcement

---

[89] MEMO/11/44, 'Statement on the suspension of the EU ETS national registries', 25 January 2011; MEMO/11/254, 'Update on transitional measure: EU ETS registries of Cyprus, Hungary, Liechtenstein and Malta to resume operations on 20 April', 18 April 2011; see also e.g. MEMO/11/106, 'Update on transitional measure: EU ETS registries of Belgium, Estonia and Luxembourg to resume operations on 24 February', 22 February 2011; MEMO/11/85, 'Update on transitional measure: Spain's EU ETS registry to resume operations on 16 February', 14 February 2011.

[90] Commission Communication of 21 December 2010.

[91] MEMO/10/697, 'Emissions Trading: Statement by Commissioner for Climate Action Connie Hedegaard on regulatory oversight of the EU carbon market', 21 December 2010.

[92] See Chapter 4.

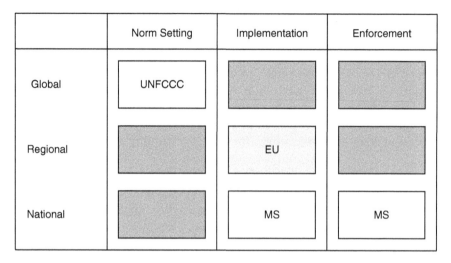

FIGURE 3.1 *Competence allocation in Phases I and II of the EU ETS*

strategies. This complex situation of EU ETS competence allocation is reduced to a schematic representation in Figure 3.1. As this figure shows, the competence allocation in Phases I and II of the EU ETS can be described as consisting of global norm setting, combined with national implementation and enforcement, with a limited role for the European Union in the implementation stage – mostly through oversight activities.

## 2 Regulatory functioning

The allocation of norm setting competences during Phases I and II of the EU ETS follows our first-best regulatory scenario insofar as it is based on global norm setting. However, the combination of this global norm setting with national implementation and enforcement does not mimic the allocative optimum. In this section we assess the regulatory effects of competence allocation in the EU ETS, both in terms of the individual allocation, and with respect to welfare improving and reducing interactions.

*A Competence allocation*

1 Norm setting

In our theoretically optimal competence allocation scenario, norm setting at the global level is considered the first-best allocation, since this is the only allocation that ensures the capture of all externalities caused by climate change. The global, disproportionate and dispersed causes and effects of greenhouse gas emitting activities call for the centralization of policy-making as a means to capture the positive and negative externalities of these activities. Through this allocation, possibilities to externalize the costs of climate change are reduced. Despite its inclusive membership, however, the UNFCCC and Kyoto Protocol system has not yet been successful in committing the most important contributors to climate change to concrete reduction goals. Key examples of this have been the failure to include the United States in the Kyoto Protocol, and the choice of Canada to leave the Kyoto Protocol in 2011 after stating that it had no intention to fulfil its commitments under the Protocol.[93]

In terms of our second-order considerations, the accommodation of heterogeneous conditions and preferences, global norm setting also renders certain benefits. Since we focus particularly on the mitigation of climate change through emissions trading, the instrument choice itself addresses some of the heterogeneity concerns. More generally, the different set of options provided by the UNFCCC and Kyoto Protocol and the differentiated approach with respect to regional and national commitments under these two instruments reflect an awareness of the different interests and circumstances of the parties. The two most important examples of this include the 'common but differentiated responsibilities' approach of the UNFCCC,[94] and the country-specific reduction goals of Annex I of the Protocol.[95]

With respect to economies of scale and scope, we see that large economies of scale and scope have been achieved by the centralization of information gathering through the IPCC. This is not to say that the creation and maintenance of the IPCC is without cost, but the synergies that can be created by the collection of information and the ability of the IPCC to relay information back to regional or local bodies is crucial. Moreover, many of the countries affected by climate change belong to the group of 'Least Developed Countries', which would not be able to perform such research independently. In terms of economies of scope, there have been attempts by the Conference of the Parties (COPs) to link measures for climate change mitigation and adaptation with those of poverty reduction and sustainable development.[96] Some have argued

---

[93] Kyoto Protocol, Canada: Withdrawal. C.N.796.2011.TREATIES-1 (Depositary Notification), 15 December 2011.
[94] Article 4 (1) and (2) of the UNFCCC.
[95] Article 17 and Annex I of the Kyoto Protocol (2005).
[96] See P. A. Sanchez, 'Linking Climate Change Research with Food Security and Poverty Reduction in the Tropics' (2000) 82(1) *Agriculture, Ecosystems & Environment* 371–383; N.

that this reduces the efficiency and effectiveness of the measures in respect of mitigating climate change.[97] Even so, the UNFCCC's location within the UN framework offers significant potential for a more effective combination of policies.

It is difficult to give a precise estimate of the economies of scale achieved in terms of the administrative costs of obtaining consensus at the global level, compared to the national or regional level since there are few reports on these specific types of cost.[98] For the UNFCCC's COP in Copenhagen in 2009, the estimated costs for the host country of Denmark were $62 million and $2 million for the UNFCCC Secretariat.[99] These numbers do not cover the (travel) costs of the tens of thousands of delegates and representatives that attended the COP. Nevertheless, it is unlikely that the alternative of decentralized norm setting would be less costly in terms of administration. This type of policy-making would require several regional meetings and coordination between these meetings, which most likely would lead to more complex coordination problems in terms of policy substance and policy-making since there may not be a pre-existing institutional structure such as the United Nations (UN) on which parties can rely. This option would moreover ignore any pre-existing knowledge of UN bodies such as the United Nations Environmental Programme (UNEP) and the United Nations Development Programme (UNDP), and more generally the experience of the UN system in providing a platform for comparable international efforts.

## 2 Implementation

Prima facie, the EU ETS appeared to have elements of implementation at both the regional and the national level: the implementation decisions regarding cap-division and allowance allocation took place predominantly at the Member State level with limited opportunity for the regional European level to influence these decisions. Given that

---

Bega *et al.* 'Linkages between Climate Change and Sustainable Development' (2002) 2(2) *Climate Policy* 129–144.

[97] E.g. the 'equitable' distribution of emissions rights may not mirror the 'efficient' distribution of emission rights, see T. Hayward, 'Human Rights versus Emissions Rights: Climate Justice and the Equitable Distribution of Ecological Space' (2007) 21 (4) *Ethics & International Affairs* 431–450.

[98] Most estimates focus on the complete cost of mitigating and/or adapting to climate change as a percentage of GDP (global or national), see e.g. N. Stern, *The Stern Review on the Economics of Climate Change* (Cambridge University Press, 2006); F. Ackerman and E. A. Stanton (eds.), *The Cost of Climate Change: What We'll Pay if Global Warming Continues Unchecked* (New York: Natural Resources Defense Council, 2008).

[99] These figures are based on estimates from the UNFCCC Secretariat.

the ultimate locus of discretion remained with the national level, we have labelled implementation as *national*. This allocation may have detrimental effects in terms of externalities caused by the sub-optimal distribution of the norm among industries. As opposed to the externalities dimension involved with norm setting, these externalities do not (necessarily) result in under- or over-abatement of greenhouse gas emissions, but rather reduce the cost-effectiveness of the regulation through a sub-optimal distribution of the norm. National implementers may consider this distribution as a method of giving effect to the heterogeneity between national economies in terms of their reliance on ETS sectors, and the relative costs of emission reductions in these sectors. However, this heterogeneity is supposed to be internalized at the industry level, facilitated through the possibility of emissions trading. Taking this heterogeneity into account at the cap-division stage of implementation is likely to result in protectionist distributions, which would undermine the cost-effectiveness of the EU ETS.

As predicted, the decentralization of cap-division competences, especially during Phases I and II, did lead to attempts by Member States to protect their industries from the costs involved with emission reduction. The differentiation in policy between the ETS and non-ETS sectors fed into the possibility for national implementers to choose sub-optimal distributions. Since the marginal abatement costs are typically higher for non-ETS sectors, these sectors were initially excluded from the ETS system in favour of sectors that could reduce pollution more efficiently.[100] But the rise in costs of services provided by the ETS sectors, which importantly included the energy sectors, also meant an increase in consumer prices and potential losses in competitiveness of Member State industries. This created additional incentives for Member States to shelter their ETS sectors by shifting part of the reduction burden to the non-ETS sectors, which undermines the cost-effectiveness of the EU ETS.[101] This would increase the overall reduction costs of that Member State and lead to a distortion of the European internal market since the

---

[100] The marginal abatement costs are the costs of preventing or reducing the polluting effect of a product or an activity per unit produced or activity performed. These costs can differ substantially per activity, per greenhouse gas and per production method. It is considered economically efficient for the abatement to take place at minimum cost, which means that those sectors that can reduce most cheaply should do so before other more cost-intensive actions are taken.

[101] Commission Impact Assessment of 23 January 2008 accompanying the Proposal for a Directive of the European Parliament and of the Council amending Directive 2003/87/EC so as to improve and extend the EU greenhouse gas emission allowance

competitive position of those ETS sectors would be disproportionately strong as compared to other Member States.[102] Their competitive position is strengthened not only by relatively lower abate requirements for these industries but also by the possibility of selling the excess of allowances, which in extreme cases made industries net sellers of emissions on the European market.[103]

Many Member States did allocate very generously to their ETS sectors, creating a situation of over-allocation in the first trading phase.[104] The Commission recognized early on that Member States have a national interest in maximizing their national cap despite the collective interest in setting restrictive caps for optimal reductions in the EU.[105] The resulting over-allocation had meant that Phase I was a failure in respect of actual emissions reductions despite its success in creating an emission allowances market; a failure that the Commission officially attributed to the limited availability of verified data.[106] Early analyses of the

trading system, COM(2008) 16 final, at 90. See also Clò, 'The Effectiveness of the EU Emissions Trading Scheme', 238 ('By definition, over-allocation implies that the ETS sectors have to bear an emissions reduction burden less than proportional to their percentage of produced emissions. Therefore, MS where over-allocation has been detected will reach their emissions reduction targets only if another agent – usually non-ETS sectors – reduces the emissions that the ETS sectors are not legally required to abate. In this case, the main side-effect of the over-allocation of allocations is a shift of the reduction burden from ETS to non-ETS sectors; this form of cross-subsidization is not cost-effective.')

[102] See also Commission Impact Assessment of 23 January 2008, at 90.

[103] Criterion five of Council Directive 2003/87/EC, Annex III did allow the Commission to reject NAPs in breach of Articles 87 and 88 of the EC on State Aid, but the information necessary to determine such a breach may well have been out of the reach of the Commission, letting less manifest breaches go unnoticed.

[104] See e.g. A. D. Ellerman and B. Buchner, 'The European Union Emissions Trading Scheme: Origins, Allocation, and Early Results' (2007) 1 *Review of Environmental Economics and Policy* 66–87. Ellerman and Buchner use the level of 2005 Business as Usual emissions as a benchmark; for an analysis using economic efficiency, proportionality and the polluter pays principle as benchmarks in order to test cap stringency, see Clò, 'Assessing the European Emissions Trading Scheme'. The subsequent confirmation of the suspected over-allocation through the release of verified emissions data caused a dramatic price drop for European Union Allowances (EUAs) at the end of the first trading phase. Analysis of 2005–06 emissions data suggests that there has *also* been an abatement of emissions during Phase I, which could be explained by decisions of affected facility managers to incorporate $CO_2$ prices into their production decisions. See A. D. Ellerman and B. Buchner, 'Over-allocation or Abatement? A Preliminary Analysis of the EU Emissions Trading Scheme based on the 2006 Emissions Data' (2008) 41 *Environmental and Resource Economics* 267–287.

[105] Commission Impact Assessment, COM(2008) 16 final, at 90.

[106] Commission Proposal of 23 January 2008 for a Directive amending Directive 2003/87/ EC so as to improve and extend the greenhouse gas emission allowance trading system of the Community, COM(2008) 30 final, at 2.

approved Phase II NAPs indicated that these NAPs would again result in an excess of allowances that would lead to a low(er) carbon price and little investment in low-carbon technology.[107] The European Commission tried to address the issue of over-allocation through a stricter review of the NAPs for the second trading phase.[108]

The European Commission does play a role in cap-division through the review of NAPs. However, even during the first trading phase, the Member States raised numerous objections before the European courts regarding the extent of this review power.[109] Many of the Phase I cases concern the design of the NAPs and the procedural steps involved in their creation: regardless of the subject, the courts held consistently that the Commission exceeded their power of review or applied the criteria incorrectly. This suggests that the Member States' discretion with respect to the NAPs was rather broad, which was to the detriment of cost-effective norm distribution.

In our theoretical framework, we highlighted the danger of sub-optimal norm distribution in case of national implementation. However, the extent to which this might occur and how it relates to other advantages of national allocation, such as lower costs of information for benchmarking and allocation decisions cannot be determined without knowledge of the specific regulatory context. Arguably, the initial creation of NAPs required a high level of expertise regarding local industries in order to create benchmarks and compose overviews of the relevant installations, which strengthens the case for national implementation. Also the relationship between ETS and non-ETS sectors at the national level constitutes information more readily available at the national level. Nevertheless, recent evaluations of the system show that there continue to be high administrative costs for the Member States, the Commission and the installations covered by the system.[110] Moreover, some Member States may be considered more capable of

---

[107] See primarily: K. Neuhoff, *et al.*, 'Emission Projections 2008–2012 versus National Allocation Plans II' (2006) 6 *Climate Policy* 395–410 at 395 and 403; K. Neuhoff, *et al.*, 'Implications of Announced Phase II National Allocation Plans for the EU ETS' (2006) 6 *Climate Policy* 411–422.

[108] Reductions imposed by the Commission represented 11.8 per cent of the allowances on the EU ETS market. See G. Dari-Mattiacci and J. A. W. van Zeben, 'Legal Uncertainty and Market Uncertainty in Market-Based Instruments: The Case of the EU ETS' (2012) 19(2) *New York University Environmental Law Journal* 101–139.

[109] See generally J. A. W. van Zeben, 'The European Emissions Trading Scheme Case Law' (2009) 18 *Review of European Community & International Environmental Law* 119–128.

[110] Commission Impact Assessment of 23 January 2008, 91.

## 132   REGULATORY COMPETENCE ALLOCATION IN THE EU ETS (2005–2012)

shouldering these costs than others.[111] In sum, we find that the over-allocation in Phases I and II was so severe, and the consequences for the EU ETS market so extreme,[112] that the second-order considerations of economies of scale/scope cannot compensate for this inefficiency. This makes national implementation sub-optimal to regional implementation, since the latter would have been better able to overcome most of the externality-related problems of norm distribution.

## 3 Enforcement

In our first-best competence allocation scenario, the market oversight element of enforcement was underlined as being potentially problematic due to the possibility of externalizing the costs of faulty oversight onto other jurisdictions when the geographic scope of the market is greater than that of the enforcer.[113] Within the EU ETS, there have

---

[111] Poland's registry did not go online until eighteen months after the start of the EU ETS; and Romania and Bulgaria, who became participants in the trial period in its last year, did not have everything in place in time to participate effectively in trading in 2007 (Ellerman and Buchner, 'Over-allocation or Abatement?', 6). Moreover, two EU Member States (Bulgaria, Greece) were found to be in non-compliance with the national system requirements under the Kyoto Protocol and were temporarily suspended from trading under the three market mechanisms (JI, CDM and emissions trading). Two other participating Member States – Romania and Lithuania –submitted reports to show their adherence to the implementation requirements following earlier findings on non-compliance. See full reports from the Eighteenth Meeting of Kyoto Protocol Compliance Committee Enforcement Branch, 2012, Informal Information notes on Questions of Implementation, retrieved 26 January 2012 at http://unfccc.int/kyoto_protocol/compliance/items/2875.php.

[112] See Dari-Mattiacci and van Zeben, 'Legal Uncertainty and Market Uncertainty'.

[113] There was some initial discussion about establishing a European-wide market rather than a national one in the preparatory documents for the EU ETS. The Commission stressed that a Community approach would prevent the distortion of competition, could take into account existing (environmental) policies, and lead to important costs-savings. See European Commission, COM (2000) 87 final, at 4 ('[A] coherent and co-ordinated framework for implementing emissions trading covering all Member States would provide the best guarantee for a smooth functioning internal emissions market as compared to a set of uncoordinated national emissions trading schemes'); and Commission Communication, Proposal of 23 October 2001 for a Directive of the European Parliament and of the Council establishing a scheme for greenhouse gas emission allowance trading within the Community and amending Council Directive 96/61/EC, COM(2001) 581 final, at 6. Moreover, the Commission's economic analysis, developed as part of the Green Paper of 2000, shows that if there were only trading at the national level, and no trading between Member States, the total cost for the EU to reach the Kyoto targets would be around €9 billion in 2010. With EU-wide trading among the energy producers and energy-intensive industries, these costs would be reduced to €6.9 billion in 2010. See European Commission, COM (2000) 87 final, Annex I, at 27 (since the models used to estimate these figures assume that

indeed been instances of VAT fraud,[114] and allowances theft, which have had implications for the entire EU ETS market, such as the closure of several national registries and the suspension of trading.[115]

With respect to enforcement related to the surrendering of allowances, i.e. ensuring that installations have enough allowances to cover their emissions, and other more 'traditional' enforcement duties, the variances in the technical ability of Member States to detect violations may also result in different outcomes between Member States. The Commission has tried to overcome the capacity differences between Member States through discussion forums and establishment of best practices.[116] The initial lack of harmonization with respect to accreditation standards for verifiers potentially increases the heterogeneity in the quality and reliability of verified reports in different Member States.[117]

The allocation of monitoring and reporting duties at the national level may furthermore overlook possible economies of scale at the European level. In terms of economies of scope, the explicit references made to the IPCC Directive and the opportunity for Member States to use authorities established under this directive show that use could be made of pre-existing European arrangements.[118] At the moment, these economies of scope have not materialized in all Member States. In the Netherlands, for example, the implementation and enforcement of the EU ETS Directive, especially the permitting and oversight elements, have been assigned to the national government, whereas similar European-based programmes, such as those under the IPCC, are in

---

Member States would be able to allocate reduction costs at least-cost between their sectors, the real costs are expected to be even higher, up to €20 billion a year).

[114] See Commission Communication, COM(2010) 796 final, at 6. See also EurActiv, 'EU moves to tackle carbon trading fraud'; EurActiv, 'EU approves revised ETS rules to combat cyber crime'.

[115] MEMO/11/44; MEMO/11/85.

[116] See e.g. information regarding the Verification Forum of 19 November 2008, available at http://ec.europa.eu/clima/documentation/ets/monitoring_monitoring_En.htm

[117] See M. Peeters, 'Inspection and Market-Based Regulation through Emissions Trading: The Striking Reliance on Self-Monitoring, Self-Reporting and Verification' (2006) 2(1) *Utrecht Law Review* 177–195 at 187 (stating that some progress has been made in this regard). See also Commission Regulation No. 600/2012 of 21 June 2012 on the verification of greenhouse gas emission reports and tonne-kilometre reports and the accreditation of verifiers pursuant to Directive 2003/87/EC of the European Parliament and of the Council, OJ (2012) L181, 1–29 (12 July 2012).

[118] European Commission, COM (2001) 581 final, at 8.

the hands of the municipalities.[119] This anecdotal evidence suggests that additional efficiency gains may be achieved.

Overall, the potential for the externalization of under-enforcement suggests that the capture of externalities remains important at the enforcement stage and that the allocation of enforcement competences at a governance level with a geographical scope equal to that of the market is preferable. It is moreover unclear whether economies of scale or scope are being achieved at the national level when available. In practice, it is difficult to verify information regarding actual national enforcement activities. For example, the Dutch Emissions Authority, which is the Dutch authorized body that deals with most EU ETS-related matters, has extensive data on its website regarding its enforcement policies,[120] together with publicly accessible data regarding the compliance behaviour of all permitted installations in the Netherlands.[121] This data suggests a 100 per cent compliance rate among Dutch installations, which means there are yet to be any enforcement procedures in the Netherlands. The UK Environment Agency, another competent authority, has also published guidelines on civil penalties for non-compliance, but no compliance data of individual installations.[122] In Poland, penalty provisions are included in the Polish Act on the greenhouse gas emissions trading scheme, but no additional guidance is offered.[123]

In addition, in Poland, the competence to fine for offences such as excessive emissions,[124] the failure to submit an annual report[125] and emitting without a permit[126] lie with the so-called 'Institutes for Environmental Protection', which are active at the provincial level. In turn, these Institutes have to report to the national centre for environmental protection, which reports to the environment minister.[127] In the Netherlands, the Emissions Authority has the competence to issue permits, as well as to impose penalties. In the United Kingdom, these

---

[119] Peeters, 'Inspection and Market-Based Regulation', at 191–192.

[120] See Dutch Emissions Authority, *Sanction strategy* (in Dutch), 2008 at www.emissieautoriteit.nl/toezicht/handhaving/sanctiestrategie.

[121] See Dutch Emissions Authority, *CO2 – emissions and compliance 2008–2010 per installation*, 2011 at www.emissieautoriteit.nl/mediatheek/afsluiten-handelsjaar/publicaties/co2-emissies-en-naleving-2008–2010-per-bedrijfslocatie%20%2816–05–2011%29/view?searchterm=naleving.

[122] See Environment Agency, 'EU Emissions Trading Scheme: Guidance to Operators on the application of Civil Penalties', 2009.

[123] Act 695 on the greenhouse gas emissions trading scheme, Journal of Law (Poland) 122, 28 April 2011, Chapter 11, Articles 70–77.

[124] *Ibid.*, Article 73.  [125] *Ibid.*, Article 70, para. 1.  [126] *Ibid.*, Article 72.

[127] *Ibid.*, Articles 76–77.

competences are both located at the same authority (the Environment Agency). The division of competences at the national level is beyond the scope of our analysis but, for future research, the effects of these sub-national competence divisions may shed further light on enforcement behaviour.

## B Interactions

Based on experiences from the first two trading phases, we can also reflect on the types of 'agencies' that are active at the national and European level. These categorizations enable us to determine whether the interaction between these agencies could be altered in a way that would be welfare improving. Our discussion will focus primarily on the interaction between norm setting and implementation since most of the available information concerns implementation practices. Due to the over-allocation during the first phase, and the financial crisis during the second phase, there has not been a situation of scarcity on the market, which makes non-compliance through excessive emission less likely. In addition, this type of non-compliance is least problematic with respect to enforcement externalities; problems with externalizing the cost of under-enforcement are most likely with respect to market oversight. By categorizing the type of behaviour displayed by EU ETS agencies (e.g. the Commission, the Member States), we are able to suggest changes to the allocation of implementation and enforcement competences, in light of their interaction with norm setting and each other, respectively.

## 1 A typology of agencies in the EU ETS

With respect to implementation, the divergence in types between the European Commission and the Member States was made explicit through the Commission's review of the Member States' NAPs. Many Commission attempts to alter NAP provisions were challenged by the Member States on the basis of the Commission's lack of competence to prescribe certain changes. For instance, in *United Kingdom* v. *Commission*, the Court of First Instance had to decide whether the Commission was entitled to reject amendments to a NAP if these amendments had not previously been included in the provisional NAP that was submitted by a Member State.[128] The court examined the roles and powers of the Commission and the Member States under the directive, and found that

---

[128] Case T-178/05, *United Kingdom* v. *European Commission* [2005] ECR II-4807.

136 REGULATORY COMPETENCE ALLOCATION IN THE EU ETS (2005–2012)

with respect to amendments to NAPs, the Commission cannot restrict a Member State's right to propose amendments but that any proposed amendment must be adopted by the Commission in order to become effective.[129]

*United Kingdom* v. *Commission* is one of the few cases between the Commission and a Member State that does not directly concern the issue of cap distribution.[130] Despite the court's repeated confirmation of the division of powers in favour of the Member States, the Commission persisted in its review, and rejection, of NAPs whenever over-allocation was suspected, for Phase II as well as Phase I. Member States responded to these rejections by bringing actions to the General Court requesting an annulment of the Commission decisions.[131] In September 2009, the landmark cases of *Poland* v. *Commission* and *Estonia* v. *Commission* were decided in favour of the Member States.[132] In these cases, Poland

[129] The Commission may test the amendments in light of the criteria of Annex III of the directive and Article 10 of the EC Treaty. Also with respect to public consultation duties, the court confirmed that there were two mandatory rounds of public consultation: one before the NAP was completed and one after the Commission has authorized the allocation but before the national decision of allocation, Case T-178/05, *United Kingdom* v. *European Commission* [2005] ECR II-4807.

[130] One of the first cases on this issue was Case T-374/04, *Germany* v. *European Commission* [2007] ECR II-4431, in which the Commission questioned Germany's decision to include an *ex post* adjustment mechanism in its NAP, which would allow the German government to take back allowances from installations under five different scenarios and to place them in the new entrants reserve. According to the Court of First Instance (now General Court), the Commission did not prove that the German *ex post* adjustment mechanism was incompatible with criteria 5 and 10 of Annex III to Directive 2003/87/EC. Specifically, the court held that the arguments of the Commission were neither 'factually substantiated nor legally well founded'. See Case T-374/04, *Germany* v. *European Commission* [2007] ECR II-4431, at paras. 151–164. Regarding the incompatibility with criterion 10 of Annex III, the court applied a four-part analysis (previously applied in Case T-251/00, *Lagardere and Canal + v. European Commission* [2002] ECR II-4825), consisting of a literal interpretation; a historical interpretation; a contextual interpretation; and a teleological interpretation (Case T-374/04, *Germany* v. *European Commission* [2007] ECR II-4431, paras. 92–150). The mere fact that 'the practice of ex-post adjustments are liable to deter operators from reducing their production volume and, therefore, their emission rates is not sufficient to call into question the adjustments' legality in light of the directive's objectives as a whole' (Case T-374/04, *Germany* v. *European Commission* [2007] ECR II-4431, at para. 148).

[131] Case T-499/07, *Bulgaria* v. *Commission* [2008] OJ (C64) 50; Case T-500/07, *Bulgaria* v. *Commission* [2008] OJ (C64) 51; Case T-483/07, *Romania* v. *Commission* [2008] OJ (C51) 56; Case T-484/07, *Romania* v. *Commission* [2008] OJ (C51) 57; Case T-369/07, *Latvia* v. *European Commission* [2011] ECR II-01039.

[132] Case T-183/07, *Poland* v. *European Commission* [2009] ECR II-03395 and Case T-263/07, *Estonia* v. *European Commission* [2009] ECR II-03463.

and Estonia requested an annulment of the Commission's decisions regarding their NAPs. These decisions instructed Poland and Estonia to reduce the amount of allocated emissions by 26.7 per cent and 47.8 per cent, respectively. The Member States submitted that the Commission had exceeded (the limits of) its powers under Article 9(3) of Directive 2003/87. Specifically, Poland submitted that the Commission had overstepped its powers under the directive by replacing the data and economic model used by Poland by its own and consequently, used its own data and economic assessment to conclude that the NAP was incompatible with the directive and imposed a ceiling for the total quantity of allowances that could be allocated in the NAPs.[133] A similar claim was made by Estonia.[134] The cases were decided in favour of the Member States with the court confirming that it was for the Member States and not the Commission to decide on the total quantity of allowances.[135]

As the court annulled the decisions,[136] the Commission was forced to take a new decision on each NAP. In the consequent political struggle between the Commission and the Member States, the Commission initially rejected both NAPs again, on different legal grounds.[137] After a revision of the NAPs by Poland and Estonia, the Commission approved the new NAPs on 19 April 2010 – two years into the second trading phase.[138] The new Polish NAP maintained the total amount of allowances at 208.5 Mt per year, the amount that the Commission had previously contested. Alongside this political process, the Commission also launched an appeal with the Court of Justice.[139] The Court of Justice dismissed the appeals in both cases, emphasizing that the method of allowance calculation was part of the discretion of the Member States, and that this need not be harmonized by the Commission in order to ensure equal treatment between the Member States.[140] In sum, the

---

[133] Case T-183/07, *Poland v. European Commission* [2009] ECR II-03395, paras. 120–121.
[134] Case T-263/07, *Estonia v. European Commission* [2009] ECR II-03463, para. 41.
[135] See Order in C-503/07 P (2008), para. 75, as referred to in *Poland v. European Commission*, para. 126.
[136] *Poland v. European Commission*, para. 163 and Case T-263/07, *Estonia v. European Commission*, para. 114.
[137] European Commission (11 December 2009).
[138] See European Commission (19 April 2010).
[139] Cases lodged under Case number C-504/09P, *European Commission v. Poland* [2011] OJ (C370) and C-505/09P *European Commission v. Estonia* (2009). For the latter, see http://curia.europa.eu/juris/liste.jsf?language=en&num=C-505/09%20P.
[140] Judgment (Poland), paras. 65–66; Judgment (Poland), para. 67; Judgment (Estonia), para. 68. See further J. A. W. van Zeben, 'Cases C-504/09 P, Commission v Poland, and C-505/09 P, Commission v Estonia, Judgment of the European Court of Justice

Member States have successfully resisted attempts by the Commission to indirectly tighten the caps for their national ETS sectors during the first two trading phases.[141] This has come at the cost of increased uncertainty regarding the number of allowances on the market and thus a less stable carbon price.[142]

In terms of allowance allocation to specific installations, the practice of grandfathering in the first and second phases, combined with the Business as Usual standard and the continued reliance on historic emission data for Member States' allowance allocation decisions, has provided perverse incentives for installation owners to increase emissions in the base years.[143] Moreover, the use of grandfathering as a method of allocation provided firms with windfall profits due to their ability to raise consumer prices without having to pay for (most of) their allowances: put differently, the costs of abatement were externalized on to the consumer, which is arguably in line with the polluter pays principle but also lowers firms' incentives to innovate and/or abate.[144] The Commission recognized this obvious danger of the 'historical emissions' allocation method as early as 2006, and moreover stressed that

---

(Second Chamber) of 29 March 2012 (annotation)' (2013) 50 *Common Market Law Review* 231–246.

[141] There have also been attempts by private parties to influence implementation, particularly allowance allocation decisions, through actions before the European Courts but they have been largely unsuccessful. A large number of cases concerned the Commission decisions regarding Member States' NAPs, with private parties objecting to a reduction in the number of allocatable allowances. These cases have all failed based on the lack of standing of these parties to appeal a Commission Decision. The court held that since it is the allocation decision taken by the Member States once the NAP has been approved, and not the actual NAP which impacts on the companies' rights, these companies are not considered 'individually concerned' with respect to the Commission Decisions. See for instance Case T-387/04, *EnBW Energie Baden-Württemberg* v. *Commission* [2007] ECR II-1195 and Case T-27/07, *U.S. Steel Kosice* v. *European Commission* [2007] ECR II-128.

[142] See Dari-Mattiacci and van Zeben, 'Legal Uncertainty and Market Uncertainty'. The Commission also recognized that the legal and political disagreement regarding NAPs created elements of uncertainty and a lack of predictability, negatively affecting the market price and its stability, see Impact Assessment, COM(2008) 16 final, at 91.

[143] Neuhoff, *et al.*, 'Implications of Announced Phase II National Allocation Plans'.

[144] See for instance J. Nash, 'Too Much Market? Conflict between Tradable Pollution Allowances and the "Polluter Pays" Principle' (2000) 24 *Harvard Environmental Law Review* 465–535. For a critique of this paper and other literature on the polluter pays principle, see Woerdman, Arcuri and Cló, 'Emissions Trading and the Polluter-Pays Principle'.

many of the NAPs fell short of setting standards that would ensure compliance with the Kyoto commitments.[145]

Overall, these experiences show that the interests advocated by the European Commission are closely aligned to the norms set at the global level, i.e. of the COPs under the UNFCCC and Kyoto Principle. The Member States protested the Commission's attempts to correct what it considered to be sub-optimal distributions in the NAPs. The consequent claims against the Commission were mirrored by cases brought by private parties,[146] which suggests that the Member States' interests are more closely aligned to private interest groups than with the norms set at the global level. These global norms may be considered to reflect the global social optimum (or as close to the social optimum as possible considering imperfect information and the need to reach consensus among 193 countries). They point towards the Member States acting as rent-seeking agencies, whereas the European Commission's actions are closer to that of a benevolent agency. In the next sub-section, we will consider the implications of this typology and how we could improve on the allocation in Phases I and II.

## 2 Interactions and welfare enhancing allocations

The authority vested in the agencies (i.e. the European institutions and the Member States) under the implementation and enforcement of the EU ETS is a positive one: they authorize an activity (the emission of greenhouse gases) through the issuing of permits.[147] In addition, the norm setter and the implementer hold concurrent competences: both actions (cap setting and cap distribution) are needed to give effect to the positive authority installed with the agencies, and the act of cap setting leaves exploitable rents for the implementer during norm distribution. Implementation and enforcement competences are imperfectly concurrent since enforcement cannot alter cap-division, but rents can still be available to the enforcer if he chooses to under-enforce a cap-division that is sub-optimal from the perspective of an individual installation.

Positive authority, (imperfectly) concurrent competences, and the fact that the national agencies can be categorized as rent-seeking together

---

[145] European Commission, 'Building a Global Carbon Market' Report pursuant to Article 30 of Directive 2003/87/EC COM 676 (2006).

[146] See note 141.

[147] Another important effect of the authority vested in these agencies is that parties now have to pay for the right to emit.

become the least favourable combination from a welfare perspective.[148] Since the positive regulatory authority of the Member State is in no way tempered by the actions of the norm setter, the Member States are compelled to act in an inefficient manner.[149] Altering the relationship between the competences so that they were alternative, rather than concurrent, would signify a great welfare improvement. However, the complementary nature is inherent to the competences and impossible to change. In terms of enforcement, one may expect similar practices of under-enforcement to arise since it is possibile to externalize the costs of non-compliance on other parties, especially with respect to market oversight.

The only other welfare improving option is to create a system of unified regulatory powers. Hypothetically, a system of unified regulatory powers would represent a slight improvement over the current situation. A unified system could be created concentrating norm setting, implementation and enforcement at the national, global or regional level. Doing so would have several drawbacks at the individual competence level, inter alia, the inability to capture the externalities inherent to climate change when setting norms at the sub-global level, or the loss of efficiency through global implementation and/or enforcement. In addition, this unification would not change the typology of the agencies involved and is likely to magnify the free-riding tendencies of national actors to the point where some Member States may not take mitigating action at all.

The negative interactions between regulatory levels and competences are further enabled through the discretion given to Member States in their implementation and enforcement practices. This discretion allows for the accommodation of heterogeneity and a potential lowering of costs but also makes it more difficult for the European Commission to correct the behaviour of the Member States, for example. The position of the Member States has been strengthened further by the fact that there was relatively little information available on emissions during the first trading phase. This situation is improving and European institutions are trying to reduce the information dissymmetry. An example of this is the Union's involvement in fulfilling the UNFCCC requirement for Annex I parties to submit national greenhouse gas inventories since 1996.[150] The European Environment Agency assists the Commission

---

[148] See Chapter 1, section 3.B.    [149] See also Parisi, Schulz, and Klick, 'Two Dimensions', 64.
[150] Articles 4 and 12 of the UNFCCC.

in this area, especially with regards to the Community inventory system.[151] Based on the European Community's annual greenhouse gas inventory, the Commission moreover prepares a short communication for the European Parliament and the Council, the so-called Progress Report.[152] However, these reports continue to be based on information supplied by the national registries, rather than on independent data.[153] Despite the importance of these measures, these endeavours to create additional oversight over national practices cannot be equated with the reallocation of competences to the European level, as is evidenced by the Commission's failure to adjust the NAPs, even in light of conflicting national and European data.

## 3 Conclusions

The application of a theoretical framework to a real-life situation is challenging since no model can capture all the nuances of reality. In this chapter, we set out to translate the implications of the competence allocation framework to norm setting under the UNFCCC and Kyoto Protocol, and to its implementation and enforcement under the EU ETS. Despite its flaws – such as the failure to commit some of the major greenhouse gas emitters – the UNFCCC and Kyoto Protocol mirror

---

[151] The European Environment Agency was established in 1993 (the regulation establishing the agency was adopted in 1990) and its mandate is to support countries to make informed decisions about environmental policy and to coordinate the European environment information and observation network ('Eionet'), see Council Regulation 401/2009 of 23 April 2009 on the European Environment Agency and the European Environment Information and Observation Network, OJ 2009 No. L126/13.

[152] These Progress Reports assess the actual and projected progress of Member States and the Community towards fulfilling their emission reduction commitments under the UNFCCC and the Kyoto Protocol. They also summarize any progress on Community policies and measures resulting from the European Climate Change Programme (ECCP). See Commission Decision 2004/156/EC. Full reports are available on http://ec.europa.eu/clima/documentation/eccp/index_En.htm.

[153] In addition, although the Member States have a responsibility to record the emission transactions in their registries, they are not required to *track* the emissions of the different installations, which means they have to rely on the work of third party verifiers (Annex V, para. 12 of Council Directive 2003/87/EC). Considering the cost of this verification, estimated at €4,000 to €6,000 for small sites and €10,000 to €17,000 for more complex sites, this looks to become a significant industry. Until 2008, Member States were able to set relatively independent standards regarding the person of the verifier but the situation has changed with the new guidelines on monitoring and reporting of 2007. See Commission Decision 2007/589/EC and also Commission Regulation SEC/2012/0176, final.

our first-best scenario of global norm setting. However, the national approach taken to implementation and enforcement in the EU ETS causes several problems with respect to different types of externalities associated with the implementation and enforcement processes, such as the sub-optimal distribution of the cap, and the failure to put in place sufficient market oversight provisions, resulting in transboundary damages. Several suggestions were made to improve this sub-optimal situation of competence allocation, most of which involved the reallocation of implementation and enforcement competences to the European level, given the evident difference in interests and type between the European Commission and the Member States.

This chapter highlighted several ways in which the European Commission has tried to overcome the limitations of this allocation of competence through oversight-related methods, none of which was particularly successful. The jurisprudence of the Court of Justice is witness to the (unsuccessful) attempts of the European Commission to gain greater control over the implementation and enforcement process of the EU ETS. Another expression of the Commission's efforts to maintain greater influence of the implementation and enforcement of the EU ETS has been through increasing the role of European institutions in the collection of data and other monitoring activities connected with enforcement.[154]

With respect to norm setting, the future of the UN-based framework beyond 2012 remains unclear. The refusal of the United States, at the time, the largest emitter of greenhouse gases, to sign or ratify the Kyoto Protocol; the disappointing results of the Kyoto commitments in terms of actual emission reductions in the Annex I countries; and current difficulties in securing a 'post-Kyoto' commitment from again the United States, China and other large developed or 'developing' countries complicate the process of coordinated global action. The Bali Road Map established a timeframe for the development of commitments

---

[154] It does so in line with the principle of subsidiarity, as stressed in Decision 208/2004/EC of the European Parliament and of the Council of 11 February 2004 concerning a mechanism for monitoring Community greenhouse gas emissions and for implementing the Kyoto Protocol, 10 March 2004, OJ 2004 No. L49 1, Preamble 19 ('Since the objectives of the proposed action, namely to comply with the Community's commitments under the Kyoto Protocol, in particular the monitoring and reporting requirements laid down therein, cannot, by their very nature, be sufficiently achieved by the Member States and can therefore be better achieved at Community level, the Community may adopt measures, in accordance with the principle of subsidiarity as set out in Article 5 of the Treaty.')

beyond the Kyoto Protocol.[155] The latest meetings of the COP under the UNFCCC in Copenhagen and Cancún have failed to secure binding targets for the 'post-Kyoto' period from 2012 onwards. Rather than signing an agreement with binding commitments to follow up on the Kyoto Protocol, COP 15 in Copenhagen resulted only in an 'accord' without any legally binding targets.[156] This has led many to wonder whether future action on climate change can, and should, be based around the UNFCCC framework.[157] As a result, we see a shift from our first-best scenario of global norm setting to a second-best regional norm-setting scenario with respect to the EU ETS from 2013 onwards. Moreover, European-based pressures have led to several changes to the allocation of implementation and enforcement competences.

[155] See Report of the Conference of the Parties on its thirteenth session, held in Bali from 3 to 15 December 2007, Addendum Part Two: Action taken by the Conference of the Parties at its thirteenth session [Bali Action Plan] UN Doc. FCCC/CP/2007/6/Add.1*. Decision 1/CP.13. (14 March 2008).

[156] Report of the Conference of the Parties on its Fifteenth Session, Addendum [Copenhagen Accord, December 18, 2009], UN Doc. FCCC/CP/2009/11/Add.1. Decision 2/CP.15. (30 March 2010).

[157] For critiques of the UNFCCC format, see e.g. Prins *et al.*, 'The Hartwell Paper: A New Direction for Climate Policy after the Crash of 2009' (May 2010) at http://eprints.lse.ac.uk/27939/1/HartwellPaper_English_version.pdf; R. Falkner, H. Stephan and J. Vogler, 'International Climate Policy after Copenhagen: Towards a "Building Blocks" Approach' (2010) 1 *Global Policy* 252–262. For regional incentives, see for instance The United Nations Collaborative Programme on Reducing Emissions from Deforestation and Forest Degradation in Developing Countries, see www.un-redd.org/; Australia's Carbon Pollution Reduction Scheme; the New Zealand Emissions Trading Scheme; Regional Emission Trading Initiatives in the United States include the Midwest Greenhouse Gas Reduction Accord, the Energy Security and Climate Stewardship Platform for the Midwest, the Western Climate Initiative, and the Regional Greenhouse Gas Initiative (RGGI). See also R. Abate, 'Kyoto or Not, Here We Come: The Promise and Perils of the Piecemeal Approach to Climate Change Regulation in the United States' (2006) 15 *Cornell Journal of Law and Public Policy* 369–401; J. Holtkamp, 'Dealing with Climate Change in the United States: The Non-Federal Response' (2007) 27 *Journal of Land, Resources & Environmental Law* 79–86.

# 4 Regulatory competence allocation in the EU ETS (2013 onwards)

The first two trading phases of the European Union Emissions Trading Scheme (EU ETS), running from 2005 to 2012, were aimed at implementing the reduction targets set under the Kyoto Protocol by establishing a functioning carbon market. The first commitment period under the Kyoto Protocol ran from 2008 to 2012, at the end of which the commitments of the Annex I Parties had to be fulfilled. At the time of writing, new (legally binding) reduction targets have not been agreed which leaves the future of global policy-making, with binding goals or targets, unsure.[1] At the European level, however, policy-making with respect to the post-2012 EU ETS regime has continued, building on the experiences of the first two trading phases.[2] These developments at the global and European level give rise to substantial changes in competence allocation for the post-2012 period, with a concentration of norm setting and implementation competences at the European level. In addition, some of the substantive rules within the EU ETS are set to change, with

---

[1] At the moment, parties – importantly including the United States and China – have only been willing to commit to pledges, which are not legally binding. See Copenhagen Accord, note 497; Outcome of the work of the Ad Hoc Working Group on Long-term Cooperative Action under the Convention [Cancún Agreements], UN Doc. FCCC/CP/2010/7/Add.1. Decision 1/CP.16 (15 March 2011); Draft decision [-/CP.17] Outcome of the work of the Ad Hoc Working Group on Long-term Cooperative Action under the Convention (Advance unedited version) [Durban], available on http://unfccc.int/files/meetings/durban_nov_2011/decisions/application/pdf/cop17_lcaoutcome.pdf, and section I.A. below. The latest meeting in Bonn (concluded 25 May 2013) was considered a step back from earlier, hard fought, consensus, see www.guardian.co.uk/environment/2012/may/25/bonn-climate-talks-end-disappointment.

[2] See European Commission, COM 30 (2008) 13 final, and especially Council Directive 2009/29/EC of 23 April 2009 amending Directive 2003/87/EC so as to improve and extend the greenhouse gas emission allowance trading scheme of the Community, OJ 2009 No. L140/63, 5 June 2009.

an increased emphasis on the auctioning of allowances and the inclusion of additional sectors to the ETS, such as the aviation industry.

This chapter starts by setting out the division of norm setting, implementation and enforcement competences from 2013 onwards. With respect to norm setting, the stalemate at the global level will be contrasted with the developments at the European level, which were meant to run parallel to the international system but have in fact taken its place in lieu of international action.[3] As such, the norm setting in the post-2012 regime corresponds with our second-best scenario.[4] This expanding role for the European level is also reflected in the reallocation of implementation competences to the European level. The allocation of enforcement competences has remained relatively stable at the decentralized Member State level but some lessons have been learned regarding the nature of enforcement needed regarding the ETS market, as compared to the prior, almost exclusive, focus on the verification of allowances by individual installations.

# 1 Regulatory competence allocation in the EU ETS

## A Norm setting

### 1 Inaction at the global level

The Kyoto Protocol's first commitment period expired in 2012, and the negotiations regarding a binding climate change agreement for 2013 onwards have been strained. At the 2007 UNFCCC Conference of the Parties (COP) meeting, the so-called Bali Road Map was adopted which sets out a two-year negotiation process that should have led to the conclusion of a new agreement on the future of the UNFCCC and the Kyoto Protocol. The Bali Road Map, which included the Bali Action Plan, set out the main issues that were to be agreed upon for a successful future agreement to take shape, including: a long-term global goal for emission reductions; action on mitigation; technology development and transfer for mitigation and adaptation; and financing.[5] The negotiations

---

[3] As phrased by D. H. Cole, 'From Global to Polycentric Climate Governance' (2011) 2 *Climate Law* 395–413 at 409 ('[T]he EU-ETS is not simply a Kyoto compliance mechanism for the European Union but a possibly preferable institutional alternative to Kyoto's trading mechanisms, from which the UNFCCC parties might learn valuable lessons for a post-Kyoto treaty.')

[4] See Chapter 3.

[5] H. E. Ott, W. Sterk, and R. Watanabe, 'The Bali Roadmap: New Horizons for Global Climate Policy' (2008) 8 *Climate Policy* 91–95.

on each of these issues would be exceedingly complex and to address all of them concurrently was considered highly ambitious.[6] However, the mood was optimistic: the United States had returned to the negotiations for the first time since 2001, the Adaptation Fund provided for in the Kyoto Protocol was made operational, and parties appeared to be willing to move away from the Annex I/non-Annex I divide that had before determined much of the negotiations.[7] The work on the Bali Road Map was set to proceed through a 'two-track' process with work on the UNFCCC taking place through the COP, the subsidiary bodies and the Ad Hoc Working Group on Long-term Cooperative Action, and work on the Kyoto Protocol through the CMP, the subsidiary bodies and the Ad Hoc Working Group on Further Commitments for Annex I Parties.[8]

Despite the extensive guidance provided by the Road Map, reaching a consensus proved difficult and many considered the agreement reached at the 2009 Copenhagen conference – the Copenhagen Accord – a disappointment, or even an outright failure.[9] The Accord is not a legally binding agreement in the same way as the Kyoto Protocol is, and as such does not contain any binding emission reduction targets for the parties;[10] rather, the Copenhagen Accord left open the reduction commitments of the Annex I parties and the developing country parties.[11] These commitments were to be communicated by the parties before 31 January 2010, a soft deadline which has been met by most parties.[12]

---

[6] *Ibid.*, 93.    [7] *Ibid.*, 93.    [8] Article 3(9) of the Kyoto Protocol.

[9] See BBC News 'Copenhagen deal reaction in quotes', accessed 16 January 2012, at http://news.bbc.co.uk/2/hi/8421910.stm (19 December 2009) (quoting José Manuel Barroso, EU Commission President: 'I will not hide my disappointment regarding the non-binding nature of the agreement here. In that respect the document falls far short of our expectations'; Xie Zhenhua, Head of China's Delegation, 'The meeting has had a positive result, everyone should be happy. After negotiations both sides have managed to preserve their bottom line. For the Chinese this was our sovereignty and our national interest.'; Lumumba Stanislaus Di-Aping, Head of the G-77 Group, '[The draft text] asks Africa to sign a suicide pact, an incineration pact in order to maintain the economic dominance of a few countries. It is a solution based on values, the very same values in our opinion that funnelled six million people in Europe into furnaces.'). See also J. Vidal, 'Rich and poor countries blame each other for failure of Copenhagen deal', 19 December 2009, www.guardian.co.uk.

[10] Officially, the Copenhagen conference was a joint meeting of the Fifteenth Session of the UNFCCC Conference of the Parties (COP 15) and the Fifth Session of the Kyoto Protocol Meeting of the Parties (CMP 5).

[11] See Copenhagen Accord, note 497, Appendix I and II.

[12] For the reduction targets, see Copenhagen Accord, note 497, Appendix I; see also J. Rogelj *et al.*, 'Analysis of the Copenhagen Accord Pledges and its Global Climatic

## 1 REGULATORY COMPETENCE ALLOCATION IN THE EU ETS  147

Regardless, these targets do not represent legally binding commitments, unlike the Kyoto Protocol commitments. Even more worryingly with respect to the development of global climate change policy, however, is the fact that the *mandate to create a legally binding negotiation outcome* has been deleted from the Copenhagen Accord, which means that although negotiations continue, their aim and scope is limited.[13]

The failure to come to an international agreement on the mitigation of and adaptation to climate change has strengthened existing claims regarding the inadequacies of the Kyoto Protocol,[14] and the call for a different vehicle for combating climate change.[15] The COP 17 meeting held in Durban in December 2011 has provided security regarding the continuation of a second commitment period for the Kyoto Protocol without a gap, which ensures the continuation of the Clean Development Mechanism (CDM) and Joint Implementation (JI) mechanism.[16] Moreover, a commitment has been made to 'clarifying the developed country Parties' quantified economy-wide emission reduction targets'.[17] Considering the approaching end of the first Kyoto Protocol commitment period, the failure to reach agreement on reduction commitments for the post-2012 period, specifically with respect to climate change mitigation through the setting of emission reduction targets,

---

Impacts – a Snapshot of Dissonant Ambitions' (2010) 5 *Environmental Research Letters* 1–9; D. Stern and F. Jotzo, 'How Ambitious are China and India's Emissions Intensity Targets?' (2010) 38 *Energy Policy* 6776–6783 (finding that China is likely to need to adopt ambitious carbon mitigation policies in order to achieve its stated target, and that its targeted reductions in emissions intensity are on a par with those implicit in the US and EU targets. India's target is less ambitious and might be met with only limited or even no dedicated mitigation policies).

[13] See R. S. Dimitrov, 'Inside Copenhagen: The State of Climate Governance' (2010) 2 *Global Environmental Politics* 18–24 at 22. See also D. Bodansky, 'The International Climate Change Regime: The Road from Copenhagen', Viewpoints Series, Harvard Project on International Climate Agreements (2010).

[14] D. Victor, *The Collapse of the Kyoto Protocol and the Struggle to Slow Global Warming* (Princeton University Press, 2001); D. H. Cole, 'Climate Change and Collective Action' (2008) 61 *Current Legal Problems* 229–264.

[15] See e.g. Dimitrov, 'Inside Copenhagen', 22; Pallemaerts and Oberthür (eds.), *The New Climate Policies*; H. Selin, and S. D. VanDeveer, *Changing Climates in North American Politics: Institutions, Policymaking and Multilevel Governance* (Cambridge, MA: MIT Press, 2009).

[16] A. Marcu, 'Post Durban: Moving to a Fragmented Carbon Market World?' 22 December 2011, available at: www.google.com/url?sa=t&rct=j&q=&esrc=s&source=web&cd=1&ved=0CCsQFjAA&url=http%3A%2F%2Fwww.ceps.eu%2Fceps%2Fdld%2F6530%2Fpdf&ei=NbGKUs_qH42isATbuIC4Dw&usg=AFQjCNHb_QYRGHbh8U60_OY8UWwsQHvvAw&bvm=bv.56643336,d.cWc.

[17] COP 17 (Durban) (2012), at 2.

has meant that (binding) norm setting can no longer be considered to take place exclusively, or even primarily, at the central level.[18] In our analysis of the post-2012 period, we witness a shift to norm setting at the European level.

## 2 EU action

From 2005 onwards, the growing prominence of the EU ETS helped to cement the leadership position that the EU and its Member States had adopted in lieu of action by the United States. The aspiring international leadership role of the EU has also given rise to increased policy-making on climate change and energy policy within the EU. Policy-making in these areas has always been an important *internal* issue for the EU, but has increasingly become part of the Union's external policies through attempts to influence international norm setting on climate change.[19] In March 2007, the Spring European Council under the German Presidency agreed on what would later be called the '20 20 by 2020' climate and energy package.[20] In this package, tabled by the Commission in January 2008, the EU heads of state and government agreed to:

- Achieve (at least) a 20 per cent reduction in greenhouse gas emissions from the 1990 level by 2020;

---

[18] See e.g. Ostrom, 'A Polycentric Approach for Coping with Climate Change'; Ostrom, 'Analysing Collective Action'; D. Bodansky, 'The Copenhagen Climate Change Conference: A Postmortem' (2010) 104 *The American Journal of International Law* 230–240 at 240 (stating that 'the Copenhagen Accord may well represent the high-water mark of the climate change regime for some time to come').

[19] See also C. Roche Kelly, S. Oberthür and M. Pallemaerts, 'Introduction, The EU's Internal and External Climate Policies: an Historical Overview', in M. Pallemaerts and S. Oberthür (eds.), *The New Climate Policies of the European Union* (Brussels: VUB Press, 2010) 11–26, at 14 ('In this context, three factors that have supported the EU's motivation for continued international leadership on climate change deserve particular highlighting. First, climate policy is an important driver of European integration in general ... The urgency and importance of the issue of climate change was increasing with the IPCC Fourth Assessment Report and public opinion polls showed high support for European-level action in this field ... Second, intensifying discussions on the security of energy supplies to Europe have leant strong support to the development of stringent climate policies ... Third, the position of the EU in the international system and its established strong support for multilateralism also reinforce EU leadership on climate change.'); and at 13 ('Since the early 1990s, the EU has established itself as the most prominent leader in international climate policy by pushing for stringent international commitments.')

[20] See also *ibid.*, 45 onwards.

## 1 REGULATORY COMPETENCE ALLOCATION IN THE EU ETS

- Increase the share of renewable energy sources to 20 per cent in 2020 (including a minimum target of a 10 per cent biofuel share);
- A saving of 20 per cent on the EU's projected energy consumption for 2020.

The Commission was tasked with the operationalization of these goals, which led to the 2008 Commission communication '20 20 by 2020 – Europe's climate change opportunity'.[21] The package was adopted by the Council and the Parliament on 17 December 2008, and became law in June 2009. It introduces four key pieces of legislation focusing on different elements of the EU's climate change and energy policy, all aimed at climate change mitigation through reduced greenhouse gas emissions:[22]

(i)   The large-scale revision of the EU ETS;[23]
(ii)  The Effort Sharing Agreement, setting out national emission targets for non-ETS sectors;[24]
(iii) Binding national renewable energy targets;[25] and
(iv)  A legal framework for the development and use of carbon capture and storage.[26]

Aside from setting out the internal climate change and energy policy, the 2020 package was an important signal to the international community regarding the European position for the ongoing UNFCCC and Kyoto Protocol negotiations. The European climate change and energy package may be considered as much a reaction to international policy-making efforts as an attempt to influence these efforts.[27] In a memo

---

[21] European Commission Communication of 23 January 2008, COM 30 (2008) 13 final.
[22] Alongside this legislation, the Commission also adopted a related set of amended guidelines on state aid for environmental protection. See European Commission 'Community Guidelines on state aid for environmental protection', OJ 2008 No. C82, 1 April 2008.
[23] Council Directive 2009/29/EC.
[24] Council Decision 406/2009/EC of 23 April 2009 on the effort of Member States to reduce their greenhouse gas emissions to meet the Community's greenhouse gas emission reduction commitments up to 2020, OJ 2009 No. L140 136.
[25] Council Directive 2009/28/EC of 23 April 2009 on the promotion of the use of energy from renewable sources and amending and subsequently repealing Directives 2001/77/EC and 2003/30/EC, OJ 2009 L.140 16, 5 June 2009.
[26] Council Directive 2009/31/EC. The Commission itself also adopted a set of amended guidelines on state aid for the environment.
[27] Skjærseth and Wettestad, 'The EU Emissions Trading System Revised', 86.

of November 2009, the position of the EU and its Member States for the Copenhagen climate negotiations is summarized as follows: 'The EU is pressing for a global, ambitious, comprehensive and legally binding international treaty [so that] global warming average temperature [is] kept below 2 degrees Celsius above the pre-industrial level.'[28] To achieve this goal, the European position was further specified as aiming for a peak in global greenhouse gas emissions in 2020, after which emissions should be halved from 1990 to 2050 and continue to decline thereafter. Industrialized countries should contribute to this goal with a 30 per cent reduction below 1990 levels by 2020, and developing countries should aim for a 15 to 30 per cent deviation below business-as-usual levels.[29] Aside from mitigation through greenhouse gas emission reduction, an international agreement should also include incentives to slow and stop tropical deforestation; reduce aviation and maritime transport emissions; include a Framework for Action on Adaptation; provide financing for research; and further develop financial flows through the carbon markets, the Clean Development Mechanism and Joint Implementation.[30]

Both the Revised Directive 2003/87/EC governing the ETS and the Effort Sharing Agreement refer explicitly to the consequences of a possible international agreement for EU emission reduction targets: the 20 per cent reduction target would be increased to 30 per cent, provided that other developed countries 'commit themselves to comparable emission reductions and economically more advanced developing countries commit themselves to contribute adequately'.[31] Article 28 of Revised Directive 2003/87/EC and Article 8 of the Effort Sharing Agreement furthermore provide a mandate for the Commission to report on a possible set of adjustments that would be applicable in the event of the approval of an international agreement on climate change by the EU.[32] The failure of the Copenhagen COP has meant that the conditions for the EU to move towards a 30 per cent reduction target

---

[28] Council Conclusions of 21 October 2009 on EU position for the Copenhagen Climate Conference, 2968th Environmental Council meeting. Accessed 21 January 2012 at www.consilium.europa.eu/uedocs/cms_data/docs/pressdata/en/envir/110634.pdf.

[29] *Ibid.*, at para. 8.

[30] *Ibid.*, at paras. 28, 19, 22, 25 and 41, respectively.

[31] Preamble 3 and Article 1 of Council Directive 2003/87/EC; Decision 406/2009/EC, Preamble 3, Articles 1 and 8.

[32] Article 28 of European Council Directive 2003/87/EC; Article 8(6) of Decision 406/2009/EC.

were not met.[33] Given the lack of action at the international level and by comparable economies, a move to the 30 per cent level was not considered feasible,[34] which means that the target of a 20 per cent reduction of greenhouse gas emission below 1990 levels remains in force for the period from 2013 to 2020.

In the absence of an international agreement with legally binding reduction targets, such as the Kyoto Protocol for the 2008–2012 period, this 20 per cent reduction target constitutes the policy goal underlying our analysis. The European goal of a 20 per cent reduction below 1990 levels encompasses the whole of the European economy, divided between the ETS and the non-ETS sectors. As 2005 was the first year for which reliable Member State level emissions data for the ETS and the non-ETS sectors were available, the ETS and non-ETS targets take 2005 as the base year, despite the reference to 1990 in many of the earlier policy documents.[35] A 20 per cent reduction target compared to 1990 translates to a 14 per cent reduction compared to 2005, with the ETS sectors having to reduce by 21 per cent compared to 2005,[36] and the non-ETS sectors by 10 per cent compared to 2005, as illustrated in Figure 4.1.

Between the revised ETS Directive and the new Effort Sharing Agreement, there are some important changes from the existing regulatory system for greenhouse gas reductions, such as the inclusion of all EU Member States in the Effort Sharing Agreement, as opposed to the EU15 in the comparable Burden Sharing Agreement, and the

[33] Nevertheless, the Commission published a communication regarding the risks of carbon leakage in the event that the EU moved beyond the 20 per cent reduction target, also taking into consideration the changed (global) economic circumstances since the creation of EU policy in 2008, see Commission Communication of 26 May 2010, 'Analysis of options to move beyond 20% greenhouse gas emission reductions and assessing the risk of carbon leakage', COM(2010) 265 final.

[34] Commission Communication of 26 May 2010, 'Analysis of options to move beyond 20% greenhouse gas emission reductions and assessing the risk of carbon leakage', COM(2010) 265 final, at 11, 13 (The Commission found that the economic crisis reduced the absolute costs of achieving the 20 per cent target, but the potential of the target to provide incentives for technological change is likewise reduced).

[35] N. Lacasta, S. Oberthür, E. Santos and P. Barata, 'From Sharing the Burden to Sharing the Effort: Decision 406/2009/EC on Member State Emission Targets for Non-ETS Sectors' in M. Pallemaerts and S. Oberthür (eds.), *The New Climate Policies of the European Union* (Brussels: VUB Press, 2011) 93–116, at 103.

[36] The ETS sectors now also include the aviation sector from 2012 onwards. See Council Directive 2008/101/EC. The 2012 cap was set at 97 per cent of average 2004–2006 airline emissions, and 85 per cent of allowances would be allocated for free. From 2013 onwards, the cap would be set at 95 per cent of average 2004–2006 emissions.

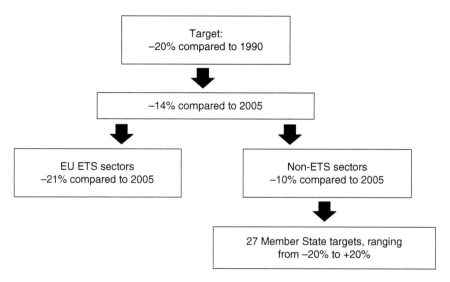

FIGURE 4.1 *The revised EU ETS Directive and the Effort Sharing Agreement*
Source: European Commission, Questions and Answers on the Effort Sharing Decision, http://ec.europa.eu/clima/policies/effort/faq_En.htm.

emphasis on per capita GDP in the setting of Effort Sharing Agreement emission reduction targets. With respect to the ETS, Article 9 of Directive 2009/29/EC introduces an EU-wide cap based on the 21 per cent reduction target (compared to 2005). This cap translates to a 1.74 per cent reduction per year from 2013 onwards, compared to the average annual total quantity issued by Member States in their NAPs for the period 2008 to 2012.[37]

In the absence of international norm setting with corresponding legally binding greenhouse gas reduction targets, the cap setting by the EU under the '20 20 by 2020' programme may be considered a decentralization of norm-setting competences from the global to the regional level. At the same time, through the translation of these norms to specific caps for the ETS and non-ETS sectors, which effectively abolishes

---

[37] See extensively Article 9 of Council Directive 2003/87/EC. For installations which are unilaterally included by Member States as an addition to the European scheme under Article 24(1) and installations carrying out activities under Annex I, which are only included from 2013 onwards, the Member States were under an obligation to submit additional data before 30 April 2010. Articles 9a(1) and (2) European Council Directive 2003/87/EC of 13 October 2003 establishing a scheme for greenhouse gas emission allowance trading within the Community and amending Council Directive 96/61/EC, OJ 2003 No. L275.

the need for National Allocation Plans (NAPs) with respect to the ETS sectors, implementation competences (cap distribution) are also moved to the European level.

## B Implementation

As in the first two trading phases, a distinction can be made between cap substantive and procedural rules, relating to cap-division and allowance allocation respectively. With respect to both sets of rules, substantive changes are foreseen for the post-2012 period. Aside from the abolition of the NAPs, the shift from grandfathering emission allowances to auctioning will have a considerable impact.

## 1 Substantive rules: cap-division

The process of cap-division has been much simplified through the abolition of the NAPs and the adoption of a yearly diminishing cap (1.74 per cent/year from 2013 onwards).[38] The competences to administer this cap have moved completely to the European level, taking an important implementation competence out of the hands of the Member States. In addition, the practice of grandfathering is to be phased out and replaced by auctioning. This means that all allowances not allocated free of charge must be auctioned from 2013 onwards. However, the move to auctioning will be gradual and full auctioning is not reached for the non-carbon leakage sensitive sectors until 2027.[39] In 2013, roughly half of the EU allowances for installations (EUAs) and 15 per cent of the EU aviation allowances (EUAAs) will be auctioned.[40]

The amount of allowances that Member States will be able to auction off depends on the division of the Community-wide cap by the Commission pursuant to Article 9, which has been subject to intense discussion and received much attention in the Proposal for the

---

[38] Article 9 of Council Directive 2003/87/EC.

[39] *Ibid.* ('The level of auctioning of allowances for non-exposed industry will increase in a linear manner as proposed by the Commission, but rather than reaching 100% by 2020 it will reach 70%, with a view to reaching 100% by 2027').

[40] MEMO/10/338, 'Emissions trading: Questions and Answers on the EU ETS Auctioning Regulation', 16 July 2010, para. 5. More generally, it should be noted that from 2013, the scope of the ETS is extended to include other sectors and greenhouse gases. Inter alia, more $CO_2$ emissions from installations producing bulk organic chemicals, hydrogen, ammonia and aluminium are included, as are nitrous oxide ($N_2O$) emissions from the production of nitric, adipic and glycolic acid production and perfluorocarbons from the aluminium sector. Installations performing activities that result in these emissions are included in the EU ETS from 2013.

Directive and the accompanying Impact Assessment.[41] The final division attempts to reconcile two policies: (i) preventing differentiation between ETS sectors in different Member States since this could lead to distortions of the internal market and lessen economic efficiency[42] and (ii) ensuring solidarity with the so-called 'low GDP per capita' Member States which may be inequitably affected by the introduction of auctioning.[43] In the end, a compromise was found between these goals in the decision to subdivide the total of the Community-wide allowances into three parts:[44]

(i) 88 per cent of the total quantity of allowances is to be divided among the Member States in shares identical to the share of verified emissions under the ETS for 2005, or the average from 2005 to 2007;

(ii) 10 per cent of the total quantity will be distributed among the 'low GDP per capita' Member States for the purpose of solidarity and growth;[45]

(iii) 2 per cent of the total quantity will be distributed among Member States whose greenhouse gas emissions in 2005 were at least 20 per cent below their respective Kyoto levels (the 'Kyoto-bonus').[46]

With the division of the cap made at the Commission level and the corresponding abolition of the NAPs, substantive implementation competences have been centralized at the European level.

## 2 Procedural rules: allowance allocation

The allocation of allowances during the first two trading phases primarily took place through grandfathering, with only 5 to 10 per cent of

---

[41] Commission Impact Assessment of 23 January 2008.

[42] Commission Proposal, COM(2008) 30 final, Preamble 17.

[43] The Commission used several models to illustrate the different (auctioning) scenarios and consider the impacts on the different countries, see Commission Impact Assessment of 23 January 2008, at 32–70. For the GDP data used for the purposes of revision of Directive 2003/87/EC, see Commission Impact Assessment of 23 January 2008.

[44] See Article 10(2) of Commission Proposal of 23 January 2008. The division of the total number of allowances can be found in Article 10 of Council Directive 2009/29/EC.

[45] The division between the low GDP Member States can be found in Commission Proposal of 23 January 2008 for a Directive amending Directive 2003/87/EC so as to improve and extend the greenhouse gas emission allowance trading system of the Community, COM(2008) 30 final, Annex IIa.

[46] This distribution can be found in *ibid.*, Annex IIb.

allowances eligible for auctioning.[47] This has changed for the post-2012 period, where the emphasis shifts to auctioning. In terms of competence allocation, the substantive rules regarding auctioning are contained in the revised Directive 2003/87/EC. The procedural rules regarding the actual auctioning of allowances are a different matter since Directive 2009/29/EC's initial guidance regarding the auctioning of allowances was limited, suggesting that the Member States would retain a large amount of discretion in respect of the auctions.[48]

However, Regulation 1031/2010 on the timing, administration and other aspects of auctioning (the Auctioning Regulation) proved to be rather prescriptive in setting out the structure of the auction system.[49] The Regulation details the nature of the auctioned products,[50] the method of bidding,[51] the auction calendar,[52] access to the auctions,[53] and the appointments of the auctioneer and auction monitor.[54] In the Impact Assessment preceding the Regulation,[55] the Commission set out three formats for the auctioning process: a centralized approach where auctions are conducted on behalf of all Member States through a single EU-wide auction process;[56] a coordinated approach consisting of a limited number of auction processes set up by Member States either individually or jointly;[57] and a hybrid approach, which would divide the auction process in two by collecting bids through individual trading places in pre-determined timeslots after which a clearing price would be determined. Consequent payment and delivery would then be completed through the individual trading places and revenues would automatically flow to the Member States.[58]

---

[47] Articles 10 and 11 of Council Directive 2003/87/EC.
[48] Article 10(4) of Council Directive 2009/29/EC (auctions are to be conducted in in an 'open, transparent, harmonized and non-discriminatory manner', open to participants of all nationalities – also from outside the European Community, and small emitters must be guaranteed access. Moreover, auctions need to be cost-efficient and the same information must be given to all participants.)
[49] Commission Regulation 1031/2010 of 12 November 2010 on the timing, administration and other aspects of auctioning of greenhouse gas emission allowances pursuant to Directive 2003/87/EC of the European Parliament and of the Council establishing a scheme for greenhouse gas emission allowances trading within the Community, OJ 2010 No. L302, 18 November 2010.
[50] *Ibid.*, Article 4.   [51] *Ibid.*, Articles 5–7.   [52] *Ibid.*, Articles 8–14.
[53] *Ibid.*, Articles 15–21.   [54] *Ibid.*, Articles 22–23 and 24–25.
[55] European Commission Impact Assessment of 8 February 2010 accompanying the Commission Regulation on the timing, administration and other aspects of auctioning of greenhouse gas emission allowances pursuant to Article 10(4) of Directive 2003/87/EC, SEC(2010).
[56] *Ibid.*, at 10.   [57] *Ibid.*   [58] *Ibid.*

In the Impact Assessment, the Commission expresses a strong preference for the centralized approach based on the efficiency of this option.[59] Most Member States also expressed their support to a centralized process, with the exception of some of the large emitters Member States – United Kingdom, Poland, Germany and Spain[60]– who prefer to control their own auctions.[61] The Auctioning Regulation reflects this lack of consensus regarding the centralized approach by providing for one auction platform to be created through a joint procurement procedure between the Commission and the Member States,[62] *and* for alternative platforms to be created through opt-outs by Member States.[63] The United Kingdom, Germany and Poland have notably opted out of the common platform.[64] They will nevertheless have to submit detailed documentation regarding the identity and operating rules of the auction platform to the Commission, which may review the notifications to a certain extent.[65] It is unclear what the nature of the Commission's review power is but there is mention of 'modified notifications'.[66] This suggests that the Commission's power of review is comparable to that of the NAPs of Phases I and II, rather than having the 'complete' centralization it preferred, as witnessed by the Impact Assessment.

## 3 Execution: institutions

The execution of the implementation of the EU ETS was always foreseen to take place at the Member State level. Article 18 of Directive 2003/87/EC provides that Member States shall make the 'appropriate

---

[59] *Ibid.*, at 23.

[60] Germany also raised several subsidiarity concerns regarding the centralized approach.

[61] Commission Impact Assessment of 8 February 2010, at 37. Other Member States are in favour of centralization but are pessimistic about the feasibility of this approach. Member States in favour of centralization include Sweden, Finland, Denmark, Austria, France, Italy and the Netherlands. The Netherlands proposed a hybrid outcome in case of a failure to agree on the centralized approach. The United Kingdom proposed an opt-out system for the initial stage with eventual convergence to the centralized approach. See Commission Impact Assessment, at 37.

[62] Articles 26–29, Commission Regulation 1031/2010.

[63] Articles 30–32, Commission Regulation 1031/2010. See also recitals 6–8 (adding that any remaining risk of reduced competition in the carbon market through a common auction platform will be mitigated through an opt-out possibility for Member States).

[64] European Commission, 'Common platform for auctioning carbon allowances in the third phase of the EU Emissions Trading System' (press release, 21 February 2011). Accessed 13 January 2012 at http://ec.europa.eu/clima/news/articles/news_2011022101_En.htm.

[65] Article 30(6) of Commission Regulation 1031/2010.   [66] *Ibid.*, Article 30(6).

administrative arrangements, including the designation of the appropriate competent authority or authorities, for the implementation of the rules of this Directive'.[67] This provision remains essentially unchanged after the adoption of Directive 2009/29/EC, only supplemented by additional provisions regarding Member States' responsibilities regarding the administration of aviation activities, which are included in the EU ETS from 2012 onwards.[68] Member States are also required to put in place registries that oversee the accounting of allowance trades.[69] In respect of the latter, there has been some centralization through the adoption of standardized electronic databases provided by the Commission.[70] Moreover, Member States are allowed to maintain their registries together with one or more other Member State.[71] Alongside the decentralized registries and authorities put in place by the Member States, the Commission is responsible for designating a Central Administrator 'to maintain an independent transaction log recording the issue, transfer and cancellation of allowances'.[72] This Central Administrator conducts automated checks on transactions and reports irregularities to the relevant Member State, who is then responsible for following up on the matter.[73]

The shift to increased auctioning also has some institutional implications. Once the legislation regarding the auctioning platforms is put in place, Member States or groups of Member States will administer the auctions. Here, a certain level of harmonization is foreseen with respect to the manner of auctioning, in contrast to the auctioning revenues, which are considered to be at the discretion of the Member States. The Auctioning Regulation stipulates that each Member State will appoint an auctioneer who will receive and distribute the auction proceeds to each Member State.[74] This confirms the provisions contained in Article 10(3) of Directive 2009/29/EC, which states that Member States shall determine the use of revenues generated from the auctioning of allowances. However, Article 10(3) also states that at least 50 per cent of the revenues made by auctioning the allowances of the 88 per cent share

---

[67] Article 18 of Council Directive 2003/87/EC.
[68] Council Directive 2008/101/EC.
[69] Article 19(1) of Commission Regulation No. 920/2010 of 7 October 2010 for a standardized and secured system of registries pursuant to Directive 2003/87/EC of the European Parliament and of the Council and Decision No 280/2004/EC of the European Parliament and of the Council, OJ 2010 L270, 14 October 2010.
[70] *Ibid.*  [71] *Ibid.*  [72] *Ibid.*, Article 20 (1).  [73] *Ibid.*, Article 20(2).
[74] Article 23(b) and (c) of Commission Regulation 1031/2010.

referred to in Article 10(2)(a) and the total amount of revenues made by auctioning the 'solidarity' ten per cent stipulated in Article 10(2)(b) should be used for certain specific aims.[75] There has been some discussion as to whether this use of revenues constituted a binding requirement on the part of the Member States after the adoption of Directive 2009/29/EC.[76] Although there is no mention of the use of revenues in the Regulation aside from the role of the auctioneer in transferring them, the preamble of the Regulation stresses that Member States determine the use of revenues, *as provided by* Article 10(3) of Directive 2009/29/EC.[77] The extent to which the Commission will be able to influence the earmarking (and spending) of auctioning revenues for certain aims remains to be seen but is likely to be (very) limited.[78]

## C Enforcement

The enforcement processes covered by Articles 14 to 16 of Directive 2003/87/EC for the first and second trading phase were modified only

---

[75] Article 10(3) of Council Directive 2009/29/EC (These aims include: (a) to reduce greenhouse gas emissions; (b) to develop renewable energies to meet the commitment of the Community to use 20 per cent renewable energies by 2020; (c) measures to avoid deforestation and increase afforestation and reforestation in developing countries that have ratified the international agreement on climate change; (d) forestry sequestration in the community; (e) the environmentally safe capture and geological storage of $CO_2$, in particular from solid fossil fuel power stations and a range of industrial sectors and subsectors, including in non-EU countries; (f) to encourage a shift to low-emission and public forms of transport; (g) to finance research and development in energy efficiency and clean technologies in the sectors covered by this Directive; (h) measures intended to increase energy efficiency and insulation or to provide financial support in order to address social aspects in lower and middle income households; (i) to cover the administrative expenses of the management of the Community scheme.)

[76] See J. A. W. van Zeben, '(De)Centralized Law-making in the EU ETS' (2009) 3 *Carbon & Climate Law Review* 340–356 at 353 ('This provision is not legally binding for the Member States; the use of the words "should be" makes it clear that it is a non-legally binding suggestion, which the Commission will not be able to enforce. That said, Article 10(3) also states that Member States "shall be deemed to have fulfilled the[se] provisions [...] if they have in place and implemented fiscal or financial support policies [...] Member States shall inform the Commission as to the use of revenues and actions taken pursuant to this paragraph in their reports." The obligation to report is real and the words "shall be deemed to have fulfilled" suggests that there is a more binding character to Article 10(3) than one would prima facie expect.')

[77] Commission Regulation 1031/2010, recital 37. Emphasis added. The wording of the preamble seems to indicate a clarification of the original wording of Article 10(3) (though lacking any legal force).

[78] See also European Commission (23 November 2011), which refers to 'put[ting] in place operational rules for Member States to report on their use of revenues from the auctioning of allowances in the EU emissions trading system (EU ETS). Member States

# 1 REGULATORY COMPETENCE ALLOCATION IN THE EU ETS 159

slightly by Directive 2009/29/EC. The changes between Phases II and III were relatively limited and related primarily to the expansion of the EU ETS into additional sectors of the economy, specifically aviation. As such, the decentralization of enforcement competences appears to be a constant factor within the overall division of competences within the EU ETS.[79]

## 1 Monitoring and reporting

A key change regarding monitoring and reporting, as mentioned in the Revised Directive 2003/87, is the addition of provisions relating to the inclusion of the aviation section in the EU ETS.[80] From 2012 onwards, aviation emissions are covered by the EU ETS,[81] which requires additional monitoring and reporting by airline operators, supervised by the Member States.[82] Aside from the provisions in Revised Directive 2003/87, specific guidelines are set out in Decision 2009/339/EC which

---

have committed to spend at least half of the revenue from such auctions to fight climate change in the EU and third countries.'

[79] Combined with the highly technical and complex nature of the provisions, this may explain why most of the literature on the EU ETS has thus far focused on the policy side of the EU ETS. Monitoring, reporting, verification and penalties are seldom mentioned in academic discussions about the EU ETS and if so, only as complementary to an analysis of lawmaking within the EU ETS. Contributions focusing solely on the enforcement processes are predominantly found as policy documents by institutions such as the OECD, see for instance, S. Peterson, 'Monitoring, Accounting and Enforcement in Emissions Trading Regimes', OECD Global Forum on Sustainable Development: Emissions Trading, Concerted Action on Tradable Emissions Permits Country Forum CCNM/GF/SD/ENV(2003)5/FINAL (2008). cf. Peeters, 'Inspection and Market-Based Regulation'; Stranlund, Chavez, and Field, 'Enforcing Emissions Trading Programs'. This is in sharp contrast with the increasing criticism of the UNFCCC system as lacking reliable enforcement mechanisms and the importance of good monitoring and enforcement for the success of environmental regulation, and climate change regulation, generally. See e.g. R. B. Stewart and J. B. Wiener, *Reconstructing Climate Policy: Beyond Kyoto* (Washington, DC: Aei Press, 2007), 60; D. Victor, 'Fragmented Carbon Markets and Reluctant Nations: Implications for the Design of Effective Architectures', in J. E. Aldy and R. N. Stavins (eds.), *Architectures for Agreement: Addressing Global Climate Change in a Post-Kyoto World* (Cambridge University Press, 2007) 133–160, at 142.

[80] Council Directive 2008/101/EC.

[81] The aviation emissions covered by the scheme include emissions from all European Member States plus Iceland, Liechtenstein and Norway, the EEA Member States also covered by the EU ETS (see EEA Joint Committee Decision No 146/2007 amending Annex XX (Environment) to the EEA Agreement, OJ 2007 No. L100) 92 (2007).

[82] Article 14(3) of European Council Directive 2003/87/EC ('Member States shall ensure that each operator of an installation or an aircraft operator monitors and reports the emissions from that installation during each calendar year, or, from 1 January 2010,

amends Decision 2007/589/EC.[83] Except for the changes in terms of scope, there is little difference in the provisions for monitoring and reporting themselves. The main responsibility remains with the operators while the Member States are responsible for making sure that monitoring and verification obligations are met.

In line with the described shared responsibility for monitoring and reporting, Member States must ensure that reports submitted by operators are verified in accordance with criteria set out in Annex V to the Revised Directive 2003/87.[84] The Commission had to adopt a regulation specifying the verification process of reports based on the Annex V criteria by 31 December 2011.[85] If such verification proves to be unsatisfactory, the operator in question is barred from making further allowance transfers.[86] In light of the inclusion of aviation, Member States are now also obliged to publish the names of both operators and aircraft operators that fail to surrender sufficient allowances. Directive 2009/29/EC moreover provides that the penalty shall increase in accordance with the European index of consumer prices.[87] For the aviation sector, specific additional penalties are available, allowing Member States to request from the Commission an operating ban on an aircraft operator.[88]

## 2 Verification and penalties

The practices regarding verification and penalties have not gone through any significant changes between the second and third trading phase. The most noteworthy development in this area has been the increased awareness of the need for market oversight in addition to individual verification. Incidents involving VAT fraud and allowance theft during the second trading phase led to an increased salience of these issues and the publication of Communication 'Towards an enhanced market oversight framework for the EU Emissions Trading Scheme'.[89] This Communication covers all behaviour as defined in the Market Abuse Directive as 'market abuse', namely insider dealing and

---

the aircraft which it operates, to the competent authority after the end of that year in accordance with the regulation referred to in paragraph 1.')

[83] Commission Decision 2009/339/EC.
[84] Article 15 of Council Directive 2003/87/EC.
[85] *Ibid.*  [86] *Ibid.*  [87] *Ibid.*, Article 16(4).
[88] *Ibid.*, Article 16(5)–(10). Detailed provisions regarding the procedure surrounding this penalty have not yet developed but may be established through comitology. Whether this will in fact happen remains unclear. See *ibid.*, Article 16(12).
[89] Commission Communication, COM(2010) 796 final.

# 1 REGULATORY COMPETENCE ALLOCATION IN THE EU ETS    161

market manipulation.[90] In addition, the Communication refers to some other types of manipulation such as money laundering, terrorist financing and other criminal activities.[91] The lack of harmonized accounting standards is also considered harmful for the transparency and overall efficiency of the market, and is set to be addressed through cooperation with the International Accounting Standards Board and the Financial Accounting Standards Board.[92]

Before the Communication and the Commission's efforts to regulate in this area, trading on the EU ETS market was already subject to financial markets regulation under the Market Abuse Directive by virtue of emission allowances qualifying as a financial instrument in a regulated market.[93] Similarly, emission allowance derivatives are also subject to regulation under the Markets in Financial Instruments Directive (MiFID) when traded on a regulated market or a 'multilateral trading facility'.[94] These two instruments impose a number of operational and reporting requirements, yet due to the differences between the national provisions for allowance trading, not all emission allowances are covered by the same regime.[95] Overall, the Commission concludes that the liquidity of the ETS market is satisfactory and that a major part of the market is already subject to market regulation through the financial markets regulation.[96] Some blind-spots remain, however, including, spot trading, which is currently regulated at the Member State level, if at all, and the future primary auctioning market, which will be covered by the Auctioning Regulation.[97] With respect to verification and penalties, the Member States will continue to hold most executory powers and responsibilities, which explains the existing differences in national regimes, but there will be increased guidance from the European level, particularly with respect to market regulation (as opposed to the monitoring of individual installations).

In December 2011, the Commission proposed two new regulations regarding the monitoring, reporting and verification of greenhouse gas emissions.[98] These regulations set out new provisions

---

[90] Council Directive 2003/6/EC of 28 January 2003 on insider dealing and market manipulation (market abuse), OJ 2003 No. L96 16, 12 April 2003.
[91] Commission Communication, COM(2010) 796 final, at 6.
[92] *Ibid.*    [93] *Ibid.*, at 7.    [94] Council Directive 2004/39/EC.
[95] Commission Communication of 21 December 2010, at 8.    [96] *Ibid.*, at 9.
[97] *Ibid.*, at 10.
[98] Commission Communication, Proposal of 20 October 2011 for a Directive of the European Parliament and of the Council on markets in financial instruments repealing Directive 2004/39/EC of the European Parliament and of the Council

with respect to verification, in order to ensure that the criteria for competent verifiers are the same in all Member States, and verifiable, objective and transparent.[99] The criteria for verification in all Member States have thereby been harmonized since January 2013. The proposed Regulation on monitoring and enforcement builds on the 2007 Commission Decision establishing guidelines on monitoring and reporting and sets out future harmonization in this area.[100] Significantly, the Regulation requires Member States with more than one competent authority to coordinate the work of these authorities in order to prevent duplication.[101]

## D  EU ETS competence allocation – Phase III

Despite their shortcomings, the UNFCCC and Kyoto Protocol were able to capture an international consensus with legally binding emission reduction commitments, which formed the basis for the first two trading periods of the EU ETS. The international negotiations that were meant to secure similar, or even more extensive, commitments for the post-2012 period have so far failed to secure legally binding targets. As a result, the competence allocation for the third trading phase of the EU ETS moves away from our first-best scenario of global norm setting to our second-best scenario with regional norm setting. For implementation and enforcement, the allocation situation has become increasingly complex. With respect to implementation, discretion regarding substantive rules has also shifted to the European level with the abolition of the NAPs. The procedural rules and execution remain primarily in the hands of the Member States. Since these elements are both crucial for successful implementation, this must be considered a shared allocation at the European and Member State level. Similarly, enforcement by European institutions exercises increased control over market oversight enforcement, while the enforcement competences with respect

---

(Recast), COM(2011) 656 final, and Commission Regulation No. 601/2012 of 21 June 2012 on the monitoring and reporting of greenhouse gas emissions pursuant to Directive 2003/87/EC of the European Parliament and of the Council.

[99] Commission Proposal, 20 October 2011.

[100] The proposed Regulation represents the first binding document on monitoring and enforcement aside from the provisions in Directive 2003/87 and warrants further discussion. However, given the scope of this publication, we focus only on those aspects that pertain to competence allocation.

[101] Commission Regulation No. 601/2012 of 21 June 2012 on the monitoring and reporting of greenhouse gas emissions pursuant to Directive 2003/87/EC of the European Parliament and of the Council, at Preamble 4 and Article 10.

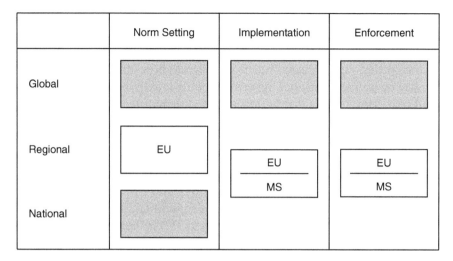

FIGURE 4.2 *Competence allocation in Phase III of the EU ETS*

to insufficient allowances remain with the Member States, as reflected in Figure 4.2.

## 2 Regulatory functioning

Broadly speaking, the picture that emerges of Phase III of the EU ETS is one of competence concentration at the European level. Both norm setting and substantial implementation – specifically norm distribution – are placed in the hands of the European institutions, and the European role in market oversight elements of enforcement is similarly increased. In terms of norm setting, the system of competence allocation for Phase III corresponds more closely to our second-best scenario of regional norm setting.[102] In this section, individual competence allocations are analysed in light of our allocation criteria (section 2.A) and we consider changes in competence interactions and their welfare implications (section 2.B).

### A Competence allocation

#### 1 Norm setting

For the period between 2013 and 2020, norm-setting competences have moved from the global to the regional European level. Depending on

---

[102] See Chapter 2.

how international action on climate change and its mitigation develops, this situation is likely to continue after 2020.[103] With respect to our first-order consideration as to the ability of the allocation to capture externalities, this regional norm is a second-best allocation: the desirability of an international agreement with legally binding cap-setting and reduction targets is inherent to the externalities problem posed by climate change.[104] In its preparatory documents for the international negotiations under the UNFCCC and Kyoto Protocol,[105] the European Union explicitly makes the tightening of the European target from 20 to 30 per cent conditional on the existence of a legally binding international agreement. In doing so, it underlines that – in this classic collective action problem – the willingness of individual, or groups of, countries to act depends on the action of others.[106] The consequent failure of the international community to reach such a binding agreement leads to a second-best scenario of coordinated regional action, in this case through the EU's '20 20 by 2020' policy. The resulting regional norm-setting process fails to capture the externalities of European greenhouse gas emitting activities due to:

(i) The ability for European companies to move (part of) their activities outside the EU to other countries that do not impose similar restrictions (i.e. carbon leakage); and

(ii) The possibility of European countries overburdening non-ETS sectors. This can moreover result in a loss of cost-effectiveness given heterogeneous abatement costs between sectors.

[103] The '20 20 by 2020' package runs until 2020 but some policy goals have already been expressed until 2050, see Commission Communication of 8 March 2011, 'A Roadmap for moving to a competitive low carbon economy in 2050', COM(2011) 112 final. Moreover, the next trading period for the EU ETS runs from 2013 to 2020 but is foreseen to continue indefinitely thereafter.

[104] The failure of the international community to take coordinated and effective action on climate change has led to calls for a more 'bottom-up' approach to the problem. Examples of alternative methods of regulation are presented by, e.g., Ostrom, 'Analysing Collective Action'; Cole, 'From Global to Polycentric Climate Governance'; and Stewart, Oppenheimer and Rudyk, 'Building Blocks for Global Climate Protection'.

[105] Council Conclusions of 21 October 2009 on EU position for the Copenhagen Climate Conference, 2968th Environmental Council meeting. Accessed 21 January 2012 at www.consilium.europa.eu/uedocs/cms_data/docs/pressdata/en/envir/110634.pdf.

[106] See F. Parisi and N. Ghei, 'The Role of Reciprocity in International Law' (2003) 36 *Cornell International Law Journal* 93–123; Cole, 'Climate Change and Collective Action'; Ostrom, 'Analysing Collective Action', and J. Paavola, 'Climate Change: The Ultimate "Tragedy of the Commons"?' in D. Cole and E. Ostrom (eds.), *Property in Land and Other Resources* (Cambridge, MA: Lincoln Institute of Land Policy, 2011) 417–433.

Carbon leakage depends on many factors, including the development and form of a post-Kyoto binding international agreement and any parallel or alternative action taken by (groups of) countries with greenhouse gas emission targets.[107] However, the uncertainty regarding the development of climate change mitigation policies in other regions may complicate industries' policies with respect to production levels and emission reduction investment decisions, which are typically made with long time horizons. Apart from policies in non-EU countries, industries must also consider the possibility of additional European policies that would charge goods imported from, and produced in, non-EU countries with lower environmental standards.[108] If these policies were to become a reality, the move of production to non-EU countries would become less beneficial. In addition, carbon leakage is a major point of contestation for European industries, which have lobbied extensively for European benchmarks for 'carbon leakage sensitive' sectors.[109] This has resulted in extensive carbon leakage reports issued by the European Commission, which are the basis for free allocation benchmarks.[110]

Within the EU, the externalization of costs between the ETS and non-ETS sectors has proven problematic in the first two trading phases, aggravated by the over-allocation with respect to the ETS sectors. The combined EU norm for ETS and non-ETS sectors through the Effort Sharing Agreement holds several advantages over the pre-2013 situation. With respect to the ETS sectors, the move away from the NAP system is a marked improvement since there fewer possibilities to undercut country targets.[111] The NAPs now only cover

---

[107] Stewart, Oppenheimer and Rudyk, 'Building Blocks for Global Climate Protection'.

[108] Commission Communication, COM(2011) 112 final, at 7. See also R. V. Anuradha, 'Unilateral Carbon Border Measures: Key Legal Issues', ICRIER Policy Series, No. 2 (2011); B. Dhar and K. Das, 'The European Union's Proposed Carbon Equalization System: Can it be WTO Compatible?' Research and Information System for Developing Countries, Discussion Paper 15 (2009); C. Fisher and A. Fox, 'Comparing Policies to Combat Emissions Leakage' Resources for the Future Discussion Paper 09–0 (2009).

[109] See also Chapter 5.

[110] See e.g. M. Bergmann, A. Schmitz, M. Hayden and K. Kosonen, 'Imposing a Unilateral Carbon Constraint on Energy-Intensive Industries and its Impact on their International Competitiveness: Data and Analysis', European Economy Economic Papers 298 (2007); Council Directive 2009/31/EC; Commission Decision of 17 December 2012 amending Decisions 2010/2/EU and 2011/278/EU as regards the sectors and subsectors which are deemed to be exposed to a significant risk of carbon leakage, OJ 2012 No. L241/52, 7 September 2012. See also Article 10 of Council Directive 2009/29/EC.

[111] Commission Proposal, COM(2008) 30 final, at 2 (stating that the over-allocation had meant that Phase I was a failure in respect of actual emissions reductions despite

the non-ETS sectors, which are less likely to be overburdened by the Member States due to the additional enforcement procedures introduced by Article 7 of Decision 406/2009/EC. In general, the wider availability of reliable data makes the monitoring and verification of Member State efforts more effective, limiting the scope for detrimental implementation.[112]

Under global norm setting, the heterogeneity of conditions in different regions and countries was taken into account through the differentiation of norms for these regions and countries on the basis of historic and current emission levels. At the European level, norms can take specific account of the individual Member State's economic situation, beyond what had been possible at the international level, where benchmarks were set based on past industry emissions. Aside from the (increasingly controversial)[113] distinction between developed and developing countries, no special notice was (or arguably could be) taken of countries' economic circumstances.[114] The EU's attempt to address some of the inequities and inefficiencies of the Kyoto reduction targets through the 1998 Burden Sharing Agreement was only partly successful; marginal abatement costs among Member States were not fully equalized since this would have resulted in (even) higher emissions allowances for relatively poorer Member States.[115] For the post-2013 period,

---

its success in creating an emission allowances market). The Commission's official position regarding the cause of failure was that the limited availability of verified data made it difficult to estimate the number of allowances correctly (Commission Proposal, at 2), but analyses of the approved NAPs for Phase II indicate that, based on several models of emission projections, these NAPs would also result in an excess of allowances which would lead to a low carbon price and low investment in low-carbon technology despite improved information availability. See primarily Neuhoff, *et al.*, 'Emission projections'; Neuhoff, *et al.*, 'Implications of Announced Phase II Plans'.

[112] One of the key points of contestation in the *Poland/Estonia* v. *Commission* cases was the use of data. The Commission argued that their data regarding the emissions of these countries was more reliable than that used by the respective Member States. See Case T-183/07, *Poland* v. *European Commission* [2009] ECR II-03395 and Case T-263/07, *Estonia* v. *European Commission* [2009] ECR II-03463.

[113] Stewart, Oppenheimer and Rudyk, 'Building Blocks for Global Climate Protection', at 10.

[114] For the benchmarking system used in the UNFCCC process, see J. P. Bruce, H. Lee and E. F. Haites (eds.), *Economic and Social Dimensions of Climate Change: Contribution of Working Group III to the Second Assessment Report of the IPCC* (Cambridge University Press, 1995), 32–33.

[115] Lacasta, Oberthür, Santos and Barata, 'From Sharing the Burden to Sharing the Effort', 97.

the marginal abatement costs have been equalized across all Member States and all sectors, both for greenhouse gas emission reductions as well as for the deployment of renewable energy.[116] The consequent possibility for Member States to trade allowances inter se for the non-ETS sectors can be considered an improvement to the Burden Sharing Agreement as available under the global norm-setting regime.[117]

In terms of economies of scope, the simultaneous shift of cap distribution competences at the implementation stage to the European level has blurred the divide between norm setting (cap setting) and implementation (cap distribution). This has resulted in improved coordination between the norm and its distribution through the Effort Sharing Decision, and more generally the ability to integrate the EU ETS further into the climate change and energy policy of the European Union.[118]

## 2 Implementation

National implementation through NAPs limited the system's ability to capture externalities, both with respect to externalities caused by greenhouse gas emitting activities and externalities caused by their regulation. During the first two trading phases, the NAPs resulted in over-allocation to national industries by Member States and a sub-optimal distribution between ETS and non-ETS sectors, aided by a lack of transparency regarding non-ETS emissions. The reallocation of cap distribution competences to the European level is expected to reduce the externalization of these regulatory costs onto other countries and industries. The interest of the European regulator in cap distribution is to maintain a successful internal market and to ensure the cost-effective achievement of emission reduction goals,[119] which means that there is no incentive for the European agencies to shield one specific (national) economy or industry. Moreover, the harmonization of free allocation rules closes an important avenue for Member State protectionism in lieu of the NAPs. Member States may use some of their auctioning revenues to temper the effects of increased auctioning on their national industries and consumers. This is not necessarily a harmful development since some consumers can be disproportionally affected by rises

---

[116] *Ibid.*, at 99.    [117] Article 3(4) of Decision 406/2009/EC.

[118] See generally European integration principles: Article 11, Article 13 (animal welfare) and Article 194(2) (energy policy) of the TFEU. See N. Dhondt, *Integration of Environmental Protection into other EC Policies: Legal Theory and Practice* (Groningen: Europa Law Publishing, 2003).

[119] See e.g. Preamble 5 and 18 of Directive 2003/87/EC.

in e.g. energy prices, as is evidenced by the frequent discussions on 'fuel poverty'.[120] In addition, any redistribution by Member States is subject to European state-aid conditions.[121]

Member States retain control of the procedural implementation that is needed for the introduction of auctioning from the start of Phase III. These implementation measures do not include auction design, which has been mostly centralized through the Auctioning Regulation.[122] The Regulation prescribes a system of 'closer bid' auctions, a method of auctions that allows bidders to enter only one bid, and requires all bidders to pay the same clearing price.[123] This type of uniform price auction prevents bidders from reacting *ex post* to the bids of their rivals and mitigates the risk of over-paying for a good, but its format also precludes allocative efficiency insofar that the bidder with the highest valuation of the good does not necessarily receive it.[124] Another advantage of this format of auctioning is that it prevents in-auction cartel formation or intimidation.[125] The latter is particularly relevant for the EU ETS auctions for which it has been suggested that there could be manipulation through demand reduction by, for instance, energy companies, which hold the vast majority of allowances in several Member States and operate in oligopolistic markets.[126] Given the prescriptive nature of the Auction Regulation with respect to the format of the auctions,

---

[120] Fuel poverty refers to the situation where households have to spend a disproportionate amount of their income on heating and other energy-intensive activities. For an academic discussion of the problem, see e.g. B. Boardman, *Fuel Poverty: From Cold Homes to Affordable Warmth* (London: Belhaven Press, 1991) and B. Boardman, *Fixing Fuel Poverty: Challenges and Solutions* (Oxford: Earthscan, 2013).

[121] Articles 107–108 of the TFEU concern the EC provisions on state aid and its relation to anti-competitive behaviour. In principle any aid granted by a Member State, which (threatens to) distort(s) competition within the internal market is incompatible with the Treaty provision on the common market. There are certain exceptions to this rule (found in Articles 107(2) and (3) of the TFEU). Moreover, all aid systems of the Member States are subject to constant control by the Commission, in cooperation with the Member States (Article 108(1) of the TFEU). For the EU ETS, see specifically Article 10a(6) of Council Directive 2003/87/EC. For the *ex ante* benchmarks, see Commission Impact Assessment, COM(2008) 16 final, at 1.

[122] Commission Regulation 1031/2010.

[123] See S. Weishaar and E. Woerdman, 'Auctioning EU ETS Allowances: An Assessment of Market Manipulation from the Perspective of Law and Economics' (2012) 3 *Climate Law* 247–263, for a general outline of some of the different types of auctions that would have been available to the European legislator.

[124] *Ibid.*, 4.   [125] *Ibid.*

[126] K. Zwingmann, 'Ökonomische Analyse der EU-Emissionshandelsreichtlinie, Bedeutung und Funktionsweisen der Primärallokation von Zertifikaten' in *Ökonomische Analyse des Rechts* (Wiesbaden: DUV Gabler Edition Wissenschaft, 2007),

## 2 REGULATORY FUNCTIONING 169

there appears to be little room for disruptive heterogeneity between the Member States, while the option for Member States to create their national Platform accommodates national preferences.[127] Moreover, a race-to-the-top scenario may occur where Member States will try to create an auctioning climate that attracts desirable market players to their auctions.[128] Overall, the planned system appears to combine local expertise building and mutual learning by the Member States.

Although respectful of heterogeneous preferences of Member States, and potentially leading to increased experimentation and learning, the decentralized implementation of auctioning procedures comes at the cost of potential scale and scope economies. The Commission underlined the cost-efficiency advantage of a centralized approach to auctioning,[129] stressing that this approach would minimize the combined costs to public authorities and bidders.[130] The selection of auction platforms through public procurement is one of the main costs of implementation, and will have to take place at least eight times under a coordinated approach as compared to only once under a European approach. The coordinated approach moreover carries a higher workload for the Commission since it is responsible for the verification of these procurement procedures.[131] A centralized approach would also lead to increased transparency and simplicity, sustained competition

---

308 (referring to the case of Germany) as quoted in Weishaar and Woerdman, 'Auctioning EU ETS Allowances', 5.

[127] Commission Regulation 1031/2010.

[128] Member States will of course have differing views on what they consider to be 'desirable parties' in their respective auctions. These players need not be the biggest European players in terms of market shares or revenues. For instance, Member States with relatively small numbers of allowances to auction might specialize in attracting small to medium-sized businesses. In this respect, the local preferences for auctions are local only to certain types of businesses or size of businesses.

[129] See Commission Impact Assessment, COM(2008) 16 final, at 122. References to the consultation documents are contained within the Impact Assessment and available at https://quickplace.icfconsulting.com/QuickPlace/eu-ets-auctions-consultation/Main. nsf/h_Toc/8D02319760086AD086257635004F5913/?OpenDocument. See also Impact Assessment, at 16–23 (the criteria for the format of auctions included: cost-efficiency, risk of market abuse, non-discrimination, openness and effects on the secondary market). Concerning the central role of cost-effectiveness in the context of the EU ETS generally, see Article 1, para. 1 of Council Directive 2003/87/EC of 13 October 2003 establishing a scheme for greenhouse gas emission allowance trading within the Community and amending Council Directive 96/61/EC, OJ 2003 No. L275.

[130] Commission Impact Assessment, COM(2008) 16 final, at 16.

[131] *Ibid.* See also 17 (considering the hybrid approach as it would allow reliance on pre-existing exchanges as established during Phases I and II).

between trading places in the carbon market and the international aspects of the trading scheme.[132] Nevertheless, the United Kingdom, Germany and Poland, some of the largest emitters, have opted to create their own Auctioning Platform. This leads to a further fragmentation of competences between these national Platforms, the European Platform, the Auction Monitor,[133] the national institutions that supervise the financial sector,[134] and the European Commission. Depending on the success of the Commission's efforts to streamline these processes, this may lead to inefficient duplication of actions.[135]

## 3 Enforcement

The allocation of enforcement competences remains largely unaltered for the third trading phase. The most significant change stems from the increased activity regarding market oversight, especially through European harmonization in this area. The Commission has proposed to extend the coverage of the directive on financial instruments (the MiFID) to include emission allowances, as well as derivatives.[136] Despite this prima facie improvement of a previously unregulated or at best under-regulated financial market, the effect of this extension depends on its application by national and European institutions.[137] Overall the harmonization of market oversight rules at the European level should create a more level playing field and increased certainty in the market regarding the standards throughout the EU. However, this will only be the case when all Member States are able to uphold comparative

---

[132] See *ibid.*, at 20–22. The Commission also stressed possible future advantages of the centralized system in case of future linkage with other systems, see Impact Assessment, at 22.

[133] Commission Regulation 1031/2010.

[134] These are the competent national authorities charged with the tasks under Directive 2004/39/EC, Directive 2003/6/EC and Directive 2005/60/EC of 26 October 2005 on the prevention of the use of the financial system for the purpose of money laundering and terrorist financing, OJ 2005 No. L309, 15, 2005, 25 November 2005.

[135] See Weishaar and Woerdman, 'Auctioning EU ETS Allowances' for a complete analysis of this concurrence of competence.

[136] Commission Proposal, COM(2011) 656 final, Annex I, section C, point 4 (to include not only derivatives but also emission allowances under the MiFID Directive).

[137] It has been argued that the continuing fragmentation of enforcement competences makes it difficult to assess the market-wide implementations of transactions, see N. J. Clausen and K. E. Sørensen, 'Reforming the Regulation of Trading Venues in the EU Under the Proposed (MiFID II) – Leveling the Playing Field and Overcoming Market Fragmentation?' Nordic & European Company Law Working Paper No. 10–23 (2012), as quoted by Weishaar and Woerdman, 'Auctioning EU ETS Allowances'.

standards of enforcement; the market abuses of the second phase originated in national markets where enforcement capacity was relatively low compared to other Member States.[138] A harmonized approach also acknowledges the possibility, and willingness, of Member States to externalize their oversight problems onto other Member States. Since 'national' allowances markets do not cater solely to national buyers, some of the costs of under-enforcement are born by other European Member States and their industries. The Commission's choice to standardize this area through the use of regulations – which are prescriptive for the Member States both in method and result – restricts the flexibility of Member States in this area and limits the system's ability to deal with heterogeneity. However, the Regulations also provide scope for additional efficiencies through the streamlining of procedures and reduce duplicate institutions and/or improve coordination.[139]

## B Interactions

In Chapter 3, I developed a typology of agencies in the EU ETS, focusing on the Member States and the European Commission. Based on their policy choices in the first two phases of the EU ETS, the Member States' behaviour most closely resembled that of a rent-seeking agency, whereas the European institutions, particularly the Commission, behaved in a predominantly benevolent way.[140] This typology has not changed substantially going into the third trading phase; the European Union continues to be the engine behind most of the climate change policy-making and the further development of the EU ETS. Member State behaviour is not completely homogeneous; there are some clear advocates and opponents of the EU ETS.[141] However, with respect to norm distribution, virtually all Member States have engaged in over-allocation to their respective industries.[142] The EU ETS advocacy appears

---

[138] Bulgaria and Greece have been found to be in non-compliance with the national system requirements under the Kyoto Protocol. Two other Member States – Romania and Lithuania –were asked to submit reports to show their adherence to the implementation requirements following earlier findings of non-compliance. Improvements were shown to have been made. See full reports on Eighteenth meeting of Kyoto Protocol Compliance Committee Enforcement Branch (2012).

[139] Commission Proposal, COM(2011) 656 final, and Commission Regulation No 601/2012 of 21 June 2012 on the monitoring and reporting of greenhouse gas emissions pursuant to Directive 2003/87/EC of the European Parliament and of the Council.

[140] See Chapter 3, section 2.B.1.  [141] See Chapter 5.

[142] See discussion in Chapter 5, section 2.A.3, at note 128.

to be limited to the 'high' politics of its continued existence and fundamental design principles. With respect to the latter, a telling example is given by the United Kingdom, which vigorously supported the introduction of auctions, but later also opted for a decentralized method of auctioning.[143]

The move from our first-best situation of global norm setting to the second-best regional norm setting is mitigated by the EU's commitment to the international process and its (aspired) leadership position therein, since the EU clearly strives to maintain the norms that would have been imposed on it under a global regime.[144] However, it continues to be difficult for the Commission to convince all Member States to act in line with its ambitious policies. Interestingly, there was relatively little objection with respect to this centralization of competences in the run-up to the third trading phase. In 2005, a majority of the EU15 preferred 'a decentralized system with respect to the cap (i.e. cap division), free allocation of allowances based on historic emissions and full access to external credits'.[145] These preferences appear to have changed in the period leading up to the proposal for a revised directive in 2008.[146] However, this does not signal a change in type, rather the lack of protest can be explained by the more stringent reductions in their non-ETS sectors that Member States faced in exchanged for the continuation of the NAP system.[147]

---

[143] Commission Impact Assessment of 8 February 2010 accompanying the Commission Regulation on the timing, administration and other aspects of auctioning of greenhouse gas emission allowances pursuant to Article 10(4) of Directive 2003/87/EC, SEC(2010), at 37.

[144] Council Conclusions of 21 October 2009 on EU position for the Copenhagen Climate Conference, 2968th Environmental Council meeting, at para. 8.

[145] Skjærseth and Wettestad, 'The EU Emissions Trading System Revised', 78–79.

[146] *Ibid.* See also Commission Proposal of 23 January 2008, COM(2008) 30 final. This Proposal was published as part of the Article 30 review process. Article 30 sets out the review process of the EU ETS, including timelines and report dates. Specifically, Article 30(2) stipulates that review of the ETS should culminate in a report drafted by the Commission, to be submitted to the European Council and Parliament by 30 June 2006. Together with this proposal an impact assessment was published. See Commission Impact Assessment, COM(2008) 16 final.

[147] Skjærseth and Wettestad, 'The EU Emissions Trading System Revised', 79 ('Brussels' insiders refer to the cap as the firewall in the ETS. It is likely that lack of attention reflects the strong call for more harmonization and the already settled overall 20 percent target. If Member States really had questioned this part of the reform, they would likely have faced demands for further emission reductions from non-ETS sectors instead.')

2 REGULATORY FUNCTIONING 173

For Phases I and II of the EU ETS, the combination of the agency types that were at the global, regional and national level with the (imperfectly concurrent) competences that carried positive authority with them resulted in a least favourable situation from a welfare perspective.[148] A unified regulatory system represents the most viable alternative to the allocation of competences in the first two trading phases, since the concurrent nature of the competences is intrinsic to the system and therefore cannot be altered. In the third trading phase, there is increased concentration (and in some ways, unification) at the European level, which now holds norm-setting competences, substantive implementation competences, and some enforcement competences related to market oversight. Member States retain procedural implementation competences and those enforcement competences related to individual compliance.

As in the first two trading phases, the competences vested in the agencies with respect to norm setting and substantive implementation are concurrent: both actions (cap setting and cap distribution) are needed to give effect to the positive authority of permitting the emission of greenhouse gases. Since the act of cap setting created exploitable rents for the implementer during norm distribution, the concentration of these competences at the European level is welfare improving. Implementation and enforcement remain imperfectly concurrent: enforcement cannot alter cap-division, but rents can still be available to the enforcer if he chooses to under-enforce a cap-division that is sub-optimal from the perspective of an individual installation. The centralization of some enforcement competences to the European level, particularly with respect to market oversight, combined with the improved possibility for data gathering at the European level with respect to individual compliance, represents an improvement compared to the competence allocation in Phases I and II. There is no direct need therefore to suggest the move from the remaining implementation and enforcement competences to the European level, provided that the information asymmetries between these levels continue to decrease and that the discretion given to the Member States is coupled with the possibility for corrective action from the European agencies.

---

[148] See Chapter 3, section 2.B.2.

## 3 Conclusions

The start of Phase III of the EU ETS heralded the start of a more 'centralized' system of competence allocation change, with a concentration of authority at the European level. This can partly be explained by exogenous factors, such as the failure to reach international consensus with respect to legally binding norms for the post-Kyoto period. 'Internal' factors, such as the difficulties with the NAPs in the first two trading phases, provided additional information for the partial redesign of the EU ETS. Based on our allocation considerations, the shift to regional norm setting falls short of satisfying our first-order consideration with respect to externalities capture. However, the fact that the European institutions can be categorized as benevolent agencies and the combination with European-level norm distribution (substantive implementation) means that this second-best norm-setting scenario is a welfare improvement as compared to the situation in Phases I and II. The same conclusions may be drawn for the market oversight elements of enforcement, which have also been increasingly moving to the European level. Even if their execution remains in the hands of the Member States, increased harmonization through the adoption of regulations signifies a de facto shift to the European level.

Thus far our analysis has focused on the implications of competence allocation for the functioning of a regulatory system in terms of its ability to capture externalities, accommodate heterogeneity and achieve economies of scale/scope. We also considered the welfare implications of divergences from the optimum as distilled in our theoretical framework. Having studied all three trading phases of the EU ETS, we are moreover able to consider changes in competences and their possible effects – although our intuitions regarding the effects of these changes for Phase III cannot yet be confirmed. Thus far, some pre-existing problems have carried over into the third trading phase, and new ones have come to the fore due to the prolonged impact of the economic crisis. In short, the changes in competence allocation do not seem to have cured the EU ETS of all its institutional problems, which raises the question whether optimal competence allocation – if this were to take place – is enough to ensure optimal regulatory functioning. In order to answer this question, the next chapter turns to the missing link in our analysis: an explanatory mechanism for the divergences between the theoretically optimal competence allocation and our observed competence allocation strategy under the EU ETS. Put differently, the identification of the process that determines competence allocation itself. In keeping with the law and economics perspective adopted throughout this book, Chapter 5 explains competence allocation within the EU ETS through the application of political economy theory.

# 5 A political economy explanation for competence allocation in the EU ETS

This book offers an additional perspective on the functioning of climate change mitigation policies, such as the EU Emissions Trading Scheme (EU ETS). When norm setting, implementation and/or enforcement competences are allocated in ways that are second- or third-best, additional room is created for rent-seeking behaviour, externalization of damaging behaviour and other inefficiencies. As such, a competence allocation analysis can explain the existence of some of these problems and present alternative strategies to ameliorate them. In the abstract, it can also prescribe a first-best allocation for a certain policy problem given a set of actors, policy instruments and normative parameters. It does not, however, explain the consequent divergence between a theoretical first-best allocation and the second- or third-best allocation that takes place in real life. For the EU ETS, unsurprisingly, neither the Phase I and II nor the Phase III allocations reflect the theoretical optimum, and the system incorporates several inefficiencies, for example, regarding norm distribution (cap-division among industries) and its enforcement (particularly, fraudulent activities and market abuse). In this chapter, we construct one possible explanation of this divergence through the application of political-economy theory to the case of the EU ETS.

Political economy may be defined as 'the study of the collective or political processes through which public economic decisions are made'.[1] It provides positive theories that refer to the role of different societal interest groups in the *creation* of policies, including environmental ones, which is an important tool in explaining the gap between our theoretical optimum and the practice of competence allocation

---

[1] Oates and Portney, 'The Political Economy of Environmental Policy', 327.

and policy design.[2] Political economy scholarship builds primarily on economic, legal and political science research and covers a wide range of topics. A common feature of this literature is the focus on power relations, including the relationship between the government and interest groups, and governments and interest groups *inter se*. Public choice theory is an important influence on those streams of political economy research that present economic models of political processes. The recasting of politicians', bureaucrats' and individuals' actions as maximizers of their individual utility rather than social welfare maximizers has not only been very influential both for the second generation of federalism,[3] but also for some streams within political economy.[4] Additional political economy explanations of policy outcomes have focused on inter alia the role of transaction costs,[5] and the role of culture.[6] In this chapter, the main streams of thought within political economy are set out, focusing on their application to environmental policy-making. From this theoretical basis, we identify the main interest groups involved in the EU ETS, their respective goals with respect to the EU ETS and their inter-relationships. This political economy analysis explains the changes in EU ETS competence allocation and design through the needs and preferences of certain interest groups at different stages of its development.

## 1  A political economy perspective of environmental policy

In this section we highlight those contributions to the vast political economy literature that hold particular explanatory power for the

---

[2] An early example of explaining this gap is the 1975 paper by Buchanan and Tullock, 'Polluters' Profits and Political Response', which shows that firms will prefer emission standards to taxes, even though the latter are considered more efficient, since standards result in higher profits due to their ability to serve as a barrier for entry for other firms.

[3] As discussed in Chapter 1, section 1.A.2.

[4] For instance, in the context of our theoretical framework and the resulting optimal competence allocation, we assume that the global norm setter is a benevolent agency that, with full information, 'designs and implements social programs for environmental protection with the sole objective of promoting the well-being of the polity as a whole' (Oates and Portney, 'The Political Economy of Environmental Policy', 328). Put differently, a benevolent agency is also a social welfare optimizing agency.

[5] See e.g. A. K. Dixit, *The Making of Economic Policy: A Transaction Cost Politics Perspective* (Cambridge, MA: The MIT Press, 1998).

[6] See M. Lederer, 'Market Making via Regulation: The Role of the State in Carbon Markets' (2012) 6 *Regulation & Governance* 1–21 at 5 for additional referencing.

development of environmental programmes.[7] Specifically, we focus on models that explain (and try to predict) the interaction between different societal interest groups and the regulatory process.[8] These include demand- and supply-side theories of regulation, which refer to the political process itself, and more specific theories regarding instrument choice within environmental policy design. A final stream of literature takes note of the institutional setting in which regulation is developed and applied, akin to our focus on competence allocation.[9]

### A Positive theories of regulation

Positive theories of (environmental) regulation are characterized by their focus on how the political process results in certain types of policies. In this setting, the 'political process' refers to all interactions between societal actors that are of interest for a particular policy initiative. As this field developed, the explanatory and predictive power of these models and theories increased as they incorporated greater detail as to specific characteristics of a given policy. A distinction can be made between three strands: demand-side explanations, supply-side explanations, and equilibrium explanations that are the result of the interaction between demand and supply.[10]

*Demand-side explanations* view regulation as a product of pressure, i.e. lobbying, applied by (industrial) interest groups. Joseph Stigler, one of the founders of this research area, stated that 'regulation is acquired by the industry and is designed and operated primarily for its benefit'.[11] As a consequence, measures adopted by 'captured' agencies will, directly or indirectly, benefit the incumbents, for instance through subsidies or foreclosure of the market.[12] Regulatory capture of the policy process

---

[7] See generally W. A. Magat, A. J. Krnpnick and W. Harrington, *Rules in the Making: A Statistical Analysis of Regulatory Agency Behavior* (Washington, DC: Resources for the Future, 1986); R. D. Congleton (ed.), *The Political Economy of Environmental Protection: Analysis and Evidence* (Ann Arbor, MI: University of Michigan Press, 1996), 31–43; B. Dijkstra, *The Political Economy of Environmental Policy: A Public Choice Approach to Market Instruments* (Cheltenham: Edward Elgar, 1999); G. T. Svendsen, *Public Choice and Environmental Regulation* (Cheltenham: Edward Elgar, 1998); and N. Wallart, *The Political Economy of Environmental Taxes* (Cheltenham: Edward Elgar, 1999).

[8] Oates and Portney, 'The Political Economy of Environmental Policy', 330 ('It seems to us that approaches that explicitly recognize this interaction of different interest groups are the most promising for an understanding of environmental policy.')

[9] Oates and Portney, 'The Political Economy of Environmental Policy', 331.

[10] Keohane, Revesz and Stavins, 'The Choice of Regulatory Instruments', 319.

[11] Stigler, 'The Theory of Economic Regulation', 3.

[12] See also R. Posner, 'Theories of Economic Regulation' (1974) 5 *Bell Journal of Economics and Management Science* 335–358, S. Peltzman, 'Towards a More General Theory of

# 1 A POLITICAL ECONOMY PERSPECTIVE OF ENVIRONMENTAL POLICY 179

is considered a mostly negative by-product of the interaction between interest groups and policymakers since it diminishes the likelihood that policies maximize social welfare, also referred to as 'resource allocation efficiency'.[13] This view of regulation as a form of wealth transfer has led to much discussion with respect to environmental regulation.

Some have taken issue with Stigler's finding of the industry as a beneficiary of regulation, arguing that there is no systematic proof of regulation in favour of strong interest groups, such as producers.[14] Oates and Portney go as far as to say that '[I]t seems misleading at best to describe environmental measures as instigated by regulatees – that is by polluting industries. We surely find certain cases where such measures have been manipulated into a form that provides specific benefits to at least some regulatees, but to argue that environmental policy has its basic impetus in the designs of polluting industries seems misplaced.'[15] Conversely, Elliott, Ackerman and Millian show that the Clean Air Amendments in 1970 resulted from pressure from industry for federal standards as a means of inhibiting states from setting non-uniform (and more stringent) standards.[16] Other work has found that the political debate over scrubber installation for power plants – a method for cleaning dirty coal emissions – as opposed to the burning of cleaner coal, can result in a coalition forming between environmentalists and

Regulation' (1976) 19 *Journal of Law and Economics* 211–240, and G. S. Becker, 'A Theory of Competition among Pressure Groups for Political Influence' (1983) 98 *The Quarterly Journal of Economics* 371–400. As suggested by Keohane, Revesz and Stavins, 'The Choice of Regulatory Instruments', 320, the capture theory of regulation was already well developed in political science. Stigler's main contribution was the application of this theory to economic scholarship and the application of economic models of behaviour to explain policy formulation.

[13] N. K. Komesar, *Imperfect Alternatives: Choosing Institutions in Law, Economics, and Public Policy* (University of Chicago Press, 1994), 14. It is difficult, however, to ascertain the actual effects of regulatory capture on regulatory outcomes. One way of approximating the effects of regulation is through reference to nationwide measures of corruption, which may be correlated to regulatory capture. Another way to analyse the connection between capture and outcomes is to look at whether influence in the form of campaign contributions to politicians matters. If one accepts that the costs and presence of corruption are a valid proxy to the existence of regulatory capture, the effects of capture are very detrimental and its effects should be curbed. On the costs of corruption, see Dal Bo, 'Regulatory Capture', 221.

[14] E. Rolph, 'Government Allocation of Property Rights: Who Gets What?' (1983) 3(1) *Journal of Policy Analysis and Management* 45–61.

[15] Oates and Portney, 'The Political Economy of Environmental Policy', 330.

[16] E. D. Elliott, B. A. Ackerman and J. C. Millian, 'Toward a Theory of Statutory Evolution: The Federalization of Environmental Law' (1985) 1 *Journal of Law, Economics & Organization* 313–340.

coal producers in favour of scrubber installation, even if this is a more expensive form of regulation with few environmental results.[17]

A less divisive objection to the demand-side theories is that they essentially ignore the role of actors on the supply-side, i.e. the legislative process, in policy creation. Buchanan and Tullock's seminal paper on industrial preferences for standards over taxes simply assumes that these preferences will prevail over politicians' legislative preferences.[18] Similarly, the model designed by Stigler, and expanded by Peltzman, represents the policymaker as an economic agent that is interested only in collecting political contributions, ignoring pressure from the electorate, variation between policymakers *inter se* and policymakers and bureaucrats, and other characteristics of the suppliers of regulation.[19]

*Supply-side explanations* move away from these assumptions and focus on voting behaviour and the institutional structure of legislation. Voting behaviour plays a central role in determining legislators' incentives.[20] In turn, institutional factors, such as agenda setting and methods of voting can influence the outcome of these votes.[21] The predictions of the work in this area are very context-specific since the institutional setting will differ from jurisdiction to jurisdiction.[22] Variations in voting styles and representation, i.e. the manner in which legislators are elected,

---

[17] B. A. Ackerman and W. Hassler, *Clean Coal/Dirty Air or How the Clean Air Act Became a Multibillion-Dollar Bail-Out for High-Sulfur Coal Producers and What Should Be Done About It* (Binghamton, NY: Vail-Ballou Press, 1981).

[18] Buchanan and Tullock, 'Polluters' Profits and Political Response'; J. M. Buchanan and G. Tullock, 'Polluters' Profits and Political Response: Direct Controls versus Taxes' in R. D. Congleton (ed.), *The Political Economy of Environmental Protection: Analysis and Evidence* (Ann Arbor, MI: University of Michigan Press, 1996), 42: 'The public-choice approach, which concentrates attention on the individual's choice as between policy instruments, allows us to construct hypotheses that explain the prevalence of direct regulation.' See also Becker, 'A Theory of Competition among Pressure Groups'.

[19] See generally Hahn, 'Political Economy of Environmental Regulation', 26; M. P. Fiorina, 'Legislative Choice of Regulatory Forms: Legal Process or Administrative Process?' (1982) 39 *Public Choice* 33–61; Peltzman, 'Towards a More General Theory'. See also J. E. L. Campos, 'Legislative Institutions, Lobbying, and the Endogenous Choice of Regulatory Instruments: A Political Economy Approach to Instrument Choice' (1989) 5 *Journal of Law, Economics, & Organization* 333–353 at 341 ('The theory of economic regulation situates lobbying by special interest groups as the fundamental stimuli to generating a regulatory policy'). Keohane, Revesz and Stavins, 'The Choice of Regulatory Instruments', 320, describe the Stigler–Peltzman model as a 'policy auction'.

[20] P. Pashigian, 'Environmental Regulation: Whose Self-interests Are Being Protected?' (1985) 23 *Economic Inquiry* 551–584.

[21] See Keohane, Revesz and Stavins, 'The Choice of Regulatory Instruments', 321–322.

[22] See also *ibid.*, 323, on the market for votes within a legislature: the exchange of votes between legislatures, or similar agreements where several legislators agree to vote for each other's bills.

# 1 A POLITICAL ECONOMY PERSPECTIVE OF ENVIRONMENTAL POLICY    181

will also have a bearing on the outcome.[23] Most theories assume that regulating agencies seek to maximize their own interests, for instance through budget maximization, re-election through the 'buying' of votes and increased political influence. That said, altruistic motivations, such as the contribution to social welfare, have also proven very effective and pervasive among certain groups.[24]

Finally, so-called *equilibria analyses* focus on the interaction between demand- and supply-side behaviour. Public choice literature had provided a method of describing the political competition between interest groups, based on the central premise that policy is determined through political and economic self-interest.[25] Early work on this topic shows that groups will compete in order to obtain those distributions of resources that are most favourable to them. As a consequence, every regulation results in 'winners' and 'losers' and during the regulatory process, politicians act as 'brokers' between these two groups.[26] This competition can result in a political equilibrium that is economically efficient.[27] Inefficient distributions are rationalized as the 'most efficient distribution possible given the presence and pressure of the interest groups'.[28] Similarly, Toke Aidt formalizes his hypothesis that environmental policy

---

[23] See e.g. literature on the median-voter model. Under this model, it is assumed that social choices that are made directly by voters or through their elected representatives reflect the median of the most preferred outcomes of the individuals in the relevant social group (Oates and Portney, 'The Political Economy of Environmental Policy',328–329). See also D. Black, 'On the Rationale of Group Decision-making' (1948) 56 *Journal of Political Economy* 23–34, a first modern treatment of median-voter theorem, and D. C. Mueller, *Public Choice II* (Cambridge University Press, 1989) for a survey on recent literature on the median-voter model). When this model is extended to include several political parties competing for votes, the policy outcomes also converge to the preferred outcome of the median voter (A. Downs, *An Economic Theory of Democracy* (New York: Harper Collins, 1957)). In some cases, the outcome of this median-voter model is in line with the social choices recommended by the normative economic theories, based on efficiency. See e.g. T. Bergstrom, 'When Does Majority Rule Supply Public Goods Efficiently?' (1979) 8 *Scandinavian Journal of Economics* 216–227, who shows that under certain conditions, the median-voter model satisfies the first-order conditions for Pareto efficiency.

[24] T. S. Aidt, 'Political Internalization of Economic Externalities and Environmental Policy' (1998) 69 *Journal of Public Economics* 1–16; G. Van Houtven, 'Bureaucratic Discretion in Environmental Regulations: The Air Toxics and Asbestos Ban Cases', in R. D. Congleton (ed.), *The Political Economy of Environmental Protection: Analysis and Evidence* (Ann Arbor, MI: University of Michigan Press, 1996).

[25] See also Buchanan and Tullock, 'Polluters' Profits and Political Response'.

[26] C. K. Rowley, (ed.), *Public Choice Theory* (Cheltenham: Edward Elgar, 1993), xviii.

[27] Becker, 'A Theory of Competition among Pressure Groups'.

[28] Hahn, 'Political Economy of Environmental Regulation', 23–4. In addition, M. P. Leidy and B. M. Hoekman, 'Pollution Abatement, Interest Groups, and Contingent Trade Policies', in R. D. Congleton (ed.), *The Political Economy of Environmental Protection:*

## 182 A POLITICAL ECONOMY EXPLANATION OF THE EU ETS

is a product of self-interest and that competition between interest groups is an important source for internalization of economic externalities,[29] through the use of the common agency model.[30] The premise of his analysis is that the presence of different lobby groups ensures the consideration and incorporation of all relevant qualities into the eventual policy: i.e. a 'political internalization of externalities'.[31] In a common agency model with perfect information, we can find an efficient equilibrium for all active players, such as lobby groups and the government.[32] If lobby groups do in fact represent all relevant interests in society, the equilibrium is socially efficient and there is complete internalization of externalities.[33] However, some citizens will typically not be organized in lobby groups, which means that this equilibrium is often incomplete, and will favour groups that have organized themselves in terms of the distributional effects of the policy.[34]

### B Instrument choice

In 1975, Buchanan and Tullock explained the widespread use of source-specific standards, as compared to fees or taxes, by their potential profitability for the affected industry; since emissions standards can act as a barrier to entry for new firms, they result in higher profits than emission taxes.[35] Industrial interest groups are especially supportive of tradable permits that are distributed free of charge to existing sources (i.e. grandfathered), a practice which was used extensively within the EU ETS.[36] Some authors have even shown that incumbents may prefer

---

*Analysis and Evidence* (Ann Arbor, MI: University of Michigan Press, 1996), at 44, argue that 'the social costs associated with the adoption of an inefficient environmental regime are likely to be compounded by consequent restrictions on trade when the affected industries are import competing'.

[29] Aidt, 'Political Internalization', 2.

[30] G. Grossman and E. Helpman, 'Endogenous Innovation in the Theory of Growth' 8 (1994) *Journal of Economic Perspectives* 22–44.

[31] Aidt, 'Political Internalization', 2. He furthermore argues that this approach of self-interest 'bridges the Coasian and Pigouvian approach to environmental policy'.

[32] B. D. Bernheim and M. D. Whinston, 'Common Agency' (1986) 54 *Econometrica* 923–942.

[33] Aidt, 'Political Internalization', 4.

[34] The reason why some parties do not organize themselves into lobby groups can be explained through free riding and organization costs. See generally Olson, *The Logic of Collective Action* (arguing that potential beneficiaries of policies will be more likely to form a lobbying group than potential losers).

[35] Buchanan and Tullock, 'Polluters' Profits and Political Response'.

[36] D. N. Dewees, 'Instrument Choice in Environmental Policy' (1983) 21 *Economic Inquiry* 53–71.

1 A POLITICAL ECONOMY PERSPECTIVE OF ENVIRONMENTAL POLICY          183

regulation over no regulation, provided they are stricter for new than for old plants.[37] More generally, industrial interest groups prefer instruments that present: the lowest aggregate costs to the industry as a whole; increased profits through the generation of rents or erection of trade barriers; or that keep individual compliance costs under the industry average.[38] Grandfathered permits create barriers to entry in much the same way as standards, since incumbents will receive permits based on past emissions, or a similar benchmark, whereas newcomers in the market are likely to be charged for some, or all, of their emissions.[39] An example of this can be found under the United States Clean Air Act, which established sulphur dioxide allowance trading and allocated virtually all allowances to existing sources for 'free'.[40] Even within the practice of grandfathering, some designs will espouse stronger industry support than others: a benchmark that is based on a 'best available technology' standard favours firms that have already invested in abatement prior to regulation, whereas benchmarks based on historic emissions favour more heavily producing firms.[41] Based on these preferences, industry groups rank instruments as follows: (i) command-and-control or subsidies; (ii) licences that are grandfathered to incumbents;[42] (iii) auctioned licences; (iv) taxes.[43]

---

[37] *Ibid.*

[38] Keohane, Revesz and Stavins, 'The Choice of Regulatory Instruments', 347.

[39] G. Kirchgässner and F. Schneider, 'On the Political Economy of Environmental Policy' (2003) 115 *Public Choice* 369–396 at 378. See also R. W. Hahn and A. M. McGartland, 'The Political Economy of Instrument Choice: An Examination of the U.S. Role in Implementing the Montreal Protocol' (1989) 83 *Northwestern University Law Review* 203–229 (showing that a rent-seeking model explains the positions of large producers that support grandfathered permits over other implementation schemes, including auctions).

[40] P. L. Joskow, R. Schmalensee and E. M. Bailey, 'The Market for Sulfur Dioxide Emissions' (1998) 88 *American Economic Review* 669–685 at 671.

[41] R. W. Hahn and R. G. Noll, 'Environmental Markets in the Year 2000' (1990) 3 *Journal of Risk and Uncertainty* 347–363 at 359.

[42] As will be discussed in more detail with respect to the EU ETS, grandfathering has been the predominant form of permit allocation in most trading schemes. For observations regarding the U.S. Clean Air Act, see E. M. Bailey, 'Allowances Trading Activity and State Regulatory Rulings: Evidence from the U.S. Acid Rain Program', 4 MIT Working Paper No. MIT-CEEPR 96–002 (1996) (finding that auctions involved less than 3 per cent of the total allocation); and P. L. Joskow, *et al.*, 'Auction Design and the Market for Sulfur Dioxide Emissions', National Bureau of Economic Research Working Paper No. 5745 (1996) (stating that auctions have proven to be a trivial part of the overall programme).

[43] Hepburn, 'Regulation by Prices, Quantities, or Both', 236.

On the (semi-) supply side, economists have long since advocated the use of market-based instruments, such as taxes, in environmental policy.[44] The cost-effectiveness of market-based instruments is typically higher than that of traditional command-and-control regulation. However, the distribution of costs between society as a whole and industry is different under command-and-control regulation and market-based instruments. More precisely, industry has to pay for its residual emissions under taxes or tradable permits with auctioning,[45] while it does not have to do so under command and control.[46] From a demand-side perspective, this makes taxes and tradable permits much less desirable than command-and-control regulation, which may explain why the bulk of environmental regulation is implemented by command-and-control instruments.[47] However, the industry's perspective that command-and-control regulation is more costly *for them* should not be taken as proof that this type of regulation is more costly *for society*. In fact, Cole and Grossman convincingly show that, both as a matter of theory and practice, command and control is sometimes more economically efficient than so-called 'market-based' instruments.[48]

The environmental interest groups are a final building block of any political economy analysis of environmental regulation.[49] These groups have traditionally also advocated in favour of command-and-control-type regulation rather than market-based approaches such as taxes or tradable permits. This can partly be explained by the symbolism that surrounds market-based instruments, namely the perceived monetization of the environment and that people are given a 'licence to pollute'. Supporting market-based instruments may therefore cause environmental groups to alienate their members,[50] which in turn may endanger the group's budget or donations and eventually its continued existence.[51] The perception of environmental interest group members

---

[44] For an overview of the argument see Hahn, 'Economic Prescriptions for Environmental Problems'. For an overview of the literature, see Keohane, Revesz and Stavins, 'The Choice of Regulatory Instruments', 316, fn. 19.
[45] Dewees, 'Instrument Choice', 59.
[46] Kirchgässner and Schneider, 'Political Economy of Environmental Policy', 378.
[47] See Hahn, 'Economic Prescriptions for Environmental Problems'.
[48] D. H. Cole and P. Z. Grossman, 'When is Command-and-Control Efficient? Institutions, Technology, and the Comparative Efficiency of Alternative Regulatory Regimes for Environmental Protection' (1999) *Wisconsin Law Review* 887–938.
[49] One could also consider labour groups or other societal interests, see Keohane, Revesz and Stavins, 'The Choice of Regulatory Instruments'.
[50] Oates and Portney, 'The Political Economy of Environmental Policy', 338.
[51] Keohane, Revesz and Stavins, 'The Choice of Regulatory Instruments', 350.

of market-based instruments as 'licences to pollute' is flawed, especially since standards under command-and-control give a comparable licence, for free. This perception is slow to change, although environmental interest groups are increasingly supportive of quantity-based economic instruments, such as permits, since they confer a certain environmental benefit, as opposed to price instruments such as taxes where the environmental result is unclear.[52] An example has been the Environmental Defense's support of the sulphur-trading scheme in the United States.[53] Other contributing factors are the perception that it might be harder to alter market-based instruments once they have been put in place – the market is supposed to run itself – and the concern that practice will diverge from theory, which can result in, for example, the presence of hot spots under trading schemes.[54] Generally environmental interest groups are considered less successful in their lobbying efforts than industry groups due to the dispersed character of the interests and the relatively small individual payoffs, which has also limited their influence on the policy choice between command-and-control regulation and market-based regulation.[55]

The perceptions of voters, some of which may unite under environmental interest groups, regarding the costs of regulation also have some influence on policymakers' decisions.[56] Since it is easier to 'hide' the costs of regulation through command-and-control mechanisms, policymakers may opt for this type of regulation in order to secure more votes.[57] Moreover, the distributional effects of market-based instruments are more uncertain, which may cause risk-averse policymakers

[52] Oates and Portney, 'The Political Economy of Environmental Policy', 338.
[53] Keohane, Revesz and Stavins, 'The Choice of Regulatory Instruments', 354.
[54] *Ibid.*
[55] Buchanan and Tullock, 'Polluters' Profits and Political Response', at 142 ('[A] small concentrated identifiable and intensely interested pressure group may exert more influence on political choice making than the much larger majority of persons, each of whom might expect to secure benefits in the second order of smalls'). See also Kirchgässner and Schneider, 'Political Economy of Environmental Policy', 375 ('Thus voters might be (partly) held responsible for the undersupply of environmental policies, but they can hardly be held responsible for the lack of market oriented measures in this policy.')
[56] Even if real technological and monitoring costs in the end seem to outweigh these political considerations, see D. H. Cole, *Pollution and Property: Comparing Ownership Institutions for Environmental Protection* (Cambridge University Press, 2002), chapters 3 and 4. See also Richards, 'Framing Environmental Policy' (discussing the technical requirements of regulatory instruments more generally).
[57] Keohane, Revesz and Stavins, 'The Choice of Regulatory Instruments', 359.

to prefer standards.[58] The familiarity of (predominantly) legally trained policymakers with command-and-control regulation may also predispose them to these instruments as opposed to economically 'complex' market-based instruments.[59] Similarly, regulators' extensive experience with command-and-control instruments means they can use the existing human capital in their development and application, whereas the development of market-based instruments calls for additional investment in human capital. The position of the policymaker must be nuanced insofar that we have thus far referred to elected officials, rather than career bureaucrats. The latter group will have different backgrounds and different goals in the development of policy. Moreover, the awareness regarding market-based instruments appears to be increasing among policymakers in the field of environmental policy. This is particularly true within the EU due to the development of the EU ETS.[60]

## C  Institutional settings

Most political economy scholarship focuses on the interaction between interest groups and policymakers with respect to the creation of policy and the consequent instrument design choices. These analyses centre on the initial policy-making and norm-setting phase and are limited to the interaction between interest groups and the policymaker. However, in practice many environmental policies, especially those related to climate change, involve multiple levels of governance in various jurisdictions. For transboundary environmental policies, this fragmentation already takes place at the policy-making stage: treaty negotiations, which are the predominant means of creating transboundary policy, can be modelled as a two-level game in which nation states' positions at the global level are in turn a product of national-level politics.[61] Treaty negotiations thus comprise two sets of interactions between the

---

[58] *Ibid.*, 359.    [59] *Ibid.*, 357.

[60] Cf. Kirchgässner and Schneider, 'Political Economy of Environmental Policy', 380, who claim that 'many members of the public environmental bureaucracy are in strong opposition against the application of market based instruments of environmental policy', especially within Europe. However, the history of the development of the EU ETS indicates the opposite trend, at least at the European level.

[61] J. Wiener, 'Global Environmental Regulation: Instrument Choice in Legal Context' (1999) 108 *The Yale Law Journal* 677–800 at 751; R. D. Putnam, 'Diplomacy and Domestic Politics: The Logic of Two-Level Games' (1988) 42(3) *International Organization* 427–460.

interest groups and the policymakers: one at the national level and one at the international level. The success of industrial and environmental interest groups at these levels will differ depending on their relative composition and budget.

Industrial interest groups are typically smaller and all members have significant and identifiable economic interests that diminish the risk of free riding. Traditionally, the diffuse nature of public environmental interests has made them more vulnerable to free-rider problems and thus less able to effectively influence the creation of regulation.[62] However, the large increase in global, regional and national environmental regulation suggests that environmental interest groups have overcome some of the free-riding problems traditionally associated with them. Some environmental non-governmental organizations (NGOs) have been referred to as 'potent enough to act as global regulatory entrepreneurs'.[63] Any scale economies of functioning on a central, global or federal level is negated by the need to lobby at many decentralized levels.[64] In these smaller geographical units, it is difficult for environmental interest groups to reach critical mass by mobilizing the public.[65] As a consequence, the activities of environmental NGOs are generally more focused at the global level than industry groups.[66]

Industry groups are more likely to support transnational environmental policy-making regardless, since this may be in their private self-interest.[67] As on the national level, the creation of barriers to entry through regulation will motivate certain industrial interest groups to act in support of international environmental standards since this could foreclose their relevant market to rivals or generally create a competitive

---

[62] Wiener, 'Global Environmental Regulation', 752.
[63] T. Brenton, *The Greening of Machiavelli: The Evolution of International Environmental Politics* (London: Royal Institute of International Affairs, 1994), at 356–357, as cited in J. B. Wiener, 'On the Political Economy of Global Environmental Regulation' (1999) 87 *Georgetown Law Journal* 749–794.
[64] R. Stewart, 'Pyramids of Sacrifice? Federalism Problems in Mandating State Implementation of Federal Environmental Controls' (1977) 86 *Yale Law Journal* 1196–1272 at 1213–1214. See Olson, *The Logic of Collective Action*, 5–65.
[65] Stewart, 'Pyramids of Sacrifice', 1213–1214 and Esty, 'Revitalizing Environmental Federalism', 649–651.
[66] Wiener, 'Global Environmental Regulation', 763.
[67] See generally G. Tullock, 'The Welfare Costs of Tariffs, Monopolies, and Theft' (1967) 5 *Western Economic Journal* 224–232; A. Krueger, 'The Political Economy of the Rent-seeking Society' (1974) 64 *American Economic Review* 291–303.

advantage.[68] For complex technical issues, industrial groups also hold a substantial informational advantage, which increases the likelihood of capture since the regulator's resources are seldom sufficient to gather all information independently from the regulated industry.[69] Even if they are, efficiency considerations may still persuade the regulator to rely on information provided by the regulated, increasing the risk of capture.[70]

In the setting of international policies, political actors are held accountable by several different constituencies, which may have heterogeneous preferences as to the properties of the negotiated policy. Leading up to the Copenhagen agreements, the international community was under tremendous pressure from international civil society to come to an agreement on the post-Kyoto regime. National representatives had to balance this pressure with their domestic mandates and preferences, which were not necessarily in favour of an international agreement, especially not one with binding reduction targets.[71] This tension can result in the explicit renunciation of a ratified treaty – e.g. Canada renouncing its commitments under the Kyoto Protocol[72] – or the effective undercutting of such an agreement through faulty implementation and/or enforcement. In fact, some policies at the international level may be agreed precisely because parties know that their non-compliance is likely to go unnoticed and/or unpunished due to a

---

[68] See S. C. Scalop and D. T. Scheffman, 'Raising Rivals' Costs' (1983) 73 *American Economic Review* 267–271; J. R. Macey, 'Federal Deference to Local Regulators and the Economic Theory of Regulation: Toward a Public-Choice Explanation of Federalism' (1990) 76 *Virginia Law Review* 265–291 at 273.

[69] See e.g. Dal Bo, 'Regulatory Capture', 214–215 (discussing the effects of the 'revolving door' phenomenon, where regulators may come from, or are later employed by, the industry that they have to regulate).

[70] This is especially true for regulatory regimes that involve some type of private enforcement, for instance in situations where private parties may instigate regulatory action by filing a claim or providing certain types of information, since people are more likely to invest in the political process when it is 'closer' to them. See Inman and Rubinfeld, 'Federalism', at 661.

[71] Yang, 'International Treaty Enforcement'; A. Benvenisti, *Sharing Transboundary Resources: International Law and Optimal Resource Use* (Cambridge University Press, 2002). See also Wiener, 'Global Environmental Regulation', 788, who offers an additional explanation for the counter-intuitive expansion of international environmental regulation (given the collective action problem it presents): the civic republican theory, which encompasses high-minded altruism.

[72] Canada Withdrawal, UN Docs. C.N.796.2011.TREATIES-1 (Depositary Notification), 15 December 2011.

# 1 A POLITICAL ECONOMY PERSPECTIVE OF ENVIRONMENTAL POLICY     189

lack of effective oversight at the international level.[73] The exceedingly common combination of international norm setting with decentralized implementation and enforcement in environmental policy and its relative success in overcoming the initial collective action problem must therefore be balanced against the likelihood of failure in its domestic implementation and enforcement. Aside from ineffective oversight, this failure may be caused by, for example, the failure of governments or agencies to agree on specific primary or secondary norms; diverging interpretation of these norms by domestic courts; or a lack of administrative capacity.[74]

For local or national environmental problems, policy-making is usually confined to the jurisdiction of one particular legislator. Even so,

---

[73] See e.g Benvenisti, *Sharing Transboundary Resources*; Stewart, 'Enforcement of Transnational Public Regulation', (2012) 6 ('Second governments or agencies may decide for a variety of political and policy reasons not to carry out their undertakings. They may wish to avoid imposing regulatory burdens on, or otherwise favor, domestic producers and prefer to free ride on other states' efforts.'). See generally on international treaties A. L. Hillman and H. W. Ursprung, 'Domestic Politics, Foreign Interests, and International Trade Policy: Reply' (1994) 84(5) *American Economic Review* 1476–1478; R. D. Congleton, 'Ethnic Clubs, Ethnic Conflict, and the Rise of Ethnic Nationalism' in A. Breton and J.-L. Galeotti (eds.) *Nationalism and Rationality* (Cambridge University Press, 1995) 71–97; A. Michaelowa, 'Impact of Interest Groups on EU Climate Policy' (1998) 8(5) *European Environment* 152–160; and A. Endres and M. Finus, 'Quotas may Beat Taxes in a Global Emissions Game' (2000) 9(6) *International Tax and Public Finance* 687–707. An important exception is the Montreal Protocol on Ozone Depleting Substances 1989, the effects of which have now become clear. See e.g. R. E. Benedick, *Ozone Diplomacy: New Directions in Safeguarding the Planet* (Boston, MA: Harvard University Press, 1998); K. Raustiala, 'Compliance and Effectiveness in International Regulatory Cooperation' (2000) 32 *Case Western Reserve Journal International Law* 387–440 at 419–420. See generally O. Yoshida, 'Soft Enforcement of Treaties: The Montreal Protocol's Noncompliance Procedure and the Functions of Internal International Institutions' (1999) 10 *Colombia Journal International Environmental Law & Policy* 95–142; Wiener, 'Global Environmental Regulation', 757 (who argues that, thus far, much theoretical work in this area 'has been done with only casual reference to observation'). This task is complicated by the lack of data regarding this phenomenon and the relative youth of most transnational environmental regimes, which means that most references to practice are anecdotal.

[74] Stewart, 'Enforcement of Transnational Public Regulation', (2012) 6 ('First, governments or agencies may fail to agree on specific primary or secondary norms, either because of disagreement or uncertainty over norms, bargaining failures, or the need for flexibility to deal with future changes in political and economic circumstances and information. Subsequently, different domestic agencies and courts in different jurisdictions may interpret the agreed but general or ambiguous norms in different ways ... Third, states or agencies may lack legal and administrative capacity to effectively implement the agreed norms. Fourth, the agreed regulatory instruments and strategies may have intrinsic efficacy limitations.')

interest group interactions regarding implementation and enforcement can still weaken or strengthen the effectiveness of earlier determined environmental policy.[75] Moreover, it is common for implementation and enforcement to be in the hands of bureaucratic institutions that are not politically appointed, or for the judiciary to play an important role in certain enforcement activities.[76] The self-interest of these bodies will not be served through the accumulation of votes, but rather through budget-maximization or through the consolidation of their own position within the regulatory system by creating a position of expertise or authority.[77]

## 2 A political economy perspective of the EU ETS

In order for any policy to successfully pass through a political decision-making process, its goals and design need to balance the interests of the most powerful interest groups with those of society (as represented by government).[78] In the preceding chapters, our analysis has focused on the desirability of allocating competences at different levels of governance in terms of externalities capture, accommodation of heterogeneity and scale/scope economies. Our political economy analysis will instead focus on the intra-European aspects of the EU ETS,[79] demonstrating a link between, on the one hand, competence allocation, implementation practices, especially instrument design choices, and enforcement; and, on the other hand, the influence of different interest groups in determining these competence allocations.

[75] Oates and Portney, 'The Political Economy of Environmental Policy', 331 ('Environmentalists, business trade organizations, and other interest groups interact first in the determination of environmental legislation ... The implementation of such legislation by environmental agencies provides another arena in which divergent interests must be reconciled in the actual design, administration, and enforcement of policy. Through the selective enforcement of specific environmental measures, regulatory agencies may either weaken the measures or expand their scope and effectiveness.')

[76] Macey, 'Federal Deference', 267 (arguing that in the United States, the federal government is only willing to delegate competences to the states when the political support it obtains from deferring to the states is greater than the political support it obtains from regulating itself). See also Oates and Portney, 'The Political Economy of Environmental Policy', 331.

[77] See e.g. Niskanen, 'Nonmarket Decision Making' and Niskanen, *Bureaucracy and Representative Government*.

[78] P. Markussen and G. T. Svendsen, 'Industry Lobbying and the Political Economy of GHG Trade in the European Union' (2005) 33 *Energy Policy* 245–255 at 245.

[79] When relevant, the interaction between the EU, its Member States and the bodies under the United Nations framework is also discussed.

## 2 A POLITICAL ECONOMY PERSPECTIVE OF THE EU ETS 191

This section is divided into two parts, each discussing a particular step in the development of the EU ETS. We focus on how the positions of the main actors – EU institutions, Member States and industry groups – were reflected in the eventual shape of the EU ETS.[80] There have been several analyses on the emergence and shape of the EU ETS, which highlight different aspects of the process.[81] For example, Markussen and Svendsen consider whether the shape of the EU ETS Directive can be explained by the potential industrial winners and losers involved in the policy-making process.[82] Anger, Bohringer and Oberndorfer instead focus on the political economy of allowance allocation, finding that industries with high lobbying power face a lower regulatory burden, which can result in inefficient regulation.[83] The analysis in this chapter takes the difference between 'market creation' and 'market consolidation' as the starting point for changes in the position of different actors in Phases I and II, and III, respectively.[84]

The distinction between market creation and market consolidation refers to the difference in circumstance between the first two phases, where the European institutions had to introduce (market-based) regulation of an activity that had gone unregulated,[85] as contrasted to the

---

[80] Chowdhury and Wessel, 'Conceptualising Multilevel Regulation in the EU', 339: 'On the basis of their actions within the entire regulatory life cycle, it is possible to identify the relative importance of the actors in terms of principals (who are involved in rule formulations), participants (who are receivers of rules and are involved in the rule implementation and enforcement) and "residual actors" (who may only play a reactive role in terms of following the rules)'.

[81] See in particular Skjærseth and Wettestad, *EU Emissions Trading*; J. B. Skjærseth and J. Wettestad, 'Implementing EU Emissions Trading: Success or Failure?' (2008) 8 *International Environmental Agreements* 275–290; and Skjærseth and Wettestad, 'The EU Emissions Trading System Revised'; Markussen and Svendsen, 'Industry Lobbying'; Lederer, 'Market Making via Regulation'.

[82] Markussen and Svendsen, 'Industry Lobbying', 246.

[83] N. Anger, C. Bohringer, and U. Oberndorfer, 'Public Interest vs. Interest Groups: Allowance Allocation in the EU Emissions Trading Scheme', ZEW – Centre for European Economic Research Discussion Paper No. 08–023 (2008). NB: This paper ignores the role of environmental lobbies, looking only at industrial lobbies.

[84] See also Stavins, 'The Problem of the Commons',100 ('Cap and trade leaves distributional issues up to politicians, and thereby provides a straightforward means to compensate burdened sectors. Of course, this political advantage is also an economic disadvantage in that it invites rent-seeking behavior… A cap-and-trade system leads to battles over the allowance allocation, but these do not raise the overall cost of the program nor affect its climate impacts.')

[85] In the run-up to the 1992 Earth Summit, the Commission attempted to have a system of Community-wide carbon taxation (The Greenhouse Effect and the Community: Commission work programme concerning the evaluation of policy options to deal with the 'greenhouse effect'). However, the unanimity requirement for tax-related measures meant that the tax proposal failed, together with the related legislative

192    A POLITICAL ECONOMY EXPLANATION OF THE EU ETS

third trading phase, where the majority of included industries had been 'locked in' by the EU ETS system. This 'lock in' effect will be shown to facilitate the European Commission's efforts to improve the EU ETS as the industries' preferences are now based on their respective positions within the system, whereas no investment in the system had yet been made during the first two phases.

### A Market creation: EU ETS Phases I and II

The European Commission and Parliament, the Member States (also in the form of the Council), and the industry groups were the most important stakeholders in the debate on the EU ETS Directive (the Directive).[86] Generally speaking, the interests of the European Commission and Parliament for the first two phases were aligned, with both institutions favouring a centralized, i.e. European-centred, EU ETS with auctioning as the main method of allocation and limited scope for the import of credits through the link with the Clean Development Mechanism (CDM) and Joint Implementation (JI) initiatives. Conversely, the Member States wanted a decentralized, i.e. national, system with grandfathering based on historic emissions and full access to external credits.[87] Industry lobbies supported a voluntary system, preferably bypassing any mandatory trading, be it centralized or decentralized.[88] We will trace the political decision-making process of the Directive – starting with the 2000 Green Paper,[89] the 2001 Directive proposal,[90] the 2002 Draft Report of the Parliament (Parliament's first reading),[91] the 2002 Council Common Position,[92] the second reading in 2003,[93] and the final Directive.[94] The

---

agenda on greenhouse gas reduction measures. As a consequence, the European Union lacked any internal policy for greenhouse gas reduction at the time of ratification of the UNFCCC.

[86] The role of environmental NGOs was rather limited in the run-up to the first trading phases since their position was mainly one of opposition towards emissions trading as a mechanism. Moreover, there is empirical work suggesting that their lobbying success during this period was limited at the European level. See C. Daugbjerg and G. Svendsen, *Green Taxation in Question: Politics and Economic Efficiency in Environmental Regulation* (London: Palgrave Macmillan, 2001) and see generally C. Woll, 'Lobbying in the European Union: From sui generis to a Comparative Perspective' (2006) 13 *Journal of European Public Policy* 456–469 (setting out the general theoretic arguments regarding European lobbying based on several empirical studies).

[87] See Skjærseth and Wettestad, 'The EU Emissions Trading System Revised', 79.

[88] Markussen and Svendsen, 'Industry Lobbying', 253.

[89] European Commission, COM (2000) 87 final.

[90] European Commission, COM (2001) 581 final.

[91] European Parliament (2002).   [92] Common Position, 15792/1/02/REV1.

[93] European Parliament (2003).   [94] Council Directive 2003/87/EC.

## 2 A POLITICAL ECONOMY PERSPECTIVE OF THE EU ETS    193

relative success of the different groups can be measured by the extent to which the final Directive reflects their interests.

## 1 The political process

Initially, the European institutions and Member States had been sceptical,[95] and even opposed to, the UNFCCC flexible mechanisms, as initially supported by the United States. According to some, 'the EU was [...] against the [global] trading of pollution credits because such measures diluted its own unique advantage. Having enjoyed nothing like America's heady economic growths since 1990, and being less reliant on coal, making cutbacks in emission levels was always going to be easier for the Europeans.'[96] Thus, the pre-1998 position of the EU had supported the use of technology standards and other command-and-control type regulation.[97] Once flexible mechanisms did become an integral part of the Kyoto Protocol, the European Commission decided to embrace this development. The first mention of emissions trading was made in the 1998 Communication where the Commission noted that '[a]n EC-wide approach to emissions trading could [...] facilitate the administrative implementation of the system and prevent new barriers to trade.'[98] The Commission also submitted that emissions trading would be the most cost-effective method for achieving the reduction targets set by the Kyoto Protocol.[99]

In the 2000 Green Paper, 'Greenhouse Gas Emissions Trading within the European Union', the Commission proposed an emissions trading scheme that was clearly based on the relatively centralized US Clean Air Program aimed at $SO_2$.[100] The Green Paper launched the European Climate Change Programme (ECCP) working groups, which provided important input for the 2001 directive proposal.[101] The working groups included representatives from the Commission, Member States, private sectors and NGOs. As a result of ECCP feedback, the 2001 proposal no longer included the option of auctioning for Phase I, and its introduction in Phase II was made dependent on the experiences in the

---

[95] Skjærseth and Wettestad, *EU Emissions Trading*.
[96] Wiener, 'Global Environmental Regulation', 779
[97] Skjærseth and Wettestad, 'The EU Emissions Trading System Revised', 67.
[98] European Commission (1998), at 2.
[99] European Commission (1998), at 18. The consequent Communication on the 'Implementation of the Kyoto Protocol' (European Commission, COM (1999) 230) led to the launch of the first European Climate Change Programme.
[100] Ellerman *et al.*, 'Markets for Clean Air'.
[101] European Commission, COM (2000) 87 final.

first phase.[102] Also, allowance allocation was placed in the hands of the Member States with limited oversight by the Commission.[103] Finally, some important industries were taken out of the scope of the EU ETS, aluminium and chemical industries, and $CO_2$ was the only greenhouse gas included.[104] The main concerns of the Commission were that decentralized emissions trading could lead to state aid violations, if Member States strategically allocated allowances to favoured industries, or possible distortions to the level playing field in the internal market.[105] In the end, the proposal advocated a centralized EU ETS with auctioning and limited scope for the use of CDM and JI credits.[106]

The first reading in Parliament suggested more than eighty amendments.[107] Most importantly, Parliament reverted back to the inclusion of all six greenhouse gases suggested in the Green Paper, and to the original set of industries, including aluminium and chemicals. Auctioning was foreseen at 15 per cent in both phases, with allocation by the Member States in line with the provisions of the Burden Sharing Agreement. Subject to these amendments, the Parliament approved the Directive 448 to 24, after which the Council of Environmental Ministers (Council) had to approve the Directive. The Council agreed to only a third of the proposed amendments by the Parliament, reducing the scope of the Directive back to one greenhouse gas ($CO_2$) and introducing a temporary opt-out for aluminium and chemical plants. Other important changes included provisions regarding initial allocation: 100 per cent grandfathering in Phase I, followed by an optional 10 per cent auctioning in Phase II. The Council also altered the penalty provisions under the Directive. Thus far, the penalties had been set at €50 (Phase I) or €100 (Phase II), or twice the market price (Phases I and II).[108] Under the Council's position, the penalties were reduced to a flat rate of €40 and €100 respectively for Phases I and II. This would have led installations to choose to pay the penalty rather than adhere to the quotas if the market prices rose above the penalty prices.[109]

---

[102] European Commission (2001), at 11 ('By 30 June 2006 the Commission will review the experience gained during the allocation of allowances for the period 2005–2007 with a view to ascertaining which harmonised method would be most appropriate in future.')
[103] European Commission (2001), at 11.
[104] Markussen and Svendsen, 'Industry Lobbying', 254.
[105] European Commission, COM (2000) 87 final, at 19.
[106] Skjærseth and Wettestad, 'The EU Emissions Trading System Revised', 81.
[107] Skjærseth and Wettestad, *EU Emissions Trading*, 4.
[108] European Commission (2001), at 14 and 27, and European Parliament (2002).
[109] D. H. Cole, 'A Glimmer of Hope: The EU's Emissions Trading Scheme' unpublished manuscript on file with author (2009), at 11.

The second reading by Parliament took place under intense time pressures since major amendments to the Directive would have meant the delay of the implementation of the Directive beyond 2005.[110] An agreement was brokered between the Council and Parliament by Jorge Moreira da Silva, which led to several compromises.[111] First, the scope of the EU ETS would be limited to $CO_2$ and six industrial sectors,[112] excluding aluminium and chemicals. Second, Member States would decide on competence allocation through NAPs, following the Burden Sharing Agreement and in line with the criteria set out in the Directive.[113] Third, auctioning would be allowed (but not mandatory) up to 5 per cent in Phase I and 10 per cent in Phase II.[114] Member States were moreover allowed to exclude specific installations, but not entire industries, until 31 December 2007.[115] Finally, penalties were set at a flat rate of €40 (Phase I) and €100 (Phase II), rather than be linked to the market price. After this 'coordinated' second reading by Parliament – which endorsed the Directive on 2 July 2003 – the Council approved the final Directive three weeks later without further amendments.

## 2 Winners and losers

Most European ETS sectors perceived of the trading scheme as a threat to their competitiveness, both with other European industries as with extra-European competitors. All industries included under the EU ETS, except for the large and renewable electricity producers and small-scale combined heat and power plants, looked to be net buyers of allowances.[116] Thus, for all but a few industries, any form of mandatory emissions trading constituted a loss, which could be mitigated by the design of the scheme.[117] This led to a powerful lobby to undercut implementation and enforcement rules at the national level.[118] The

---

[110] Skjærseth and Wettestad, *EU Emissions Trading*, 5.

[111] Parliament (2003).

[112] Energy production, ferrous metals production and processing (iron and steel), cement, pulp and paper plants, and the mineral industry.

[113] Article 9 of Council Directive 2003/87/EC.

[114] *Ibid.*, Article 10.

[115] *Ibid.*, Article 27.

[116] Markussen and Svendsen, 'Industry Lobbying', 248.

[117] Driesen, 'Is Emissions Trading an Economic Incentive Program?', 4 ('No economic reason exists for a polluter to agree to an allowance trading program absent a credible government ability to impose a traditional regulatory program. Allowance trading only reduces costs; it does not eliminate them.')

[118] See generally D. Demailly *et al.*, 'Differentiation and Dynamics of EU ETS Competitiveness Impacts', Climate Strategies, Research Theme 1.3 Interim Report

initial allocation rules (grandfathering), the flat-rate penalties, and the exclusion of the aluminium and chemical industries, together with the possibility of excluding certain specific installations, plays into the relevant industrial interests, especially regarding the mitigation of private reduction costs. The free initial allocation is particularly favourable to industry interests as it minimizes private costs and creates a barrier to entry for new entrants, which are forced to buy all their permits from incumbents.[119]

These provisions were the result of amendments suggested by the Council, which indicates that Member State and industry interests were closely aligned with respect to the first two trading phases.[120] During the initial UNFCCC negotiations, many of the EU Member States were strongly opposed to the development of an emissions trading scheme as a means of fulfilling their emission reduction commitments.[121] Conversely, the European Commission and Parliament strongly supported a centralized system of trading with limited linking and auctioning as an initial allocation method as soon as this was included in the UNFCCC system.[122] Their position received little support from environmental interest groups, some of which were markedly hostile

---

(2007); G. Klepper and S. M. Peterson, 'The EU Emissions Trading Scheme. Allowance Prices, Trade Flows, Competitiveness Effects', FEEM Working Paper No. 49.04 (2004); M. Grubb and K. Neuhoff, 'Allocation and Competitiveness in the EU Emissions Trading Scheme: Policy Overview' (2006) 6 *Climate Policy* 7–30; D. Demailly and P. Quirion, 'European Emission Trading Scheme and Competitiveness: A Case Study on the Iron and Steel Industry' (2008) 30 *Energy Economics* 2009–2027; R. Smale *et al.*, 'The Impact of $CO_2$ Emissions Trading on Firm Profits and Market Prices' (2006) 6 *Climate Policy* 29–46; U. Oberndorfer and K. Rennings, 'Costs and Competitiveness Effects of the European Union Emissions Trading Scheme' (2007) 17 *European Environment* 1–17.

[119] See e.g. Nash, 'Too Much Market?' and cf. Woerdman, Arcuri and Clò, 'Emissions Trading and the Polluter-Pays Principle'. See generally Buchanan and Tullock, 'Polluters' Profits and Political Response'.

[120] Oates and Portney, 'The Political Economy of Environmental Policy', 339 ('Systems of tradable permits with a free initial distribution can thus achieve support from various interest groups that may not be forthcoming for other forms of incentive-based instruments.')

[121] See e.g. Skjærseth and Wettestad, 'Implementing EU Emissions Trading', 282 ('In the negotiations leading up to the Kyoto Protocol, Germany was one of the leading sceptics within the EU to the use of the flexibility mechanisms.') Even Member States which were considered relative frontrunners only had experience with voluntary trading schemes. This experience was limited to Denmark and the United Kingdom.

[122] The Members of the European Parliament are elected through national elections, but once in Parliament they are grouped with party-counterparts of different Member States rather than with their countrymen. This means that national interests are fragmented by party policy not by national interest – a practice referred to as Party

towards emissions trading.[123] Significantly, consumer interest groups played virtually no part in the debates surrounding the EU ETS but would later emerge as significant 'losers'. Despite the free allocation of allowances, many industries did pass on 'higher' costs to the consumer, which resulted in higher electricity bills and other elevated prices.[124]

The Commission and Parliament were unsuccessful in securing their preferences in the final EU ETS Directive. However, they did manage to get concessions regarding the review of the EU ETS for the third trading phase, particularly with respect to the inclusion of additional industries and greenhouse gases,[125] as well as the method of allocation.[126] Moreover, the Directive was successful in creating an emissions trading scheme, which is now the largest in the world. In this market creation phase, the concessions made to the Council (and indirectly to the industries) may have been necessary to overcome the political opposition to the EU ETS.[127]

## 3 Explaining competence allocation

The most notable divergence between the theoretically optimal competence allocation and the actual competence allocation strategy in the first and second phases of the EU ETS was the decentralization of implementation at the national level. As predicted by the Commission, the Member State-level implementation resulted in over-allocation

Grouping. The Parliament therefore has a different constituency to consider than the national representatives in the Council. See F. Attina, 'The Voting Behavior of the European Parliament Members and the Problem of the Europarties' (1990) 18 *European Journal of Political Research* 557–579 (analysing data from roll-call votes in order to test Party Group cohesion and voting line-ups of Party Groups); S. Hix, A. Noury and G. Roland, 'Power to the Parties: Cohesion and Competition in the European Parliament, 1979–2001' (2005) 35 *British Journal of Political Science* 209–234.

[123] Skjærseth and Wettestad, 'The EU Emissions Trading System Revised', 81. See e.g. Sandbag, 'ETS S.O.S.: Why the flagship "EU Emissions Trading Policy" needs rescuing' (2009), available at www.sandbag.org.uk/site_media/pdfs/reports/Sandbag_ ETS_SOS_Report.pdf (finding that permits and offsets that can be bought before 2012 can be banked and used to cover nearly 40 per cent of the effort required to cover 2020 caps, without further cuts to domestic emissions taking place).

[124] See J. P. M. Sijm, *et al.*, 'The Impact of the EU ETS on Electricity Prices', Final report to DG Environment of the European Commission, ECN-E – 08-007 (2008), 12–13.

[125] Article 30(1) of Council Directive 2003/87/EC.

[126] *Ibid.*, Article 30(2).

[127] N. Gunningham and D. Sinclair, 'Policy Instrument Choice and Diffuse Source Pollution' (2005) 17 *Journal of Environmental Law* 51–81 at 75–77 ('Thus a phased approach has the potential to overcome, or at least reduce, much of the political opposition likely to eventuate if negative incentives were adopted in the first instance.')

198     A POLITICAL ECONOMY EXPLANATION OF THE EU ETS

to most sectors; the first verified emission figures (for 2005) showed that seventeen countries were 'long' (meaning that more permits were allocated than necessary), and only five countries were 'short'.[128] The situation did not improve significantly in preparation for the second trading phase and only the UK's NAP was unconditionally accepted by the Commission.[129] Regardless, the Commission's predictions of over-allocation were an insufficient counter weight to the Council's position to secure European-level implementation.

Some Member States, specifically Denmark and the United Kingdom, already had national registries in place, which facilitated the implementation of the EU ETS in these countries.[130] However, the vast majority of Member States did not have such prior experience, which made them more dependent on potentially unreliable information supplied by the industries. In some Member States, not only the information itself was lacking but also the legal provisions to obtain this information, which meant that Member States were dependent on information voluntarily submitted.[131] Most industries did cooperate with this data gathering but the benchmark of historic emissions heightened the chance of over-estimated past emissions.[132] Other avenues through which industry groups attempted to influence the process included the allocation between the ETS sectors and the non-ETS sectors. In Germany, which had been a leading sceptic of the EU ETS in the negotiations leading up to the Kyoto Protocol and whose industries were strongly opposed to mandatory trading,[133] the allocation decisions were based on fifty-two factors that led to 'a largely incalculable allocation result and to a hazy situation for many plant operators'.[134] The Commission had limited success in reducing the abuse of the NAPs; with respect to the first trading

[128] Skjærseth and Wettestad, 'Implementing EU Emissions Trading', 279. Large variations existed between the countries that were 'short'. Germany was short by just 0.2 per cent, whereas Ireland and the United Kingdom were short by 16.4 and 17.7 per cent respectively.
[129] *Ibid.*, 280.   [130] *Ibid.*, 282.   [131] Cole, 'A Glimmer of Hope'.   [132] *Ibid.*
[133] See Skjærseth and Wettestad, 'Implementing EU Emissions Trading', 282.
[134] F. C. Matthes and F. Schafhausen, 'Germany' in A. Ellerman, B. Buchner and C. Carraro (eds.), *Allocation in the European Emissions Trading Scheme: Rights, Rents and Fairness* (Cambridge University Press, 2007), 72–105, at 102, as quoted in Cole, 'A Glimmer of Hope', fn. 80. Cf., at 101 ('Nevertheless, some observers considered Germany's first NAP a remarkable achievement in light of that country's 'strong corporatist policy style and ... diversity of diverging interests,' as well as the limited ability of Germany's political system to 'manage complex political processes of this kind, on the basis of very uncertain and incomplete information ...').

phase, 4.5 per cent of the total allocation was shaved off, for the Phase II NAPs allocation was reduced by an average of 9.5 per cent.[135]

These experiences have confirmed the Commission's reservations regarding Member State implementation and in part explain the competence allocation during the first two trading phases. Both the NAPs (distribution at the Member State rather than European level) and the concession to grandfathering based on historic emissions (allowance allocation) represent wealth transfers to national industries that were included in the EU ETS.[136] Without these side-payments, the acceptance of the EU ETS by industry and Member States would have been unlikely. Moreover, these concessions had a clear expiration date: after the review provided for in Article 30 of the Directive, large-scale alteration of the EU ETS was foreseen.[137]

Enforcement played a far smaller role in the political process running up to the Directive. In fact, 'most member states paid very little attention to the crucial importance of a well developed and implemented system of monitoring, reporting, verification, inspection, and enforcement … [T]hese elements of the compliance chain were generally underestimated and undervalued by practically all parties.'[138] This may be explained by the focus on the political rather than practical aspects of the EU ETS, combined with the prevalent perception of emissions trading as requiring less monitoring.[139] The Commission did consider compliance monitoring and enforcement a salient issue, as is evidenced by the guidelines on the monitoring and reporting of greenhouse gases a few months after the adoption of the Directive.[140]

---

[135] Skjærseth and Wettestad, 'Implementing EU emissions trading', pp. 285 and 280. See also Cole, 'A Glimmer of Hope', at 22 ('It is difficult to imagine how the Commission possibly concluded that these allocations put member states on a 'path towards achieving' their Kyoto/Burden-sharing Agreement targets.')

[136] The incorporation of the polluter pays principle through auctioning was an important aspect for Parliament, which they were not able to incorporate in the final directive. See Markussen and Svendsen, 'Industry Lobbying', 253. See also E. Woerdman, O. Couwenberg and A. Nentjes, 'Energy Prices and Emissions Trading: Windfall Profits from Grandfathering?' (2009) 28 *European Journal of Law and Economics* 185–202.

[137] Article 30 of Council Directive 2003/87/EC.

[138] C. Dekkers and M. Oudenes, 'EU ETS in the Post-2012 Regime: Lessons Learned' in W. Th. Douma *et al.* (eds.), *The Kyoto Protocol and Beyond: Legal and Policy Challenges of Climate Change* (The Hague: TMC Asser Press, 2007) 185, at 189, as quoted in Cole, 'A Glimmer of Hope', at 28.

[139] See e.g. Chapter 1, note 174.

[140] Commission Decision 2004/156/EC.

In terms of competence allocation, enforcement competences are best shared between the national and regional levels in case of a regional carbon market, with compliance monitoring placed at the national level and market oversight at the regional level. Enforcement was not discussed in sufficient detail to conclude that such a shared allocation would have been unacceptable for the parties involved. Moreover, the market oversight problems that transpired through the VAT fraud cases and double-selling of credits were arguably part and parcel of the 'learning by doing' nature of especially the first trading phase.[141]

The positions of the Commission, Parliament, Council and industry groups during the EU ETS Directive's legislative process support the categorization of Phases I and II as 'market creation' phases. Both the division of competences and the substantive implementation provisions (especially the provisions pertaining to the scope of the EU ETS, the initial allocation provisions and linking) reflect a compromise between the ideal structure of the EU ETS as envisaged by the Commission and Parliament in the Green Paper, Proposal and parliamentary reports, and the relative hostility of the Member States and the industries towards a market-based mechanism. Importantly, even of those Member States that supported the introduction of emissions trading, and thus represented important allies to the Commission, only one was in favour of centralization (Denmark), while the others (United Kingdom, the Netherlands and Ireland) clearly preferred a decentralized system.[142] This compromise has been described as crucial in the creation of the EU ETS; Carbon Trust stated that 'the most fundamental political deal that enabled the EU ETS to be launched as a European-wide venture was that the Member States would retain the right to allocate allowances'.[143] The windfall profits and barriers to entry created by the free initial allocation represent important rents for the industries, and politically the discretion provided by the NAPs strengthened the Member States' domestic positions. For the third phase, we expect a power shift away

---

[141] More generally, national enforcement allows for some experimentation with an instrument, which is very new to the administrations. See Gunningham and Sinclair, 'Policy Instrument Choice', 76 ('A further benefit of a phased approach is that by sequencing the introduction of policy instruments, we can enjoy the benefits of regulatory pluralism without degenerating into a smorgasbord approach, or worse, counterproductive instrument clashes.').

[142] J. Wettestad, 'European Climate Policy: Toward Centralized Governance?' (2009) 26 *Review of Policy Research* 311–328 at 318.

[143] Carbon Trust Report, *Cutting Carbon in Europe – The 2020 Plans and the Future of the EU ETS* (London: Carbon Trust Publication, CTC 734, June 2009), at 21.

from the Member States and industries in favour of the Commission and the Parliament for several reasons. Firstly, the industries are now locked in to the system and are thus benefiting from its continued existence; the investments in CDM and JI projects plays an important role in this respect. Secondly, the position of the Commission and Parliament is strengthened by the availability of verified information and the increased visibility of the EU ETS. These developments confirm earlier predictions of over-allocation and harness the pressure of environmental and consumer interest groups that demand a more equitable EU ETS, particularly with regard to free allocation.

## B Consolidating the EU ETS: Phase III onwards

In order to understand the complete political process under which Directive 2009/29/EC was developed and adopted, it is important to note that the political climate in which the revisions to the EU ETS took place was very different from that in which it was developed. Since 2005, the European Union's influence over energy and climate policy had increased significantly and the issue had become increasingly salient for European citizens.[144] This increased awareness provided a counterbalance to industrial pressure in favour of a more lenient EU ETS. Moreover, the EU ETS had been earmarked as the centrepiece of the European climate change policy, and its success was key to maintaining the front-runner status that the EU had appropriated for itself with respect to the international climate change negotiations under the UNFCCC. Furthermore, Directive 2009/29/EC was developed as part of a broader energy and climate change package which created a possibility for compromises between different Member State interests beyond the scope of the Directive itself, for instance relating to renewable energy commitments or commitments for the non-ETS sectors. The resulting political decision-making process surrounding the revision of the EU ETS was highly complex and moreover under significant time pressure due to the then impending UNFCCC COP meeting in December of 2009.

[144] Skjærseth and Wettestad, 'The EU Emissions Trading System Revised', 71 (showing that the percentage of Eurobarometer respondents who listed climate change as their main worry increased from 39 per cent in 2003 to 57 per cent in 2007). The most recent report from October 2011 shows that 89 per cent of respondents consider climate change to be a serious problem with 68 per cent considering it a very serious problem, see DG Communication, 'Climate change' *Special Eurobarometer* 372, 2011, accessed 29 January 2012 at http://ec.europa.eu/public_opinion/archives/ebs/ebs_372_en.pdf, at 4.

## 1 The political decision-making process

The EU ETS is currently the largest trading scheme in existence, and acquired this status incredibly soon after its creation.[145] Article 30 of the original EU ETS Directive provided that a review of the EU ETS was to be drawn up by the Commission by 30 June 2006. In this review process, it was confirmed that the choice for decentralized implementation through NAPs, coupled with free initial allocation and several other design flaws, was undermining the credibility and functioning of the system.[146] Initial consultations were made through a web survey in the autumn of 2005, and the Commission published several policy documents regarding the further development of the EU ETS. The Communication 'Building a Global Carbon Market' of November 2006 showed the international ambition of the Commission with respect to the exemplary function of the EU ETS.[147] The consequent Communication on the integrated energy and climate package ('20 20 by 2020') was adopted by the Council in March 2007, confirming the central place of the EU ETS within a broader energy and climate package of the EU.[148]

In 2007, four consultation rounds on the review of the EU ETS were held within the second ECCP working group on emissions trading.[149] These consultation rounds involved the main stakeholders in the EU ETS (governmental and non-governmental) and focused on four specific themes within the EU ETS review: the scope of the Directive (industries and gases); compliance and enforcement; possible further harmonization of the EU ETS (potentially through a centralized cap); and the linkage to other emissions trading schemes of non-EU countries, CDM and JI projects.[150] With respect to competence allocation, the debates

---

[145] As early as 2006 trading volumes and value were more than double those of 2005. See Skjærseth and Wettestad, 'Implementing EU Emissions Trading', 280.

[146] C. Egenhofer, *et al.*, 'The EU Emissions Trading System and Climate Policy towards 2050: Real Incentives to Reduce Emissions and Drive Innovation?', CEPS Special Report (2010), at v ('There were numerous weaknesses in the initial pilot phase (2005–07) as well as the second phase (2008–12). Most of these have been addressed to be ready for the third phase starting in 2013. However, the perception of inefficiency and ineffectiveness continues to exist because most of the analysis in the literature is based on phases 1 and 2.')

[147] Commission Communication of 13 November 2006 on Building a Global Carbon Market – Report pursuant to Article 30 of Directive 2003/87/EC, COM(2006) 676 final.

[148] Presidency Conclusions adopted by the Council on 8/9 March 2007, 7224/1/07, CONCL 1/REV 1, 2 May 2007; European Commission, COM 30 (2008) 13 final.

[149] Consultations available at http://ec.europa.eu/clima/consultations/ consultations_archives_En.htm#ETS.

[150] Skjærseth and Wettestad, 'The EU Emissions Trading System Revised', 71-72.

regarding harmonization, both of the cap and of enforcement and monitoring activities, are most relevant. In the second meeting under the ECCP II, there seemed to be a relatively easy agreement on the need for further harmonization in the areas of enforcement and compliance.[151] At the third meeting, the issue of harmonization regarding other aspects of the EU ETS was discussed, particularly cap setting and allowance allocation.

This third meeting may be considered a turning point for the review of the EU ETS since this meeting made clear that most Member States would not necessarily oppose a centralized cap. The official report speaks of a 'unanimous call for improved cap setting [...] a general, very strong message calling for more harmonization, if not a centralized cap'.[152] Power generators, carbon traders and NGOs supported this point of view, stating explicitly that harmonization would 'take away the discretion of Member States resulting in adverse and distorting effects' and 'underpin the political leadership of the EU' to the outside world.[153] However, some (new) Member States had reservations, which may be linked to the discussion regarding increased use of auctioning within the EU ETS and the relative development of their industries. The official report states that 'albeit not against more harmonization, some Member States consider it important to take into account specific national circumstances, such as level of economic development, impact on economic growth, but also how the energy intensive or export dependent industry would be affected.'[154]

Allocation issues proved more controversial, with strong opposition from the industries regarding the introduction of auctioning and the weakening of benchmarks.[155] Several Member States indicated that they were open to supporting benchmarks, but also acknowledged their complexity and the risk of over-allocation to efficient installations.[156] Much of the debate on benchmarking was directly linked to the parallel discussion on auctioning. As was to be expected, industry representatives were strongly opposed to any auctioning before the completion

---

[151] *Ibid.*, 71.
[152] European Commission report of the 3rd meeting of the ECCP working group on emissions trading on the review of the EU ETS on further harmonization and increased predictability (21–22 May 2007), 070521–22 final report M3, at 3.
[153] *Ibid.*   [154] *Ibid.*   [155] *Ibid.*, at 15.
[156] *Ibid.* This was supported by NGOs who highlighted the risk of distortions arising from the implementation of benchmarks, which may result in 27 rather than one benchmark in one sector.

of a global agreement, citing impacts on competitiveness due to less investment in research and development as compared to the United States and Japan, and likening the auctioning to the imposition of a 'variable and unpredictable tax'.[157] From the perspective of the Member States, autonomy with respect to auction revenues appeared to be non-negotiable, although the option of reserving part of the proceeds for environmental projects was left open.[158] In his conclusions, the chairman – Mr Jos Delbeke from the European Commission – found that '[t]here is a lot of support for auctioning because of its merits in terms of transparency, delivering a clear price signal, avoiding windfall profits and others. The merits have to be balanced against the concerns relating to international competitiveness, however, this would not apply to all sectors, but only those which can adequately demonstrate that they are exposed to international competition or which cannot pass through their costs.'[159]

On 23 January 2008, the Commission put forward a proposal for a revised post-2012 EU ETS.[160] Building on the 2007 consultation process, the Commission proposal included a EU-wide cap based on fully harmonized rules for the 2013–2020 period.[161] Furthermore, auctioning was introduced as the main principle for allocation.[162] A distinction was made between the industrial installations and installations involved in electricity production, and only the latter would be exposed to full auctioning from 2013 onwards.[163] Energy-intensive industries would be allowed a transitional period starting with 20 per cent auctioning in 2013 to zero in 2020. Some industries and sub sectors that were found to be 'carbon leakage sensitive' would be eligible for 100 per cent free allocation if no international agreement would be in place.[164] The EU ETS reform proposal was not submitted in isolation; three other proposals were submitted at the same time, confirming that the EU ETS was now an integrated part of a broader EU energy and climate package. Due to the presentation of these proposals as a single package, possible political compromises were not restricted to the EU ETS Directive but also included Member State duties regarding emission reductions in the non-ETS sectors,[165] renewable energy shares,[166] and carbon capture and storage development.[167]

[157] Commission Report, 070521–22 final report M3,19.
[158] *Ibid.*, at 21.   [159] *Ibid.*, at 23.   [160] Commission Proposal, COM(2008) 30 final.
[161] *Ibid.*, Article 9.   [162] *Ibid.*, Article 10.   [163] *Ibid.*   [164] *Ibid.*
[165] Council Decision 406/2009/EC.   [166] Council Directive 2009/28/EC.
[167] Council Directive 2009/31/EC.

As mentioned, the impending COP meeting in Copenhagen put the decision-making process under considerable pressure. By mid-October 2008, the French EU Presidency announced that the energy and climate package, including the ETS reform, would be decided at the European Council meeting in December.[168] This announcement followed the meeting of the Parliament's Environmental Committee debate on the ETS proposal in early October. Parliament supported the reform, particularly the move towards centralization and more auctioning, but did call for an earmarking of auctioning revenues for climate-related purposes, the funding of carbon capture and storage projects through the new entrant reserve, and the exclusive use of 'high quality' CDM credits.[169] In the remaining month leading up to the December Council meeting, there were several 'trialogue' meetings between the Commission, Parliament and Council in which the final negotiations regarding the package took place.

The revised EU ETS as adopted at the December Council meeting largely follows the January proposal of the Commission. Summarizing the main changes with respect to cap setting and allowance allocation, we see that Article 9 of Directive 2009/29/EC introduces the centralized cap,[170] and that auctioning becomes the main allocation method.[171] With respect to auctioning, only the electricity producing sectors will experience full auctioning from 2013 onwards. Other industries will have to buy 20 per cent of their allowances in 2012, increasing to 70 per cent in 2020, with a view to 100 per cent in 2027.[172] Industries that are considered carbon leakage sensitive will receive free allowances, based on benchmarks rather than historical emissions.[173] Additional distributional provisions were included regarding auctioning revenues, with 10 per cent of revenues of Member States of high per capita GDP redistributed to low income Member States.[174] The use of CDM and JI credits is allowed to be used for up to 50 per cent of EU-wide reductions in the 2008–2020 period, without additional quality criteria for non-EU projects.[175]

Although monitoring and enforcement has become a more prominent feature for the EU ETS, little attention was paid to this issue in the ETS reform. Most developments regarding this issue were introduced

---

[168] Skjærseth and Wettestad, 'The EU Emissions Trading System Revised', 74.
[169] *Ibid.*    [170] Council Directive 2009/29/EC, Article 9.
[171] *Ibid.*, Article 10.    [172] *Ibid.*
[173] *Ibid.*, Article 10(a) and (b) on carbon leakage. See also Council Directive 2009/31/EC.
[174] Article 10, Council Directive 2009/29/EC.    [175] *Ibid.*

through Commission monitoring and reporting guidelines, starting from 2004,[176] and a Commission Communication on enhanced market oversight, which was published in December 2010.[177] In this Communication, the potential for market abuse in the now significant carbon market was recognized and an agenda was set for further consultation on the issue in line with Article 12(a) of the original ETS Directive.[178] In October 2011, proposals were submitted for directives and regulations on financial instruments, market abuse and criminal sanctions for market abuse.[179] The central role of the Commission in these initiatives reflects the consensus in the second EPPCII consultation on enforcement and monitoring.

## 2 Winners and losers

The first EU ETS Directive was substantially different from the Green Paper and the proposal on which it was based.[180] The differences between the January 2008 proposal for the revised directive and the version that was adopted in December of that year appear to be much smaller, indicating that the positions of the Member States, Parliament and Commission were relatively aligned from the beginning of the review. Considering the differences between the original and revised EU ETS directives, and the fact that these differences relate to hard-earned compromises in the first directives, this shift deserves further examination. This sub-section sets out the winners and losers of the reform, showing the important role of the additional proposals included in the energy and climate package with which the ETS reform was introduced and the changes in Member State interests.

Experience had shown that NAPs did not work due to free riding between Member States and sectors, were politically problematic for Member States who experienced extreme lobbying and were

---

[176] Commission Decision 2004/156/EC.
[177] Commission Communication, COM(2010) 796 final.    [178] *Ibid.*, at 2–3.
[179] Commission Proposal, COM(2011) 656 final; Commission Communication, Proposal of 20 October 2011 for a Regulation of the European Parliament and of the Council on markets in financial instruments and amending Regulation [EMIR] on OTC derivatives, central counterparties and trade repositories, COM(2011) 652 final; Commission Communication, Proposal of 20 October 2011 for a Regulation of the European Parliament and of the Council on insider dealing and market manipulation (market abuse), COM(2011) 651 final; Commission Communication, Proposal of 20 October 2011 for a Directive of the European Parliament and of the Council on criminal sanctions for insider dealing and market manipulation, COM(2011) 654 final.
[180] See section 2.A.1.

administratively draining.[181] The first expression of Member State interest in a more harmonized EU ETS came during the review of the Phase II NAPS, when the Climate Change Committee, composed of Member State representatives, called for the assessment of NAPs on a 'consistent, coherent, and robust basis',[182] referring to the verified emissions of 2005 as a basis for comparison.[183] During the 2007 consultations rounds, the Member States also did not express any strong desire to keep the decentralized system of NAPs. That said, an important distinction must be made between the 'old' and 'new' Member States, i.e. the western and eastern European Member States. Front-runner Member States such as the United Kingdom had become increasingly frustrated with laggard countries such as Poland and Estonia and were worried about the distorting effects of the NAPs.[184] Conversely the new Member States were worried that a central cap would restrict their economic growth and would impose unequal mitigation burdens.[185]

This divide was first vocalized in the 2007 consultation rounds,[186] and spilled over into the negotiations on the emission targets for the non-ETS sectors. Some central and eastern European Member States, led by Hungary, argued against the 2005 baseline adopted by the Commission, saying that this would not take sufficient account of early action by Member States and instead argued in favour of 1990 as a base year.[187] Although a base year of 1990 was not considered a feasible demand, this position opened the door for concessions with respect to the ETS requirements, for example the possibility for Member States to transfer part of their greenhouse gas allocation to subsequent years and other Member States, and the possibility to use CDM and JI credits for up to 3 per cent of emissions in the 2005 base year.[188] Moreover, electricity

---

[181] Wettestad, 'European Climate Policy'. See also Carbon Trust, *Cutting Carbon in Europe*, 21 ('[T]he process of National Allocation Plans proved to be fraught with such difficulty that most Member States will be glad to see them fade into history.')

[182] Wettestad, 'European Climate Policy', 319.

[183] Commission Communication on the assessment of national allocation plans for the allocation of greenhouse gas emission allowances in the second period of the EU Emissions Trading Scheme, 29 November 2006, COM(2006) 725 final, at 2.

[184] Wettestad, 'European Climate Policy', 319.

[185] Commission Impact Assessment, COM(2008) 16 final (for analysis of the distribution of costs related to mitigation).

[186] Commission Report, 070521–22 final report M3, 3.

[187] Lacasta, Oberthür, Santos and Barata, 'From Sharing the Burden to Sharing the Effort', 105.

[188] S. Oberthür and M. Pallemaerts, 'The EU's Internal and External Climate Policies: An Historical Overview', in Pallemaerts and Oberthür, *The New Climate Policies* 27–64, at 49–50.

providers to low GDP Member States could opt for free allocation (with a maximum of 70 per cent in 2013), if they provided more than 30 per cent of national electricity.[189]

Distribution-related compromises made it possible for the cap-setting centralization reform to pass without too much protest. This change represents a win for the Commission, which was confirmed in its earlier predictions regarding the undermining effect of the NAPs and would be relieved from some of the administrative burden placed on it through the complex review system.[190] Parliament supported most of the reforms of the EU ETS, in line with the pressures from environmental and consumer lobbying groups with respect to grandfathering. However, its concerns regarding the questionable environmental integrity of many CDM and JI projects were not reflected in the final directive. With respect to the non-ETS sectors, Parliament was more successful, ensuring that the use of international offsets was limited to 8 per cent rather than the 24 per cent suggested by the Commission.[191] Industrial interest groups have had to accept the introduction of auctioning, but the many exceptions in Article 10 of the Directive, combined with the Commission Decision on carbon leakage sensitive industries means that this introduction allows for substantial derogations.[192]

## 3 Explaining competence allocation

The reforms for Phase III, particularly with respect to cap-setting and allowance allocation but also regarding enforcement, move the division of competences within the EU ETS closer to our theoretical optimum. In line with our qualification of the first two trading phases as 'market creating', Phase III may be described as 'market consolidating': since the necessary elements for trading have been secured – registries, property right regimes – and significant investments have been made in the market and external credits, steps can be taken to improve the market's functioning. Based on this typology, we predicted a move towards the optimal allocation, as preferred by the Commission and Parliament, since (i) parties are now locked in to the system and are

---

[189] Article 10(c) of Council Directive 2009/29/EC.
[190] Wettestad, 'European Climate Policy', 321.
[191] European Parliament (2008), at 34–37.
[192] Commission Decision 2010/2/EC of 24 December 2009 determining, pursuant to Directive 2003/87/EC of the European Parliament and of the Council, a list of sectors and subsectors which are deemed to be exposed to a significant risk of carbon leakage, OJ 2010 No. L1, 5 January 2010.

thus benefiting from its continued existence, due to inter alia investments in CDM and JI projects; and (ii) the availability of verified information and the increased visibility of the EU ETS increases the political acceptability of certain measures since more information is available regarding their effects.

The negative experiences of the Member States with the NAPs meant they were also increasingly in favour of centralization. The perceived inequity between the Member States as a result of the failure or unwillingness of some Member States to adhere to the deadlines and requirements, together with the intense domestic pressure related to cap-division and competence allocation further strengthened the case for centralized implementation. The position of the ETS within the broader energy and climate package made negotiation with different-minded Member States easier since concessions could be made in other areas. That said, industrial lobbying has also been intense at the European level and these groups have no doubt influenced benchmarking and carbon leakage standards. The transition provisions contain important ad hoc concessions made to certain Member States and sectors, which suggests that norm distribution at EU level is not immune from pressures comparable to those subjected on the NAPs. Nevertheless, the playing field is arguably more level since all industries now have to lobby at the European level, which reduces the divergence caused by differing national circumstances.

The locked-in effect of the market consolidation stage also explains some of the changes in allowance allocation rules, most notably the move to auctioning. The recent inclusion of the aviation sector is also accompanied by large-scale grandfathering: 85 per cent in 2012, decreasing to 82 per cent in 2020.[193] This is another example of initial wealth transfer to newly included ETS sectors in order to secure political acceptability. Similarly, investments in CDM and JI have been very profitable for many Member States, mostly as buyers but also as sellers. This is reflected in the EU's position in the UNFCCC and Kyoto Protocol negotiations, and reflected in the outcome of Durban, which included agreement on a second commitment period for the Kyoto Protocol without a gap, which confirms that the CDM and JI mechanisms can continue.[194] More generally, credibility and successful functioning of

---

[193] Airlines with relatively new, and thus clean, aeroplanes were some of the first to favour very strict requirements and early inclusion dates.
[194] Conference of the Parties 17 (Durban) (November/December 2011).

the EU ETS is an important part of the EU's external climate policy, as it is the basis of the EU's 'green leadership' position. From this self-proclaimed leadership position the EU has recently taken unilateral action to include non-EU based aviation companies into the EU ETS, to the dismay of the international community.[195]

## 3 Conclusions

The political process of decision-making determines whether and how certain activities are regulated. Academic scholarship may try to influence the outcomes of political decision-making by providing information about the effects of certain types and methods of regulation, for instance through cost-benefit analyses, but ultimately the decisions are taken by political bodies representing societal and private interests. In the same vein, our theoretical framework of competence allocation can set out the optimal division of powers among several levels of governance based on normative criteria inspired by the economic and legal theories of federalism. However, the eventual distribution of competences will depend on political compromise between the relevant stakeholders, which may or may not be in line with the theoretical optimum. It is therefore important to supplement our prescriptive analysis of competence allocation with an explanatory study of political decision-making in the EU ETS. By applying a political economy perspective to these developments, the idea that markets can exist as economic processes born out of economic necessity without political intervention is explicitly rejected.[196] A carbon market such as the one created in the EU ETS is a market that exists solely due to government intervention, and as such is inherently political.[197]

By analysing the political decision-making process surrounding the creation and reform of the EU ETS, we find several explanations for its design. All actors involved in this process were subject to both 'internal'

---

[195] C-366/10 *Air Transport Association of America and Others* v. *The Secretary of State for Energy and Climate Change*, OJ 2010 C 260/12, of 21 December 2011.

[196] R. Gilpin, *Global Political Economy: Understanding the International Economic Order* (Princeton: Princeton University Press, 2001) and H. Chang, 'Breaking the Mould: an Institutionalist Political Economy Alternative to the Neo-Liberal Theory of the Market and the State' (2002) 26 (5) *Cambridge Journal of Economics* 539–559 at 547.

[197] See also Lederer, 'Market Making via Regulation', 6.

and 'external' pressures, such as domestic and European/international political commitments. The way in which these different interests and pressures were accommodated in the original and revised EU ETS Directive depends on the relative position of the different actors *inter se*, i.e. the political economy of the EU ETS. In turn, these positions can for a large part be explained by the stage of development of the EU ETS itself. The 'market creation' nature of the original Directive strengthened the position of the Member States and the industries since an EU ETS with centralized cap setting and auctioning would have been politically unacceptable for these groups. Since the creation of a market was more important for the Commission and Parliament than the creation of the 'perfect' market, the compromises with respect to cap setting, allocation and some other aspects such as fines and the use of external credits, were acceptable, especially given the foreseen review of the EU ETS.

For the revised EU ETS starting in Phase III, the new situation of market consolidation provides for very different compromises. The revised EU ETS Directive moves closer to a fully centralized system and starts to reduce the rents of the industries through the introduction of auctioning. The experiences with the EU ETS leading up to its review – especially over-allocation and windfall profits – have made the problems of decentralization self-evident and provide Member States with politically acceptable grounds for deferring to the European level for cap setting and restricting free allocation. Moreover, the positioning of the EU ETS within the broader energy and climate package enabled distributional compromises that are not reflected in the EU ETS Directive itself.

Despite these changes, it is too early to conclude that the functioning of the EU ETS has markedly improved. The financial crisis has significantly lowered the demand for emission allowances, which has led to a situation of low prices. Efforts of the Commission to remedy this situation through the 'back loading' of allowances,[198] where allowances are temporarily withheld from the market, have met with much resistance. Significantly, the European Parliament initially voted against the proposal despite its overall support of the EU ETS.[199] This raises two

---

[198] This proposal was supported by the United Kingdom and twelve other Member States, see www.gov.uk/government/news/uk-rallies-12-eu-countries-behind-backloading-twin-track-emissions-trading-system-ets-reform.

[199] The proposal was later approved on 3 July 2013, by 344 votes to 311.

questions: whether a first-best allocation of competences, enabled by a favourable political climate, is sufficient to create a well-functioning regulatory regime; and what can be said about the future of the EU ETS in light of our analysis.[200]

[200] Congleton, *The Political Economy*, at 66: 'The political economy of the regulatory process teaches us that it is not enough to formulate "optimal" or efficient policies in the abstract. Policy relevance requires that such solutions be packaged with those institutional-legal changes needed to make them politically feasible. If the lessons of this model are robust, there is likely to be a strong and pervasive distaste for efficiency among interest groups in the area of environmental policy. And this aversion appears to be exacerbated by existing institutions and practices in commercial policy, particularly the rules for contingent protection. Interest-groups support for the inefficient policy is not terribly surprising since efficiency implies the absence of rents, which are the lifeblood of such groups. The challenge for policymakers (and policy economists) is to redirect the efforts of pressure groups toward socially desirable policies without also initiating new opportunities for rent seeking.'

# Epilogue
## Climate realities and regulatory theories

During its relatively short life, roughly coinciding with the period in which this book was written, the European Union Emissions Trading Scheme (EU ETS) has experienced varying degrees of success and failure. In analysing the functioning of the EU ETS, I have focused on the consequences of regulatory competence allocation. My interest in competence allocation is based on a broader ambition to bring existing theories of federalism (both legal and economic) more closely in line with the increasingly complex, multi-level governance reality that surrounds us. As the fragmentation of the regulatory process becomes the rule rather than the exception, our understanding of competence allocation should move beyond the binary choice of centralizing or decentralizing 'policy' and start to distinguish the roles of norm setting, implementation and enforcement in the regulatory process.

The application of this general interest to the EU ETS led to a consideration of the confrontation between the first-best world of ideal competence allocation and the second-best world of regulatory reality. In 1964, in a slightly different but relevant context, Ronald Coase argued that society's various mechanisms for organizing social relations are all 'more or less failures'.[1] His statement highlights the shortcomings of recommendations based on models that assume a first-best world, composed of rational actors with perfect information striving towards 'optimality'. The regulation of social interactions necessarily takes place in a second-best world, where much of the model's optimality

---

[1] R. H. Coase, 'The Regulated Industries', in 'Papers and Proceedings of the Seventy-sixth Annual Meeting of the American Economic Association' (1964) 54 *American Economic Review* 192–197 at 195.

is lost. The goal, then, is to structure our solutions 'in ways that under the circumstances, are least likely to fail or are likely to fail the least'.[2] A first-best model allows us to identify the most important failings of our regulatory strategies even if our subsequent recommendations are implemented in a second-best world.

The development of the EU ETS also shows that the link between regulatory functioning and competence allocation is an indirect one: for instance, the problem of over-allocation in Phases I and II of the EU ETS was the direct consequence of a design choice in favour of National Allocation Plans (NAPs). That design choice in turn was the result of implementation by the Member States, who favoured this particular approach, rather than implementation through a European-level cap-setting process. The rules of the EU ETS 'game' have undergone continuous change. Some of these changes are internal to the EU ETS – conscious alterations to its design, aimed at improving its functioning by the respective norm setters and/or implementers. Other changes have been inspired and/or necessitated by external events, such as a widespread economic recession that has had a profound impact on the energy and production needs of European companies and consumers. The interrelatedness of competence allocation and instrument design choices does not imply a causal link between competence allocation and regulatory functioning. There are numerous internal and external factors that contribute to optimal or sub-optimal functioning of a regulatory instrument – such as design variations[3] or economic recession – and competence allocation is one of these factors. Recognizing the modest part played by competence allocation within the EU ETS, what may be said about the future development of the EU ETS and the role of competence allocation within regulatory theory generally?

---

[2] Cole, *Pollution and Property*.

[3] These ongoing changes cause a level of legal uncertainty with respect to the design of the EU ETS, which some parties consider harmful, especially when allowance allocation rules are involved – see e.g. Dari-Mattiacci and van Zeben, 'Legal Uncertainty and Market Uncertainty' (showing that it is not legal uncertainty in itself that is harmful – this is an intrinsic feature of artificial markets – but rather the tools available to the European Courts in dealing with this uncertainty). Conversely, legal uncertainty may also be considered essential for flexibility, allowing for improvements to the design of the EU ETS in ways that would have been impossible under the international Kyoto Protocol regime where lack of consensus has stalled any progress and prevented constructive change to the regime. See Cole, 'From Global to Polycentric Climate Governance' (arguing relatedly that this is one of the elements that speaks in favour of a polycentric approach, where several regimes would develop simultaneously, allowing for more experimentation and learning).

# 1 The EU ETS: Taking the long way home?

The first two trading phases most clearly showed divergences between competence allocation in the EU ETS and the optimized allocation in our stylized theoretical framework. The national implementation and enforcement of the norms set through the UNFCCC and Kyoto Protocol processes left sufficient room for European Member States to externalize costs and/or to free ride on others' efforts through sub-optimal implementation and enforcement choices.[4] These choices have been explained at the hand of a political economy analysis of the decision-making process surrounding the EU ETS, within which the developmental stages of the EU ETS market played a significant role.[5] As the EU ETS market matured, abuses of implementation and enforcement lapses have increasingly been understood and corrected. Nonetheless, improved competence allocation, greater information availability and a deeper understanding of the emissions trading instrument overall have not prevented problems to carry over from Phase II to Phase III, which started in January 2013. Pre-existing over-allocation, continuing financial downturn, and, ironically, the EU's own Energy Efficiency programmes,[6] have resulted in a surplus of more than one billion allowances and a resulting drop in allowance prices of 83 per cent, of which 69 per cent took place in the year from mid-2012 to mid-2013.[7]

The European Commission was concerned that the over supply of allowances would persist past 2020, especially with additional allowances coming onto the market again in 2013. In November 2012, the European Commission acted upon its concerns by proposing to set aside 900 million allowances over the 2013–2015 period, to be 'back loaded' (reintroduced) into the market in 2019 and 2020.[8] 'The State

---

[4] See Chapters 3 and 4.    [5] See Chapter 5.

[6] These programmes have further reduced the demand for allowances, already in decline since 2011. See S. Moore, 'If the Cap Fits: Reform of European Climate Policy and the EU Emissions Trading System', Policy Exchange (2013), available at www.policyexchange.org.uk/publications/category/item/if-the-cap-fits-reform-of-european-climate-policy-and-the-eu-emissions-trading-system, at 40.

[7] Measured between 2008 and 2013, see W. Burns, 'The European Union's Emissions Trading System: Climate Model, Now Climate Muddle?', posted 15 July 2013, www.ourenergypolicy.org/the-european-unions-emissions-trading-system-climate-model-now-climate-muddle/.

[8] European Commission, 'Commission submits draft amendment to back load 900 million allowances to the years 2019 and 2020' (press release, 12 November 2012), http://ec.europa.eu/clima/news/articles/news_2012111203_en.htm.

of the European Carbon Market in 2012' report that was published in the same month put forward several additional options for structural reform, including the permanent withdrawal of the set-aside allowances.[9] In a bid to delay the auction of some allowances and to revive the allowance price, the Commission pushed for an expedited vote on the 'back loading' proposal, separate from and before the complete EU ETS review.[10] On 16 April 2013, the European Parliament voted against the back loading proposal, which forced a plenary debate of the proposal, as had been advocated by the energy-intensive industries,[11] and caused significant delays in its eventual adoption. Following the rejection of the Commission's proposal, twelve Member States explicitly united in favour of back loading, calling for the costs of back loading to be clarified and on Parliament to schedule a second vote by July 2013, as well as for the Commission to propose structural reforms by the end of 2013.[12] Ultimately, the European Parliament passed an amended proposal on 7 July 2013.[13]

Some commentators took the back loading proposal, and its initial rejection, to signal the demise of the EU ETS in its entirety.[14] The European Parliament has become increasingly vocal within certain policy areas, such as climate change, but has seldom used its influence to vote against Commission proposals that are ostensibly in favour of the environment, such as the back loading proposal. In terms of competence allocation, the Parliament's actions raise again questions

---

[9] Commission Communication of 14 November 2012, 'The State of the European Carbon Market in 2012', COM(2012) 652 final, at 7–8.

[10] Some separate review moments are explicitly provided for in the Directive (Council Directive 2009/29/EC), for instance in Article 9 with respect to the possible revision of the cap by 2025, as well as harmonization rules (Article 24a).

[11] Dutch Emission Authority, Nieuwsbrief emissiehandel No. 108, 28 February 2013, http://m15.mailplus.nl/genericservice/code/servlet/React?wpEncId=DiLARC4Cny&wpM essageId=10731&userId=315100072&command=viewPage&activityId=test&encId=1#a rtikel1.

[12] Statement by environmental ministers of the United Kingdom, Germany, France, the Netherlands, Sweden, Denmark, Portugal, Finland and Slovenia, 7 May 2013, www.gov.uk/government/news/european-ministers-set-out-timetable-for-eu-ets-reform.

[13] MEMO/13/653, 'Climate Action Commissioner Connie Hedegaard welcomes the European Parliament's positive vote on the carbon market "backloading" proposal', 3 August 2013.

[14] 'ETS, RIP?', *The Economist*, 20 April 2013; Editorial Board, 'Europe is becoming a green-energy basket case', *Washington Post*, 22 April 2013; F. Harvey, 'EU urged to revive flagging emissions trading scheme', *The Guardian*, 15 February 2013; Point Carbon, 'Backloading voted down, EU ETS in disarray', www.pointcarbon.com/aboutus/pressroom/pressreleases/1.2287282.

regarding interactions between actors at the same regulatory level and to what extent their interests are indeed aligned. In this specific case, the initial disagreement between the Commission and Parliament led to an (arguably) better back loading plan with stricter conditions and earlier, more predictable, reintroduction of credits, 600 million of which are now earmarked for innovation purposes.[15] Both interactions within regulatory levels as well as feedback effects must thus be considered important avenues for future research.

Back loading has not been the only controversial feature of the future of the EU ETS. In lieu of action by the international community, the EU has taken unilateral action in several areas that had been part of the international negotiation agenda, such as the regulation of aviation and maritime emissions.[16] The EU's self-assigned competence in this area has met with political and legal resistance,[17] and creates another type of interaction that has not yet been discussed. Any divergences between the Member States regarding the EU ETS have thus far been played out in the European political process and the European courts; for instances of disaccord between the EU and external regional or national actors it is unlikely that the international political process, or courts, can offer the same structured dialogue.[18] As such, the 'external' dimension of competence allocation within the EU ETS raises new questions about the action radius of agencies' decisions. In allocating competences, the impact on third party actors requires additional attention.

Finally, our discussion of competence allocation has thus far excluded the role of private parties, with the exception of those elements of the EU ETS that rely on private party action, particularly with respect to monitoring and verification. These duties directly feed back into the enforcement duties of national authorities that often have to rely on this information when making their enforcement decisions. Much of the information needed for private actors to be more involved with the EU ETS, for instance through monitoring activities outside those

---

[15] www.europarl.europa.eu/news/nl/pressroom/content/20130617IPR12344/html/ Environment-Committee-reaffirms-support-for-emissions-trading-fix.

[16] Council Conclusions of 21 October 2009 on EU position for the Copenhagen Climate Conference, 2968th Environmental Council meeting. Accessed 21 January 2012 atwww.consilium.europa.eu/uedocs/cms_data/docs/pressdata/en/envir/110634.pdf, at para. 28.

[17] B. Mayer, 'Case C-366/10, *Air Transport Association of America and Others* v. *Secretary of State for Energy and Climate Change*, Judgment of the Court of Justice (Grand Chamber) of 21 December 2011', (2012) 49 *Common Market Law Review* 1113–1140.

[18] See also Cole, 'From Global to Polycentric Climate Governance'.

mandated by the EU ETS Directive, is already available through the EU Pollutant Emissions Register and the Community Transaction Log.[19] This increased access to information also allows for more efficient use of third party verifiers as 'certifiers' for the reliability of certain actors on the market.[20] Encouraging active participation of private actors, when desirable,[21] requires a deeper understanding of the incentives of these parties, and the institutional prerequisites for their participation. Given that the implementation of the EU ETS has moved primarily to the European level, the limited access of private parties to the European courts forms a stumbling block for their full participation since it makes it harder to question European decision-making on the EU ETS.[22]

[19] Commission Decision 2000/479/EC of 17 July 2000 on the implementation of a European pollutant emission register (EPER) according to Article 15 of Council Directive 96/61/EC concerning integrated pollution prevention and control (IPCC) (notified under document number C(2000) 2004) (2000) OJ No. L192 36. Originally designed to 'fulfil the public's right to know about the releases of pollutants in their neighbourhood', it provides public parties web-based access to water and air emissions of fifty pollutants from large and medium-sized industrial point sources in the EU. Member States must report every three years. See www.eea.europa.eu/data-and-maps/data/eper-the-european-pollutant-emission-register-4. Now supplemented by the European Pollutant Release and Transfer Register (E-PRTR) as put in place by Regulation No. 166/2006 of the European Parliament and the Council of 18 January 2006 concerning the establishment of a European Pollutant Release and Transfer Register and amending Council Directives 91/689/EEC and 96/61/EC. This combined register collects information for ninety-one substances released into air and water as well as the transfer of waste from industrial facilities across sixty-five sectors. The register covers 29,000 facilities in 32 countries (the EU28 (excluding Croatia), Iceland, Liechtenstein, Norway, Switzerland and Serbia).

[20] This could also affect the secondary markets in which the ETS sectors are active since consumers may exercise their buying power in response to environmental misconduct. See Badrinath and Bolster, 'The Role of Market Forces'; and van Aaken, 'Effectuating Public International Law' (arguing for a more active role of the market in the enforcement of public international law. Markets here refer to final consumer markets, for instance regarding the diamond trade.)

[21] See M. Cohen, 'Monitoring and Enforcement of Environmental Policy', in T. Tietenberg and H. Folmer (eds.), *International Yearbook of Environmental and Resource Economics* (Cheltenham: Edward Elgar Publishers, 1998/1999) 44–106 (who finds that private enforcement of environmental law may lead to over-deterrence and may be used in order to further private interests. He discusses empirical studies on the situation where EPA enforcement fell in the United States and that an argument can be made that private enforcement may fill the gap in enforcement against public polluters.)

[22] These parties fail to fulfil the requirements for legal standing as the directive does not convey any 'unconditional' or 'sufficiently precise' rights to them vis-à-vis the European institutions. In the context of the EU ETS, actions could be brought against national authorities issuing, for instance, allocation decisions during Phases I and II

The development of the EU ETS fits in rather well with a second-best world inhabited by different types and degrees of regulatory failure. That said, through these failings, the EU ETS is slowly improved and arguably moved closer to the theoretical first-best design. Ultimately, it may not be desirable for the EU ETS to strive to, or conform with, that first-best model, even if this were possible. The living reality of the EU ETS is much richer than the model. However, taking the long way home may prove beneficial to both the design and longevity of the EU ETS as we learn which policy recommendations survive real world application.

## 2 Regulatory theories: Extensions

Rather than break down the existing structures of economic and legal theories of federalism, the perspective of competence allocation as developed in this book attempts to construct an additional level of analysis. As such, the theoretical framework developed here is not case-specific to the mitigation of greenhouse gas reductions through emissions trading; the normative values applied in the current analysis may be replaced by any other value. The relevant policy area should inform the choice and ranking of the normative standards applied to different competence allocations. For instance, democratic legitimacy or accountability could be taken as a first-order consideration. The question then becomes: which allocation best ensures a high level of legitimacy or accountability with respect to norm setting, implementation and enforcement? While this may change the implications for the architecture of the regulatory system, the system of analysis remains the same.[23] Aside from changing the normative perspective applied

---

since these decisions would address a specific group of plaintiffs. See generally J. Jans and H. Vedder, *European Environmental Law* (Groningen: Europa Law Publishing, 3rd revised edn, 2008), at 169. See also Case C-72/95, *Aannemersbedrijf P.K. Kraaijeveld BV e.a.* v. *Gedeputeerde Staten van Zuid-Holland* [1996] ECR I-05403; Case C431/92, *Commission* v. *Germany* [1995] ECR I-2189 and Case C236/92, *Comitato di Coordinamento per la Difesa della Cava and others* v. *Regione Lombardia and others* [1994] ECR I-03463. In this last case, the distinct nature of environmental law and directives is hardly recognized. Similarly, actions between private parties also miss a legal basis in the directive since the directive does not have so-called 'horizontal direct effect'.

[23] Similarly, this analysis may be applied to policy domains that are exclusively national. The multi-level nature of the analysis can be restricted to two levels, contained within one national system.

to competence allocation decisions, several other extensions to the current theoretical framework may be proposed.

*Shared competences* – In refining the framework of analysis, we can relax the assumption of competence allocation as an either/or choice and incorporate the sharing of competences among regulators at different levels. In our analysis of the EU ETS, we have already touched upon this issue with respect to enforcement, where a distinction can be made between enforcement activities with respect to individual installations and market oversight activities. More subtle forms of competence sharing can be envisaged: with respect to norm setting, the new citizen's initiative within the EU provides an interesting example. Under Article 11(4) of the TEU, a minimum of one million citizens from a significant number of Member States may invite the Commission to create a legislative proposal. Once the European Commission proposes a new law, the European Parliament and the Council of the European Union must adopt it.[24] This new initiative to give power to citizens raises the question as to the allocation of norm-setting powers; can it be considered 'shared' among the private and European level?[25] Once the possibility of shared competences is included in our framework, the lessons of polycentric theory become increasingly relevant. A polycentric system would divide regulatory competences among many different levels, which can be both public and private, with varying degrees of responsibility and authority.[26] Similarly, more attention could be paid to the possibility of delegation (as opposed to allocation).

*Feedback and 'repeat players'* – Another element that deserves further analysis is the consequence of repeated interaction between regulatory agencies.[27] The changed competence allocation structure in the EU ETS for the third trading phase is greatly influenced by the experiences in the first two periods with respect to NAPs and enforcement problems.

---

[24] The Council needs to vote by qualified majority, see Articles 289 and 294 of the TFEU.

[25] Another important element of sharing could be the role of voting behaviour at different levels. See Rose-Ackerman, 'Does Federalism Matter?', 157 (finding that without constitutional limits, a majority of citizens may be so unhappy with the mixture of independent state choices under federalism that they favour a more powerful central government than they would in a unitary system).

[26] See Ostrom, Tiebout and Warren, 'The Organization of Government in Metropolitan Areas'; Ostrom, 'A Polycentric Approach for Coping with Climate Change'; Cole, 'From Global to Polycentric Climate Governance'.

[27] Thanks to Ariel Porat for highlighting this interaction. Another important aspect in this interaction is the role of trust and knowledge building, see Ostrom, 'Reflections on "Some Unsettled Problems of Irrigation"'.

This has been addressed primarily through shifts in competence allocation. In some settings, changes in competence allocation are not feasible but we may still encounter certain 'feedback effects' between different regulatory competences. For instance, norms might be tightened beyond the optimal level if the norm setter knows that under-enforcement has taken place in the past.[28] This feedback effect could be an interesting extension of the current framework, pertaining to the content of the regulatory competences as well as to their position within the system of governance.

*Comparative research* – Competence allocation provides an additional basis for comparative research. Although the relationship between the United States federal government and its states differs substantially from that between the European Union and its Member States, lessons may be learned with respect to the competence allocation under the US $SO_2$ system and the EU ETS. As highlighted by Sigman, 'public policies for pollution control in the United States are a hybrid of centralized standard setting and decentralized implementation and enforcement'.[29] This is comparable to the situation we have encountered in the EU with respect to the EU ETS in the first two phases, and with respect to environmental law more generally.[30] However, there are also important differences, for instance with respect to the role of the Environmental Protection Agency (EPA) in the United States, which may step in if states fail to enforce environmental policy.[31] The role of the European Environment Agency is not (yet) comparable to that of the EPA, even though, based on the United States experience, it could

---

[28] See E. Hutchinson and P. W. Kennedy, 'State Enforcement of Federal Standards: Implications for Interstate Pollution' (2008) 30 *Resource and Energy Economics* 316–344 (arguing that in order to ensure enforcement of US federal policy on transboundary air pollutants under the US Clean Air Act by states, stricter than first-best standards may be instrumental whereas location-based standards should be avoided since this can exacerbate the enforcement problem). See cf. D. M. Driesen, 'Choosing Environmental Instruments in a Transnational Context' (2000) 27 *Ecology Law Quarterly* 1–52 at 27 (on *ex ante* rather than *ex post* checks on compliance efforts by an international body on a national authority).

[29] Sigman, 'Transboundary Spillovers', 82. On this form of competence allocation see also Lin, 'How Should Standards Be Set' (conjoint federalism is a form of federal governance where the central government sets the standard (norm setting), while the local governments meet the standard (implementation and enforcement).

[30] See e.g. T. Konstadinides, *Division of Powers in European Union Law: The Delimitation of Internal Competence between the EU and the Member States* (The Hague: Kluwer Law International, 2009), 25–26.

[31] Sigman, 'Transboundary Spillovers', 84–85.

improve enforcement practices in the EU. By focusing primarily on the de facto and functional division of powers, rather than constitutional differences, competence allocation can present a complementary basis for comparative research.

In conclusion, regardless of its global climate change setting, our analysis of the EU ETS is primarily an EU-based reflection on the role of agencies in a multi-level governance structure. Since the European treaties are not founded on a principle of separation of powers, but rather one of 'institutional balance',[32] this European context makes the exercise particularly challenging and worthwhile. Questions remain regarding action taken 'within' the European level, where the roles of the European institutions are well defined but nevertheless frequently overlap.[33] Similarly, the relationship between the European, national and sub-national levels offers a rich area of future research. Our political economy explanation for competence allocation within the EU ETS only scratches the surface of the complex top-down and bottom-up interactions within the EU that are only tentatively moderated by, inter alia, the subsidiarity principle.[34] The conscious decision to adopt an extra-legal perspective on the division of competence within the EU does not deny, or belittle, the 'constitutional' issues that competence allocation raises. Fundamental questions regarding democracy, representation and responsiveness must be addressed,[35] and an allocation criterion based on the capture of externalities – however analytically sound – is unlikely to capture the hearts of European citizens.

---

[32] R. Grzeszczak, 'Executuve Power in the European Union', in R. Grzeszczak and I. Karolewski (eds.), *The Multi-Level and Polycentric European Union: Legal and Political Studies* (Lit Verlag, 2012) 77–102.

[33] See also H. M. Osofsky, 'The Intersection of Scale, Science, and Law in Massachusetts v. EPA', in W. G. Burns and H. M. Osofsky (eds.) *Adjudicating Climate Change: State, National, and International Approaches* (Cambridge University Press, 2009) 129–144 on the interplay between scale and policy in the American context.

[34] The concept of subsidiarity is currently underused, despite being ubiquitous in the political debate, due to the continuing vagueness of the criteria for competence allocation. See e.g. Frey and Eichenberger, 'FOCJ', 323 ('"Subsidiarity" as proclaimed in the Maastricht Treaty is generally recognized to be more a vague goal than a concept with content'). On European constitutionalism generally, see e.g. J. H. H. Weiler, 'The Reformation of European Constitutionalism' (1997) 35 *Journal of Common Market Studies* 97–131; B. Kohler-Koch and R. Eising (eds.), *The Transformation of Governance in the European Union* (London: Routledge, 2004); C. Reh, 'De-Constitutionalizing the European Union?' (2009) 47 *Journal of Common Market Studies* 625–650.

[35] See J. A. W. van Zeben, 'A Polycentric European Union' (on file with author).

Before being able to move forward with improving the European project, clear criteria should be set for our assessment of the division of powers within the European Union. Marie Curie (1894) rightly observed that in the end, 'one never notices what has been done. One can only see what remains to be done'.

# Bibliography

Aaken, A. van 'Effectuating Public International Law Through Market Mechanisms?' (2009) 165 *Journal of Institutional and Theoretical Economics* 33–57

Abate, R. 'Kyoto or Not, Here We Come: The Promise and Perils of the Piecemeal Approach to Climate Change Regulation in the United States' (2006) 15 *Cornell Journal of Law and Public Policy* 369–401

Abbot, C. *Enforcing Pollution Control Regulation – Strengthening Sanctions and Improving Deterrence* (Oxford: Hart Publishing, 2009)

Ackerman, B. and Hassler, W. *Clean Coal/Dirty Air or How the Clean Air Act Became a Multibillion-Dollar Bail-Out for High-Sulfur Coal Producers and What Should Be Done About It* (Binghamton, NY: Vail-Ballou Press, 1981)

Ackerman, B. and Stewart, R. 'Reforming Environmental Law' (1985) 37 *Stanford Law Review* 1333–1366

Ackerman, F. and Stanton, E. A. (eds.) *The Cost of Climate Change: What We'll Pay if Global Warming Continues Unchecked* (New York: Natural Resources Defense Council, 2008)

Adger, W. N., Paavola, J., Huq, S. and Mace, M. J. (eds.) *Fairness in Adaptation to Climate Change* (Cambridge, MA: MIT Press, 2006)

Adler, J. H. 'Jurisdictional Mismatch in Environmental Federalism' (2005) 14 *New York University Environmental Law Journal* 131–178
'When Is Two a Crowd? The Impact of Federal Action on State Environmental Regulation' (2007) 31 *Harvard Environmental Law Review* 67–114

Aidt, T. S. 'Political Internalization of Economic Externalities and Environmental Policy' (1998) 69 *Journal of Public Economics* 1–16

Alesina, A., Angeloni, I. and Etro, F. 'International Unions' (2005) 95(3) *American Economic Review* 602–615

Alesina, A., Angeloni, I. and Schuknecht, L. 'What Does the European Union Do?' (2005) 123 *Public Choice* 275–319

Alesina, A. and Wacziarg, R. 'Is Europe Going Too Far?' (1999) 51(1) *Carnegie-Rochester Conference Series on Public Policy* 1–42

Alonso, R., Dessein, W. and Matouschek, N. 'When does Coordination Require Centralization?' (2008) 98(1) *American Economic Review*, 145–179

Amundsen, E. S., Bjorndal, T. and Conrad, J. M. 'Open Access Harvesting of the Northeast Atlantic Minke Whale' (1995) 6(2) *Environmental and Resource Economics* 167–185

Andres, R. J., Fielding, D. J., Marland, G., Boden, T. A., Kumar, N. and Kearney, A. T. 'Carbon Dioxide Emissions from Fossil-Fuel Use, 1751-1950' (1999) 51B *Tellus* 759–765

Anger, N., Bohringer, C. and Oberndorfer, U. 'Public Interest vs. Interest Groups: Allowance Allocation in the EU Emissions Trading Scheme', ZEW – Centre for European Economic Research Discussion Paper No. 08-023 (2008)

Anuradha, R. V. 'Unilateral Carbon Border Measures: Key Legal Issues', ICRIER Policy Series, No. 2 (2011)

Arcuri, A. and Dari-Mattiacci, G. 'Centralization versus Decentralization as a Risk-Return Trade-off' (2010) 53 *Journal of Law and Economics*, 359–378

Arrhenius, S. 'On the Influence of Carbonic Acid in the Air upon the Temperature of the Ground' (1896) 41(5) *Philosophical Magazine and Journal of Science* 237–276

Arrow, K. 'The Organization of Economic Activity: Issues Pertinent to the Choice of Market Versus Non-Market Allocation', in Joint Economic Committee, *The Analysis and Evaluation of Public Expenditures: The PPB System*, vol. I (Washington, DC: U.S. GPO, 1970)

Arrow, K. *Social Choice and Individual Values* (New Haven, CT: Yale University Press, 1951)

Attina, F. 'The Voting Behavior of the European Parliament Members and the Problem of the Europarties' (1990) 18 *European Journal of Political Research* 557–579

Azoulai, L. 'The "Retained Powers" Formula in the Case Law of the European Court of Justice: EU Law as Total Law?' (2011) 4(2) *European Journal of Legal Studies* 192–219

Badrinath, S. G. and Bolster, P. J. 'The Role of Market Forces in EPA Enforcement Activity' (1996) 10 *Journal of Regulatory Economics* 165–181

Bailey, E. M. 'Allowances Trading Activity and State Regulatory Rulings: Evidence from the U.S. Acid Rain Program' 4 MIT Working Paper No. MIT-CEEPR 96-002 (1996)

Baldwin, R. and Cave, M. *Understanding Regulation: Theory, Strategy and Practice* (Oxford University Press, 1999)

Bator, F. M. 'The Simple Analytics of Welfare Maximization' (1957) 47(1) *The American Economic Review* 22–59

Baumol, W. J. and Oates, W. E. 'The Use of Standards and Prices for Protection of the Environment' (1971) 73(1) *The Swedish Journal of Economics* 42–45

Becker, G. S. 'A Theory of Competition among Pressure Groups for Political Influence' (1983) 98 *The Quarterly Journal of Economics* 371–400

## BIBLIOGRAPHY

Becker, G. S. and Stigler, G. J. 'Law Enforcement, Malfeasance, and Compensation of Enforcers' (1974) 3 *Journal of Legal Studies* 1–18

Bega, N., Morlota, J. C., Davidson, O., Afrane-Okesseb, Y., Tyanib, L., Dentonc, F., Sokonac, Y., Thomasc, J. P., Lèbre La Rovered, E., Parikhe, J. K., Parikhe, K. and Atiq Rahmanf, A. 'Linkages between Climate Change and Sustainable Development' (2002) 2(2) *Climate Policy* 129–144

Ben-Shahar, O. and Bradford, A. 'The Economics of Climate Enforcement', John M. Olin Law and Economics Working Paper No. 512 (2010)

Benedick, R. E. *Ozone Diplomacy: New Directions in Safeguarding the Planet* (Boston, MA: Harvard University Press, 1998)

Benson, D. and Jordan, A. 'Understanding Task Allocation in the European Union: Exploring the Value of Federal Theory' (2008) 15 *Journal of European Public Policy* 78–97

Benvenisti, A. *Sharing Transboundary Resources: International Law and Optimal Resource Use* (Cambridge University Press, 2002)

Bergh, R. van den, Faure, M. and Lefevere, J. 'The Subsidiarity Principle in European Environmental Law: An Economic Analysis', in E. Eide and R. van den Bergh (eds.) *Law and Economics of the Environment* (Oslo: Juridisk Forlag, 1996) 121–166

Bergmann, M., Schmitz, A., Hayden, M. and Kosonen, K. 'Imposing a Unilateral Carbon Constraint on Energy-intensive Industries and its Impact on their International Competitiveness: Data and Analysis', European Economy Economic Papers 298 (2007)

Bergstrom, T. 'When does Majority Rule Supply Public Goods Efficiently?' (1979) 8 *Scandinavian Journal of Economics* 216–227

Bermann, G. 'Taking Subsidiarity Seriously: Federalism in the European Community and the United States' (1994) 94 *Columbia Law Review* 331–456

Bernheim, B. D. and Whinston, M. D. 'Common Agency' (1986) 54 *Econometrica* 923–942

Besley, T. and Coate, S. 'Centralized Versus Decentralized Provision of Local Public Goods: A Political Economy Approach' (2003) 87 *Journal of Public Economics* 2611–2637

Biermann, F. and Boas, I. 'Preparing for a Warmer World: Towards a Global Governance System to Protect Climate Refugees' (2010) 10 *Global Environmental Politics* 60–88

Bird, R. M. 'Threading the Fiscal Labyrinth: Some Issues in Fiscal Decentralization' (1993) 46 *National Tax Journal* 207–227

Black, D. 'On the Rationale of Group Decision-making' (1948) 56 *Journal of Political Economy* 23–34

Boardman, B. *Fixing Fuel Poverty: Challenges and Solutions* (Oxford: Earthscan, 2013)

*Fuel Poverty: From Cold Homes to Affordable Warmth* (London: Belhaven Press, 1991)

Bodansky, D. 'The Copenhagen Climate Change Conference: A Postmortem' (2010) 104 *The American Journal of International Law* 230–240

'The International Climate Change Regime: The Road from Copenhagen', Viewpoints Series, Harvard Project on International Climate Agreements (2010)

Bogojević, S. *Emissions Trading Schemes: Markets, States and Law* (Oxford: Hart Publishing, 2013)

Borgerson, S. G. 'Artic Meltdown: The Economic and Security Implications of Global Warming' (2008) 87 *Foreign Affairs* 63–77

Börzel, T. A. and Risse, T. 'Who is Afraid of a European Federation? How to Constitutionalise a Multi-Level Governance System', Harvard Jean Monnet Working Paper (Symposium), No. 7/00 (2000)

Bowman, A. O'M. 'Horizontal Federalism: Exploring Interstate Interactions' (2004) 14 *Journal of Public Administration Research and Theory* 535–546

Braithwaite, J., Coglianese, C. and Levi-Faur, D. 'Can Regulation and Governance Make a Difference' (2007) 1 *Regulation and Governance* 1–7

Bray, M. 'Centralization/Decentralization and Privatization/Publicization: Conceptual Issues and the Need for More Research' (1994) 21 *International Journal of Educational Research* 817–824

Brennan, G. and Buchanan, J. *The Power to Tax: Analytical Foundations of a Fiscal Constitution* (Cambridge University Press, 1980)

Brenton, T. *The Greening of Machiavelli: The Evolution of International Environmental Politics* (London: Royal Institute of International Affairs, 1994)

Bruce, J. P., Lee, H. and Haites, E. F. (eds.) *Economic and Social Dimensions of Climate Change: Contribution of Working Group III to the Second Assessment Report of the IPCC* (Cambridge University Press, 1995)

Brus, M. T. A., Raimond, R. R. and Drupsteen, T. G. 'Balancing National and European Competence in Environmental Law' (1994) 9 *Connecticut Journal of International Law* 633–674

Buchanan, J. M. and Tullock, G. 'Polluters' Profits and Political Response: Direct Controls Versus Taxes' (1975) 65 *The American Economic Review* 139–147

'Polluters' Profits and Political Response: Direct Controls versus Taxes' in R. D. Congleton (ed.) *The Political Economy of Environmental Protection: Analysis and Evidence* (Ann Arbor, MI: University of Michigan Press, 1996)

Búrca, G. de 'Reappraising Subsidiarity's Significance after Amsterdam', Harvard Jean Monnet Working Papers, No. 7/99 (1999)

Burniaux, J-M., Chateau, J., Dellink, R., Duval, R. and Jamet, S. 'The Economics of Climate Change Mitigation: How to Build the Necessary Global Action in a Cost-Effective Manner', Economics Department Working Papers No. 701 (2009)

Burris, S., Kempa, M. and Shearing, C. 'Changes in Governance: A Cross-Disciplinary Review of Current Scholarship' (2008) 41 *Akron Law Review* 1–66

Butler, H. N. and Macey, J. R. 'Externalities and the Matching Principle: The Case for Reallocating Environmental Regulatory Authority' (1996) 14 *Yale Law & Policy Review* 24–66

Buzbee, W. B. 'Climate as an Innovation Imperative: Federalism, Institutional Pluralism and Incentive Effects', Public Law & Legal Theory Research Paper Series, No. 10-125, Emory University School of Law (2010)
  'Recognizing the Regulatory Commons: A Theory of Regulatory Gaps' (2003) 89 *Iowa Law Review* 1-64
Calabresi, G. and Melamed, A. D. 'Property Rules, Liability Rules and Inalienability: One View of the Cathedral' (1972) 85 *Harvard Law Review* 1089-1128
Camerer, C. F. *Behavioral Game Theory: Experiments in Strategic Interaction* (Princeton, NJ: Cloth, 2003)
Campos, J. E. L. 'Legislative Institutions, Lobbying, and the Endogenous Choice of Regulatory Instruments: A Political Economy Approach to Instrument Choice' (1989) 5 *Journal of Law, Economics, & Organization* 333-353
Carbon Trust *Cutting Carbon in Europe – The 2020 Plans and the Future of the EU ETS* (London: Carbon Trust Publication, CTC 734, June 2009)
Carbonara, E., Luppi, B. and Parisi, F. 'Optimal Territorial Scope of Laws', University of Minnesota Law School, Legal Studies Research Paper No. 08-44 (2008)
Carlton, D. W. and Loury, G. C. 'The Limitations of Pigouvian Taxes as a Long-Run Remedy for Externalities' (1980) 97 *The Quarterly Journal of Economics* 559-566
Chang, H. 'Breaking the Mould: An Institutionalist Political Economy Alternative to the Neo-liberal Theory of the Market and the State' (2002) 26 (5) *Cambridge Journal of Economics* 539-559
Chang, H., Sigman, H. and Traub, L. 'Endogenous Decentralization in Federal Environmental Policies', U. of Penn, Inst. for Law and Economics Research Paper No. 12-25 (2012)
Chinn, L. N. 'Can the Market be Fair and Efficient? An Environmental Justice Critique of Emissions Trading' (1999) 26(1) *Ecology Law Quarterly* 80-125
Chowdhury, N. and Wessel, R. A. 'Conceptualising Multilevel Regulation in the EU: A Legal Translation of Multilevel Governance?' (2012) 18 *European Law Journal* 335-357
Clausen, N. J. and Sørensen, K. E. 'Reforming the Regulation of Trading Venues in the EU Under the Proposed (MiFID II) – Leveling the Playing Field and Overcoming Market Fragmentation?' Nordic & European Company Law Working Paper No. 10-23 (2012)
Clò, S. 'Assessing the European Emissions Trading Scheme Effectiveness in Reaching the Kyoto Target: An Analysis of the Cap Stringency', Rotterdam Institute of Law and Economics Working Paper Series, No.14 (2008)
  'The Effectiveness of the EU Emissions Trading Scheme' (2009) 9 *Climate Policy* 227-241
Close, G. 'Harmonisation of Laws: Use or Abuse of the Powers under the EEC Treaty?' (1978) 3 *European Law Review* 461-481
Coase, R. H. 'The Problem of Social Cost' (1960) 3 *The Journal of Law and Economics* 1-44

'The Regulated Industries', in 'Papers and Proceedings of the Seventy-sixth Annual Meeting of the American Economic Association' (1964) 54 *American Economic Review* 192–197

Cohen, J. M. and Peterson, S. B., *Administrative Decentralization: Strategies for Developing Countries* (West Hartford, CT: Kumarian Press, 1999)

Cohen, M. 'Monitoring and Enforcement of Environmental Policy', in T. Tietenberg and H. Folmer (eds.) *International Yearbook of Environmental and Resource Economics* (Cheltenham: Edward Elgar Publishers, 1998/1999) 44–106

Cole, D. H. 'Climate Change and Collective Action' (2008) 61(1) *Current Legal Problems* 229–264

'From Global to Polycentric Climate Governance' (2011) 2 *Climate Law* 395–413

'A Glimmer of Hope: The EU's Emissions Trading Scheme', unpublished manuscript on file with author (2009)

*Pollution and Property: Comparing Ownership Institutions for Environmental Protection* (Cambridge University Press, 2002)

Cole, D. H. and Grossman, P. Z. 'Toward a total-cost approach to environmental instrument choice' (2002) 20 *Research in Law and Economics* 223–241

'When is Command-and-Control Efficient? Institutions, Technology, and the Comparative Efficiency of Alternative Regulatory Regimes for Environmental Protection' (1999) *Wisconsin Law Review* 887–938

Collier, U. 'The European Union's Climate Change Policy: Limiting Emissions or Limiting Powers?' (1996) 3 *Journal of European Public Policy* 122–138

Condorcet, J. M. *Essay on the Application of Analysis to the Probability of Majority Decisions* (Paris, 1785)

Congleton, R. D. 'Ethnic Clubs, Ethnic Conflict, and the Rise of Ethnic Nationalism' in A. Breton and J.-L. Galeotti (eds.) *Nationalism and Rationality* (Cambridge University Press, 1995) 71–97

Congleton, R. D. (ed.) *The Political Economy of Environmental Protection: Analysis and Evidence* (Ann Arbor, MI: University of Michigan Press, 1996)

Congressional Budget Office *Federalism and Environmental Protection: Case Studies for Drinking Water and Ground-level Ozone* (Washingtom, DC: Congress of the United States, 1997)

Conrad, K. and Schroder, M. 'Choosing Environmental Policy Instruments Using General Equilibrium Models' (1993) 15 *Journal of Policy Modeling* 521–544

Cooter, R. D. 'Three Effects of Social Norms on Law: Expression, Deterrence, and Internalization' (2000) 79 *Oregon Law Review* 1–22

Corwin, E. S. 'The Passing of Dual Federalism' (1950) 36 *Virginia Law Review* 1–24

Costello, C., Gaines, S. D. and Lynham, J. 'Can Catch Shares Prevent Fisheries Collapse?' (2008) 321 *Science* 1678–1681

Crook, R. and Manor, J. 'Democratic Decentralization', OED Working Paper Series (2000)

Dal Bo, E. 'Regulatory Capture: A Review' (2006) 22 *Oxford Review of Economic Policy* 203–225

Dales, J. H. 'Land, Water and Ownership' (1968) 1 *Canadian Journal of Economics* 791–804
 *Pollution, Property, and Prices* (University of Toronto Press, 1968)

Dari-Mattiacci, G., Hendriks, E. S. and Havinga, M. 'A Generalized Jury Theorem', Amsterdam Law School Research Paper No. 2011-39, University of Amsterdam (2011)

Dari-Mattiacci, G. and van Zeben, J. A. W. 'Legal Uncertainty and Market Uncertainty in Market-Based Instruments: The Case of the EU ETS' (2012) 19(2) *New York University Environmental Law Journal* 101–139

Dasgupta, P. *The Control of Resources* (Cambridge, MA: Harvard University Press, 1982)

Daugbjerg, C. and Svendsen, G. *Green Taxation in Question: Politics and Economic Efficiency in Environmental Regulation* (London: Palgrave Macmillan, 2001)

Dawes, R. M. 'The Commons Dilemma Game' 13 *ORI Research Bulletin* (1973) 1–12

Dekkers, C. and Oudenes, M. 'EU ETS in the Post-2012 Regime: Lessons Learned', in W. Th. Douma, L. Massai and M. Montini (eds.) *The Kyoto Protocol and Beyond: Legal and Policy Challenges of Climate Change* (The Hague: TMC Asser Press, 2007) 185

Demailly, D., Grubb, M., Hourcade, J.-C., Neuhoff, K. and Sato, M. 'Differentiation and Dynamics of EU ETS Competitiveness Impacts', Climate Strategies, Research Theme 1.3 Interim Report (2007)

Demailly, D. and Quirion, P. 'European Emission Trading Scheme and Competitiveness: A Case Study on the Iron and Steel Industry' (2008) 30 *Energy Economics* 2009–2027

Dewatripont, M., Jewitt, I. and Tirole, J. 'The Economics of Career Concerns, Part II: Application to Missions and Accountability of Government Agencies' (1999) 66 *Review of Economic Studies* 199–217

Dewees, D. N. 'Instrument Choice in Environmental Policy' (1983) 21 *Economic Inquiry* 53–71
 'Tradable Pollution Permits', in P. Newman (ed.) *The New Palgrave Dictionary of Economics and the Law*, vol. III (London: MacMillan, 1998) 596–601

Dhar, B. and Das, K. 'The European Union's Proposed Carbon Equalization System: Can it be WTO Compatible?' Research and Information System for Developing Countries, Discussion Paper 15 (2009)

Dhondt, N., *Integration of Environmental Protection into other EC Policies: Legal Theory and Practice* (Groningen: Europa Law Publishing, 2003)

Dijkstra, B. *The Political Economy of Environmental Policy: A Public Choice Approach to Market Instruments* (Cheltenham: Edward Elgar, 1999)

Dimitrov, R. S. 'Inside Copenhagen: The State of Climate Governance' (2010) 2 *Global Environmental Politics* 18–24

Dixit, A. K. *The Making of Economic Policy: A Transaction Cost Politics Perspective* (Cambridge, MA: The MIT Press, 1998)

Downs, A. *An Economic Theory of Democracy* (New York: Harper Collins, 1957)

Driesen, D. 'Is Emissions Trading an Economic Incentive Program?: Replacing the Command and Control/Economic Incentive Dichotomy' (1998) 55 *Washington and Lee Law Review* 289–350

Driesen, D. M. 'Choosing Environmental Instruments in a Transnational Context' (2000) 27 *Ecology Law Quarterly* 1–52

Dwyer, J. 'The Practice of Federalism under the Clean Air Act' (1995) 54 *Maryland Law Review* 1183–1225

Dyke, B. Van 'Emissions Trading to Reduce Acid Deposition' (1991) 100 *Yale Law Journal* 2707–2726

Egenhofer, C., Alessi, M., Georgiev, A. and Fujiwara, N. 'The EU Emissions Trading System and Climate Policy towards 2050: Real Incentives to Reduce Emissions and Drive Innovation?' CEPS Special Report (2010)

Eggleston, S., Buendia, L., Miwa, K., Ngara, T. and Tanabe, K. (eds.) '2006 IPCC Guidelines for National Greenhouse Gas Inventories', Intergovernmental Panel on Climate Change (2006)

Eising, R. and Kohler-Koch, B. (eds.), *The Transformation of Governance in the European Union* (London: Routledge, 2004)

Elazar, D. J. *The American Partnership: Intergovernmental Co-operation in the Nineteenth-Century United States* (University of Chicago Press, 1962)

  *Exploring Federalism* (Tuscaloosa: The University of Alabama Press, 1987)

Ellerman, A. D. and Buchner, B. 'The European Union Emissions Trading Scheme: Origins, Allocation, and Early Results' (2007) 1 *Review of Environmental Economics and Policy* 66–87

  'Over-allocation or Abatement? A Preliminary Analysis of the EU Emissions Trading Scheme Based on the 2006 Emissions Data' (2008) 41 *Environmental and Resource Economics* 267–287

Ellerman, A. D., Joskow, P. L., Schmalensee, R., Montero, J.-P. and Bailey, E. M. *Markets for Clean Air: The U.S. Acid Rain Program* (Cambridge University Press, 2000)

Elliott, E. D. 'Goal Analysis versus Institutional Analysis of Toxic Compensation Systems' (1985) 73 *Georgetown Law Journal* 1357–1376

Elliott, E. D., Ackerman, B. A. and Millian, J. C. 'Toward a Theory of Statutory Evolution: The Federalization of Environmental Law' (1985) 1 *Journal of Law, Economics & Organization* 313–340

Endres, A. and Finus, M. 'Quotas may Beat Taxes in a Global Emissions Game' (2000) 9(6) *International Tax and Public Finance* 687–707

Engel, K. H. 'Harnessing the Benefits of Dynamic Federalism in Environmental Law' (2006) 56 *Emory Law Journal* 159–188

Environment Agency, 'EU Emissions Trading Scheme: Guidance to Operators on the application of Civil Penalties' (2009)

232 BIBLIOGRAPHY

Estache, A. and Sinha, S. 'Does Decentralization Increase Spending on Public Infrastructure?' World Bank Policy Research Working Paper No. 1457 (1995)

Esty, D. 'Revitalizing Environmental Federalism' (1996) 95 *Michigan Law Review* 570–653

Esty, D. and Geradin, D. (eds.) *Regulatory Competition and Economic Integration, Comparative Perspectives* (Oxford University Press, 2001)

European Commission, 'Community Guidelines on state aid for environmental protection', OJ 2008 No. C82, 1 April 2008

 'Impact Assessment Guidelines', SEC(2009)

 'Impact Assessment of 8 February 2010 accompanying the Commission Regulation on the timing, administration and other aspects of auctioning of greenhouse gas emission allowances pursuant to Article 10(4) of Directive 2003/87/EC', SEC(2010)

 'Report of the 3rd meeting of the ECCP working group on emissions trading on the review of the EU ETS on further harmonization and increased predictability', 070521-22 final report M3 (21–22 May 2007)

Falkner, R., Stephan, H. and Vogler, J. 'International Climate Policy after Copenhagen: Towards a "Building Blocks" Approach' (2010) 1 *Global Policy* 252–262

Faure, M. and Nollkaemper, A. 'International Liability as an Instrument to Prevent and Compensate for Climate Change' (2007) 26 *Stanford Environmental Law Journal* 123–179

Fiorina, M. P. 'Legislative Choice of Regulatory Forms: Legal Process or Administrative Process?' (1982) 39 *Public Choice* 33–61

Fisher, C. and Fox, A. 'Comparing Policies to Combat Emissions Leakage', Resources for the Future Discussion Paper 09-0 (2009)

Fiske, E. *Decentralization of Education: Politics and Consensus* (Washington, DC: World Bank, 1996)

Fleurke, F. 'Effecten van Decentralisatie' (1995) 49(2) *Bestuurswetenschap* 101–137

Fourier, J. 'Mémoire sur les Températures du Globe Terrestre et des Espaces Planétaires' (1827) 7 *Mémoires de l'Académie Royale des Sciences* 569–604

Freeman, J. and Rossi, J. 'Agency Coordination in Shared Regulatory Space' (2012) 125(5) *Harvard Law Review* 1131–1211

Frey, B. and Eichenberger, R. 'FOCJ: Competitive Governments for Europe' (1996) 16 *International Review of Law and Economics* 315–327

Friedman, R. M., Downing, D. and Gunn, E. M. 'Environmental Policy Instrument Choice: The Challenge of Competing Goals' (2000) 10 *Duke Environmental Law & Policy Forum* 327–387

Gilbert, A., Bode J. W. and Phylipsen, D. *Analysis of the National Allocation Plans for the EU Emissions Trading Scheme* (London: Ecofys, 2004)

Gilpin, R., *Global Political Economy: Understanding the International Economic Order* (Princeton University Press, 2001)

Golub, J. 'Sovereignty and Subsidiarity in EU Environmental Policy' (1996) 44 *Political Studies* 686–703

Goulder, L. H. 'The Cost-Effectiveness of Alternative Instruments for Environmental Protection in a Second-Best Setting' (1999) 72 *Journal of Public Economics* 329–360

Goulder, L. H. and Parry, I. W. H. 'Instrument Choice in Environmental Policy' (2008) 2 *Review of Environmental Economics and Policy* 152–174

Grande, E. 'The State and Interest Groups in a Framework of Multi-level Decision-making: The Case of the European Union' (1996) 3 *Journal of European Public Policy* 365–390

Griffin, K. 'Economic Development in a Changing World' (1981) 9 *World Development* 221–320

Grodzins, M. *The American System: A New View of the Government of the United States* (New York: Rand McNally, 1966)

'The Federal System', in *The Goals for Americans: Report of President's Commission on National Goals* (New York: Prentice Hall, 1960) 256–282

Grossman, G. and Helpman, E. 'Endogenous Innovation in the Theory of Growth' 8 (1994) *Journal of Economic Perspectives* 22–44

Grubb, M. and Neuhoff, K. 'Allocation and Competitiveness in the EU Emissions Trading Scheme: Policy Overview' (2006) 6 *Climate Policy* 7–30

Grzeszczak, R. 'Executuve Power in the European Union' in R. Grzeszczak and I. Karolewski (eds.) *The Multi-Level and Polycentric European Union: Legal and Political Studies* (Zurich: Lit Verlag, 2012) 77–102

Gunningham, N. and Sinclair, D. 'Policy Instrument Choice and Diffuse Source Pollution' (2005) 17 *Journal of Environmental Law* 51–81

Haagsma, A. 'The European Community's Environmental Policy: A Case-Study in Federalism' (1989) 12 *Fordham International Law Journal* 311–359

Hahn, R. W. 'Economic Prescriptions for Environmental Problems: How the Patient Followed the Doctor's Orders' (1989) 3 *The Journal of Economic Perspectives* 95–114

'The Political Economy of Environmental Regulation: Towards a Unifying Framework' (1990) 65 *Public Choice* 21–47

Hahn, R. W. and McGartland, A. M. 'The Political Economy of Instrument Choice: An Examination of the U.S. Role in Implementing the Montreal Protocol' (1989) 83 *Northwestern University Law Review* 203–229

Hahn, R. W. and Noll, R. 'Designing a Market for Tradable Emissions Permits', in W. Maget (ed.) *Reform of Environmental Regulation* (Cambridge: Ballinger, 1982) 119–146

'Environmental Markets in the Year 2000' (1990) 3 *Journal of Risk and Uncertainty* 347–363

Hahn, R. W. and Stavins, R. N. 'Economic Incentives for Environmental Protection: Integrating Theory and Practice' (1992) 82(2) *The American Economic Review* 464–468

Hardin, G. 'The Tragedy of the Commons' (1968) 162 *Science*, 1243–1248

Hayward, T. 'Human Rights versus Emissions Rights: Climate Justice and the Equitable Distribution of Ecological Space' (2007) 21(4) *Ethics & International Affairs* 431–450

## BIBLIOGRAPHY

Hendriks, E. S. 'Modelling Subsidiarity Applying a Continuous CJT to Determine the Optimal Level of Decision Making for Standard Setting', PhD thesis, University of Amsterdam (2010)

Hepburn, C. 'Regulation by Prices, Quantities, or Both: a Review of Instrument Choice' (2006) 22 *Oxford Review of Economic Policy* 226–247

Hillman, A. L. and Ursprung, H. W. 'Domestic Politics, Foreign Interests, and International Trade Policy: Reply' (1994) 84(5) *American Economic Review* 1476–1478

Hirschman, A., *Exit, Voice, and Loyalty: Responses to Decline in Firms, Organizations, and States* (Cambridge, MA: Harvard University Press, 1970)

Hix, S., Noury, A. and Roland, G. 'Power to the Parties: Cohesion and Competition in the European Parliament, 1979–2001' (2005) 35 *British Journal of Political Science* 209–234

Holder, J. and Lee, M. *Environmental Protection, Law and Policy: Texts and Materials* (Cambridge University Press, 2007)

Holland, K. M., Morton, F. L. and Galligan, B. (eds.) *Federalism and the Environment: Environmental Policymaking in Australia, Canada, and the United States* (Westport, CT: Greenwood, 1996)

Holt, C. A. *Markets, Games, and Strategic Behavior* (Boston, MA: Pearson-Addison Wesley, 2007)

Holtkamp, J. 'Dealing with Climate Change in the United States: The Non-Federal Response' (2007) 27 *Journal of Land, Resources & Environmental Law* 79–86

Homans, R. F. and Wilen, J. E. 'A Model of Regulated Open Access Resource Use' (1997) 32(1) *Journal of Environmental Economics and Management* 1–21

Homeyer, I. von 'The Evolution of EU Environmental Governance', in J. Scott (ed.) *Environmental Protection: European Law and Governance* (Oxford University Press, 2009)

Hooghe, L. and Marks, G. 'Types of Multi-level Governance', in H. Enderlein, S. Wälti and M. Zürn, *Handbook on Multi-Level Governance* (Cheltenham: Edward Elgar, 2010) 17–31

Hoogzaad, J. and Streck, C. 'A Mechanism with a Bright Future: Joint Implementation', in D. Freestone and C. Streck (eds.) *Legal Aspects of Carbon Trading: Kyoto, Copenhagen, and Beyond* (Oxford University Press, 2009) 176–194

Houtven, G. Van 'Bureaucratic Discretion in Environmental Regulations: The Air Toxics and Asbestos Ban Cases', in R. D. Congleton (ed.) *The Political Economy of Environmental Protection: Analysis and Evidence* (Ann Arbor, MI: University of Michigan Press, 1996)

Huffman, J. L. 'Making Environmental Regulation more Adoptive through Decentralization: The Case for Subsidiarity' (2005) 52 *University of Kansas Law Review* 1377–1400

Hutchcroft, P. D. 'Centralization and Decentralization in Administration and Politics: Assessing Territorial Dimensions of Authority and Power' (2001) 14 *Governance* 23–53

Hutchinson, E. and Kennedy, P. W. 'State Enforcement of Federal Standards: Implications for Interstate Pollution' (2008) 30 *Resource and Energy Economics* 316–344

Hutter, B. *Compliance: Regulation and Environment* (Oxford: Clarendon Press, 1997)

Inman, R. 'Transfers and Bailouts: Enforcing Local Fiscal Discipline with Lessons from U.S. Federalism' in J. Rodden (ed.) *Enforcing the Hard Budget Constraint* (Cambridge, MA: MIT Press, 2003) 35–83

Inman, R. and Rubinfeld, D. 'Rethinking Federalism' (1997) 11(4) *The Journal of Economic Perspectives* 43–64

Inman, R. and Rubinfeld, D. L. 'Federalism', in B. Bouckaert and G. De Geest (eds.) *Encyclopedia of Law and Economics* (Cheltenham: Edward Elgar Publishing, 2000), 661–691

Jaffe, J., Ranson, M. and Stavins, R. N. 'Linking Tradable Permit Systems: A Key Element of Emerging International Climate Policy Architecture' (2009) 36 *Ecology Law Quarterly* 789–808

Jans, J. and Vedder, H. *European Environmental Law* (Groningen: Europa Law Publishing, 3rd revised edn, 2008)

Joskow, P. L., Schmalensee, R. and Bailey, E. M. 'Auction Design and the Market for Sulfur Dioxide Emissions', National Bureau of Economic Research Working Paper No. 5745 (1996)

'The Market for Sulfur Dioxide Emissions' (1998) 88 *American Economic Review* 669–685

Kaplow, L. 'Taxes, Permits, and Climate Change', NBER Working Papers 16268, National Bureau of Economic Research (2010)

Kefer, J. V. 'Warming up to an International Greenhouse Gas Market: Lessons from the U.S. Acid Rain Experience' (2001) 20 *Stanford Environmental Law Journal* 221–300

Keohane, N. and Olmstead, S. M. *Markets and the Environment* (Washington, DC: Island Press, 2007)

Keohane, N., Revesz, R. L. and Stavins, R. N. 'The Choice of Regulatory Instruments in Environmental Policy' (1998) 22 *Harvard Environmental Law Review* 313–367

Kersbergen, K. van and Verbeek, B. 'The Politics of Subsidiarity in the European Union' (1994) 32 *Journal of Common Market Studies* 215–236

Kimber, C. J. M. 'A Comparison of Environmental Federalism in the United States and the European Union' (1995) 54 *Maryland Law Review* 1658–1690

Kingsbury, B., Krisch, N. and Stewart, R. B. 'The Emergence of Global Administrative Law' (2005) 68 *Law and Contemporary Problems* 15–61

Kirchgässner, G. and Schneider, F. 'On the Political Economy of Environmental Policy' (2003) 115 *Public Choice* 369–396

Klepper, G. and Peterson, S. M. 'The EU Emissions Trading Scheme. Allowance Prices, Trade Flows, Competitiveness Effects', FEEM Working Paper No. 49.04 (2004)

Knight, F. H. *Risk, Uncertainty, and Profit* (Boston, MA: Hart Schaffner and Marx, 1921)

Kohler-Koch, B. 'Catching up with Change: The Transformation of Governance in the European Union' (1996) 3 *Journal of European Public Policy* 359–380

Kohler-Koch, B. and Eising, R. (eds.) *The Transformation of Governance in the European Union* (London: Routledge, 2004)

Komesar, N. K. *Imperfect Alternatives: Choosing Institutions in Law, Economics, and Public Policy* (University of Chicago Press, 1994)

Konstadinides, T. *Division of Powers in European Union Law: The Delimitation of Internal Competence between the EU and the Member States* (The Hague: Kluwer Law International, 2009)

Kosolapova, E. 'Liability for Climate Change-Related Damage in Domestic Courts: Claims for Compensation in the USA', in M. Faure and M. Peeters (eds.) *Climate Change Liability* (Cheltenham: Edward Elgar, 2011) 189–205

Krämer, L. *EC Environmental Law* (London: Sweet & Maxwell, 6th edn, 2007)

Krey, M. and Santen, H. 'Trying to Catch up with the Executive Board: Regulatory Decision-making and its Impact on CDM Performance', in D. Freestone and C. Streck (eds.) *Legal Aspects of Carbon Trading: Kyoto, Copenhagen, and Beyond* (Oxford University Press, 2009) 231–247

Krueger, A. 'The Political Economy of the Rent-seeking Society' (1974) 64 *American Economic Review* 291–303

Kumar Sharma, C. 'Decentralization Dilemma: Measuring the Degree and Evaluating the Outcomes' (2006) 1 *The Indian Journal of Political Science* 49–64

Lacasta, N., Oberthür, S., Santos, E. and Barata, P. 'From Sharing the Burden to Sharing the Effort: Decision 406/2009/EC on Member State Emission Targets for Non-ETS Sectors', in M. Pallemaerts and S. Oberthür (eds.) *The New Climate Policies of the European Union* (Brussels: VUB Press, 2011) 93–116

Lederer, M. 'Market Making via Regulation: The Role of the State in Carbon Markets' (2012) 6 *Regulation & Governance* 1–21

Lee, M. 'From Private to Public: The Multiple Roles of Environmental Liability' (2001) 7 *European Public Law* 375–397

Lefeber, R. *An Inconvenient Responsibility* (Amsterdam: Eleven International Publishing, 2009)

Leidy, M. P. and Hoekman, B. M. 'Pollution Abatement, Interest Groups, and Contingent Trade Policies', in R. D. Congleton (ed.) *The Political Economy of Environmental Protection: Analysis and Evidence* (Ann Arbor: University of Michigan Press, 1996)

Lenaerts, K. 'Constitutionalism and the Many Faces of Federalism' (1990) 38 *American Journal of Comparative Law* 205–264

  'The Principle of Subsidiarity and the Environment in the European Union: Keeping the Balance of Federalism' (1994) 17 *Fordham International Law Journal* 846–895

Lin, C. 'How Should Standards Be Set and Met?: An Incomplete Contracting Approach to Delegation in Regulation' (2010) 10 *The B.E. Journal of Economic Analysis & Policy* 1–17

Lomas, O. 'Environmental Protection, Economic Conflict and the European Community' (1988) 3(3) *McGill Law Journal* 506–539

Loprieno, M. 'Data Consistency between National GHG Inventories and Reporting under the EU ETS: Differences and Similarities, Outlook to Changes', Second Workshop, Copenhagen (13 September 2007)

Macey, J. R. 'Federal Deference to Local Regulators and the Economic Theory of Regulation: Toward a Public-Choice Explanation of Federalism' (1990) 76 *Virginia Law Review* 265–291

Maddick, H. *Democracy, Decentralisation and Development* (London: Asia Publishing House, 1963)

Maher, I. 'Legislative Review by the EC Commission: Revision without Radicalism', in J. Shaw and G. More (eds.) *New Legal Dynamics of European Union* (Oxford: Clarendon Press, 1995) 235–253

Magat, W. A., Krnpnick, A. J. and Harrington, W. *Rules in the Making: A Statistical Analysis of Regulatory Agency Behavior* (Washington, DC: Resources for the Future, 1986)

Marchant, G. E. 'Global Warming: Freezing Carbon Dioxide Emissions: An Offset Policy for Slowing Global Warming' (1992) 22 *Environmental Law* 623–684

Marcu, A. 'Post Durban: Moving to a Fragmented Carbon Market World?' 22 December 2011, available at: www.google.com/url?s a=t&rct=j&q=&esrc=s&source=web&cd=1&ved=0CCsQFjAA&url= http%3A%2F%2Fwww.ceps.eu%2Fceps%2Fdld%2F6530%2Fpdf&ei =NbGKUs_qH42isATbuIC4Dw&usg=AFQjCNHb_QYRGHbh8U60_ OY8UWwsQhVvAw&bvm=bv.56643336,d.cWc

Marklund, P. and Samakovlis, E. 'What is Driving the EU Burden-sharing Agreement: Efficiency or Equity?' (2007) 85 *Journal of Environmental Management* 317–329

Marks, G. 'An Actor-centred Approach to Multi-level Governance' (1996) 6 *Regional & Federal Studies* 20–38

   'Structural Policy and Multilevel Governance in the EC: The State of the European Community', in A. Cafruny and G. Rosenthal (eds.) *The State of the European Community: The Maastricht Debate and Beyond* (Boulder, CO: L. Rienner Publishers, 1993) 391–411

Marks, G., Hooghe, L. and Blank, K. 'European Integration from the 1980s: State-centric v. Multi-level Governance' (1996) 34 *Journal of Common Market Studies* 341–378

Markussen, P. and Svendsen, G. T. 'Industry Lobbying and the Political Economy of GHG Trade in the European Union' (2005) 33 *Energy Policy* 245–255

Massai, L. *The Kyoto Protocol in the EU: European Community and Member States under International and European Law* (The Hague: T.M.C. Asser Press, 2011)

Matthes, F. C. and Schafhausen, F. 'Germany', in A. Ellerman, B. Buchner and C. Carraro (eds.) *Allocation in the European Emissions Trading Scheme: Rights, Rents and Fairness* (Cambridge University Press, 2007) 72–105

Mayer, B. 'Case C-366/10, *Air Transport Association of America and Others* v. *Secretary of State for Energy and Climate Change*, Judgment of the Court of Justice (Grand Chamber) of 21 December 2011' (2012) 49 *Common Market Law Review* 1113–1140

McGartland, A. and Oates, W. E. 'Marketable Permits for the Prevention of Environmental Deterioration' (1985) 12 *Journal of Environmental Economics and Management* 207–228

McGinnis, M. and Hanisch, M. 'Analyzing Problems of Polycentric Governance in the Growing EU', Paper presented at the Transcoop Workshop on Problems of Polycentric Governance in the Growing EU, Humboldt University, Berlin (on file with the author) (2005)

McGinnis, M. and Ostrom, E. 'Reflections on Vincent Ostrom, Public Administration, and Polycentricity' (2012) 72 *Public Administration Review* 15–25

Metcalf, G. 'Reacting to Greenhouse Gas Emissions: A Carbon Tax to Meet Emission Targets', Discussion Paper Series, Department of Economics 0731, Tufts University (2009)

Michaelowa, A. 'Impact of Interest Groups on EU Climate Policy' (1998) 8(5) *European Environment* 152–160

Montesquieu, C. de *The Spirit of the Laws*, trans. T. Nugent (New York: MacMillan, 1949)

Montgomery, W. D. 'Markets in Licenses and Efficient Pollution Control Programs' (1972) 5(3) *Journal of Economic Theory* 395–418

Moore, S. 'If the Cap Fits: Reform of European Climate Policy and the EU Emissions Trading System', Policy Exchange (2013), available at www.policyexchange.org.uk/publications/category/item/if-the-cap-fits-reform-of-european-climate-policy-and-the-eu-emissions-trading-system

Mueller, D. C. *Public Choice II* (Cambridge University Press, 1989)
  *Public Choice III* (Cambridge University Press, 2003)

Musgrave, R. *The Theory of Public Finance* (New York: McGraw Hill, 1959)
  'The Voluntary Exchange Theory of Public Economy' (1939) 53 *Quarterly Journal of Economics* 213–237

Nash, J. 'Too much Market? Conflict between Tradable Pollution Allowances and the "Polluter Pays" Principle' (2000) 24 *Harvard Environmental Law Review* 465–535

Netto, M. and Schmidt, K. U. B. 'The CDM Project Cycle and the Role of the UNFCCC Secretariat', in D. Freestone and C. Streck (eds.) *Legal Aspects of Carbon Trading: Kyoto, Copenhagen, and Beyond* (Oxford University Press, 2009) 213–230

Neuhoff, K., Åhman, M., Betz, R., Cludius, J., Ferrario, F., Holmgren, K., Pal, G., Grubb, M., Matthes, F., Rogge, K., Sato, M., Schleich, J., Sijm, J., Tuerk, A., Kettner, C. and Walker, N. 'Implications of Announced Phase II National Allocation Plans for the EU ETS' (2006) 6 *Climate Policy* 411–422

Neuhoff, K., Ferrario, F., Grubb, M., Gabel, E. and Keats, K. 'Emission Projections 2008–2012 versus National Allocation Plans II' (2006) 6 *Climate Policy* 395–410

Newell, R. G. and Pizer, W. A. 'Uncertain Discount Rates in Climate Policy Analysis' (2004) 32(4) *Energy Policy* 519–529

Newell, R. G. and Stavins, R. N. 'Cost Heterogeneity and the Potential Savings from Market-Based Policies' (2003) 23(1) *Journal of Regulatory Economics* 43–59

Nicolaisen, J., Dean, A. and Hoeller, P. 'Economics and the Environment: A Survey of Issues and Policy Options', OECD Economics Studies No. 16 (1991)

Niskanen, W. A. *Bureaucracy and Representative Government* (Chicago: Aldine Atherton, 1971)

'Nonmarket Decision Making: The Peculiar Economics of Bureaucracy' (1968) 58 *The American Economic Review* 293–305

Nollkaemper, A. and Jacobs, D. 'Shared Responsibility in International Law: A Concept Paper', ACIL Research Paper No 2011–07 (SHARES Series) (2011)

Nordhaus, R. R. and Danish, K. W. 'Assessing the Options for Designing a Mandatory U.S. Greenhouse Gas Reduction Program' (2005) 32 *Boston College Environmental Affairs Law Review* 97–164

Oates, W. E. 'On Environmental Federalism' (1997) 83(7) *Virginia Law Review* 1321–1329

'An Essay on Fiscal Federalism' (1999) 37 *Journal of Economic Literature* 1120–1149

*Fiscal Federalism* (New York: Harcourt Brace Jovanovich, 1972).

'A Reconsideration of Environmental Federalism', Resources for the Future, Discussion Paper No. 01–54 (2001)

'A Reconsideration of Environmental Federalism', in J. List and A. de Zeeuw (eds.) *Recent Advances in Environmental Economics* (Cheltenham: Edward Elgar, 2002)

'Searching for Leviathan: An Empirical Study' (1985) 75 *The American Economic Review* 748–757

'Toward a Second-Generation Theory of Fiscal Federalism' (2005) 12 *International Tax and Public Finance* 349–373

Oates, W. E. and Portney, P. R. 'The Political Economy of Environmental Policy', in K.-G. Maler and J. R. Vincent (eds.) *Handbook of Environmental Economics* (Amsterdam: Elsevier Science B.V., 2003)

Oates, W. E. and Schwab, R. M. 'Economic Competition Among Jurisdictions: Efficiency Enhancing or Distortion Inducing?' (1988) 35 *Journal of Public Economics* 333–354

Oberndorfer, U. and Rennings, K. 'Costs and Competitiveness Effects of the European Union Emissions Trading Scheme' (2007) 17 *European Environment* 1–17

Oberthür S. and Pallemaerts, M. 'The EU's Internal and External Climate Policies: An Historical Overview', in M. Pallemaerts and S. Oberthür (eds.) *The New Climate Policies of the European Union* (Brussels: VUB Press, 2010) 27–64

Olson, M. *The Logic of Collective Action: Public Goods and the Theory of Groups* (Cambridge, MA: Harvard University Press, 1965)

'The Principle of "Fiscal Equivalence": The Division of Responsibilities among Different Levels of Government' (1969) 59 *American Economic Review, Papers and Proceedings* 479–487

Osofsky, H. M. 'The Intersection of Scale, Science, and Law in Massachusetts v. EPA', in W. G. Burns and H. M. Osofsky (eds.) *Adjudicating Climate Change: State, National, and International Approaches* (Cambridge University Press, 2009) 129–144

'Is Climate Change "International"?: Litigation's Diagonal Regulatory Role' (2009) 49 *Virginia Journal of International Law* 585–650

'Multiscalar Governance and Climate Change: Reflections on the Role of States and Cities at Copenhagen' (2010) 25 *Maryland Journal of International Law* 64–85

Ostrom, E. 'Analysing Collective Action' (2010) 41(s1) *Agricultural Economics* 155–166

*Governing the Commons* (Cambridge University Press, 1990)

'A Polycentric Approach for Coping with Climate Change', World Bank Policy Research Working Paper Series, No. 5095 (2008)

'Reflections on "Some Unsettled Problems of Irrigation"' (2011) 101(1) *American Economic Review* 49–63

Ostrom, V. *The Intellectual Crisis in American Public Administration* (Tuscaloosa: University of Alabama Press, 1974)

Ostrom, V. and Bish, R. *Comparing Urban Service Delivery Systems: Structure and Performance* (Beverly Hills, CA: Sage, 1977)

Ostrom, V. and Ostrom, E. 'Public Good and Public Choices', in M. McGinnis and E. Ostrom (eds.) *Polycentricity and Local Public Economies* (Ann Arbor: University of Michigan Press, 1999) 75–103

Ostrom, V., Tiebout, C. and Warren, R. 'The Organization of Government in Metropolitan Areas: A Theoretical Inquiry' (1961) 55 *American Political Science Review* 831–842

Ott, H. E., Sterk, W. and Watanabe, R. 'The Bali Roadmap: New Horizons for Global Climate Policy' (2008) 8 *Climate Policy* 91–95

Paavola, J. 'Climate Change: The Ultimate "Tragedy of the Commons"?' in D. Cole and E. Ostrom (eds.) *Property in Land and Other Resources* (Cambridge, MA: Lincoln Institute of Land Policy, 2011) 417–433

Pachauri, R. K. and Reisinger, A. (eds.) *Climate Change 2007: Synthesis Report. Contribution of Working Groups I, II and III to the Fourth Assessment Report of the Intergovernmental Panel on Climate Change* (Geneva: Intergovernmental Panel on Climate Change, 2008)

Pallemaerts, M. and Oberthür, S. (eds.) *The New Climate Policies of the European Union* (Brussels: VUB Press, 2010)

Parisi, F. and Ghei, N. 'The Role of Reciprocity in International Law' (2003) 36 *Cornell International Law Journal* 93–123

Parisi, F., Schulz, N. and Klick, J. 'Two Dimensions of Regulatory Competition' (2006) 26 *International Review of Law and Economics* 56–66

Parker, A. 'Decentralization: The Way Forward for Rural Development?' The World Bank Policy Research Working Paper 1475 (1995)

Pashigian, P. 'Environmental Regulation: Whose Self-interests are being Protected?' (1985) 23 *Economic Inquiry* 551–584

Paulsson, E. 'A Review of the CDM Literature: from Fine-tuning to Critical Scrutiny?' (2009) 9(1) *International Environmental Agreements: Politics, Law and Economics* 63–80

Pedersen, W. F. 'Using Federal Environmental Regulations to Bargain for Private Land Use Control' (2004) 21 *Yale Journal On Regulation* 1–66

Peeters, M. 'Inspection and Market-based Regulation through Emissions Trading: The Striking Reliance on Self-monitoring, Self-reporting and Verification' (2006) 2(1) *Utrecht Law Review* 177–195

Peltzman, S. 'Towards a More General Theory of Regulation' (1976) 19 *Journal of Law and Economics* 211–240

Peterson, S. 'Monitoring, Accounting and Enforcement in Emissions Trading Regimes', OECD Global Forum on Sustainable Development: Emissions Trading, Concerted Action on Tradable Emissions Permits Country Forum CCNM/GF/SD/ENV(2003)5/FINAL (2008)

Pigou, A. C. *The Economics of Welfare* (London: Macmillan, 4th edn, 1932) 'The Laws of Diminishing and Decreasing Costs' (1927) 37 *The Economic Journal* 188–197

Porter, G. 'Trade Competition and Pollution Standards: "Race to the Bottom" or "Stuck at the Bottom"' (1998) 8 *Journal of Environment and Development* 133–151

Posner, R. 'Theories of Economic Regulation' (1974) 5 *Bell Journal of Economics and Management Science* 335–358

Poteete, A. R., Janssen, M. A. and Ostrom, E. (eds.) *Working Together: Collective Action, the Commons, and Multiple Methods in Practice* (Princeton University Press, 2010)

Prins, G., Galiana, I., Green, C., Grundmann, R., Hulme, M., Korhola, A., Laird, F., Nordhaus, T., Pielke Jnr, R., Rayner, S., Sarewitz, D., Shellenberger, M., Stehr, N. and Tezuka, H. 'The Hartwell Paper: A New Direction for Climate Policy after the Crash of 2009' (May 2010) available at http://eprints.lse.ac.uk/27939/1/HartwellPaper_English_version.pdf

Prud'homme, R. 'The Dangers of Decentralization' (1995) 10 *The World Bank Research Observer* 201–220

Putnam, R. D. 'Diplomacy and Domestic Politics: The Logic of Two-Level Games' (1988) 42(3) *International Organization* 427–460

Qian, Y. and Weinga, B. R. 'Federalism as a Commitment to Preserving Market Incentives' (1997) 11 *Journal of Economic Perspectives* 83–92

Raustiala, K. 'Compliance and Effectiveness in International Regulatory Cooperation' (2000) 32 *Case Western Reserve Journal International Law* 387–440

Reh, C. 'De-constitutionalizing the European Union?' (2009) 47 *Journal of Common Market Studies* 625–650

Revesz, R. *Environmental Law and Policy* (New York: Foundation Press, 2008) 'The Race to the Bottom and Federal Environmental Regulation: A Response to Critics' (1997) 82 *Minnesota Law Review* 535–564

Revesz, R. and Engel, K. 'State Environmental Standard-Setting: Is there a "Race" and is it "To the Bottom"?' (1997) 48 *Hastings Law Journal* 271–398

Revesz, R. and Stavins, R. N. 'Environmental Law', in A. M. Polinsky and S. Shavell (eds.) *The Handbook of Law and Economics* (Amsterdam: Elsevier Science, 2007), 499–589

Richards, K. R. 'Framing Environmental Policy Instrument Choice' (2000) 10 *Duke Environmental Law and Policy Forum* 221–286

Riedel, R. 'Silesian Representations in Brussels: How the Sub-national Authorities Utilise Opportunity Structures in the Multi-level Governance of the EU', in R. Grzeszczak and I. Karolewski (eds.) *The Multi-level and Polycentric European Union: Legal and Political Studies* (Zurich: Lit Verlag, 2012) 57–76

Roche Kelly, C., Oberthür, C. and Pallemaerts, M. 'Introduction, The EU's Internal and External Climate Policies: an Historical Overview', in M. Pallemaerts and S. Oberthür (eds.) *The New Climate Policies of the European Union* (Brussels: VUB Press, 2010) 11–26

Rogelj, J., Chen, C., Nabel, J., Macey, K., Hare, W., Schaeffer, M., Markmann, K., Höhne, N., Andersen, K. K. and Meinshausen, M. 'Analysis of the Copenhagen Accord Pledges and its Global Climatic Impacts – A Snapshot of Dissonant Ambitions' (2010) 5 *Environmental Research Letters* 1–9

Rolph, E. 'Government Allocation of Property Rights: Who Gets What?' (1983) 3(1) *Journal of Policy Analysis and Management* 45–61

Rondinelli, D. A. 'Government Decentralization in Comparative Perspective: Theory and Practice in Developing Countries' (1981) 47 *International Review of Administrative Sciences* 133–145

Rondinelli, D. A. and Nellis, J. R. 'Assessing Decentralization Policies in Developing Countries: The Case for Cautious Optimism' (1986) 4 *Development Policy Review* 3–23

Rooij, B. van *Regulating Land and Pollution in China: Lawmaking, Compliance, and Enforcement; Theory and Cases* (Leiden University Press, 2006)

Rose-Ackerman, S. 'Does Federalism Matter? Political Choice in a Federal Republic' (1981) 89 *Journal of Political Economy* 152–165

Ross, S. A. 'The Economic Theory of Agency: The Principal's Problem' (1973) 63 *American Economic Review* 134–139

Rowley, C. K. (ed.) *Public Choice Theory* (Cheltenham: Edward Elgar, 1993)

Sadeleer, N. de 'Principle of Subsidiarity and the EU Environmental Policy' (2012) 9 *Journal for European Environmental & Planning Law* 63–70

Samuelson, P. A. 'Diagrammatic Exposition of a Theory of Public Expenditure' (1955) 37 *Review of Economics and Statistics* 350–356

   *Foundations of Economic Analysis* (Cambridge, MA: Harvard University Press, 1947)

   'The Pure Theory of Public Expenditures' (1954) 4 *Review of Economics and Statistics* 387–389

Sanchez, P. A. 'Linking Climate Change Research with Food Security and Poverty Reduction in the Tropics' (2000) 82(1) *Agriculture, Ecosystems & Environment* 371–383

Sandbag, 'ETS S.O.S.: Why the flagship "EU Emissions Trading Policy" needs rescuing' (2009), available at www.sandbag.org.uk/site_media/pdfs/reports/Sandbag_ETS_SOS_Report.pdf

Scalop, S. C. and Scheffman, D. T. 'Raising Rivals' Costs' (1983) 73 *American Economic Review* 267–271

Schemmel, M. L. and de Regt, B. 'The European Court of Justice and the Environmental Protection Policy of the European Community' (1994) 17 *Boston College International & Comparative Law Review* 53–84

Scott, J. *EC Environmental Law* (New York: Longman Publishing Group, 1998)
'In Legal Limbo: Post-Legislative Guidance as a Challenge for European Administrative Law' (2011) 48 *Common Market Law Review* 329–355
'The Multi-Level Governance of Climate Change', in P. Craig and G. de Búrca (eds.) *The Evolution of EU Law* (Oxford University Press, 2011) 805–835

Seabright, P. 'Accountability and Decentralisation in Government: An Incomplete Contracts Model' (1996) 40 *European Economic Review* 61–89
'Centralised and Decentralised Regulation in the European Union', in P. Newman (ed.) *The New Palgrave Dictionary of Economics and the Law* (London: Macmillan, 1998) 214

Selin, H. and VanDeveer, S. D. *Changing Climates in North American Politics: Institutions, Policymaking and Multilevel Governance* (Cambridge, MA: MIT Press, 2009)

Sen, A. K. *Choice, Welfare and Measurement* (Cambridge, MA: MIT Press, 1982)
'Distribution, Transitivity and Little's Welfare Criteria' (1963) 73 *Economic Journal* 771–778

Shapiro, S. A. and Glicksman, R. L. 'Goals, Instruments, and Environmental Policy Choice' (2000) 10 *Duke Environmental Law and Policy Forum* 297–325

Shapiro, S. A. and McGarity, T. 'Not so Paradoxical: The Rationale for Technology-based Regulation' (1991) 40 *Duke Law Journal* 729–752

Shavell, S. 'Liability for Harm versus Regulation of Safety' (1984) 13 *Journal of Legal Studies* 357–374

Sigman, H. 'Decentralization and Environmental Quality: An International Analysis of Water Pollution', National Bureau of Economic Research Working Papers 13098 (2007)
'Transboundary Spillovers and Decentralization of Environmental Policies' (2005) 50 *Journal of Environmental Economics and Management* 82–101

Sijm, J. P. M., Hers, S. J., Lise, W. and Wetzelaer, B. J. H. W. 'The Impact of the EU ETS on Electricity Prices', Final report to DG Environment of the European Commission, ECN-E – 08-007 (2008), 12–13

Simonetti, S. 'Access to Justice for the Private Sector in Joint Implementation Projects under the Kyoto Protocol: A Brief Study of Possible Disputes and Remedies Available to Private Participants in International Carbon Emission Reduction Projects', Robert Schuman Center for Advanced Studies Florence School of Regulation 2010/08, EUI (2010)

Skjærseth, J. B. 'The Climate Policy of the EC: Too Hot to Handle?' (1994) 32 *Journal of Common Market Studies* 25–45

## BIBLIOGRAPHY

Skjærseth, J. B. and Wettestad, J. *EU Emissions Trading: Initiation, Decision-making and Implementation*, (Aldershot: Ashgate Publishing Limited, 2008)

'The EU Emissions Trading System Revised (Directive 2009/29/EC)', in M. Pallemaerts and S. Oberthür (eds.) *The New Climate Policies of the European Union: Internal Legislation and Climate Diplomacy* (Brussels: VUB Press, 2010) 65–93

'Implementing EU Emissions Trading: Success or Failure?' (2008) 8 *International Environmental Agreements* 275–290

Slaughter, A. *A New World Order* (Princeton University Press, 2004)

Smale, R., Hartley, M., Hepburn, C., Ward, J. and Grubb, M. 'The Impact of $CO_2$ Emissions Trading on Firm Profits and Market Prices' (2006) 6 *Climate Policy* 29–46

Smith, D. M. and Wilen, J. E. 'Economic Impacts of Marine Reserves: The Importance of Spatial Behavior' (2003) 46(2) *Journal of Environmental Economics and Management* 183–206

Smith, V. L. *Rationality in Economics: Constructivist and Ecological Forms* (Cambridge University Press, 2008)

Solomon, B. D. and Lee, R. 'Emissions Trading Systems and Environmental Justice' (2000) 42(8) *Environmental Justice* 32–45

Spagnolo, G. 'Divede et Impera: Optimal Leniency Programmes', CEPR Discussion Papers 4840, C.E.P.R. (2004)

Spulber, D. E. 'Effluent Regulation and Long-Run Optimality' (1985) 12 *Journal of Environmental Economics and Management*, 103–116

Stavins, R. N. 'Experience with Market-Based Environmental Policy Instruments', Resources for the Future Discussion Paper 01–58 (2001)

'Market-Based Environmental Policies', Resources for the Future Discussion Paper 98–26 (1998)

'Policy Instruments for Climate Change: How Can National Governments Address a Global Problem?' Resources for the Future Discussion Paper 97–11 (1997)

'The Problem of the Commons: Still Unsettled after 100 Years' (2011) 101 *American Economic Review* 81–108

Stern, D. and Jotzo, F. 'How Ambitious are China and India's Emissions Intensity Targets?' (2010) 38 *Energy Policy* 6776–6783

Stern, N. *The Stern Review on the Economics of Climate Change* (Cambridge University Press, 2006)

Stewart, R. B. 'Economics, Environment, and the Limits of Legal Control' (1985) 9 *Harvard Environmental Law Review* 1–22

'Enforcement of Transnational Public Regulation', EUI Working Papers, Robert Schuman Centre for Advanced Studies, Private Regulation Series-06 no. 2011/49 (2011)

'Enforcement of Transnational Public Regulation', in F. Cafaggi (ed.) *Enforcement of Transnational Regulation: Ensuring Compliance in a Global World* (Cheltenham: Edward Elgar Publishing, 2012) 41–74

'Environmental Law in the United States and the European Community: Spillovers, Cooperation, Rivalry, Institutions' (1992) 39 *University of Chicago Legal Forum* 44–46

'Environmental Quality as a National Good in a Federal State' (1997) *University of Chicago Legal Forum* 199–230

'Environmental Regulation and International Competitiveness' (1993) 102 *The Yale Law Journal* 41–75

'Pyramids of Sacrifice? Federalism Problems in Mandating State Implementation of Federal Environmental Controls' (1977) 86 *Yale Law Journal* 1196–1272

Stewart, R. B., Oppenheimer, M. and Rudyk, B. 'Building Blocks for Global Climate Protection' NYU Law and Economics Research Paper No. 12–43 (2012)

Stewart, R. B. and Wiener, J. B. *Reconstructing Climate Policy: Beyond Kyoto* (Washington, DC: Aei Press, 2007)

Stigler, G. J. 'The Tenable Range of Functions of Local Government', in Joint Economic Committee, Subcommitee on Fiscal Policy, U.S. Congress (ed.) *Federal Expenditure Policy for Economic Growth and Stability* (Washington, DC: US Government Printing Office, 1957) 213–219

'The Theory of Economic Regulation' (1971) 2 *The Bell Journal of Economics and Management Science* 3–21

Stranlund, J. K., Chavez, C. A. and Field, B. 'Enforcing Emissions Trading Programs: Theory, Practice and Performance' (2002) 30(3) *Policy Studies Journal* 343–361

Streck, C. 'The Governance of the Clean Development Mechanism: The Case for Strength and Stability' (2007) 2 *Environmental Liability* 91–100

Strumpf, K. and Oberholzer-Gee, F. 'Endogenous Policy Decentralization: Testing the Central Tenet of Economic Federalism' (2002) 110 *Journal of Political Economy* 1–36

Sunstein, C. R. 'Political Equality and Unintended Consequences' (1994) 94 *Columbia Law Review* 1390–1414

Svendsen, G. T. *Public Choice and Environmental Regulation* (Cheltenham: Edward Elgar, 1998)

Swenson, K. M. 'A Stitch in Time: The Continental Shelf, Environmental Ethics, and Federalism' (1987) 60 *Southern California Law Review* 851–896

Sykes, A. O. 'Regulatory Competition or Regulatory Harmonization? A Silly Question?' (2000) 3(2) *Journal of International Economic Law* 257–264

Tabau, A-S. *La mise en œuvre du Protocole de Kyoto en Europe* (Paris: Bruylant, 2011)

Tiebout, C. 'A Pure Theory of Local Expenditures' (1956) 64 *The Journal of Political Economy* 416–424

Tiersman, D. 'Decentralization and the Quality of Government', UCLA Political Science Working Paper (2002)

Tietenberg, T. *Emissions Trading: An Exercise in Reforming Pollution Policy* (Washington, DC: Resources for the Future, 1985)

'Tradable Permits in Principle and Practice' (2006) 14 *Pennsylvania State Environmental Law Review* 251–281

'The Tradable-Permits Approach to Protecting the Commons: Lessons for Climate Change' (2003) 19(3) *Oxford Review of Economic Policy* 400–419

Tocqueville, A. de *Democracy in America*, vol. I, ed. J. P. Mayer, trans. G. Lawrence (London: Fontana Press, 1994)

Tol, R. S. J. 'The Economic Effects of Climate Change' (2009) 23 *Journal of Economic Perspectives* 29–51

Tol, R. S. J., Downing, T. E., Kuik, O. J. and Smith, J. B. 'Distributional Aspects of Climate Change Impacts' (2004) 14 *Global Environmental Change* 259–272

Tomassi, M., Spiller, P. T. and Stein, E. 'Political Institutions, Policymaking Processes, and Policy Outcomes: An Intertemporal Transactions Framework', Leitner Program in International and Comparative Political Economy Working Paper 2003-03, Yale University (2003)

Toth, L. 'Agency Issues within Public Agencies: Performance Effects of External Budget Assignment', University of Amsterdam (2012)

Trachtman, J. P. 'Regulatory Competition and Regulatory Jurisdiction' (2000) 3(2) *Journal of International Economic Law* 331–348

Tullock, G. 'The Welfare Costs of Tariffs, Monopolies, and Theft' (1967) 5 *Western Economic Journal* 224–232

Turner, G. 'Value of the Global Carbon Market Increases by 5% in 2010 but Volumes Decline', *Bloomberg New Energy Memo* (6 January 2011)

Unger, M. von and Streck, C. 'An Appellate Body for the Clean Development Mechanism: A Due Process Requirement' (2009) 1 *Carbon and Climate Law Review* 31–44

Vasa, A. and Michaelowa, A. 'Uncertainty in Climate Policy – Impacts on Market Mechanisms', in G. Gramelsberger and J. Feichter (eds.) *Climate Change and Policy* (Heidelberg: Springer, 2011) 127–144

Vedder, H. 'The Treaty of Lisbon and European Environmental Law and Policy' (2010) 22 *Journal of Environmental Law* 285–299

Verchick, R. R. M. 'Feathers or Gold? A Civic Economics for Environmental Law' (2001) 25 *Harvard Environmental Law Review* 95–150

Victor, D. *The Collapse of the Kyoto Protocol and the Struggle to Slow Global Warming* (Princeton University Press, 2001)

'Fragmented Carbon Markets and Reluctant Nations: Implications for the Design of Effective Architectures', in J. E. Aldy and R. N. Stavins (eds.) *Architectures for Agreement: Addressing Global Climate Change in a Post-Kyoto World* (Cambridge University Press, 2007) 133–160

Vinuales, J. E. 'Legal Techniques for Dealing with Scientific Uncertainty in Environmental Law' (2010) 43 *Vanderbilt Journal of Transnational Law* 437–503

Wallart, N. *The Political Economy of Environmental Taxes* (Cheltenham: Edward Elgar, 1999)

Wennerås, P. E. 'State Liability for Decisions of Courts of Last Instance in Environmental Cases' (2004) 16(3) *Journal of Environmental Law* 329–340

Watts, R. L. 'The Theoretical and Practical Implications of Asymmetrical Federalism', in R. Agranoff (ed.) *Accommodating Diversity: Asymmetry in Federal States* (Baden-Baden: Nomos Verlagsgesellschaft, 1999)

Weiler, J. H. H. 'The Reformation of European Constitutionalism' (1997) 35 *Journal of Common Market Studies* 97–131

Weishaar, S. and Woerdman, E. 'Auctioning EU ETS Allowances: An Assessment of Market Manipulation from the Perspective of Law and Economics' (2012) 3 *Climate Law* 247–263

Weitzman, M. L. 'Prices vs. Quantities' (1974) 41 *Review of Economic Studies* 477–491

Werlin, H. 'Linking Decentralization and Centralization: A Critique of the New Development Administration' (1992) 12(3) *Public Administration and Development: An International Journal of Training, Research, and Practice* 223–236

Wettestad, J. 'European Climate Policy: Toward Centralized Governance?' (2009) 26 *Review of Policy Research* 311–328

Wheare, K. C. *Federal Government* (London: Oxford University Press, 1953)

Wiener, J. 'Global Environmental Regulation: Instrument Choice in Legal Context' (1999) 108 *The Yale Law Journal* 677–800

'On the Political Economy of Global Environmental Regulation' (1999) 87 *Georgetown Law Journal* 749–794

Woerdman, E., Arcuri, A. and Cló, S. 'Emissions Trading and the Polluter-Pays Principle: Do Polluters Pay under Grandfathering?' (2008) 4(2) *Review of Law and Economics* 565–590

Woerdman, E., Couwenberg, O. and Nentjes, A. 'Energy Prices and Emissions Trading: Windfall Profits from Grandfathering?' (2009) 28 *European Journal of Law and Economics* 185–202

Woll, C. 'Lobbying in the European Union: From sui generis to a Comparative Perspective' (2006) 13 *Journal of European Public Policy* 456–469

Yandle, B. 'Creative Destruction and Environmental Law' (2002) 10 *Penn State Environmental Law Review* 155–174

Yang, T. 'International Treaty Enforcement as a Public Good: Institutional Deterrent Sanctions in International Environmental Agreements' (2006) 27 *Michigan Journal of International Law* 1131–1184

Ylvisaker, P. 'Some Criteria for a "Proper" Areal Division of Governmental Powers', in A. Maass (ed.) *Area and Power: A Theory of Local Government* (Glencoe, IL: Free Press, 1959)

Yoshida, O. 'Soft Enforcement of Treaties: The Montreal Protocol's Noncompliance Procedure and the Functions of Internal International Institutions' (1999) 10 *Colombia Journal of International Environmental Law & Policy* 95–142

Zeben, J. A. W. van 'Cases C-504/09 P, Commission v Poland, and C-505/09 P, Commission v Estonia, Judgment of the European Court of Justice (Second Chamber) of 29 March 2012 (Annotation)' (2013) 50 *Common Market Law Review* 231–246

'(De)Centralized Law-making in the EU ETS' (2009) 3 *Carbon & Climate Law Review* 340–356

'The European Emissions Trading Scheme Case Law' (2009) 18 *Review of European Community & International Environmental Law* 119–128

'A Polycentric European Union' (on file with author)

'Research Agenda for a Polycentric European Union', The Vincent and Elinor Ostrom Workshop in Political Theory and Policy Analysis Working Paper Series, W13–13 (2013)

'The Untapped Potential of Horizontal Private Enforcement within EC Environmental Law' (2010) 5 *The Georgetown International Environmental Law Review* 241–269

Zimmerman, J. F. 'Nation-State Relations: Cooperative Federalism in the Twentieth Century' (2001) 31 *Publius* 15–30

Zwingmann, K. 'Ökonomische Analyse der EU-Emissionshandelsreichtlinie, Bedeutung und Funktionsweisen der Primärallokation von Zertifikaten', in *Ökonomische Analyse des Rechts* (Wiesbaden: DUV Gabler Edition Wissenschaft, 2007)

# Index

accountability, 26, 79, 219
activity-specific approach, 121
administration, 47, 128
  centralized, 61
  costs, 62
  market, 96
  public, 28, 49
  standard-setting, and, 88
agencies
  administrative, 46
  behaviour, 67
  benevolent, 68–72, 139, 171, 174
  categorizations, 135
  concurrent competences, 173
  diversity, 67
  enforcement abilities, 95
  governmental, 26, 31
  incentives, 66
  interacting competences, 65
  interests of, 66
  power, exercising, 70
  public, 38
  regulatory, 66, 68, 69, 220
  rent-seeking, 68–72, 100, 104,
    139, 171
  typology, 135–139, 171
allocative criteria
  identifying, 54
  questions, and, 56
  ranking, 64
  third phase, 163–171
allowance allocation, 17, 115
  changes, 205, 208, 209
  first phase, 118
  harmonization, 203
  method of, 105, 138, 192, 197
  national, 128, 138, 194
  political economy of, 191
  procedural rules, 153
  second phase, 154–156

specific, 138
allowances theft, 124, 133
aluminium industry, 194–195
anthropogenic interference, 110
auctioning, 195, 203
  Auctioning Regulation, 155–158,
    161, 168
  centralization, 156, 211
  decentralization, 172
  eligibility, 155
  emphasis, 145
  impact, 153
  institutional implications, 157
  introduction of, 154, 203
  main method, as, 192, 205
  market, 161
  permits, 87
  prescriptive nature, 168
  procedural rules, 115
  revenues, 157, 158, 167, 205
  transition, 153
authority, 71, 157, 220
  agency, 68, 139
  competence, 119
  creation of, 190
  dividing, 20
  European level, 174
  informing, 123
  Member State, 122, 162
  positive, 70–73, 99, 103, 104, 139, 173
  regional, 90
  regulatory, 68–72, 74, 99–102, 140
aviation industry, 122, 145, 150, 159, 217
  administration, 157
  allowances, 153
  inclusion, 159, 160, 209

Bali Road Map, 145, 146
Burden Sharing Agreement, 111, 112, 116,
  166, 194, 195

## 250  INDEX

bureaucratic institutions, 190
Business as Usual, 119, 138

cap distribution
  concurrent, 139, 173
  implementation, as, 115, 167
  level, 153, 167
cap-division, 116
  decentralization, 129
  first phase, 116–118
  level, 116, 125
  national, 128
  pressures, 209
  procedural rules, 153
  second phase, 153–154
  under-enforcement, 139, 173
cap setting, 17
  binding, 164
  centralization, 208, 211
  changes, 205, 208
  concurrent, 139, 173
  decentralization, 152
  European level, 211, 214
  harmonization, 203
  norm setting, as, 115, 167
carbon
  leakage, 115, 153, 164, 165, 204–208
  market, 144, 170, 200, 206, 210, 216
  pricing, 87
centralization
  agencies, 68
  allowance trades, 119
  assumptions, 23
  auctioning, and, 205
  choices, 28, 54
  considerations, 32
  decentralization, and, 24, 30
  definition, 49
  degree, 19
  devolution, as, 51
  electronic databases, 157
  enforcement, 173
  externalities, 45
  increasing favour of, 209
  information, 127
  instrument choice, 59
  policy-making, 9, 29, 127
  political economy, and, 27
  preference, 31
  public goods, 21
  race-to-the-bottom, 34
  recommendations, 73
  reform, 208
  regulatory powers, of, 43
  regulatory process, 44, 64
  science, 29, 60
  trade-offs, 26

uniformity, and, 59
chemical industry, 194–195
Clean Development Mechanism
  (CDM), 84–85
climate change
  adaptation, 2, 127, 147
  costs, 77, 79
  effects of, 3, 79, 91
  environmental issues, 2
  ideal policy, 79
  impact, 1
  mitigation, 75, 108, 111, 127, 147, 165
  nature, 3, 78
  regulatory characteristics, 106
  regulatory problem, as, 75, 77–79, 90
  scientific uncertainties, 76
  unequal distribution, 76
collective action
  agreement, 27
  balancing, 189
  externalities, 44
  incentives, and, 78
  norm setting, 92
  problem, 3, 79, 90, 164
command-and-control regulation, 57–63,
  95, 184, 186
  choice, 185
common but differentiated responsibilities approach, 127
comparative research, 221
competence allocation, 6–11
  economic views, 31
  individual, 74
  legal views, 43
  optimal, 75
  overview, 5
  scenarios, 89
  theory, 39
  treaties, in, 41
complexity, regulatory, 105
Conference of the Parties (COP), 80, 110,
  143, 145, 146
consumer interest groups, 201
  grandfathering, 208
  losers, as, 197
Copenhagen Accord, 146
costs
  administrative, 61, 63, 128, 131
  auctioning, 169
  compliance, 63
  different industries, 92
  enforcement, 95
  externalized, 215
  flexibility, 45
  private, 196
  public/social, 28, 184, 185
  regulatory, 59–73, 92, 105, 167

# INDEX    251

sector, 129
Council of the European Union, 82, 83, 220

data collection, 92, 130, 134, 198
decentralization, 9
  definition, 49
  devolution, as, 51
  enforcement, 103
  fiscal, 51
  functional, 49
  implementation, 103
  national implementation, and, 197
  territorial, 49
  trade-offs, 26
Decentralization Theorem, 22, 24, 59
deconcentration, 51
deforestation, 150
democratic legitimacy, 79, 219, 222
developing/developed countries, 79
devolution, process of, 51
discretion
  allowance calculation, 137
  amount, 47, 72, 155
  centralization, and, 51
  community, 40
  enforcement, 88
  information, 64, 72
  instruments, 72
  interacting competences, 140
  Member State, 129, 157, 173, 200
  National Allocation Plans, 131
  norm implementation, 47
  operationalization, 88
  penalties, 123
  permits, 118
  political, 203
  rules, 162
distribution
  optimal, 99, 109, 129
  sub-optimal, 103, 104, 129, 131,
    142, 167
division of powers, 19, 44, 125, 136, 145,
  210, 222

economies of scale/scope, 12, 128,
  133, 167
  centralization, 29, 43, 60, 127
  decentralization, 63
  instrument choice, 65
  level, 134
  maximizing, 12, 13, 31, 44, 45, 74, 75,
    90, 97
  norm setting, 92
  overlooking, 133
  second-order considerations, 91, 93,
    107, 132
  theory, 11

Effort Sharing Agreement, 149, 150, 152,
  165, 167
emission reduction goals, 86, 167
emissions trading, 14, 60, 63, 88, 106
  behaviour, 94, 106
  binding, 107
  desire for scheme, 115
  goals, and, 115
  heterogeneity, and, 129
  instrument choice, and, 127
  introduction, 193
  mandatory, 195
  meaning, 86
  method, as, 108
  reality, 110
  results, 4
  role, 114
energy
  consumption patterns, 2, 77, 149
  sector, 129, 204
enforcement, 47, 52
  competence-specific allocation, 94–97
  decentralization, 159
  definition, 88
  EU Emissions Trading Scheme, 120–125,
    132–135
  global, 104
  implementation, and, 103
  political process, 199
  reform, 208
  regional, 104
  sub-optimal, 94, 95, 104, 106
  third phase, 170–171
  under, 135
environmental interest groups, 2, 184,
  185, 187, 201
  composition, 187
  emissions trading, and, 196
  grandfathering, 208
environmental tax, 114
European Commission, 82, 83, 171, 220
  allocation, 118
  back loading, 16, 211, 216,
  behaviour, correcting, 140
  cap-division, 131
  carbon leakage, 165
  concerns, 215
  data, 15
  emissions trading, 193
  fragmentation, 170
  industry preferences, and, 192
  interests, 139
  Kyoto Protocol, and, 114
  limitations, 142
  Member States, and, 135, 142
  over-allocation, 131
  review power, 156

## INDEX

European Council, 82
 climate and energy package, 148
European Court of Justice, 82, 83
 jurisprudence, 142
 National Allocation Plans, and, 137
European Parliament, 16, 82, 83, 211, 220
 back loading, 216
European Union, 81–84
 history, 111
 legal system, 20
 procedure, 83
 specialized bodies, 82
 structure, 82
European Union Emissions Trading
 Scheme (EU ETS), 11, 19, 74, 97,
 106, 176
 aim, 75
 changes, 214
 competence allocation, 126
 compromises, 200, 201, 211
 conflict, political, 207
 criticisms, 108
 early phases political process, 193–195
 first phase, 116–120, 138
 framework, 141
 functioning, 213
 model, 116
 overview, 4, 108
 phases, 5, 109, 144
 power shifts, 201
 problems, 174
 second phase, 138, 153–158
 stakeholders, 192
 supervision of, 124
 targets, 148
 third phase, 174
 third phase political process, 202–206
execution, 115
 first phase, 119
 second phase, 156–158
externalities, 43, 45, 55
 centralization, and, 105
 competence allocation, and, 66
 costs of regulation, 92
 definition, 7
 diverging, 100
 economic, 90, 182
 effect, 8
 enforcement, 97, 135, 140
 environmental, 55
 European activities, 164
 focus, 55
 global, 90, 91
 implementation, and, 93
 importance, 90
 information, 35
 interjurisdictional, 42

jurisdictions, and, 9, 38
 local problems, and, 64
 national norm setting, and, 91
 norm setting, 164
 political internalization, 182
 problem, 7
 regulated activities, and, 12
 transboundary, 78

federalism, 177, 210
 assumptions, 25
 economic, 6–9, 21–31
 fiscal, 22–25
 legal, 9–11, 21, 32–44
 literature, 28
 meaning, 20
 second generation theory, 25–31
feedback, 220
financial crisis, 135, 211, 215
fragmentation, 13, 213
 competence allocation, 103
 increasing, 105

governance, levels of, 51–54, 96, 109,
 186, 210
 fragmentation, 71, 74, 105
 global nature, 3
 legal approach, 9
 private parties, 14, 120
 relativity, 73
 single, 105
grandfathering, 153, 183
 concession, 199
 consumer groups, 208
 history, 154
 Member States, 192
 permits, 87, 115
 problems, 138
 procedural rules, 115
 scale, 209
greenhouse gases, 78, 88, 91, 101,
 106, 173
 causes, 76
 changes in regulation, 161
 concentration, 110
 effect, 77
 emissions, 90
 EU Emissions Trading Scheme, and, 197
 reduction of, 3, 75, 108, 111
 specific sectors, and, 116
 time spent in atmosphere, 78
 UN framework, and, 80
 unequal distribution, 127
 United States, 142

harmonization, 43, 157, 203
 centralization, and, 51

European, 170, 171
free allocation rules, 167
future, 162
increasing, 174
standards, and, 133
heterogeneous conditions, 44
accommodating, 12, 45, 59, 64, 74, 90
instrument choice, and, 127
national, 92, 129
norm setting, and, 59, 166
role, 36

implementation, 46, 52, 73
changes to, 144
competence-specific allocation, 92–94
decentralization, and, 197
definition, 88
enforcement, and, 100–103
EU Emissions Trading Scheme, 114–120, 128–132
Kyoto Protocol, 111
norm setting, and, 100–103
practices, 190
procedural, 168
regional, 97, 104, 106, 132
third phase, 167–170
incentive-based regulation, 58
incentives, 3, 13, 94, 129
structures, 39
industrial interest groups, 182, 187
auctioning, and, 204
composition, 187
free initial allocation, and, 196
influence, 209
net buyers, as, 195
preferences, 192
industries, 117, 129
information, 127
availability, 36
costs, 29, 30, 43, 60, 61
externalities, 35
increase, 215
industry, 61, 198
private actors, 217
role of, 25, 28
technology, and, 96
infringement procedures, 47
institutional balance, 222
instrument choice, 45, 57
competence interaction, 64
discretion, and, 72
economists, 184
effects, 59–73
environmental groups, 184
heterogeneous preferences, 93
importance, 74

industrial interest groups, 183
influences, 59
ranking, 183
voters, 185
interactions of competences, 65, 98
assumptions, 65–66
competences, 68–72
instrument choice, 72–73
regulators, 66–68
Intergovernmental Panel on Climate Change (IPCC), 81, 127
interjurisdictional competition, 34

Joint Implementation (JI), 84
jurisdictions, 24

Kyoto Protocol, 111–115, 147, 188, 209, 215
Adaptation Fund, 146
commitment periods, 144, 145
commitments, 86, 113, 125, 143, 147
consensus, 162
flexible instruments, 117, 193
global norm setting, 100, 109
importance, 4
market-based mechanisms, and, 114
reduction norms, 84
second commitment period, 147
stabilizing gases, 80
targets, 4, 84, 115, 166, 193

largest greenhouse gas emitters, 78
locked-in effect, 192, 209

maritime industry, 150, 217
market
abuse, 73, 94, 95, 160, 176, 206, 215
consolidation, 191, 208, 209, 211
creation, 108, 191, 197, 200, 208, 211
design, 210
distorting, 129
improvements, 209
integrity, 124
regulation, 161, 170
market-based instruments, 57, 62
behaviour, 95
choice, 185
distribution, 185
environmental groups, 184
European Union, and, 84
implementation, 86
industry groups, 184
introduction, 4
monitoring, 95
private parties, 14
unique, 105
minimum harmonization, 43

## 254 INDEX

monitoring
  approach, 121
  changes in, 159–160
  obligations, 120–122, 133
  plans, 122
  private parties, 217
  procedures, 121
multi-level governance, 37–40
  levels, 51
  scholarship, 21
  structure, 222
  theory, 21, 32
  types, 38

National Allocation Plans (NAPs), 116–118,
  135–139
  abolition of, 153, 154
  design choice, 214
  difficulties, 174
  externalities, 167
  failure, 206
  introduction, 131
  Member States, and, 209
  overview, 116
norm setting, 46, 52, 73
  best scenario, 143, 162
  changes to, 144
  competence-specific allocation, 90–92
  definition, 88
  EU Emissions Trading Scheme, 110–113,
    126–128
  failures, 164
  global, 98–107, 109, 126, 127, 142, 166,
    167, 172
  implementation, and, 102
  level, moving, 163
  national, 126
  regional, 75, 97–105, 107, 109, 162–164,
    172, 174
  third phase, 90–92
  UN-based framework, 142

operationalization, 48, 88, 115, 149
optimality, 11–13, 74, 90, 213
  competence-specific allocation, 97
  determinants, 12
  interactive allocations, 104–105
  norms, 100
over-allocation
  costs, 165
  design choice, 214
  extent, 171
  first trading phase, 130, 132, 135
  incentives, 15
  National Allocation Plans, 136, 167
  overcoming, 16
  pre-existing, 215

review, 211
risk, 203
second phase, 197
sectors, 197

penalties, 14, 94, 110, 122
  aviation sector, 160
  changes to, 160–162
  civil, 134
  early phases, 194
  flat rate, 196
  Member State, 123
  notifying of, 124
  third parties, 120
policy-making, 189
political decision-making process,
  178, 210
political economy, definition, 176
pollution, 129, 184
polycentric theory, 18, 39
principal–agent model, 25, 27
private parties, 120, 139, 217
public choice, 16, 21, 24–27
  theory, 177
public goods, 22–25
public sector regulation, 22

race-to-the-bottom hypothesis, 32–36
reduction targets, 85, 111–113, 147, 188
  agreement, 150
  binding, 151, 164
  combining, 125
  country-specific, 81, 127
  decentralization, 152
  implementing, 144
  meeting, 4
  Member State, 112
  setting, 80, 152
regulated activities
  activity, 59
  characteristics, 56
  complexity, 60
  externalities, 105
  first-order consideration, 12
  local, 52
  meaning, 101
  nature, 59
  ranking, 56, 64
regulated financial markets, 170
rent extraction, 69
repeat players, 220
reporting
  changes in, 159–160
  obligations, 120–122, 133
risk diversification, 30
rules
  creation, 115

## INDEX

key, 116
primary, 120
procedural, 115, 118, 154–156
responsibility, 115
substantive, 116–118, 144, 153–154

sanctions, 47
criminal, 206
scientific research, 3, 29, 60, 76
self-interest, 3, 181, 187, 190
separation of powers, 19
shared competences, 220
social optimum, 8, 12, 98, 99, 139
global, 101
social welfare, 22–26, 31, 66, 68, 177,
179, 181
standards
accreditation, 133
performance, 57
source-specfic, 182
technology, 57, 60, 63, 92, 193
sub-regions, 60
subsidiarity, principle of, 6, 9, 20, 41, 42,
44, 46
surrendering allowances, 133

taxes, 39, 57, 63, 64, 180, 184
theories of regulation
demand-side, 178–180
equilibria analyses, 181
supply-side, 180
tradable permits, 19, 57, 63, 73, 106,
182, 184
appropriateness, 109
auctioning, and, 184
cap, 86
enforcing, 94
schemes, 4, 86, 92, 96, 114
trade-offs, 42, 56, 59
normative, 45, 54, 64, 74

translation, legal, 110
Treaty of Lisbon, 83

under-permitting, 101–105
unequal distribution, 3
uniformity, 6, 23, 26, 59, 140
competence allocation, 103
United Nations, 80–81
United Nations Framework Convention on
Climate Change (UNFCCC)
Conference of the Parties
(COP), 110
development, 111
history, 80
importance, 4, 142
obligations, 111
overall objective, 84
success, 127

variables, 45
enforcement, 73
regulatory competence, as, 45
weight, 108
VAT fraud, 124, 133, 160, 200
verification, 14, 145
changes to, 160–162
enforcement, 96, 110
focus, 124
private parties, 217
procedures, 121, 123
process, 160
responsibility, 169
voting-with-the-feet model, 23

wealth transfer, 209
welfare
implications, 70, 71, 106, 163
improving, 70–72, 101–105, 126, 135,
140, 173
windfall profits, 138, 204, 211

For EU product safety concerns, contact us at Calle de José Abascal, 56–1°, 28003 Madrid, Spain or eugpsr@cambridge.org.

www.ingramcontent.com/pod-product-compliance
Ingram Content Group UK Ltd.
Pitfield, Milton Keynes, MK11 3LW, UK
UKHW020454090825
461507UK00007B/222